COMMUNICATION AND
COMMUNICATION SYSTEMS
In Organization, Management, and
Interpersonal Relations

The Irwin Series in Management

Consulting Editor   John F. Mee   Indiana University

MOORE   *Manufacturing Management*   4th ed.

NIEBEL   *Motion and Time Study*   4th ed.

ROSCOE   *Organization for Production: An Introduction to Industrial Management*   4th ed.

JUCIUS   *Personnel Management*   6th ed.

CRUICKSHANK & DAVIS   *Cases in Management*   3d ed.

FILIPETTI   *Industrial Management in Transition*   rev. ed.

SPRIEGEL & MYERS (Editors)   *The Writings of the Gilbreths*

TERRY   *Principles of Management*   5th ed.

VORIS   *Production Control Text and Cases*   3d ed.

SIMONDS & GRIMALDI   *Safety Management: Accident Cost and Control*   rev. ed.

JONES   *Executive Decision Making*   rev. ed.

NIEBEL & BALDWIN   *Designing for Production*   rev. ed.

PATTON, LITTLEFIELD, & SELF   *Job Evaluation: Text and Cases*   3d ed.

SHULL & DELBECQ (Editors)   *Selected Readings in Management: Extensions and Modifications*   Second Series

BRENNAN   *Wage Administration: Plans, Practices, and Principles*   rev. ed.

JUCIUS & SCHLENDER   *Elements of Managerial Action*   rev. ed.

HANEY   *Communication and Organizational Behavior: Text and Cases*   rev. ed.

JOHNSON   *Personal and Industrial Relations*

DEPHILLIPS, BERLINER, & CRIBBIN   *Management of Training Programs*

MORRIS   *The Analysis of Management Decisions*   rev. ed.

ROSCOE   *Project Economy*

EELLS & WALTON   *Conceptual Foundations of Business*

HOUSTON   *Manager Development: Principles and Perspectives*

SEIMER   *Cases in Industrial Management*

REED   *Plant Layout: Factors, Principles, and Techniques*

AMMER   *Materials Management*

BROOM   *Production Management*   rev. ed.

SCOTT   *Organization Theory: A Behavioral Analysis for Management*

SIEGEL   *Industrial Psychology*

TIMMS   *The Production Function in Business: Fundamentals and Analysis for Management*   rev. ed.

NADLER   *Work Design*

FOX   *The Management Process: An Integrated Functional Approach*

CHAMPION & BRIDGES   *Critical Incidents in Management*

MOORE & KIBBEY   *Manufacturing: Materials and Processes*

MCDONOUGH & GARRETT   *Management Systems: Working Concepts and Practice*

GREENE   *Production Control: Systems and Decisions*

FARMER & RICHMAN   *Comparative Management and Economic Progress*

LING   *The Management of Personnel Relations: History and Origins*

RICHARDS & GREENLAW   *Management Decision Making*

PRINCE   *Information Systems for Management Planning and Control*

MEGGINSON   *Personnel: A Behavioral Approach to Administration*

THAYER   *Communication and Communication Systems: In Organization, Management, and Interpersonal Relations*

COMMUNICATION
and
COMMUNICATION SYSTEMS

In Organization, Management, and
Interpersonal Relations

LEE THAYER, Ph.D.

Center for the Advanced Study of Communication
University of Missouri at Kansas City

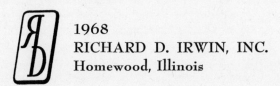
1968
RICHARD D. IRWIN, INC.
Homewood, Illinois

THIS BOOK IS BASED IN PART ON THE AUTHOR'S PREVIOUS
TEXT *Administrative Communication*.

First Printing, February, 1968

Library of Congress Catalog Card No. 67–26285
PRINTED IN THE UNITED STATES OF AMERICA

For Cassy and Stephanie

Preface

THIS IS a new book. Like all books, it has its intellectual history. My *Administrative Communication* preceded this book intellectually as well as in time. But for all of its debt to its predecessor, this is a completely new book.

There were a number of good reasons for writing a new book rather than simply revising an old one. The field has changed greatly since 1960. Those changes have come in the form of new ideas, new concepts, new perspectives. These could not have been successfully appliquéd to an earlier conceptual framework. They called for a complete reformulation; and this is what I have tried to provide in this book.

A new book called for a new title as well. Communication doesn't belong solely to the practice of administration any more than it does to the practice of teaching or psychology. A much broader scope was necessary to incorporate ideas which transcend the boundaries of traditional disciplines—and of conventional ways of thinking about human communication.

An area of study that could properly be labeled *communication and communication systems* is rapidly evolving. Its rich and exciting challenges have drawn scholars and thoughtful practitioners from disciplines ranging from neurology to sociology, from cybernetics to psycholinguistics, from the communicative arts to general systems theory, from organization and management theory to the simulation of self-organizing automata. The fruits of this now emerging movement will have application in all of man's personal and social and economic and aesthetic endeavors, indeed, for the ultimate understanding of his very existence.

This is just the beginning. There are no final answers in this book. But it presents a view in scope and depth that should be of value to any person who has either a professional or a practical interest in communication and communication systems—wherever and however he concerns himself with the essential issues of people and their relationships and their organizations.

A task of that sort called for a completely new book, a new effort to integrate some of these rich new ideas. This is the result.

THIS IS NOT an easy book. If the cause of that difficulty were wholly attributable to the author's ineptness in presentation, that would indeed be a grievous fault. But I have tried to present my ideas as straightforwardly and as simply as I could. The source of the difficulty, rather, is the subject itself.

To quote Albert Upton (since it would undoubtedly be in bad taste to quote oneself in his own preface), ". . . communication is difficult because it is the most complex operation known to man." Thus the reader should expect to encounter at least some of the same difficulties in this book that he might expect to encounter in a book about nuclear physics or abstract mathematics (unless, of course, he's already conversant with the conceptual subtleties of those fields!).

Add to that a compounding difficulty. Things are difficult to understand in reverse order to their familiarity to us. The more commonplace or universal something is, the more difficult it is for us to gain a scientifically sound understanding of it. And there is probably nothing we take for granted more than the process of communication—and the ways in which we understand that process.

It is not a difficult book to read. But the nature of the subject—and our conventional biases about it—are such that getting the full measure of the ideas presented here, and of their implications, may call for a little special effort on the part of the reader, just as they have on the part of the author.

Can that be an unfair tip?

THIS IS NOT a theoretical book. It may seem so from a distance. But what I have tried to present here are not theoretical statements, but simply some useful *tools* for *thinking* about communication and communication systems—whether for theoretical or practical ends.

Thus this book is addressed to the practicing manager, the practicing public administrator, the practicing educational, religious, and military administrator, indeed the *practicing* human being whatever his special role—as well as to the scholar, the teacher, and the researcher. Even our most casual dealings with family or friends often give us occasion to *think about* human communication, how it sometimes works and sometimes doesn't.

There is no good reason why the tools we use to *think about* communication should be any different for the scholar than for the practitioner.

We are all of us practitioners of communication. We are probably all of us therefore communication theorists—or we at least have our homespun philosophies about it. Thus this book has been written with all of us in mind. There is perhaps something about our communication experiences, or about communication in general, we'd each like to understand a little bit better. Hopefully there are a few of these kinds of ideas and insights in this book for each of those who would undertake to read it seriously.

THIS IS finally a book which owes an unusual intellectual debt to an unusually large number of people. It is always impossible to acknowledge appropriately every source of knowledge and inspiration from which an author has freely drawn. Where it has been possible to acknowledge these debts (or when they could be remembered), I have done so in the text itself. Yet I have attempted to avoid cluttering these pages with excessive documentation. I was guided by these thoughts: Would a reader like to pursue this idea elsewhere? Would a reader like to know how this particular idea was derived, or how it contrasts with other closely related ideas? Would a reader like to have some suggestions for reading further into the general topics covered? In those cases, there are references. In others, there are not.

I am particularly grateful to those scholars and practitioners who participated in the first two international symposia on communication theory and research held in Kansas City, to all of those who directly or indirectly have shared dialogues with me about the ideas herein, and to the many military, government, and corporate managers and executives from whom I have learned so much over the several years I have presumed to serve as consultant to them. They must go unnamed, but not forgotten. If I have failed to take advantage of all of these rich resources in this book, the responsibility is totally mine.

To my students, colleagues, deans and administrators, and especially to the graduate assistants who have contributed in no small way over the years to these proceedings, I would communicate a hearty "Thank you!"

And to Nancy Thayer, for all of those incommunicable things along the way, some subtle gesture of a shared and difficult task completed; for she would understand the meaning of that, and of this.

LEE THAYER

Kansas City, Missouri
January, 1968

Table of Contents

Large Numbers." The Implications of "On-behalf-of. . . ." A Recapitu-
lation: People, Behavior, Communication.

Communication: Levels of Analysis: The Intrapersonal Level. Inter-
communication: The Interpersonal Level. Organizational Communication:
The Third Level. Interorganizational Communication. Communication
Systems and Data Systems. Control Systems. Metacommunication.
The Occasions of Communication. The Consequences of Communi-
cation. The Communication Event. The Communication Sequence.
The Basic Facilitators and Barriers in Human Communication:
Communicative Facilitators and Barriers. Metacommunicative Facilitation.
The Role of Intention and Expectation. Two Modes of Inter-
communication. Media and Channels of Communication. Communi-
cation Competence and Communication Control.

PART II.   COMMUNICATION, MESSAGES, AND COMMUNICATION SYSTEMS: QUALITIES AND CHARACTERISTICS

The Sources of Confusion. One-Person and Two-Person Communication Effectiveness. Determining the Effectiveness of Organizational Communication. Communication Satisfaction. The Role of
Purpose. Communication Effectiveness and Behavior. Message Validity, Utility, and Consequence. Effectiveness in Being Communicated-With. On Communicating Effectively.

Intrapersonal Factors. Interpersonal Factors. Organizational and
Technological Factors. Communication Efficiency: Message Efficiency. Channel Efficiency. Media Efficiency. System Efficiency. Economy
and Effectiveness: Two Further Issues.

Comprehensibility: Comprehensibility and Ambiguity. Validity. Utility.

Basic Processes: Acquisition. Transportation/Distribution. Processing.
Display/Presentation. Some Further Dimensions of System Efficacy:
Adequacy. Adaptability. Reliability. Compatibility. Viability and Effi-
cacy.

PART III.   THE FUNCTIONS OF COMMUNICATION

Importance of the Information Function. On the Nature of Information. Individual and Organizational Information. Information and Information Systems. Needs for and Uses of Information.
The Concept of "Education." Intentional and Unintentional Information. Some Further Obstacles to Informative Communication: Organizational Barriers. Interpersonal Barriers. Individual Barriers.
Economic, Geographic, and Temporal Barriers. Channel and Media Barriers. A Basic Technological Barrier.

INDEXES

PART I

On the Nature and
Dynamics of
Human Communication

1

The Study of Communication:
Some Basic Premises

PEOPLE have always held queer beliefs about human communication. They still do.

The Greeks accounted for the phenomenon of communication very simply: Their wingfooted god Mercury would pluck the appropriate idea from the speaker's brain and plunge it on the end of his spear into the brain of the listener. Given the way explanations in communication typically go, that's not a bad one. But it wouldn't be satisfactory today. It's doubtful that Mercury and his helpers could get appropriately licensed by the medical boards of the various states to perform the delicate brain operation required. Too, nobody could be quite sure what would happen if we started bouncing armored messengers off of the Early Bird satellite!

Not that we have made so much progress in our own understanding of the human communication process. People still have queer ideas about how communication occurs.

One reason is that we simply assume we know what we are talking about—or what the other fellow is talking about—when the term "communication" comes up. If someone talks about a communication problem, we usually nod our heads. It's all too easy to *assume* that we know what he is really talking about. It's even easier to assume that *he* knows what he is talking about. It's easier still to assume that people are referring to some specific phenomenon when they hear or use the word "communication."

Are they? For the most part, they are not. Make the test for yourself.

What is a book about communication . . . about? What am I talking about when I write "communication"? Or, much more important, what do you *think* I am talking about? What specifically is being referred to in such common statements as, "This company really has some communication problems," or "It just boils down to a communication problem between me and . . ."? When you use the word communication, what are you really talking about? Are you always referring to the same thing? Have you ever heard anyone refer to a letter or a telephone call as "a communication"? If a letter or a speech is "a communication," then what is it *to communicate*? Is comprehension a part of the process? Belief? Appropriate action? What is it that gets communicated?

If I am communicating with you at this moment, why is it that some readers will be communicated-to and some won't? What is a communication breakdown? What "breaks"? Exactly what is a communication failure—a failure to say the right thing to the right person at the right time? *His* inability to understand what we had in mind? His failure to do or say what we expected? Our dissatisfaction with his subsequent behavior? What, exactly, do people mean by communication?

Do you feel perfectly confident that you can always know what other people are talking about when they talk about communication? For that matter, are you perfectly confident that you know what you are talking about when you use the term?

Most people don't.

And there you have the most potent communication problem of all. Like walking and thinking and breathing and talking, like all of the things that we seem to be doing *naturally*, we take our understanding of the process for granted. We assume we know what we're talking about. We smile knowingly and nod knowingly at each other when we discuss communication.

As a result of the ease with which we can recognize so popular a term without stopping to establish what exactly is being referred to, we are destined either

1. to misunderstand each other; or
2. to obscure even more our casual assumptions about what is being referred to—an infinitely worse consequence.

If we misunderstand each other, at least we are alerted to the need to explore our misunderstanding. But if we blissfully assume we know what we're talking about, then we could be hopelessly off on the wrong track.

This is what has happened in the field of human communication. In the first place, it's extremely difficult to introduce vital new knowledge when everybody assumes he already knows all that needs to be known. History is replete with examples. The inquisitions and the bloodshed and the centuries it took for the population at large to accept the first scientific *fact* about our universe—that the sun and not the earth is the center of our part of that universe—is a classic piece of evidence.

Second, it is extremely difficult to find support for, or carry out, scientific research on *universal* experiences—love, death, communication. Thus, worthwhile new understandings of these common experiences are very slow in coming.

Scientifically, we know much much less about human communication than we do about animal husbandry—this in spite of the fact that our lives are infinitely more affected by communication than by the genetics of a particular breed of hogs. Yet we do have conceptually superior ways of understanding and practicing human communication.

It is not the purpose of this book simply to document the research and the principles of communication that have been expounded to date. What follows is not an academic survey of the field. Rather, the purpose of this book is to present and examine what would seem to be some of the most useful thinking and analytical tools presently available for understanding and *practicing* the art of human communication.

At best, that task is a most difficult one. If you believe you already know most of what you need to know or could know about human communication; if you think all that's left to be learned about human communication is a few techniques; if you found yourself nodding your head with an "Oh, yes, this is about communication—I know what it's about" . . . then we have a real communication problem!

The point is clear enough: We can't afford to assume we understand all there is to be known about even the most elementary and obvious aspects of human communication at this point. If we do, there is no way for us to communicate very successfully *about* communication.

Communication and Competence

As your study of this book progresses, it will likely become apparent to you that there is a close and essential tie between communicate-abilities and the kind of competencies we will be concerned with. This is true for the individual, and it is true for the organization.

One's abilities to communicate-to and to be communicated-with are both cause and consequence of his unique competencies to manage himself, his interpersonal relationships, and the organizations for which he may have some responsibility. But a word of caution: You would be wrong if you interpreted this to mean that one's vocabulary or his articulateness or his ability to speak or read or write letters are in themselves criteria of his competence. There is much more to it than that. One's ability to be-communicated-with goes far beyond his ability to read or to listen. It goes to the richness and the depth of his communication or information-processing system (or his mind, or the structure of his knowledge, if you wish). And it goes to the nature of his basic attitudes and orientations—toward himself, others, his job, his organization, and a whole complex of other factors.

In the same way, one's ability to communicate-to others goes far beyond his ability to write or speak well. These are matters we will take up in more detail in later chapters. Here it is important only to note that one's human competencies, his abilities to accomplish and to achieve his purposes and his potential in life—these depend ultimately upon his communicate-abilities, the adequacy with which he can be communicated-with, the adequacy of his internal information-processing (his thinking, decisioning, etc.), and the adequacy with which he can communicate-to others.[1]

Thus there could be no better reason for studying communication than that of improving one's personal, interpersonal, or managerial competencies. This book has been written with that premise in mind.

On the "Theory" and the "Practice" of Communication

The noted psychologist, Kurt Lewin, once remarked, "There is nothing so practical as a *good* theory" (I emphasize *good*).

The healthy skepticism that many practicing managers have of theory and theoretical approaches probably stems from two circumstances:

1. Their exposure over the years to a lot of *poor* theories; and
2. A basic misunderstanding about what theories actually are and how they should be evaluated.

---

[1] This will be made clear later, but it should perhaps not be overlooked here that a high level of personal competency may actually disadvantage an individual in certain organizations, or in the larger society. For example, it is quite possible that in some bureaucracies (e. g., the military), promotions and rewards—and hence job satisfaction—go to those who at least exhibit certain sorts of human *incompetencies*. Historically, superior minds have often been either harassed or ignored by the society at large.

In the chapters immediately following, it should become obvious to the reader why competencies and communicate-abilities are so closely interrelated.

First, the issue at stake in our development of superior knowledge about the things and the happenings of our world is not TRUTH. It is enable-ability. Whether a theory about something is *true* or *false* is not at issue. What is at issue is simply whether or not a new or a different way of understanding something would enable a person to accomplish a goal or a mission he couldn't otherwise accomplish.[2] The test of a *good* theory, therefore, is a pragmatic one. So the issue here is not whether any one approach to communication is true and the others false, but whether understanding communication in one way offers a potential advantage *in practice* over other ways of understanding communication. The concepts and analytical tools we will be examining here offer a great many potential advantages for the comprehension of human communication *and* for its practice—personally, interpersonally, and managerially. But that is a judgment you could not and should not make until you have completed your study of this book.

Second, we all have our own "theories" about people, communication, organization, and management. The question is not *whether* we are to have theories about these things, but simply *which ones*. And that takes us back to the test: Which ones will serve us best?

Ordinarily, those that fit the facts best will serve us best in practice. So, the intent here has been to offer some new concepts and analytical tools from the life and behavioral sciences and related areas which seem to fit the *empirical* facts of human communication.

Some of these will seem to run contrary to your experience. But then the notion of a revolving, wobbling, spherical earth certainly doesn't jibe with our personal experiences of walking around on it.

So the test of a useful theory is not always personal experience alone. Often we need to modify our interpretation of our personal experiences and from time to time augment those experiences with new ideas—with ways of understanding things that escape our everyday observations. That is why you have this book before you, and hopefully that is how it will serve you. Certainly the study of a book such as this could be an experience as useful as any other in developing an understanding of human communication.

On "Effective" Communication

Conventional ways of thinking about human communication have— unfortunately—led us to believe that successful or effective communication

---

[2] . . . or whether it would enable a person to accomplish the same goals or missions more efficiently, more effectively, more gratifyingly, etc.

can be achieved simply by employing superior skills or techniques. One has the impression, from the continuous barrage of articles and books on communication, that a little better listening, a little more attention to grammatical niceties in memo-writing, a little more use of color on employee posters, etc., would immediately convert communication failure to success, and poor communicators into good ones—just like that.

Technique and method-oriented approaches to communication are misleading on two counts:

a) The approach implies that the critical factors in most communication situations are techniques or methods; and
b) There is the implication in these approaches that human communication is a science, and that there are certain unequivocal laws which, if followed, lead to success, and, if not, to failure.

Human communication is not a science. It is very much still—and perhaps always will be—essentially an art. Neither successes nor failures are, at this point in the development of the field, easily explainable. Certainly no particular success or failure could be attributed to any one single factor. Furthermore, there is still considerable question about what actually constitutes success or failure. If a subordinate "misunderstands" my order, but does something which turns out to be more beneficial to the organization than behaving in keeping with my order would have been—is that success or failure?

The substantive knowledge upon which we can base a sound understanding of the processes of human and organizational communication is not to be found in the area of method and technique alone. It must be sought elsewhere as well.

We shall see that communication effectiveness—viewed in the conventional sense of communicator *doing something* to his receiver(s)—is determined:

a) First, by the communicator's understanding of the communication process;
b) Then by the communicator's attitudes and orientations; and
c) Only then by the techniques the communicator employs.

We will have occasion and good reason to depart from some conventional views of human communication. Many of those conventional views of the communication process have not served us well—in fact or in practice. We can advantageously begin by recognizing that techniques as such rarely make the difference between success and failure. There are of course many factors other than the communicator's *understanding* of the process and his *attitudes* (and orientations) toward his communication tasks. But these two factors are the only ones which are clearly within his control.

For that reason, this book has been written to contribute first to the reader's *understanding* of the processes of communication; second to the appropriateness and adequacy of his *attitudes*; and only then to his *techniques*.

It is natural to look for successful recipes for effective communication. But the evidence shows that it is the adequacy of one's understanding and not the currency of his techniques that consistently produces desired results in communication.

If the reader has a thorough understanding and comprehension of the processes of human and organizational communication, he will have much less difficulty in determining appropriate techniques. But one's techniques can never be any more effective than his basic understanding of the process.

Those are some of the basic premises behind the writing of this book. It is very important that they (and their obvious personal implications for the study of communication) be understood before proceeding.

SUGGESTIONS FOR FURTHER READING

Because communication is basic to all human behavior, concepts of and approaches to communication range as widely as the disciplines concerned. These recent collections reflect well many of those differing orientations to human communication.

CARPENTER, E., and McLUHAN, M. (eds.). *Explorations in Communication.* Boston: Beacon Press, 1960.

DANCE, F. E. X. (ed.). *Human Communication Theory: Original Essays.* New York: Holt, Rinehart & Winston, Inc., 1967.

MATSON, F. W., and MONTAGUE, A. (eds.). *The Human Dialogue: Perspectives on Communication.* New York: Free Press, 1967.

RIOCH, D. McK., and WEINSTEIN, E. A. (eds.). *Disorders of Communication.* Baltimore: Williams and Wilkins Co., 1964.

ROYCE, J. R. (ed.). *Psychology and the Symbol: An Interdisciplinary Symposium.* New York: Random House, Inc., 1965.

SCHRAMM, W. (ed.). *The Science of Human Communication.* New York: Basic Books, Inc., 1963.

Smith, A. G. (ed.). *Communication and Culture.* New York: Holt, Rinehart & Winston, Inc., 1966.

Thayer, L. (ed.). *Communication: Concepts and Perspectives.* Washington, D.C.: Spartan Books, Inc., 1967.

———, (ed.). *Communication: Theory and Research.* Springfield, Ill.: Charles C Thomas, 1967.

Weeks, F. W. (ed.) *Readings in Communication from Fortune.* New York: Holt, Rinehart & Winston, Inc., 1961.

2

People, Communication, and Organization: Some Basic Perspectives

IT WOULD BE DIFFICULT to make much sense of people and their behavior toward one another without taking communication into account. It would be even more difficult to talk about human communication without taking into account something of the nature of people.

At the same time, there is very little in the way of communication or human behavior we could talk about without taking into account the way communication and behavior contribute to and depend upon the patterns into which people get organized or organize themselves for specific purposes. Further, the direction of our individual lives and our organizations depends upon the ways they are or are not managed; and managing people in or out of formal organizations depends ultimately upon communication.

Those are the basic relationships between people, communication, organization, and management—relationships it would now be profitable to examine in more detail. Throughout the book, we will of course be concerned with how these factors are interrelated. Here we need only to establish some initial perspectives—a foundation upon which to build.

Because we could still be "miscommunicating" in the use of our basic term—and because behavior and organization depend ultimately upon communication—it would be appropriate to look first at the notion of communication.

11

Communication

Communication is a good deal more talked about than understood. It is a catchword of our times. Expressions like, "It's a communication problem" are commonplace. The popularity of communication serves as a camouflage which resists our attempts to look into that process and comprehend it in a detached way.

Technically, we can no more understand communication by being able to utter, "There's a communication problem here" than we could understand nuclear physics through our sheer ability to say: "This looks to me like a problem in nuclear physics." Listening to a noisy automobile engine and musing, "Sounds like the tappets to me," is not the same as being able to repair or adjust noisy tappets.

Great myths and systems of folklore arise as means of explaining just those experiences which are the most common—the most universal. Men for hundreds of years had seen the sun "rise" and "set." They explained this universal phenomenon in many (and, given our modern perspectives, often bizarre) ways. At one time, everyone knew that the sun was drawn across the sky by a horse-drawn chariot. It wasn't until the dawn of our modern age that the relative movement of the stars and planets began to be understood in more reliable and more useful ways.

We find it relatively easy to accept new facts regarding the behavior of atomic particles, for example, simply because these bits of energy cannot be directly experienced by masses of people. Communication can be directly experienced by any normal adult. The phenomenon of communication is a universal human experience.

Because whatever a man experiences in common with others he feels necessary to explain in some way, there has grown up around the notion of human communication successive layers of folklore and myth which must be penetrated or set aside if we are ever to develop empirically sound concepts and understandings of this vital human process. Unfounded knowledge is often worse than none at all. An even more formidable obstacle is our inclination to assume we understand human communication simply because we do it.

There is a common and universal experience of communication which we want to explain and talk about, of course. People do manage to affect one another—and be affected by one another—quite without any physical contact. We do manage to "get in touch with" each other. We are often able to comprehend and react to a play written hundreds of years ago just as we are able to comprehend and react to today's television newscast, or the boss's memo, dated yesterday.

There is this something we want to talk about. But it is of no advantage personally or professionally to talk nonsense about it. It is much to our personal advantage to talk as much sense about communication as we can. To do so, we'll need to cut through a lot of misunderstanding, untenable belief, and faulty assumption.

We can't carry that task far in this chapter, for that is the overall purpose of this book. But we can initiate it here.

On Defining Communication

Definitions of communication are legion. The issue here is not to document them, however; we need look only far enough to become wary of them. Here are four definitions more or less at random:

1. "Communication is the process of effecting an interchange of understanding between two or more people."
2. "Communication is the mutual interchange of ideas by any effective means."
3. ". . . The imparting or interchange of thoughts, opinions, or information by speech, writing, or signs" (*American College Dictionary*).
4. "Communication is the arrangement of environmental stimuli to produce certain desired behavior on the part of the organism."

There is really nothing wrong with any of these definitions. And there would be no purpose in being critical of any definition—*were it not for the fact that the way we describe and define things places limits on our ability to think about those things.*

Look back: (1.) and (2.) are similar. The first one seems to imply that the purpose of communication is to achieve understanding—the second some satisfactory exchange of ideas. Implicit in both is the requisite of *intention* and conscious awareness (or rationality). Neither author seems to concern himself with the interchange of feelings, which are an inevitable counterpart of all of our transactions with people. Too, one might ask: Exactly what is meant by an interchange? Do the authors mean that person A expresses something which person B exchanges for his expression, and conversely? Does the second definition mean that any nonmutual interchange is not communication? A boss or field commander might issue an order which is carried out with no comment. Is this sort of thing to be excluded from the meaning of communication? Suppose you misunderstand something I say; you *thought* you understood and *I* thought you understood, but what you did subsequently could only be interpreted as your misunderstanding of what I said. Did communication occur, or not? How does one interchange ideas? What specifically is interchanged, and how?

The compilers of the *American College Dictionary* (example 3.), who are trying to capture the spirit of the way people use the term, reflect our apparent desire to eat our cake and have it too when it comes to communication. According to this source, by communication we seem to want to mean *either* the interchange *or* the sheer act of expressing a thought or opinion. If I impart an opinion, but you either do not hear me or do not comprehend me, has communication occurred or not? If someone overlooks a "Bridge Out" sign and ends up in the river, has communication occurred? Was information actually imparted? What is the test of imparting? Of interchange? Of the communicability of a thought?

Example (4.) is somewhat different. Do we take this sort of definition to mean that unarranged environments do not influence our behavior? Or that, if the desired behavior does not ensue, communication has not occurred? And note again the implication of intention.

Such definitions seem reasonable and harmless enough on the surface. But perhaps this brief examination of but four representative definitions has demonstrated how potentially obscure and misleading they can be.

The point is that such definitions have not contributed much to our understanding of communication. There are a number of reasons for the general inadequacy of our typical explanations of communication.

First, our explanations and definitions—indeed our private understandings of communication—have been far too limited by the implication that communication is a process one undertakes in order to *do something to* someone else. The implication is that communication is limited to those instances in which one *intends* to affect another in some way, and that his intention is a conscious and a rational one.

Granted that this is in large part what we are concerned with in applied fields such as the management of organizations, the application should not be allowed to get in the way of developing better understandings of the process itself.

If one begins with an implicit assumption of intentionality, he is soon stuck with the problem of explaining unintended responses and interpretations as mistakes, errors, or "noise." He is then at odds with the very person he wants to communicate with.

The assumption of intentionality also implies that the communicator somehow controls all of the conditions which determine the occurrence of communication. This is obviously not true. A little reflection will provide abundant evidence that neither you nor I in fact control all of the conditions under which our communication is occurring at this moment.

So the implicit assumption that communication is something one *does* (or intends to *do*) *to* another is not a tenable one.

A second reason for the general inadequacy of our definitions and explanations of communication is that they imply far too much *rationality* and conscious awareness. We have inadvertently established a link between communication and ideas or throughts which is simply too restrictive. People react (even reliably and predictably) to far more than words or symbols as such. And they react in far more than purely cognitive ways. A general feeling of uneasiness about someone or some situation is often a major determinant of our behavior in those situations.

People may talk to each other for reasons other than interchanging ideas or information. A subordinate who cannot "size up" his boss's mood well enough to avoid asking for a raise at the wrong time would be considered fairly naïve. We get the message even though people don't consciously send the one we get. A speeding car is not only an idea or a thought; it is a reality—one that can kill or maim a person if he doesn't leap out of the way at the proper time. A that moment it is not a symbol of something. Yet we can derive a meaningful message out of those circumstances.

Conventional or shared languages are indeed a factor in communication, but we would be making a mistake to restrict our understanding of the communication process to those situations in which there was some rational and purely linguistic interchange of ideas or information.

A third basic reason for the inadequacy of our present "definitions" of human communication is that their authors have apparently looked upon communication as an incidental or occasional bit of behavior that people engage in by choice. An understanding of communication limited to that connotation implies that, from time to time, as the need arises, a person would go out and *communicate* with others. This sort of implicit assumption in our understanding of communication would—and often does—lead us far astray.

A concept of communication as something one turns on and off does a severe injustice to what is easy enough to observe: that we can't stop communicating or being communicated with any more than we can stop breathing in or breathing out and still go on living.[1] Communication is not an intermittent but a continuous function of human beings. Furthermore, communication is not an occasional enterprise in which a human being chooses to engage; it is as essential to his continuous existence as is the regulation of his heartbeat.

We have too long relegated communication to an incidental role in human affairs. In doing so, we have failed to achieve an adequate understanding of the vital functions of communication in human life and human affairs.

To gain an initial feeling for the possibilities of a somewhat different approach to communication[2]—and its potential for our understanding and application—let us reconsider the relationship between people and communication.

People and Communication

To best comprehend the relationship between people and communication we need to look at that relationship from at least three different points

---

[1] On this issue, here are some interesting points of departure for reflection or discussion:

"For him who has eyes to see and ears to hear no mortal can hide his secret; he whose lips are silent chatters with his fingertips and betrays himself through all his pores." From the title page: H. Lasswell, *Psychopathology and Politics* (New York: Viking Press, Inc., 1930).

"Man reveals himself by three languages: the language of acts, the language of words, and the language of gestures." Charlotte Wolff, *A Psychology of Gesture* (London: Methuen, 1948, p. 4).

"Why are there trees I never walk under but large and melodious/ Thoughts descend upon me?" Walt Whitman, *Leaves of Grass* (New York: Doubleday & Co., Inc., 1924).

"Have you seen a red sunset drip over one of my corn- / fields, the shore of night stars, the wave of lines of / dawn up a wheat valley?" "The prairie sings to me in the forenoon . . .," from Carl Sandburg's poem, "Prairie," in his *Complete Poems.* (N.Y.: Harcourt, Brace & World, 1950, p. 79).

The reader can perhaps recall similar personal experiences of both wordless and intentionless communication.

[2] There is no justification for simply having a different approach. This approach is different because (a) it seems to me better to fit the facts we do have about human communication and human behavior, and (b) it seems to me considerably more useful in comprehending and dealing with communication in an applied sense.

At the same time, it is not my purpose to suggest or imply that our concern with human communication should be any different from what it has always been. The phenomenon we are concerned with is the same in either case. We want to know more about how people affect, control, and influence one another. What differs is how these things are to be understood and dealt with both conceptually and in practice.

of view: individual behavior, interpersonal behavior, and organizational behavior.

At the level of the individual, the role of communication in one's intellectual and emotional (psychological) existence might well be compared to the role of eating and breathing in one's physiological processes. Communication is to human feeling and intellect what physical metabolism is to the body's physiological processes.

Thus communication can be looked upon as one of the two basic processes of all living systems—one, the transformation of food into energy; the other, the transformation of event-data into information. All living systems—people and organizations alike—exist only in and through these two basic processes.[3]

Communication may thus be conceived of as the dynamic process underlying the existence, growth, change, the behavior of all living systems—individual or organization. Communication can be understood as that indispensable function of people and organizations through which the organization or the organism relates itself to its environment, and relates its parts and its internal processes one to the other.[4]

Communication is as fundamental to the living system—the individual or the organization—as its ingestion and consumption of "food" and "fuel" to run its physical and physiological machinery. But it is more than this. It is in part that vital process by which individuals and organizations relate themselves to each other, and through which they affect and

---

[3] These two processes are not exclusive of each other, of course. We must ingest data about our environments (and our internal conditions) in order to seek out and consume the raw materials we need to run the body's (or the organization's) machinery. Similarly, the process of ingesting and processing information about our external and internal environments requires the use of small amounts of energy. For example, about 10 watts of power—albeit a strikingly small amount—is needed to support the information-processing "work" of the brain.

Given this particular view of the basic function of communication in individual behavior, we can ask a wide range of potent questions. For example, what patterns of information "consumption" lead to what conditions of thinking, problem-solving, and decision-making behavior? Why is it that intelligence and information consumption seem to be related? Just as we function physically to maintain, establish, or alter the body's relations vis-à-vis its environment—or to modify the physical environment in some way compatible with the body's needs—we function communicatively to establish, maintain, or modify our relations vis-à-vis others, or others vis-à-vis ourselves. How do we "get organized" to carry out these basic functions, and what difference does the way we get organized to carry out these functions make to our achieve-abilities as individuals or as managers of organizations?

[4] Cf. J. G. Miller, *Living Systems* (New York: John Wiley & Sons, Inc., 1968); and N. Wiener, *Cybernetics: Control and Communication in the Animal and the Machine* (New York: John Wiley & Sons, Inc., 1948).

influence the direction of their individual lives and their cooperative enterprises and endeavors.

Communication processes are thus the crucial processes which both enable and determine the conditions, the operations, and the interrelationships of all living systems. The essence of being human is thus *communicating-to* and *being communicated-with*.

A function of such scope—contrasted with the almost incidental role that is often attributed to communication in human behavior—may be difficult to comprehend or to accept at this point. But as we proceed, you may come to understand why this concept of communication is both a necessary and an advantageous one—particularly in practice.

As the focus of our attention shifts from individual to interpersonal behavior, we begin to ask another sort of question: How do two (or more) self-regulative systems (i.e., individuals) succeed or fail in their attempts to control or influence each other? At the level of the organization, we are concerned with still another set of issues. We want to know how to prescribe communication patterns between and among the members of that organization in such a way that the organization will function either more effectively or more efficiently.

Closer examination of these basic issues can be deferred to the appropriate later chapters.

Communication and Organization

Essentially what gets organized when people organize themselves into collective enterprises of one sort or another (companies, nations, etc.) is the flow of enterprise-related information (both into and out of decision points), and hence the strategic relationships between and among the working parts of those organizations. What is at stake is this: Who does what with what pieces of enterprise-related information?

The answer to that question basically describes the structure and the functioning of any enterprise—whether it be General Motors or the Republican party or the sociopolitical structure of the United States or the U.S.S.R. or a committee.

It is the communication that occurs and the patterns of intercommunication which ensue that define and determine the structure and the functioning of any organization.[5]

---

[5] Cf. K. W. Deutsch, "Communication Theory and Social Science." *American Journal of Orthopsychiatry*, 1952, 22, 469–83.

Organizations, like organisms, can be characterized by their inputs, their operations, and their outputs. But of primary interest to us here are those informational inputs, operations, and outputs which predict to the current condition, the capability, and the destiny of an organization. In a book of this sort, it is the organizational communication patterns which describe what is happening and what will happen as a consequence that are of interest to us.

There is another basic aspect of communication and organization, one which reflects something of the dilemma of human communication that we will be examining in more detail in later chapters. It is this: The way one is psychologically (conceptually) organized determines how he communicates with his world and how his world can communicate with him. But, at the same time, the communication system within which one maintains himself determines how he will be psychologically organized. Communicatively, people and those aspects of their worlds they do or would deal with co-determine each other. The same is true of collective enterprises of all sorts—of formal and informal organizations alike. The perceived environment and the enterprise's internal communication structure essentially codetermine each other.

Communication and Management

Like organization, management needs first to be understood in the abstract. Given the advantage of that proviso, there are three management tasks which are of concern to us in this volume.

The first is the task of managing oneself as an enterprise. The second is that of managing one's interpersonal relations to some end. The third task is that of managing larger organizations.

The common element in all three of these tasks is communication. At the personal level, it is a matter of organizing and managing one's communication network and patterns of communication to the end of developing the highest possible level of competence or achievement, for it is one's past and present communication patterns that largely determine his immediate and potential capabilities.[6] At the interpersonal level, it is a matter of managing and controlling one's interpersonal relations, and of insuring their productivity. One's investment is in the form of communicative time and effort, for communication is the only means available to us for achieving cooperative or productive human contacts.

---

[6] Cf. J. McV. Hunt. *Intelligence and Experience* (New York: Ronald Press Co., 1961).

At the level of the larger organization, it is a matter of designing that communication system which simultaneously enables that organization to cope with its environment, to maintan its internal functioning, and to be cognizant of and capable of carrying out necessary or opportunistic change.

Internal communication is to an organization what the psychological/ conceptual system is to the organism. It is what permits the organization to learn, to be aware of itself, to be intelligently adaptive and creatively aggressive vis-à-vis its environment. As is true of the individual, any organization's effectiveness is some function of its past and present communication patterns—both internal and external. As is true of the individual, the organization's external communication patterns determine its internal structure and functioning. The role of managing is therefore to design and implement those communication systems (information-decision systems) that will accomplish personal or organizational goals—and at the same time develop their further capabilities.[7]

Understanding the relation between management and communication in this way, it would seem there could be no greater challenge to the management of either human or organization life than that of fully comprehending the complex and often subtle processes of communication.

SUGGESTIONS FOR FURTHER READING

Something of the difficulty of ordering what has been said and written about communication is evident in the following list. These books and papers have been selected as good background reading for the serious student of human communication.

Babcock, C. Merton. "A Dynamic Theory of Communications," *Journal of Communication*, Vol. 2 (1952), pp. 64 ff.

————. *Ideas in Process: An Anthology of Readings in Communication.* New York: Harper & Bros., 1958.

Bach, R. O. (ed.). *Communication: The Art of Understanding and Being Understood.* New York: Hastings House, 1963.

Berne, Eric. "Concerning the Nature of Communication," *Psychiatric Quarterly*, Vol. 27 (1953), pp. 185–98.

---

[7] Barnard was one of the first practicing managers to articulate this basic function of managing: C. I. Barnard, *The Functions of the Executive* (Cambridge, Mass.: Harvard University Press, 1938). Cf. K. W. Deutsch, "Communication in Self-Governing Organizations." In L. Bryson, et al. (eds.), *Freedom and Authority* (New York: Harper & Row, 1952).

BLACK, JOHN W., and MOORE, WILBUR E. *Speech-Code, Meaning, and Communication.* New York: McGraw-Hill Book Co., 1955.

BOIS, J. SAMUEL. *Explorations in Awareness.* New York: Harper & Bros., 1957.

BRIGGS, HAROLD E. *Language . . . Man . . . Society: Readings in Communication.* New York: Rinehart & Co., Inc., 1949.

BROWN, ROGER. *Words and Things.* New York: Free Press, 1958.

BRYSON, LYMAN (ed.). *The Communication of Ideas.* New York: Harper & Bros., 1948.

CAMPBELL, JAMES H., and HEPLER, HAL W. (eds.). *Dimensions in Communication: Readings.* Belmont, Calif.: Wadsworth Publishing Co., Inc., 1965.

CHASE, STUART. "Communications: Up, Down, and Sideways," *Reader's Digest,* September, 1952.

EISENSON, J.; AUER, J. J.; and IRWIN, J. V. *The Psychology of Communication.* New York: Appleton-Century-Crofts, 1963.

GERBNER, G. "A Theory of Communication: . . ." in *The Nature of Teaching, A Symposium.* Milwaukee: University of Wisconsin School of Education, 1963.

HANDY, R. and KURZ, P. "A Current Appraisal of the Behavioral Sciences. Communication: Information Theory, Cybernetics, Linguistics, Sign Behavior." *American Behavioral Scientist,* Vol. 7 (1964), Supplement.

HANEY, WILLIAM V. *Communication and Organizational Behavior.* Rev. ed. Homewood, Ill.: Richard D. Irwin, Inc., 1967.

HARTMAN, FRANK R. "A Behavioristic Approach to Communication: A Selective Review of Learning Theory and a Derivation of Postulates," *A-V Communication Review,* Vol. 11 (1963), pp. 155–90.

HARWOOD, KENNETH, and CARTIER, FRANCIS. "On a General Theory of Communication," *A-V Communication Review,* Vol. 1 (1953), pp. 227–33.

HAYAKAWA, S. I. *Language in Action.* New York: Harcourt, Brace & Co., Inc., 1930.

———. *Language in Thought and Action.* New York: Harcourt, Brace & Co., Inc., 1949.

———. *Language, Meaning and Maturity.* New York: Harper & Bros., 1954.

HENLE, PAUL (ed.). *Language, Thought and Culture.* Ann Arbor: University of Michigan Press, 1958.

HIGHAM, T. M. "Basic Psychological Factors in Communication," *Occupational Psychology* (London), Vol. 31 (1957), pp. 1–10.

JOHNSON, WENDELL, H. *People in Quandaries.* New York: Harper & Bros., 1946.

KORZYBSKI, ALFRED. *Science and Sanity: An Introduction to Non-Aristotelian Systems and General Semantics* (1933). Lakeville, Conn.: Institute of General Semantics, 1948.

Lee, Irving J. (ed.).   *The Language of Wisdom and Folly.* New York: Harper & Bros., 1949.

———.   *Customs and Crises in Communication.* New York: Harper & Bros., 1954.

Mason, Stella E.   *Signs, Signals, and Symbols.* Springfield, Ill.: Charles C Thomas, 1963.

Miller, George A.   *Language and Communication.* New York: McGraw-Hill Book Co., 1951.

———.   *The Psychology of Communication.* New York: Basic Books Inc., 1966.

Mulholland, J., and Gordon, G. N.   *The Magical Mind.* New York: Hastings House, 1967.

Pierce, J. R. *Symbols, Signals, and Noise.* New York: Harper & Row, 1965.

Rose, A. M. (ed.).   *Human Behavior and Social Processes.* Boston: Houghton Mifflin Co., 1962.

Shibutani, T.   *Society and Personality.* Englewood Cliffs, N.J.: Prentice-Hall, Inc., 1961.

Skinner, B. F.   *Verbal Behavior.* New York: Appleton-Century-Crofts, Inc., 1957.

Smythe, Dallas W.   "Some Observations on Communications Theory," *A-V Communication Review,* Vol. 2 (1954), pp. 24–37.

Vickers, Sir Geoffrey.   "Human Communication," *British Management Review,* Vol. 12 (1954), pp. 71–79.

3

On the Nature of
Communication: I

TRADITIONAL VIEWS of human communication are usually variants of one basic model:

$$A \longrightarrow B = X \qquad \text{(FIGURE 1)}$$

This formula, explicit or implicit in most of our theories, and thus in the understanding of the process held by laymen and "practitioners," can be read, "A communicates something to B with X effect or result." (The →, "communicates something to," naturally embraces a number of subcategories, such as "when?" and "how?" and "in what medium?" and "under what circumstances?" etc.) Like other simple algebraic formulas, we can solve for any one of the elements given the other two. For example, if we hope to achieve a given result X with a given person or group B, then what must be the context, the manner, the delivery, the medium, etc., of the → ("communicates something to")? Or, if the → and the X and the A are given, what must be the characteristics and/or conditions of the audience B in order to complete the formula? And so on. Some writers add "noise" in the channels (→), others add the necessity of encoding by A, decoding by B, etc., but these are simply variants on the basic model.

From a practical point of view, there is nothing wrong with this kind of concept or model of the communication process. Indeed, in practice this is essentially the relationship of the elements we must deal with: I want to convince B of X; what must I say to him, or how, or when? A manager (A) must report a change in certain personnel policies to his subordinates

(*B*); given the topic and *A*'s communicate-abilities, what is likely to be the reaction (*X*) of those subordinates?

These are the things we want and need to know—in practice. But developing an empirically or conceptually sound understanding of the nature of communication from the perspective of the *practice* of communication would be somewhat like trying to develop a sound theory of nuclear fission from watching a series of atomic explosions or mushroom-shaped clouds. The formulae with which the nuclear physicist works look nothing at all like what we see when we look at a mushroom cloud or an atomic pile.

In the past we have attempted to understand the underlying nature of human communication from an *applied* model of the process. The result: a somewhat faulty and inadequate conception of nature of the process of communication.[1]

This traditional, implicit "model" of communication we carry around in our heads is faulty or inadequate on a number of counts:

First, the Stimulus → Response (*A* → *B*) model of communication simply does not fit the facts. *A* may say something to *B*. We would not want to question the "reality" of *A*'s utterance. But we also need to understand that what *B* hears or how he *interprets* what he hears is ultimately a product of *B* and not of *A*. *A*'s utterance *may* be a necessary condition of *B*'s subsequent behavior, but the *sufficient* condition is always and exclusively the manner in which *B* "processes" *A*'s statement.

Second, we have to recognize the fact that *A*'s utterance does not fall upon even a temporarily inactive or relatively "blank" mind. Quite the contrary. *A*'s statement can in fact be meaningful to *B* only to the extent that (1) *B* has developed over time the required mental "wherewithal" to apprehend and comprehend *A*'s utterance in the context in which it occurs; and (2) *B*'s "mind" is active.

What this means is that any statement to another necessarily falls upon his own busy ongoing stream of mental events having their own histories, their own system of priorities and attention, their own interactions, and so on. Whether or not *B* "hears" *A*'s utterance or reacts *appropriately* to it thus depends upon many factors besides what *A* says or how he says it. From this it is apparent that there are conditions that determine the success or failure of communication that are well beyond the control of the communicator or the receiver.

---

[1] For a further discussion of this and other problems of theory-building in communication, see L. Thayer, "On Theory-Building in Communication: I. Some Conceptual Problems." *Journal of Communication*, December, 1963, 1–27.

Third, it should be obvious that *who* is doing the communicating has considerable influence upon how *B* interprets the utterance. One can easily accept a controversial statement made by a friend, but might vehemently disagree with the same statement made by someone he dislikes or distrusts.

Fourth, the traditional view of the communication process obscures the fact that we may actually be talking about *different* things with the common label, communication. For example, what the sociologist is concerned with when he studies mass communication may be quite different from what the speech pathologist refers to when he talks about communication. What the simple $A{\rightarrow}B = X$ model of communication obscures from us is the fact that there are at least four distinct points of view (or levels of analysis) which separate those who study communication. At each level of analysis researchers are concerned with a more or less different set of basic elements or variables. The neurophysiologist would normally look at the same communication event differently than would the psychologist, the psychologist differently than the sociologist, the sociologist differently than the technologist (i.e., someone solely interested in the means of *transporting* data, etc.).[2] Each looks at different aspects of the overall process. We should have no argument with this. But we should be sensitive to the fact that those who subscribe to one or the other of the four levels of analysis are referring to a different set of basic operations or events than the other three—*even though they are using the same term, communication.*

Finally, given that neither the *A* nor the *B* nor the *X* in the basic formula is independent of any of the conditions of the $\rightarrow$ (such as the medium or the manner of communicating), it is apparent that we cannot describe communication in terms of a linear formula like the conventional one, $A{\rightarrow}B = X$. What we are confronted with is a complex *system* of elements, each of which influences and interacts with each of the other elements. Audiences, quite without saying a word, do occasionally communicate-to a speaker more successfully than he can communicate-to them! Our model or theory of the communication process simply has to accommodate these commonsense and irrefutable facts of human communication.

There are many other points that could be made to illustrate the inadequacy of our traditional concepts of human communication. But

---

[2] For some striking evidence of these differences, see L. Thayer (ed.), *Communication: Theory and Research* (Springfield, Ill.: Charles C Thomas, 1967); and L. Thayer (ed.), *Communication: Concepts and Perspectives* (Washington, D.C.: Spartan Books, Inc., 1967).

perhaps these few will be sufficient to suggest their inadequacy and the critical need for a more adequate understanding.

We are not abandoning the ultimate objective of improving the practice of human and organizational communication in the A →B = X sense, however. The point is simply that a more adequate understanding of the basic nature of the processes of human communication will serve us far better in the practice of communication than have our traditional views of the past.

The Basic Phenomenon

Let us not at this point get involved in any under-the-breath debate about what communication *is*. Definitions are easy to come by. It's a better understanding of the process and the development of more advantageous concepts of communication that we are after. These are difficult to come by, but infinitely more valuable (personally and professionally) than winning a debate on who has the best definition.

Imagine any human communication situation you wish—two friends talking, a boss and his subordinate, a conference, reading the newspaper, taking notes in class, watching television, etc. Every communication situation has one thing in common with every other communication situation. And that is the *basic phenomenon which underlies any and every human communication situation we might want to analyze or discuss.*

It is a dynamic phenomenon common to all living systems. It is the basic phenomenon of *communication*.

If this basic phenomenon does not occur, communication does not occur—however we might define communication. It is therefore the *sufficient* condition in the process of communication—whether the *necessary* condition be a friend's remark, a boss's directive, a conference member's comment, a news item in the paper, a teacher's lecture, a television program, or a headache.

It is the *basic phenomenon that occurs when a living system[3] takes-something-into-account.* Thus the phenomenon basic to and underlying every situation in which human communication occurs is simply this: that an organism (an individual) took-something-into-account, whether that

---

[3] A "living system" could be anything from a single cell to an organization like General Motors. Here, however, the living system we are most concerned with is the individual—people. Organizations are different orders of living systems and hence require a somewhat different level of analysis, but they can nonetheless be viewed as living systems. See J. G. Miller, *Living Systems* (New York: John Wiley & Sons, Inc., 1968); or his "Toward a General Theory for the Behavior Sciences." *American Psychologist*, 1955, 10, 513–31.

something was something someone did or said or did not do or say, whether it was some observable event, some internal condition, the meaning of something being read or looked at, some feeling intermingled with some past memory—literally anything that could be taken-into-account by human beings in general and that individual in particular.[4]

How does this help us understand the process of communication in the practical sense of $A \rightarrow B = X$?

For one thing, it emphasizes the sheer fact that our primary concern is whether or not B senses, registers, interprets, or identifies what A is saying (or not saying) to him. It emphasizes the fact that what A says (or doesn't say) will communicate something to B only if B takes-into-account what A is saying (or not saying).

It calls our attention to the fact that B can be communicated-to by A without regard for the logic of time and place; if someone suddenly remembers something someone else told him last week, communication is occurring just as surely as if that person were right in front of him at that moment, and just as surely as if that person had just made the statement. It calls our attention to the fact that the message B "gets" is some product of both A and B, but that it can vary to as much as 100 percent a function of B alone. (We could therefore modify the conventional formula thus: $A \longleftrightarrow$ "Message" $\longleftrightarrow B = X$, but remain aware of the fact that we could never fully diagram the communication process in this linear or algebraic fashion.)

Importantly, it reveals to us in a thoroughly irrefutable way that communication is not something that someone does to someone else, but is a process that is continuously ongoing within each of us. It permits us to dispense with the troublesome dichotomies of verbal-nonverbal communication, intentional-unintentional communication, conscious-nonconscious communication, etc. The basic phenomenon is the same—whether verbal or nonverbal, intentional or unintentional, conscious or nonconscious.[5]

It forces us to recognize the fact that communication occurs when B takes-into-account A's absence, or A's failure to say something (or the right thing) when expected by B. It forces us to recognize the fact that the critical factors in attempting to communicate-something-to someone are not such things as the truth or logicality or importance of our statements, or even the articulateness or the skill of our delivery. The critical factors

---

[4] Cf. E. Berne: "Whatever can be understood is a communication. Whatever cannot be understood is not a communication." In "Concerning the Nature of Communication," *Psychiatric Quarterly*, 1953, 27, p. 191.

[5] Cf. J. Ruesch, "Principles of Human Communication." *Dialectica*, 1957, 11, 154–65.

are *B*'s particular *take-into-account-abilities*, and his particular *take-into-account-susceptibilities*.

By take-into-account-abilities[6] we will want to mean more than a particular person's language abilities, intelligence, knowledge, listening skills, etc.—although these are certainly a part of his abilities and susceptibilities. What we need to establish here is a general comprehension of the basic phenomenon in all communication—*the process of taking-something-into-account*—and a preliminary appreciation of take-into-account-abilities and take-into-account-susceptibilities.

Again, we are not departing from the need to understand and improve one's competence to analyze and handle practical $A \rightarrow B = X$ communication situations. But even in the most *practical* circumstances, it would be disadvantageous to overlook or be unaware of the fact, for example, that the message which the receiver "gets" is *at least* as much his own creation as it is the sender's or the originator's. A concept or model of communication which is not firmly based upon an understanding of this basic phenomenon is ultimately either inadequate or misleading, or both.

Finally, whatever it is we are going to mean by communication, this basic phenomenon will have to be a part of our understanding, crucial to any view we might take of the communication process. Wherever and whenever human communication occurs, there must inevitably be one or more individuals *taking-something-into-account*.

Data, Information, Communication

With that inevitable condition of human communication in mind, let us add a further point of fundamental usefulness in studying human communication.

The world inside and outside of our skins is a hugely complex, unending sequence of events. Some of those events of the world are within the limited range of our sensory equipment (with or without amplification or translation by some technological device). These particular events or occurrences are therefore potential *data* for us. As long as these events are within range (or in the physical form necessary to be registered by our sensory equipment), they will impinge upon that equipment as data available to us about some aspect of our internal or external environments.

---

[6] The reader will perhaps forgive me for using such clumsy expressions. We simply do not have adequate terms to refer to these things. In any event, this roundabout way of referring to the two critical factors in communication we want to discuss may "communicate" my meaning better than arbitrary new terms.

At this point, however, those events exist only as raw sensory data (having been translated from their prior state as physical sound waves, light waves, etc.).

The next step in this sequence is a selective *conversion* of this sensory data into a form suitable for "consumption" or processing by our functional or psychological systems—i.e., into *information*.[7]

The worlds which we could take-into-account are infinite arrays of ongoing event data. As our eyes and our ears and our minds impose structure, meaningfulness, significance, or utility upon those data, the product is information[8]—functional units which our brains are uniquely equipped and "programmed" to process.

Information, not data, is the raw material for thinking, decisioning, problem-solving, attitude development, learning, and all of the specifically human activities that concern us about our own psychological functioning and the behavior of people. For example, if someone says something to you in your presence (or over the telephone), that person's utterance is potential data for you about an ongoing event of concern to you in your environment. Your sensory equipment translates the physical data of his speech (sound waves) into patterns of neurological data. This neurological data is then *selectively* organized and converted into patterns of information. What your friend is actually producing—physical sound waves—is now *meaningful* to you in the form of consumable or processable messages or bits of intelligence about those particular ongoing events in your external environment.

In some areas of systems engineering and information (and computer) sciences, the two terms "data" and "information" are used interchangeably. But it is very useful for those concerned with human communication (perhaps not those concerned solely with the transportation of data) to distinguish between that which is *potentially available* (data) and that which is *immediately consumable* (information).

So a second and helpful way of characterizing the basic processes of human communication is to suggest that underlying all communication is the process of organizing and converting raw sensory data into functionally-

---

[7] The elapsed time between these "steps" is so small as to be insignificant. These translation and conversion processes occur instantaneously and almost simultaneously. So they should not be conceived in a "first, this . . . then that" fashion. It is only for purposes of thoroughly understanding the communication process that these steps need to be viewed at all as separate processes.

[8] E. Berne writes, ". . . in the mind, information does not 'exist,' it 'becomes'" (*op. cit.*).

consumable or processable units of information. This is one useful way of specifying *what* goes on when a living system takes-something-into-account.

It is not always necessary to our analysis, but it is indispensable to our understanding of human communication, to recognize this crucial difference between "data" and "information."

The Four Levels of Analysis

Given this understanding of the basic processes underlying human communication, we are quite correctly forced to recognize that there are at least four different levels of analysis or points of focus from which to view communication.

There is first what we might call the *intrapersonal* level of analysis. Our focus at this level is upon individual behavior such as observing, problem-solving, thinking, listening or reading, seeking for or acquiring consumable information, speaking or writing, and so on—with particular emphasis upon the *inputting* and *processing* of information. We would study and analyze those processes of communication which occur "in" an individual or "in" people in general. We would be concerned with how an individual gets communicated-with, what that process consists of and how it might be facilitated or impeded, etc. This, of course, is the level of analysis which has to be accommodated in some way by any explanation we might make of communication at any level of analysis—simply because this is where communication occurs, *in* the individual.

The next level of analysis is the *interpersonal* level. Here we would be concerned with what might be called *intercommunication*. Our focus would be upon two-person (or *n*-person) *systems* of communication. We would of course remain cognizant of the fact that the basic processes of human communication occur *in* the individuals involved, but we would add a consideration of other variables, such as the relationship of the individuals involved, their intentions and expectations vis-à-vis each other, the rules of the interpersonal "games" they might be playing at the time, and so on. Here we would be concerned not with how an individual is affected via communication, but with how given individuals affect each other through intercommunication and thereby mutually regulate and control each other.[9]

---

[9] For our immediate purposes, we can look upon mass communication as a special case of intra- and/or interpersonal communication, but distinguished by the use of mass-produced, mass-disseminated "messages" of some sort. Cf. G. Gerbner, "An Institutional Approach to Mass Communications Research," in L. Thayer (ed.), *Communication: Theory and Research*. Springfield, Ill.: Charles C Thomas, 1967.

A third level of analysis or point of focus might be termed the *organizational*. At this level of analysis, we would be concerned with the networks of data systems that link organization members together and provide the means by which the organization relates itself to its environment—and with how these data (or communication) systems affect task-related decisioning, the efficiency and effectiveness of the organization, and so on. We should never overlook the fact, in analyzing organizational communication patterns, that the basic phenomenon is always something that occurs *in* that organization's individual members, and that intercommunication amongst certain members is constantly occurring. But it will also be useful to concern ourselves with the organization as a living system or information-decision system having some identifiable characteristics of its own.

An increasingly common level of analysis is the *technological*. When the focus is upon the technology of communication, one is concerned with equipment, apparatus, and/or the formalized "programs" for generating, storing, processing, translating, distributing, or displaying data—either for "consumption" by other pieces of equipment or for ultimate translation into information and consumption by human beings. This is a perfectly justifiable level of analysis. But we need to remember from the outset that the *languages* we use—whether verbal, graphic, or gestural—are just as much a part of the technology of communication as are telephones, radios, the teletype, xerography, paper, computers, and the ball-point pen. We should certainly not restrict our notion of communication technology to that recently invented or evolved. The ear and the eye must be considered an aspect of communication technology alongside television and space communication.

Also, while we can legitimately focus upon this level of analysis, we have to realize that there are essential technological aspects at all three of the other levels of analysis. Further, we should never neglect the fact that the "hardware" of communication handles only *data*. *Information*, which is the ultimate element of human communication, is a functional product or output of the human psychological system. Thus a data-handling system of electronic or mechanical equipment of which some human being is an indispensable part is more appropriately called a communication system. A system of equipment which simply displays its product to a human being is better referred to as a data system. If a man is an indispensable part of a particular communication system, then we can not adequately describe that system without taking into account the communicate-abilities and susceptibilities of human beings in general and that man in particular.

A great deal of confusion in studying and understanding communication arises from our failure to be alert to the particular level of analysis being employed. Perhaps the following sketch will serve as an illustrative reminder of the four levels of analysis and their relationships.

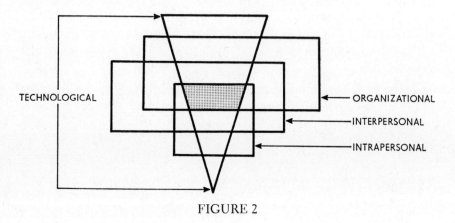

FIGURE 2

Communication "Metabolism"

At the individual or *intrapersonal level* of analysis, we will find an analogy to metabolism helpful in building a sound and adequate understanding of human communication. Metabolism is the term used to refer to the energy-processing functions of the body. The vital process in physical metabolism is the conversion of raw food and fuel into forms of energy which are consumable or usable by the body's machinery.

In some respects, communication viewed at the intrapersonal level serves the individual's nonorganic or psychological needs in a way similar to the manner in which metabolic processes serve the body's organic or physiological needs. The selective translation of raw event data into sensory data by the sense organs, and the selective conversion of that sensory data into information consumable (or usable) by the "mind" or the psychological system, could be viewed as the vital part of what might be called "communication metabolism."

From this perspective, we could easily identify four sub-processes of the communication systems in and through which the individual maintains himself: (a) the *generation*, (b) *dissemination*, (c) *acquisition*, and (d) *ingestion* or *consumption* of data. That is, data "about" the events of an individual's internal and external worlds are continuously being generated, disseminated, acquired (or not), and ingested or consumed (or not.)

The usefulness of this concept is quite simple. Metabolically, the individual is continuously and often simultaneously involved in generating and disseminating, acquiring and ingesting, data. In terms of intercommunication, if another person is generating or disseminating data for which you currently have some need or "appetite,"[10] you will acquire and ingest that data for present or future use by your psychological system. Under these circumstances, a "matching" would have occurred between your communication system and his—a condition that greatly facilitates intercommunication.

There is also a phenomenon known as "communication satisfaction"; one's feeling of satisfaction about any communication encounter will depend keenly upon the contribution that encounter makes to his basic communication metabolism.

The Basic Functions of Communication

Thus far we have been viewing human communication as a natural process quite apart from man's use of that process toward his own ends—as in his organizations. There is one further point to be made before we begin to depart from our exploration of those functions of communication common to all living systems and turn to those applied functions of communication which have evolved through man's peculiarly human endeavors.

The two *basic functions of communication* are these:

a) The dominant function of communication for all living systems is *adaptation*. The fact that we are designed and programmed to be communicated-to by our environment permits us to adapt to it and to maneuver our way through it enroute to our instinctive or purposeful ends. Our abilities to take-into-account certain features and events of our environment serve the purposes of establishing, maintaining, exploiting, or altering some relationship between us and our environment.[11]

---

[10] A metabolic (communication) need or "appetite" for information may be either conscious or nonconscious.

[11] Domestic animals demonstrate adequate abilities to be communicated-to. They can accumulate more or less adequate understandings of how we feel, what we want them to do, etc. But, without a means of intercommunication like human language, their abilities to communicate-to us or to other members of their own species is—by contrast—very poorly developed.

b) The other basic function of communication—which humans have developed to their extreme social advantage—is that of communicating-to some *living* aspect of the environment (such as a person) in such a way that we establish, maintain, exploit, or alter the relationship of that person to us.[12]

In the former instance, we *input* and process external and internal event-data with a view toward adapting ourselves to some aspect of our environment. In the latter instance, we *output* (generate or disseminate data directed at someone else) in order to adapt that someone else to us. In short, when we take-something-into-account, we do so with the consequence of establishing, maintaining, exploiting, or altering some aspect of ourselves vis-à-vis that which we take-into-account. When we attempt to get someone else to take-into-account us or our utterances, the consequence we seek is the establishment, maintenance, exploitation or alteration of the relation of that person *to us*. In the former instance, we attempt to adapt ourselves in some way to something out there. In the latter, we attempt to adapt that something out there to us. And these basic functions of communication are common to all living systems. As we move toward the top of the evolutionary ladder from phototropism through animal to man, the first function becomes less characteristic, and the second function more characteristic of behavior. In man, manipulating the environment communicatively (essentially other people) characterizes most of our self-initiated behavior. But the other basic function of communication should not be overlooked.

Instrumental and Consummatory Communication

Some of our communication and intercommunication serves as an end in itself. Often much of it is. We sometimes take-into-account some aspect of the world (a person or any other experience-able event of the world) simply for the pleasure of doing so. We sometimes "output" or "input" with no direct or indirect purpose in mind other than the sheer doing-so. Such conditions of our existence are "consumable" quite without any consequence beyond their sheer consumption. Some of our own behavior, and some of the behavior of other people, we may consume with no point in mind except the sheer consumption of it. The play of children is a good

---

[12] For eloquent testimony on this point by a leading biologist, see J. Z. Young, *Doubt and Certainty in Science* (New York: Oxford University Press, 1950). Cf. N. Wiener, *Cybernetics* (New York: John Wiley & Sons, Inc., 1948) for emphasis on the first basic function expressed above: "The process of receiving and of using information is the process of our adjusting to the outer environment. . . ."

example. Being moved by music is another. Perhaps the most common example is the fellow who talks just to hear himself talking.[13] Such communication is *consummatory*.

But a large proportion of our intercommunication, particularly, is *instrumental*. We hope to accomplish some end, directly or indirectly.[14]

In this book we will be concerned primarily with *instrumental* or *purposive* communication. But we could never afford to neglect the fact that communication of some consequence occurs even if not intended. Thus we will have to expand the notion of instrumental or purposive to include any communication which occurs *with some adaptive consequence* for someone. Silence on the part of a manager can be just as instrumental in affecting the recipient of that silence as any attempt the manager might make to communicate-to that person.

Therefore we must consider that *any communication that occurs and which is of some consequence to the interpersonal or organizational relationships of the persons involved is instrumental.*

The practical question is a simple one to ask, although a difficult one to answer: how do I as originator communicate-to the other in such a way as to achieve my objectives vis-à-vis the other, while avoiding or preventing any incidental or unintended message he might "get" which might have a contrary effect?

Anticipating accurately what *not* to do or say is as basic a competence for the effective communicator as his ability to anticipate adequately what to do or say. This is so because other people are in no sense limited merely to what we do or say in what they can take-into-account. *Anything* (including silence) that is meaningfully interpreted by some person constitutes an occurrence of communication.

And any communication occurrence which affects an adaptive relationship is instrumental, quite apart from the intentions of the persons involved.

Meaning and Message

There are two concepts (whatever the specific terms employed) which are common to most approaches to human communication. Often these

---

[13] Such behavior has technical names like *autotelic* or *autogenous*. But for a most readable exposition of the consequences for human communication, see W. H. Johnson, *Your Most Enchanted Listener* (New York: Harper & Row, 1956).

[14] To illustrate a fairly commonplace distinction between the two: spurring one's horse to move faster is *instrumental*; but if the ride is just for pleasure, then the experience of riding is *consummatory*.

concepts are left implicit. But it will be to our advantage to make as explicit as we can how we are going to understand *meaning* and *message*.

To avoid certain "mentalistic" pitfalls in our understanding of meaning, we can note first that whatever has some functional utility for an individual is potentially meaningful to him. Anything that a person *can* take-into-account, whether consciously or nonconsciously, has meaning for that person. Thus our individual take-into-account-abilities and take-into-account-susceptibilities are equivalent to our individual make-meaningful-abilities.

Any event or pattern of events (or absence thereof) which I am capable of converting into consumable or usable information is meaningful to me. What this means, of course, is that the meaning of any thing or happening will for me be somewhat different from the meaning of that same thing or event for you. This is so because no two people have the same take-into-account-abilities. But the way in which we individually process information may be similar enough to permit us to talk about things *as if* our separate experiences of them were identical—that is, we may share an adequate degree of *intersubjectivity*.

Meaning is an individual process or product. When we arrive at some agreement about what something means, what we are agreeing upon are the terms by which we will *refer* to that something in intercommunication. We simply formalize a way of referring to that something so as to share that formalization (as we do when we prepare and share dictionary "meanings").

In communication, however, what we are up against is what those things we want to talk about *mean* to you as an individual and to me as an individual. The significance or meaning you are ascribing to the marks on this page is the critical factor in what is getting communicated-to you—not what those words mean to me or how they are defined in the dictionary.

There are no intrinsic meanings in things or events. The objects and events of our worlds are totally without meaning in their raw event-data form. It is people who create and attach or assign meaningfulness to them. The way a person puts words together is a product of him. But the way in which those words are understood by a receiver is a function of the receiver, not of the originator. The originator may create the event-data; but the receiver creates the *meaning* that event-data has for him. And that's what counts in communication.

If we are to gain a fully useful understanding of the communication process, however, there is another basic concept that must be comprehended. That is the concept of *message*. One might accurately assign meaning to another's words, but still miss his point. Typically, we must comprehend the event-data of the world (such as another's statement to us) in two ways before our understanding is complete:

a) First, we must assign or impose some appropriate *meaning* upon the sense-data he makes available to us; and

b) Second, we must deduce the *import* of those data, given the originator, the situation, the timing, etc.

Or, to put it in a somewhat different way, people can ordinarily ascribe appropriate meanings to what we are saying. They do sometimes (or often) understand what we say. But they occasionally misconstrue the *why* or the *wherefrom* we speak. (Or, if one sometimes attempts to hide or veil his real intentions, another may nonetheless deduce the speaker's "ulterior" purpose and thereby "disrupt" the communication!)

The individual words or sentences of a speech or a document, for example, may be individually meaningful to the receiver. But there is another level at which this data is or is not meaningful to him. That is the level of the message, or the *import* of what he is "getting" from what the other is saying.

There is a rare degree of accuracy in the expression, "getting the message." Intuitively, we seem to have realized that there is more to communication than just comprehending the words. If you "get" what I say, you have the raw information. But if you "get" what I *intend*, if you get what I *mean*, then you are "getting the message."

But the message, like the meaning, is ultimately a product of the receiver; the originator's product is nothing but potential sense *data* for the receiver. Thus the message the originator intends and the message the receiver "gets" are often different. At best, they can only be similar, and then only by tacit agreement (again, by virtue of the intersubjectivity of the participants).[15]

The raw data—a letter or memo, another's utterance, etc.—should be understood as nothing more than potential sense data for the receiver. The *functional message*, the import the receiver "gets,"—the unit of exchange upon which most human communication revolves—is an internal, subjective creation of the receiver.

The message is thus the basic unit of communication. People may apprehend or even discuss their worlds in smaller units (such as words or

---

[15] Cf. Ruesch, *op. cit*, p. 157 ff.

automobiles or experiences). But the unit upon which all response, reaction, and behavior is based is the message—the event as understood in the perceived context of, and in terms of its *import* for, the receiver.

An originator's statement has *purport* or intention—his intention. His statement implies three things. It implies *him* as the originator, it implies *his concept* of what he is talking about, and it implies a relationship between those two. The receiver's *message* has *import*—the import of that statement, as construed, by and for the receiver. The message the receiver creates from the available event-data implies a similar triadic relationship— the receiver qua receiver, *his* concept of what the originator is referring to, and the relationship between those two factors as comprehended by him.

Words and other events of the world can mean something in a dictionary sense. But import is import *to someone*. Furthermore, only the meaning of words and a few idioms can be formalized or conventionalized, and those only apart from any particular contest. Yet we must constantly deal with much larger aggregates and patterns—sentences, paragraphs, extended conversations, books, reports, conferences, business associations, and so on. It would be impossible to get to the meaning of these larger aggregates and patterns by simply "adding up" the meaning of each individual term employed. As human beings, we must learn to make sense of—to make *messages* out of—aggregates and patterns of individual data units of an infinite variety of sizes, shapes, qualities, dimensions, etc.

Functional messages of this sort are not composed of logically-related units. Anything can be put together with anything else to comprise messages. I can "add" what you say to my interpretation of where and when you say it, to the significance I attach to the other people present, to my feeling about you as a person, to the likely consequences for me of what you are saying, to some vague notion I have of right and wrong, to a rebuff I experienced at your hands last week, to my theory of how people get ahead in this world, and so on and on. There are no logical, spatial, temporal, or any other limits on what can be taken-into-account by me in creating messages about what is going on when someone else is communicating-to me.

This sort of concept certainly doesn't simplify the task of understanding human communication, for we know far too little about how messages get created out of raw sense data to be able to predict message-formation with much reliability. But the essence of what has been described here *is* an invariant aspect of human communication. We would be wrong and equally disadvantaged if the concept of *message* were not a basic aspect of our understanding of human communication.

Communication and Communicating

We've covered a good deal of basic ground in this chapter. But the concepts discussed here are prerequisite to all that follows. How well we have communicated here will indeed determine how well we are going to communicate from here on!

As a result of the sort of education and training in communication that has been available, it seems natural for us to think in terms of how-to-communicate rather than how-to-be-communicated-with. Yet the one is no more important than the other. The ability to be communicated-with is just as important to personal or professional competence as is the ability to communicate-to others. Perhaps more so.

Further, our inclination to think of communication essentially in terms of manipulating or affecting others—of communicating-to others—stands as an obstacle to a more advantageous view of communication as something which occurs *in* the receiver. Overemphasis on the origination of statements to be transmitted detracts from the primary focus that should be placed upon the creation of the message within the receiver, the message upon which he will base *his* thinking and *his* behavior.

Again, the practical needs of our personal and professional lives are such that we do need to develop better ways of communicating-to others. But we also need to develop better ways of being communicated-with. A more empirically sound concept of the human communication process—the basis of which we have formed in this chapter—should enable us to develop our capacities and competencies in both directions.

The practical need to communicate-to will ultimately be served best by a concept of communication which better fits the empirical facts, however much at variance with traditional understandings or practical needs it seems to be at the moment.

In later chapters, we will look with more depth into some of the practical implications of these basic issues in communication. But for now, given the interconnection between communication and behavior, we need to review some facts about people and the way they function.

SUGGESTIONS FOR FURTHER READING

It would hardly be possible to identify the broad array of published thought which has been incorporated in this orientation to communication. But the documents listed below could be used to enlarge upon the perspectives outlined in this chapter.

BENTLEY, A. F.   *Behavior, Knowledge, Fact.* Bloomington, Ind.: Principia Press, 1935.

DEUTSCH, KARL W.   "Mechanism, Teleology, and Mind: The Theory of Communication," *Philosophical and Phenomenological Research*, Vol. 12 (1951), pp. 185–222.

————.   "On Communication Models in the Social Sciences," *Public Opinion Quarterly*, Vol. 16 (1952), pp. 365–80.

FEARING, FRANKLIN.   "Toward a Psychological Theory of Human Communication," *Journal of Personality*, Vol. 22 (1953), pp. 71–88.

————.   *Human Communication: An Introduction.* Report A256. Los Angeles: University of California, 1954.

GIBB, JACK R.   "Defensive Communication," *The Journal of Communication*, Vol. 11 (1961), pp. 141–48.

GIBSON, J. J.   *The Senses Considered as Perceptual Systems.* Boston: Houghton Mifflin Co., 1966.

HALL, E. T.   *The Silent Language.* Garden City, N. Y.: Doubleday & Co., Inc., 1959.

HAYAKAWA, S. I.   *Our Language and Our World.* New York: Harper & Bros., 1954.

KECSKEMETI, PAUL.   *Meaning, Communication and Value.* Chicago: University of Chicago Press, 1952.

MASLOW, A. H.   *The Psychology of Science.* New York: Harper & Row, 1966.

MILLER, J. G.   "The Individual as an Information Processing System," in W. S. FIELDS and W. ABBOTT (eds.). *Information Storage and Neural Control.* Springfield, Ill.: Charles C Thomas, 1963.

MORRIS, CHARLES W.   *Signs, Language, and Behavior.* Englewood Cliffs, N.J.: Prentice-Hall, Inc., 1946.

RUESCH, JURGEN.   "Synopsis of the Theory of Human Communication," *Psychiatry*, Vol. 16 (1953), pp. 215–43.

————.   "Principles of Human Communication," in his *Therapeutic Communication.* New York: W. W. Norton & Co., Inc., 1961.

SCHRODER, H. M.; DRIVER, M. J.; and STREUFERT, S.   *Human Information Processing.* New York: Holt, Rinehart & Winston, 1967.

SOLTIN, J. F.   *Seeing, Knowing, and Believing: A Study of the Language of Visual Perception.* London: Geo. Allen & Unwin, 1966.

SMITH, R. L.   *General Models of Communication.* (Dittoed.) Communication Research Center, Purdue University, 1962.

SWARTZ, ROBERT J. (ed.).   *Perceiving, Sensing, and Knowing.* New York: (Anchor Books), Doubleday & Co., Inc., 1965.

TOCH, H., and MACLEAN, M. S., JR.   "Perception, Communication and Educational Research: A Transactional View," *A-V Communication Review*, Vol. 10 (1962), pp. 55–77.

4

People, Behavior, and Communication:
On Being Communicated-With

PEOPLE do make sense of their worlds, and of a large proportion of what other people say to them. We have to, if we are going to adapt to or deal with other people or with the world in some way. As determined by our take-into-account-abilities and our take-into-account-susceptibilities, we organize and convert sensory experiences of our worlds into meaningful units—into *messages*. Our messages about the world (and about our own internal functioning) constitute our knowledge of the world, our understanding of it, the sum of our intelligence about it.

There is thus a "something," some set of operations within people, which serves simultaneously as the ultimate *source* of all of their knowledge about themselves and their worlds, and as the *basis* of all of their purposive behavior vis-à-vis themselves and their worlds.

To gain a thorough understanding of human communication, we don't need to know everything there is to know about the behavior of people. But we do need to have some useful concept of what makes it possible for us to make sense of the raw event-data of the world. And we do need some useful concept of why people do what they do (or don't do what they don't do) communicatively.[1] In effect, we want to develop some explanations or models of the behavior of people which will provide us with a

---

[1] Thus the purpose of this chapter is not to survey or catalog the accumulated knowledge of neurologists, psychologists, sociologists, etc., about human behavior. In fact, I have exercised considerable license both in designing basic models of human *knowing* and *doing*, and in reinterpreting standard concepts of behavior (such as

better and more useful understanding of human communication—in fact and in practice.

On Behaving Communicatively

How is it that people make sense of their worlds? Why is it that people vary in their ability to "get the message"? Why is it that an individual's behavior—particularly his communication behavior—seems to bear some persistent evidence of his personality? What is behind the fact that our motivation to communicate-to effectively and to be communicated-with varies as much as it does? What is it that determines the way take-into-account-abilities (and -susceptibilities) vary from person to person, and within the same person from time to time?

These are questions of the sort we want to have useful and reliable answers to—whether the immediate concern is with the theory or the practice of human communication. They are questions of both the "how" and the "why" variety.

The kinds of human behavior we are concerned with all imply some conscious or nonconscious comprehension of, or orientation to, those situations that a person wants to deal with communicatively. It is a particular person's interpretation of (or orientation to) the situation being taken-into-account by him that provides the essential framework upon which his behavior or actions in that situation are based.

There are thus two components of the model of human behavior to be developed here: the *comprehending-evaluating* component (or *conceptual/evaluative system*), and the *action* component (or *behavior control system*). There is no need to get deeply involved with the details of these components. Broad general conceptions will serve our purposes well.

The Conceptual/Evaluative System

One may usefully view what is "within" people that enables them to organize and make sense of their raw sensory experiences of themselves and

---

thinking and learning) in terms of those basic models. This is because our purpose here is not to study the history of knowledge about human behavior. It is to develop a sounder and more reliable approach to *understanding* human communication. This criterion, in my view, justifies the somewhat "nonacademic" manner in which the bases of human behavior are described and interpreted in this book.

their environments (i.e., to relate themselves to their environments)—as a conceptual/evaluative system.[2]

This system is an extremely complex and intricately organized multi-dimensional hierarchy of concepts, values, beliefs, etc., and of clusters of concepts, values, beliefs, etc.[3] There are thus individual beliefs or attitudes, and systems of belief and attitude, or of higher-order concepts. It is a dynamic, *self-organizing* system.[4] Its primary function is that of enabling the individual to establish, maintain, confirm, exploit, or alter a con-ceptual/evaluative relationship between himself and some aspect of his environment, or vice versa.

Viewed in the aggregate, each individual's conceptual/evaluative system is his "model" of the world: all of his assumptions, orientations, beliefs, feelings, hypotheses, constructs, etc., about what the world in general or any situation in specific is like—at least those aspects of that world he has dealt with or expects to deal with (or could potentially deal with). Simple concepts are functional interpretations of (or ways of relating to) such units of one's world as individual words or isolated bits of behavior (such as a certain facial expression). *Clusters* of simple concepts enable us to deal with larger units of our environment—to process their *import*. Still larger clusters of concepts permit us to deal with higher-order abstractions, and so on. Concepts and concept-clusters are thus hierarchically ordered.

---

[2] Probably the most commonly accepted explanation of human take-into-account-abilities or make-sense-abilities is *mind*. There is really nothing wrong with mind as an "explainer" of how people apprehend and comprehend themselves and their environ-ments. But there are a number of advantages to the notion of conceptual/evaluative system. If the reader wishes, he may translate conceptual system as mind *plus* . . . cer-tain other characteristics of a person's comprehend-abilities and evaluate-abilities, characteristics which have only recently begun to be understood in a scientific way. See, e.g., Constance Sheerer (ed.), *Cognition* (New York: Harper & Row, 1964); R. J. C. Harper, *et al.* (eds.), *The Cognitive Processes* (Englewood Cliffs, N.J.: Prentice-Hall, Inc., 1964); F. H. George, *Cognition* (London: Methuen, 1962); E. B. Hunt, *Concept Learning* (New York: John Wiley & Sons, Inc., 1962); and J. S. Bruner *et al.* (eds.), *Studies in Cognitive Growth* (New York: John Wiley & Sons, Inc., 1966). Cf. J. Scher (ed.), *Theories of the Mind* (New York: Free Press, 1962).

[3] *Concept* can be understood as a way of functionally comprehending any event, thing, idea, relationship, feeling, etc., which the organism is capable of sensing (or discriminating). A concept, thus viewed, is also a way of functionally organizing and identifying and/or interpreting the raw event-data of the nervous system. Every concept and cluster of concepts has its own evaluative dimensions. *It is not possible to conceive of something without simultaneously evaluating it.* So I will generally use the single term concept to include both the knowing and the evaluating dimensions of concepts and concept-clusters.

[4] Cf. M. C. Yovits *et al.* (eds.), *Self-Organizing Systems, 1962* (Washington, D.C.: Spartan Books, Inc., 1962), for some related concepts.

The hierarchical organization *within* concept-families permits us to classify the objects and happenings of our world. The structural relations *between* concept-families and between concepts belonging to the same concept-cluster enable us to conceive of relationships, sequences, cause-effect contingencies, and so on. The functional linkages between and within concept-clusters all have evaluative dimensions.

Other than to note finally that the structure and the operations of the conceptual system as such are *functional*—that is, not organic—we need not get further involved in just how the system develops, organizes itself, and operates. What we are concerned with are those aspects and functions of the comprehending/evaluating component which have some particular value for our understanding of human communication. It will be helpful to consider some of the more important factors one at a time.

THE NOTION OF REALITY

The "reality" which is the basis for individual behavior is not *the Reality*, but that model of it which has evolved "inside" the behaver. The issue here is not a philosophical one. It is a practical, pragmatic, matter-of-fact one. It would be a waste of time to debate the issue of whether there is a reality beyond those experiences people have of it. But it would be an exceeding error of understanding to fail to note that it is not *the Reality* upon which we base our behavior, but our own conceptions of it.

The only point of contact any human has with his world—whether things or other people—is through his senses. There is no alternative. The raw material out of which all of our comprehensions of the world are built is sensory data. The world does not come to us in the form of ideas or things or people or concepts. It comes to us *only* in the form of physical event-data which our sensory equipment translates into sensory event-data.

Every individual's behavior in every situation is based not upon *reality*, but upon reality-as-comprehended by the behaver.[5] The fact that the earth has always been round was not the determining factor in the reluctance of early sailors to venture beyond sight of land. What did in fact hold them back was their belief in the "fact" (almost universally believed to be true

---

[5] For a full treatment of this point of view, see A. W. Combs and D. Snygg, *Individual Behavior: A Perceptual Approach to Behavior.* Rev. ed. (New York: Harper & Row, 1959). Cf. H. Cantril, A. Ames, A. H. Hastorf, & W. H. Ittelson, "Psychology and Scientific Research," (in 3 parts), *Science*, 1949, Vol. 110 (Nov. 4, 11, 18); and H. Cantril, "Concerning the Nature of Perception," *Proceedings* of the American Philosophical Society, 1960, 104, 467–73.

at that time in history) that the earth was flat—and that venturing out too far would lead to the obvious fate of falling off the edge.

A significant use of our models of the world is that of speculating or hypothesizing on what *might* or *should* happen in the future. We use our conceptual/evaluative systems not only to infer the import (for us) of present and past situations, but also to determine what may be likely to happen in the future as a result of what we do or do not do in the present.

Every experience or expectation we have of those aspects of the world which we want to deal with in some way (such as another's comment to us or his likely reactions to our reply)—must be interpreted and comprehended *by an individual.* Thus the way we see the world, interpret any particular situation, or anticipate its consequences, is ultimately a product of us. The only reality upon which an individual can base his behavior is his own reality—*his* conceptual structuring of the world, *his* model or image of it, *his* expectations about the future.[6]

There is no alternative to this basic fact. The world we see and hear and comprehend depends upon how we are individually organized to convert raw event-data into information, and the sort of conceptual systems we individually have to make messages out of that information. At the same time, each one of us must proceed *as if*[7] we were comprehending the world "out there," and not simply our own conceptions of it. We do in fact communicate as if the things we talk about were gotten from some private pipeline to "Truth" rather than from our comprehensions of rather tenuous sense data about those things. We talk to each other as if we were referring to "Reality" rather than our private conceptions of it. But it is our private conceptions we must ultimately be talking about.

---

[6] For three different points of view of this issue, see J. M. Dorsey and W. H. Seegers, *Living Consciously* (Detroit: Wayne State University Press, 1959); E. Knight, *The Objective Society* (New York: George Braziller, Inc., 1960); and G. A. Kelly, *A Theory of Personality* (New York: W. W. Norton & Co., Inc., 1963). For a cogent review of some implications specifically for communication study, cf. H. Toch & M. S. MacLean, "Perception, Communication, and Educational Research: A Transactional View." *AV Communication Review*, 1962, 10, 78–108. The scholar may be reminded of what F. C. Bartlett calls *schema*, A. Ames calls *assumptions*, J. Bruner calls *hypotheses*, J. Z. Young calls *brain models*, and D. O. Hebb calls *cell-assemblies*.

[7] Cf. H. Vaihinger, *The Philosophy of 'As If'* (London: Routledge, 1911). The issue being raised here is not the age-old issue between "subjectivity" and "objectivity." The issue is the ultimate inevitability of our psychological egocentrism. We must of necessity see things in and through ourselves. It is a physiological, a psychological, an empirical, and a logical impossibility for a human to perceive his world except in and through himself. The major scientists throughout history have uniquely accepted their ultimate "subjectivity."

Sensory Reality and Normative Reality

It is sometimes helpful to recognize two different kinds of reality—sensory (or physical) *reality* and *normative* (or consensual) *reality*.[8]

The difference can and should be made distinct. Sensory reality is comprised of all of those experiences of the world which a particular individual could test or validate with his own senses. If I want to know whether I can walk through my office wall, I can test it and find out. If I want to know whether it would make me feel better physically if I walk to the office rather than drive, I could test that.

But very little of what engages the attention of the average 20th-century American adult could be categorized as sensory reality. Most of the structure and the operations of our conceptual systems are oriented to *normative* or *consensual* reality. Normative or consensual reality is in essence any concept or quality or relationship we can comprehend—*but which cannot be physically validated by one's own senses.*[9] A moment's reflection will serve to impress upon you the simple fact that most of the information processing we do—most of our thinking, speaking, listening—is not "about" anything that we could test with our own individual senses.[10] It is "about" things and ideas and qualities and conditions that are common to our individual conceptual systems *by tacit agreement* (i. e., by virtue of our intersubjectivity). We exhibit similar conceptions of the world simply because we have been similarly educated and socialized to do so—not, as it is all too easy to delude ourselves, because we are all seeing the same absolute "Reality."

A large proportion of the things we talk about are things that cannot be directly experienced by our own senses. Such things as democracy, foreign policy, the State Department, the quality of Elizabeth Taylor's screen

---

[8] The obvious similarity of consensual or normative reality to what L. Festinger referred to as "social reality" should be noted (in his "Informal Social Communication," *Psychological Review*, 1950, 57, 271–82). I prefer *normative*, however, because some connotations of social might inadvertently make the concept too restrictive.

[9] The object I call "Mary" exists. I can test that with my own senses. But whether Mary is pretty or smart or pleasant or efficient or talented or lazy or a thousand other qualities—these are part of our shared consensual realities, our intersubjectivity. They are *not* a part of the object I call "Mary," which is physically a complex pattern of event-data. I comprehend her "Mary-nesses," but these perceptions are communicatively "true" only to the extent they are consensual (i.e., intersubjectively held in common by another person).

[10] Cf. G. A. Miller, E. Galanter, and K. H. Pribram, *Plans and the Structure of Behavior* (New York: Holt, Rinehart and Winston, 1960).

performances, the campus, a decline in sales, and so on and on—such things can be talked about only to the extent that they are similarly comprehended by other people.

Even if we were to grant that a sizeable proportion of all the things one talks about (or other people talk about) could be *directly* experienced in some way, those experiences could exist only in the form of sense data and would have to be converted into information and organized into meaningful messages. So to facilitate our "getting in touch" with other other, our separate conceptual systems (either accidentally or on purpose) get structured or programmed to produce reasonably similar interpretations of normative reality.

Or, to put it in a slightly different way, there are only two ways of building a model of "reality." One is to test our assumptions and conceptions of it with our own senses. The other is to agree to more or less standardized interpretations of those things we want to talk about, and simply acquiesce to the programming of our own conceptual systems consistent with those standardized interpretations (normative concepts). Much of this is accomplished through education. An even larger part of it is accomplished indirectly; as we observe other people communicating-at each other, we inadvertently develop more and more of the conceptual elements and the conceptual relations which determine our own perceptions of the world.

Of all of those elements and relations we need or might be able to use in building an adequate "comprehending component" for ourselves, what we don't get from other people we evolve for ourselves. Communication is thus both the end and the means of organized human behavior. As we shall see, the very conditions that make intercommunication possible give rise to a number of common communication pitfalls.

CULTURE AND REFERENCE GROUPS

This brings us to two concepts of a somewhat different order—but potentially just as useful.

Culture can be thought of as that normative reality (including values, norms, assumptions, orientations, etc.) common to two or more people, and which thereby facilitates communication between them. That is, to the extent that two or more people have some part of their individual conceptual/evaluative systems in common, they belong in some sense (and in some degree) to the same culture. And those conceptions of the world two or more people have in common generally facilitate communication between them.[11] So culture is both a means and an end of communication.

It should be perfectly clear, however, that culture—from this point of view—is a characteristic of those individual conceptual systems which link people together communicatively. Every two-person relationship has some cultural aspects which are unique to it, just as our Western culture relates all of us in very subtle but no less unique ways. A culture, in other words, can be of any size or of any scope, historically or geographically. The function of culture in communication is the same whether it evolves from the unique interaction of two people or is implicitly socialized into millions of people over hundreds of years.

It is empirically unavoidable that every individual must develop his own model of the world either (1) in and through his own individual sensory experiences of it, or (2) in and through his accumulation of *standardized* interpretations of it—via education, socialization, observation and imitation, etc. It is thus our various cultures and subcultures which organize us socially; and it is that same sociocultural organization which perpetuates and evolves cultures.

As with any organization, however, the "price" of membership in a culture or subculture is the *abdication* of certain *degrees of freedom* by the individual (wittingly or not). Any individual could evolve his own private model of the world through his own private sensory experiences of it, as primitive man did. But he could not then be a full-fledged "member" of those cultural groups into which he was born. He would not be able to communicate effectively or efficiently with his peers, nor they with him. To gain full "membership," we have had (either wittingly or not) to abdicate certain uniquely individual possibilities for experiencing and interpreting our worlds in order to accommodate *normative* reality. We must necessarily experience and comprehend our worlds in more or less standardized ways *if we want to maintain our "membership"*—if we want to "belong" to our respective cultures and subcultures.

---

[11] It is worth noting that the objective of enculturation is to inculcate in new members of the group or subculture a certain kind and degree of normative reality. This process can be carried out only through communication. As adequate levels of normative or consensual reality (i.e., intersubjectivity) are attained, communication with other members of that group or society is generally facilited. This in turn permits a more efficient enculturation of *each other*, and so on. It is interesting to speculate on the possibility that, were it not for our ineffectiveness in communicatively enculturating others, we would all be much more similar in conceptual system structure and functioning than we are.

One kind of culture of particular potency is what is often referred to as reference group.[12]

A reference group is any group or aggregate, or any other categorizable set of people, with whom an individual identifies himself, or from which he derives certain aspects of his consensual (normative) reality. He may or may not be an official "member" of his reference groups. He may only privately identify himself with certain groups or classes or categories of people.

The function of a reference group in human behavior is the same as the function of any cultural network: the sharing of certain concepts, values, norms, beliefs, interpretations of the world, and so forth—as a basis for achieving normative or consensual models of the world. Or, one might view reference groups as the actual or imagined audiences which are perceived as ultimately approving or disapproving of one's behavior.[13]

A reference group is thus any cultural group or classification (such as midwesterner, professional, student, etc.) to which an individual *refers* his behavior—either before or after that behavior occurs. We assimilate, directly or indirectly, certain aspects of our comprehending and evaluating component from those values or beliefs or assumptions we assume to be common to the "members" of our particular set of reference groups. We in turn validate those aspects of our conceptual/evaluative systems by being alert to evidence of approval or disapproval of our behavior by those we believe to be members-in-good-standing of those reference groups (i. e., "reference persons"). As long as approval is forthcoming, we presume some membership security, and those aspects of our conceptual/evaluative systems derived from seeing oneself as a member of particular reference groups are thereby confirmed.[14]

RELATING AND PERCEIVING

As we have seen, the functions of the conceptual system are not only to enable us to *perceive* the world, but to enable us to *conceive* the world.

---

[12] A good summary of this concept is in P. F. Secord and C. W. Backman, *Social Psychology* (New York: McGraw-Hill Book Co., 1964, pp. 209–12). Cf. M. and Carolyn W. Sherif, "Reference Groups in Human Relations," in their *Groups in Harmony and Tension* (New York: Harper & Bros., 1953).

[13] See T. Shibutani, *Society and Personality* (Englewood Cliffs, N.J.: Prentice-Hall, 1961, esp. pp. 257 ff.). Cf. D. P. Crowne and D. Marlowe, *The Approval Motive* (New York: John Wiley & Sons, Inc., 1964).

[14] For an intriguing discussion of the same issue from a different point of view, see R. D. Laing, *The Self and Others* (Chicago: Quadrangle Books, Inc., 1962).

The purposes served by these functions are those of organizing and structuring, of "relevanting" the world in such a way that some relationship between the organism and some aspect of its environment is established, maintained, altered, or exploited. It is not some condition of us or some condition of the environment—as such—that is the object of our behavior. It is some *relationship* between the two that concerns us when some subset of the conceptual system is brought into play.

There is therefore a large degree of codetermination between what *is* and what is *conceived to be.* Neither is totally the cause of the other, and neither is totally the effect of the other. It is no more accurate to assume that "we see only what we want to see" than it is to assume that external stimuli "cause" perceptual or behavioral responses. In some as yet poorly defined way, every conception we have of the world is both consequence *and* cause of the external event to which it relates us. Our sense-data are partly dependent upon external event-data for their existence. But that which is external to us depends (in any practical or behavioral sense) upon the extent to which and the manner in which we individually attribute meaning or significance or utility to it. And it is important to note that we cannot purposefully relate ourselves to any part of our environment we cannot conceive of.[15]

For example, my dog is an undeniable physical object. But my behavior toward him (which is critical in the formation of *his* "personality" as well as mine) is based upon my conception of him. And that is in some unspecifiable way a function of me at the same time it is a function of him.

And so it is with people.

Take-into-Account-Abilities and -Susceptibilities

To what will the organism pay attention? How does one get the attention of another?

In the next chapter we will again be concerned with the nature of take-into-account-abilities and take-into-account-susceptibilities. But a brief consideration of these basic factors in communication behavior is in order here.

---

15 The implications of some corollaries of Ashby's *law of requisite variety* for our abilities to be communicated-with are intriguing for those who wish to pursue them. In one respect, Ashby's theorem would suggest that an individual's conceptual system can apprehend only that of which it is capable—not that which actually exists or occurs. See W. R. Ashby, *An Introduction to Cybernetics* (London: Chapman and Hall, 1956, esp. Ch. 11 ff.).

It is always possible (although usually not feasible) to overwhelm the receiver's sensorium in some way. The story of the farmer who tapped his mule across the brow with a fencepost "to get his attention" before starting off to town is a humorous but fairly accurate example of one means of getting another's attention.

There are some other conditions of potential attentiveness that are more characteristic of human behavior, however.

1. *People will attend to* those events external to themselves which they assume might have some relevance to their personal goals and objectives, immediate or long-range.

Students sit through dull lectures—more or less "attentively"—apparently with the expectation that they might have some future need of what the professor is saying. Subordinates are typically fairly attentive when certain superiors speak, for perhaps a similar reason. The generality of this particular condition might permit a very crude sort of formula:

$$\text{Likelihood (or extent) of attention} = \frac{\text{Expected payoff}[16]}{\text{Anticipated effort}}$$

Thus if the "motive" for attending is a conscious one, we would expect one's likelihood (or extent) of attention to vary as the ratio of what he anticipates as his payoff for doing so—to the effort he anticipates will be required by him to attend and comprehend.

In other words, there are limits, even when the "motive" for paying attention is the receiver's own. As the anticipated value of attending nears the effort required to do so, one's attention begins to lag. As the effort required to be attentive begins to balance the personally-anticipated reward for doing so (or punishment for not doing so), one's attention wanes.

This isn't the only factor which determines whether or not another person will actively "pay attention to" what we say to him. But it is one, and the reader can undoubtedly recall several instances from his own experience which seem to fit this crude formula.

2. *People will attend to* those external or internal events which serve the nonconscious, metabolic needs or "appetites" of the conceptual/evaluative system itself.

For example, individuals who have been deprived of sensory inputs for a short period of time will involuntarily have an "appetite" for almost any

---

[16] Freely adapted from W. Schramm's "Fraction of Selection," in *The Process and Effects of Mass Communication* (Urbana: University of Illinois Press, 1954, p. 19).

sort of external event-data.[17] We have probably all experienced in ourselves or others what seems to be a "hunger" to be communicated-with.

It is understandable that our conceptual/evaluative systems have their own "appetites" or needs for information quite outside our own awareness or control. Their business is information-processing. Yet their complexity and functioning are far beyond our conscious capacity to comprehend.

When one's conscious needs for information are, accidentally or not, coincidental with his nonconscious system needs for stimulation and information, the attention which ensues is unusually wholesome, natural, aggressive, unstrained, and efficient. But we could not safely assume that this sort of total attention would generally meet one's attempts to communicate-to others. At best, receivers probably attend only in partial ways.

But the fact that people are not always aware of the communicational needs of their own psychological systems does lend some logical credence, for example, to advertising based upon "depth analysis" of the target audience. And a significant proportion of all direct intercommunication serves functions which are quite outside of any intellectual pursuits of the individuals involved.

One of the continuing needs of the conceptual/evaluative system is that of confirming itself. This is particularly true of the self-concept.[18] These are needs which can divert one's attention in spite of his attempts to control his attention in the service of some conscious goal or objective. Consistency over time in our own behavior depends largely upon the continuous confirmation—by others—of who we are,[19] what we are, why

---

[17] For a general review, see P. Solomon et al. (eds.), *Sensory Deprivation* (Cambridge, Mass.: Harvard University Press, 1961).

[18] One's concept of himself is evolved and functions much the same as other major, complex concept-clusters. The self-concept encompasses all of the functional orientations one could potentially exhibit toward himself. In addition, however, one's self-concept is normally that concept cluster having the greatest "centrality"—both because it is the only concept cluster which is ultimately related in some way to all of the other elements of the conceptual/evaluative system, and because it is impossible for a "normal" person to behave, either inwardly or outwardly, without involving his self-concept in some way. Cf. Ruth C. Wylie, *The Self Concept* (Lincoln: University of Nebraska Press, 1961).

[19] For further exploration, see P. Lecky, *Self-Consistency* (New York: Island Press, 1945); and R. D. Laing, *The Self and Others* (Chicago: Quadrangle Books, Inc., 1962). This process is often described as self-definition or self-image. (A good review is "Some Interpersonal Aspects of Self-Confirmation." In W. G. Bennis et al., *Interpersonal Dynamics* [Homewood, Ill.: Dorsey Press, 1964].) Self-identity processes are also conceptually quite similar: see E. H. Erikson, *Childhood and Society* (New York: W. W. Norton & Co., Inc., 1950); and Helen M. Lynd, *On Shame and the Search for Identity* (New York: Science Editions [Wiley], 1961), for representative treatments of this concept.

we are, etc. The smallest conceptual/evaluative unit to be invoked or induced (or brought into play) as a basis for comprehending some aspect of the world one wants to deal with communicatively is thus (a) some subset of the self-concept; (b) some concept of the thing or idea being apprehended; and (c) some relationship (cognitive *and* effective or evaluative) between *a* and *b*.

This suggests why people are highly susceptible to any external or internal evidence which indicates to them unstable or unconfirmed relationships between some part of their self-concepts and some other component of the conceptual/evaluative system. For example, a manager who feels inadequate to deal effectively with his superiors or his peers might have an inordinate "appetite" for any information that might be taken as evidence of his adequacy, yet may have a very high threshold for information confirming his *in*adequacy.[20]

3. *People will therefore attend to* those things they can, but disattend to those things which are contrary or disconfirming in some way to their own models of the world—or of their expectations about the future.

Rokeach uses the term *belief system* much as the term conceptual/evaluative system is being used here. He proposes that the belief system ". . . seems to be constructed to serve both masters at once: to understand the world insofar as possible, and to defend against it insofar as necessary."[21]

The conceptual/evaluative system, in other words, accommodates external event-data and internal sense-data to the extent that it *can* (i.e., is appropriately structured and programmed to do so). But it often disaccommodates data which might be deleterious to its own stability and security.[22] An avid Republican might not "hear" all that a Democrat speaker is saying, or might grossly "distort" that which he does hear. A

[20] Cf. A. H. Maslow, "The Need to Know and the Fear of Knowing." *Journal of General Psychology*, 1963, 68, 111–25.

[21] M. Rokeach, *The Open and Closed Mind* (New York: Basic Books, Inc., 1960). Cf. E. Goffman, *Encounters* (Indianapolis: Bobbs-Merrill Co., Inc., 1961), p. 104: ". . . the individual . . . actively participates in sustaining a definition of the situation that is stable and consistent with his image of himself."

[22] The first part of this proposition harks back to the Ashby theorem: that an adaptive system maintains itself only to the extent it can exhibit a variety of responses no fewer in number than the variety of situations which it must adapt to or wishes to adapt to. The second part reminds us that the conceptual/evaluative system, like the human system of which it is a part, is itself a living system. And, as such, it will naturally exhibit its own adaptive mechanisms—operations normally quite beyond the control (or awareness) of the individual.

worker who believes management to be the enemy (or vice versa) may have a very *low* threshold for those management messages which would confirm that belief yet have a very *high* threshold for potentially disconfirmatory data.

4. *People will attend to* the unexpected. This is perhaps one of the few aspects of human and organizational communication for which Information Theory, as such, has relevance.[23]

People will normally be aware of those internal or external events[24] which fall significantly outside of their expectations. If I expect someone *not* to know my name, but he does, my attention is drawn to this discrepancy between what I expected and what is apparent at the time of the encounter.

But the converse also occurs. We are sensitive to those cues which confirm our expectations. Our expectation that a green traffic signal will change to amber and then to red provides a "set" for taking this particular sequence into account. The difference is that in the first case I become *consciously* aware of the discrepancy, but in the latter situation the "fit" of what is occurring with my expectations permits me to carry out my objectives at a nonconscious level.[25]

5. *Finally, the relationship* which obtains between an individual and some object, event, idea, or person in his environment will play some part in determining the attention which he gives to it (or to the other person).

For example, a subordinate is differently "tuned in" to his boss than he is to his fellow-workers. At the same time, he will be differently calibrated (communicatively) to the utterances of those of his peers he likes and admires than he will be to those he dislikes or those he simply does not know. A manager who hopes to be credible to his subordinates must

---

[23] A recent volume which summarizes and suggests some applications of Information Theory to human behavior is W. R. Garner, *Uncertainty and Structure as Psychological Concepts* (New York: John Wiley & Sons, Inc., 1962). Cf. a volume which approaches human cognition from an information-processing point of view: W. R. Reitman, *Cognition and Thought* (New York: John Wiley & Sons, Inc., 1965).

[24] I use external or internal events, but the reader will realize that all event-data which we could possibly take account of must ultimately be *internal* before we can convert it into functionally consumable units of information—i.e., *messages.*

[25] The implications of this view for understanding involuntary conscious awareness of our internal or external environments are probably apparent. But further discussion of this important point can be found in J. Rothstein, *Communication, Organization, and Science* (Indian Hills, Colo.: Falcon's Wing Press, 1958).

necessarily develop a relationship with them in which his credibility is a basic dimension.

LEARNING AND CHANGE

The accommodate-ability of any individual's conceptual/evaluative system is a function of the complexity of that ststem at any point in time. But our accommodate-abilities do change over time. They are constantly in the process of changing, however imperceptible those changes may be in our typical behavior.

This raises a very intriguing question: How is it that our comprehending systems grow or diminish when they can—at any point in time—cope only with those external or internal events which they are capable of or susceptible to taking-into-account? How is it that we can sometimes get across to a person a point or a concept which he is not initially equipped to comprehend?

First, the comprehending system, as a living system, is *adaptive*. It will adapt to those external or internal conditions which it *must* adapt to in some way, or which, in the service of the individual, it would be helpful to adapt to. By-and-large, any normal comprehension/evaluation system could develop almost any set of accommodate-abilities, given appropriate developmental steps and a large enough payoff (either consciously or nonconsciously) for going through the stress which accompanies the instability of that development. A "logical mind," for example, is not basically different from a normal mind; it is only *structured* somewhat differently. Thus all such abilities are more or less learnable or develop-able.

Second, our conceptual/evaluative systems are dynamically self-organizing. Their structures are not static, but are continuously changing as a consequence of their own internal processes.[26]

Third, our particular comprehend-abilities are not limited to *isomorphic* representations of the external (or internal) environment, or, perhaps, even to *homomorphic* representations.[27] They also derive from the functional properties of the system, and from the incipient or latent possibilities of that system's structure and dynamics. For example, we sometimes

---

[26] The capabilities of any system are a function "not only of the characteristics of the elements but of their interactions or interrelations": P. M. Fitts, *Notes and Selected Readings on Human Engineering* (Ann Arbor: University of Michigan, College of Engineering, 1959).

[27] See S. Beer, *Cybernetics and Management* (New York: John Wiley & Sons, Inc., 1959).

accidentally hear or read something which crystallizes a new idea or understanding. We do, and must, comprehend those things we have not previously comprehended. There is nothing we could not adequately comprehend, given the appropriate preliminary structure and conditions of our comprehending systems.

But it is extremely important to remember that—although we sometimes refer to the comprehending system as static—it is constantly changing, reorganizing itself, developing new structures, etc.

Fourth, and somewhat contrary to the above propositions, the "normal" condition of the adult human conceptual system is that of *least rate of change*.[28] While our potential comprehend-abilities are essentially unlimited, it is much more characteristic of human behavior to resist rather than to invite any but the most minor changes. Our comprehend-abilities and hence our communicate-abilities grow and develop rapidly during our early years. But as our models of the world become adequate, their rate of growth and change diminish rapidly. By-and-large, adults are less educable and less develop-able than children.[29]

There are many other aspects of learning and change that could be taken up here. But perhaps these four will be sufficiently suggestive of the nature of the conceptual/evaluative system.

FEELINGS

We have not considered the topic of feelings separately in this discussion of the relation of human behavior to communication processes. There is a good reason.

Our feelings are an inevitable part of any and all of our comprehensions and apprehensions of our environments (external or internal). Feelings are unavoidably a dimension of every linkage between and among the elements of our conceptual/evaluative systems—whether those elements be characterized as beliefs, values, assumptions, norms, models, orientations, or simply as concepts. It is not possible to conceive of the world (to understand it in some way) without simultaneously feeling in some way toward it. The fact that we sometimes "lead from" our feelings rather than our understandings attests to the *valence* or relative importance of the feeling dimensions of the way we see that particular situation.

We need to disabuse ourselves of the notion that some human com-

---

[28] Cf. J. Ruesch, "The Observer and The Observed," in R. R. Grinker (ed.), *Toward a Unified Theory of Human Behavior* (New York: Basic Books, Inc., 1956).

[29] For a discussion of some of the "problems" this fact presents, see J. W. Gardner, *Self-Renewal* (New York: Harper & Row, 1964).

munication is "visceral" and other human communication is "cerebral." All human communication inevitably has both dimensions, in greater or lesser degree. What a person says (or does not say) may indeed affect another person's feelings greatly, but only if the latter comprehends the statement or the situation in some way. And to comprehend is to feel toward . . . in some way, even though we are often not aware of the feeling component of our comprehensions.

What we must avoid is the very incorrect assumption (which occasionally arises) that we have one system for handling intellectual things and another for handling emotional things. We do not. We have but one nervous system and but one psychological system. Our feelings are an inherent and unavoidable component of every dynamic relationship that exists between and among the elements of our comprehending systems, and hence of all of our communicative behavior.

In the next chapter, we will examine a simple but useful model for understanding the other component of our "people, communication, and behavior" continuum—the behavior control system.

SUGGESTIONS FOR FURTHER READING

The complex structures and processes which enable us to be communicated-with have inspired a great body of published theory and research. Those documents selected for this list may be useful to the reader in developing his further perspectives on this rich area of study.

BLAKE, R. R., and RAMSEY, G. V. (eds.). *Perception: An Approach to Personality*. New York: Ronald Press Co., 1951.

BROADBENT, D. E. *Perception and Communication*. New York: Pergamon Press, Inc., 1958.

BROWN, ROGER. "How Shall a Thing Be Called?" *Psychological Review*, Vol. 65 (1958), pp. 14–20.

BRUNER, JEROME. *On Knowing*. Cambridge, Mass.: Harvard University Press, 1962.

————, and POSTMAN, L. "An Approach to Social Perception," in W. Dennis et al. (eds.), *Current Trends in Social Psychology*. Pittsburgh, Pa.: University of Pittsburgh Press, 1948.

CANTOR, NATHANIEL. *The Learning Process for Managers*. New York: Harper & Bros., 1958.

CHURCH, J. *Language and the Discovery of Reality*. New York: Random House, Inc., 1961.

DEWEY, JOHN, and BENTLEY, ARTHUR F. *Knowing and the Known*. Boston: Beacon Press, 1949.

DORSEY, J. M., and SEEGERS, W. H.   *Living Consciously: The Science of Self.* Detroit: Wayne State University Press, 1959.

FEARNSIDE, W. WARD, and HOLTHER, WILLIAM B.   *Fallacy.* Englewood Cliffs, N.J.: Prentice-Hall, Inc., 1959.

FELDMAN, SHEL (ed.).   *Cognitive Consistency.* New York: Academic Press Inc., 1966.

FESTINGER, L.   *A Theory of Cognitive Dissonance.* Evanston, Ill.: Row, Peterson & Co., 1957.

GARNER, W. R.   *Uncertainty and Structure as Psychological Concepts.* New York: John Wiley & Sons, Inc., 1962.

GEORGE, K. H.   *The Brain as a Computer.* London: Pergamon Press, Inc., 1962.

HARVEY, O. J. (ed.).   *Experience, Structure, and Adaptability.* New York: Springer Publishing Co., Inc., 1966.

————; HUNT, D. E.; and SCHRODER, H. M.   *Conceptual Systems and Personality Organization.* New York: John Wiley & Sons, Inc., 1961.

HAYGOOD, R. C., and BOURNE, L. E., JR.   "Attribute and Rule-Learning Aspects of Conceptual Behavior," *Psychological Review,* Vol. 72 (1965), pp. 175–95.

HEIDER, FRITZ.   "Attitudes and Cognitive Organization," *Journal of Psychology,* Vol. 21 (1946), pp. 107–12.

HUNT, E. B.   *Concept Learning.* New York: John Wiley & Sons, Inc., 1962.

JOHNSON, WENDELL H.   *Your Most Enchanted Listener.* New York: Harper & Bros., 1956.

KLAUSMEIER, H. J. et al.   *Concept Learning & Problem Solving: A Bibliography, 1950–1964.* Tech. Report No. I, Research and Development Center for Learning and Re-Education. Madison: University of Wisconsin, 1965.

LAWSON, CHESTER A.   *Language, Thought, and the Human Mind.* East Lansing: Michigan State University Press, 1958.

MACKAY, D. M.   "Towards an Information-Flow Model of Human Behavior." *British Journal of Psychology* (London), Vol. 47 (1956), pp. 30–43.

————.   "Information Theory and Human Information Systems," *Impact of Science on Society,* Vol. 8 (1957), pp. 86–101.

————.   "Operational Aspects of Some Fundamental Concepts of Human Communication," *Journal of Communication,* Vol. 21 (1961), pp. 183–219.

MEAD, GEORGE HERBERT.   *Mind, Self, and Society.* Chicago: University of Chicago Press, 1934.

MILLER, G. A.   "The Magical Number Seven, Plus or Minus Two: Some Limits on our Capacity for Processing Information," *Psychological Review,* Vol. 63 (1956), pp. 81–97.

————, and ISARD, S. "Some Perceptual Consequences of Linguistic Rules," *Journal of Verbal Learning and Verbal Behavior*, Vol. 2 (1963), pp. 217–28.

MOWRER, O. HOBART. *Learning Theory and the Symbolic Processes*. New York: John Wiley & Sons, Inc., 1960.

OSGOOD, C. E. "On Understanding and Creating Sentences," *American Psychologist*, Vol. 18 (1963), pp. 735–51.

PIKAS, A. *Abstraction and Concept Formation*. Cambridge, Mass.: Harvard University Press, 1966.

PILLSBURY, W. B., and MEADER, C. L. *The Psychology of Language*. New York: D. Appleton & Co., 1928.

QUINE, WILLARD VAN ORMAN. *Word and Object*. New York: Technology Press of Massachusetts Institute of Technology and John Wiley & Sons, Inc., 1960.

REITMAN, W. R. *Cognition and Thought: An Information Processing Approach*. New York: John Wiley & Sons, Inc., 1965.

————. "Information-Processing Models in Psychology," *Science*, Vol. 144 (1964), pp. 193–97.

SCHON, D. A. *Displacement of Concepts*. London: Tavistock, 1963.

SHANDS, H. C. *Thinking and Psychotherapy*. Cambridge, Mass.: Harvard University Press, 1960.

SHELLY, M. W., and BRYAN, G. L. (eds.). *Human Judgments and Optimality*. New York: John Wiley & Sons, Inc., 1964.

SINCLAIR, ANGUS. *The Conditions of Knowing*. London: Routledge and Kegan Paul, Ltd., 1951.

TODA, M. "Information-Receiving Behavior of Man," *Psychological Review*, Vol. 63 (1956), pp. 204–12.

URBAN, W. M. *Language and Reality*. London: George Allen and Unwin, Ltd., 1951.

WEINBERG, HARRY L. *Levels of Knowing and Existence: Studies in General Semantics*. New York: Harper & Bros., 1959.

WERNER, H., and KAPLAN B. *Symbol Formation*. New York: John Wiley & Sons, Inc., 1963.

WHORF, BENJAMIN LEE. *Language, Thought, and Reality* (J. B. CARROLL, ed.). New York: Technology Press of Massachusetts Institute of Technology and John Wiley & Sons, Inc., 1956.

WITKIN, H. A. et al. *Personality through Perception*. New York: Harper & Bros., 1954.

WOOLDRIDGE, D. E. *The Machinery of the Brain*. New York: McGraw-Hill Book Co., 1963.

5

People, Behavior, and Communication: On the Motivation and Control of Human Behavior

THE BASIC MODEL of behavior control to be presented in this chapter is, of course, as applicable to our understanding of the nature of being communicated-with as it is to our understanding of the nature of communicating-to. But while the main points and issues raised in the preceding chapter would seem to be better understood if considered from the point of view of the conditions and determinants of the input side of human communication behavior, those to be raised in the present chapter can be more easily described from the point of view of the determinants of the output side of communication behavior. What we have done in making this somewhat arbitrary point of division in what is functionally an indivisible sequence of interdependent processes could perhaps be illustrated thus: The overlapping areas may be taken as either the condition or the consequences of the organism's inputs, or as the prerequisite occurrences for its outputs or its products (such as thinking, decisioning, overt behavior, etc.).

It is the psychological system which, as we have seen, is both the ultimate source of all of the organism's comprehensions of his internal and external environments, and the basis of all of his behavior. So, while recognizing that the psychological system is a single system, it is convenient to look at the comprehending and the behavior control components

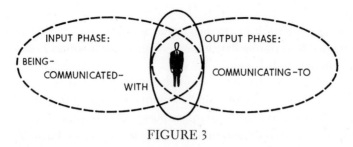

FIGURE 3

separately. In this chapter, we will be focusing upon the behavior control component. But—as will be evident—it is not possible fully to understand the behavior control component without understanding the comprehending component, and vice versa. The two function interdependently.

A Basic Model of Behavior Control

Before we examine a greatly oversimplified model of how human behavior is "motivated" and controlled, we need to realize that a complete description of the *why* of most human behavior is still beyond the reach of the behavioral sciences. It is true that we could hypothesize with some assurance about certain very limited and separate aspects of human behavior; but there is presently no way of conceptualizing adequately and accurately that immensely complex process.

At this stage of our understanding of human behavior, it is especially useful to formulate models which accommodate the known empirical facts from a wide range of separate disciplines concerned with some aspect of human behavior, and to ask, "What useful difference would it make to my understanding of human behavior if I reformulated my views in keeping with the implications of this particular model of the process?" That is exactly what we will do here.

It should be made clear that neither this simple model, nor the implications of it that we will consider, in any way constitute a formal theory of behavior. It is offered here simply as one particularly useful way of looking at certain functions within the overall process of human communication (and, of course, of other human behavior upon which communication is contingent, or which is contingent upon communication —such as problem solving).

The model we want to explore is crudely derived from a broad range of recent work in cybernetics and general systems theory, as well as earlier concepts of motivation and behavior controls.[1] But it is also derived from relatively current work in the behavioral sciences, and its design is therefore intended to accommodate a broad range of key findings from empirical research on human behavior.[2]

If we can assume that our communicative behavior at any point in time is roughly a consequence of a single dominant purpose, or some dominant set of more or less complementary purposes vis-à-vis some other person(s) or some aspect of the environment, then the basic model might appear thus:

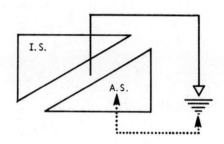

WHERE I. S. = SOME "INTENDED" OR "NEEDED"
             (CONSCIOUS OR NONCONSCIOUS)
             RELATIONSHIP VIS-A-VIS THE
             ENVIRONMENT;

      A. S.= THE "APPARENT STATE OF AFFAIRS"
             IN THE ENVIRONMENT;

          = SOME ACTION-IN-THE-ENVIRONMENT
          (E. G., SOME COMMUNICATIVE BE-
          HAVIOR DIRECTED TO ANOTHER); AND

          = FEEDBACK AND/OR "FEEDFORWARD."

FIGURE 4

A simple example may illustrate the application of this crude analytical tool.

[1] Cf. esp. S. Beer, *Cybernetics and Management* (New York: John Wiley & Sons, Inc., 1959); W. R. Ashby, *An Introduction to Cybernetics* (London: Chapman & Hall, 1956); K. W. Deutsch, "On Communication Models in The Social Sciences," *Public Opinion Quarterly*, 1952, 16, 365–80; D. P. Eckman, *Systems: Research and Design* (New York: John Wiley & Sons, Inc., 1961); R. M. Gagne (ed.), *Psychological Principles in System Development* (New York: Holt, Rinehart and Winston, 1962); J. Rothstein, *Communication, Organization and Science* (Indian Hills, Colo.: Falcon's Wing Press, 1958); and G. A. Kelly, *A Theory of Personality* (New York: W. W. Norton & Co., Inc., 1963).

[2] Those that I have drawn upon defy specification here. But the suggested references for this and the previous chapter offer some representative sources.

Suppose you want someone to know something he doesn't presently know, or to understand something in a way he doesn't presently understand it. Your evaluation of how he presently understands that something is your comprehension of the present *apparent-state-of-affairs* (A. S.). If there is a discrepancy or a deviation[3] between your *intended-state-of-affairs* (I. S.) and what you conclude to be the existing-state-of-affairs, then you will undertake that action or behavior which you expect will eliminate or at least significantly reduce the difference between your intended-state-of-affairs (I. S.) and what you see as the apparent-state-of-affairs (A. S.).[4]

We should make especial note of the fact that, as humans, we can *simulate* our behavior and its anticipated consequences—in advance of actually carrying out that behavior. Although we are not often aware of doing so, we often do run through a preliminary "dress rehearsal" or test of the probable impact of our behavior—especially when we have had little or no experience on which to base more reliable expectations.[5]

These "cybernetic machines," as they might be called,[6] comprise a *dynamic, self-generative,* and *regenerative* hierarchical set of orientations vis-à-vis the environment which by-and-large determine and channel our behavior. These machines may be short-term or long-term, large or small, ascending or descending (in the hierarchy), central or peripheral, emerging or dissolving, dominant or subordinate, etc.—depending upon the immedi-

---

[3] The notion of a discrepancy or deviation between I. S. and A. S. bears some resemblance to Festinger's well-known concept of *cognitive dissonance* (see L. Festinger, *A Theory of Cognitive Dissonance* [Evanston, Ill.: Row-Peterson, 1957]). But it does not derive from Festinger's concept, and its usefulness perhaps extends beyond the reaches of cognitive dissonance.

[4] This sort of statement, necessarily somewhat awkward, does permit us to include both conscious and nonconscious behavior within a single frame of reference. Intended-state-of-affairs should be understood broadly as target, goal, aim, steady-state, and so on. Thus whether our concern is with body temperature, a casual stroll, or an effort to change someone else's mind about something, the basic model is applicable.

[5] Cf. the "TOTE" unit of G. A. Miller, E. Galanter, and K. A. Pribram, *Plans and the Structure of Behavior* (New York: Holt, Rinehart and Winston, 1960). At the sociological level of analysis, one might be inclined to compare this to E. Goffman's "Art of Impression Management," in *The Presentation of Self in Everyday Life* (Garden City, N. Y.: Doubleday, 1959). But the issue at stake is much more than impression management, however. It is a basic function of the psychological system which is critical to its successful adaptation and survival, and hence to all of the communication *behavior* of the individual.

[6] After Beer, *op. cit.* The reader should not interpret machine to mean "mechanistic" in any pejorative sense. Functional machines of the conceptual or psychological sort we want to develop an understanding of in this book should not be looked upon as mechanistic in the negative sense we often ascribe to that term.

ate and long-term state of the organism vis-à-vis its environment (in terms of its goals or intentions or habituations). But our behavior can usefully be looked upon as some function of this extremely dynamic, constantly changing system of cybernetic machines.

When we observe someone doing something, we can conclude that his behavior is "in the service of" one or more cybernetic machines. All of our behavior is, successfully or not, directed to the resolution of a discrepancy between some *intended* or desired state-of-affairs and the perceived or *apparent-state-of-affairs*.

It may also have occurred to the perceptive reader that there are several possibilities for resolving those motivating discrepancies between our A. S.'s and I. S.'s apart from actually engaging in some overt behavior. For example, it would seem that the *modus operandi* of a great many people is simply that of generally accepting what occurs (the apparent-state-of-affairs) as a suitable intended-state-of-affairs. There are times, of course, when it is wisdom to accept that which one can't do anything about. But the distinction to be made here is one between people, and not between situations.

Another example: our conceptual abilities to simulate in advance and to rerun our experiences vis-à-vis the environment leave open the possibility of interpreting or reinterpreting an event or a person in view of the hypothesized- or apparent-state-of-affairs either before or after the event. Given this "out," it is human nature to take advantage of it from time to time. We can, and do, interpret what we perceive the existing-state-of-affairs to be in the light of our intentions, and hence often misinterpret the data in either a favorable or an unfavorable direction. Often we simply "distort" the apparent-state-of-affairs to make it appear congruous with our intended-state-of-affairs.

A third example may help further to suggest the wide-ranging implications of the operation of these cybernetic machines. They may be resolved conceptually—either without engaging in external behavior at all, or by simply ignoring the consequences of that behavior. There are two exaggerated extremes which may be considered as illustrative of the range of possibilities. A person may simulate an anticipated encounter in advance, and thereby resolve that particular discrepancy in some way without ever engaging in any actual behavior. Or, a person might replay a particularly successful or unsuccessful encounter, with the consequence of reresolving that particular situation in a way inconsistent with what had actually happened, but more satisfactory to the individual.

We don't need to ask *why* our cybernetic machines work as they do.

We need only a grasp of *how* they function sufficient to be able to use them as conceptual tools for better understanding our own and others' communication behavior.

ON THE NOTION OF MOTIVATION

"Motivation" is a very common term. All sorts of people use it in all sorts of ways to refer to a variety of different things. Like communication, however, a word that means so many different things to so many different people is at best, slippery; at worst, treacherous.

Knowing what we do at this point about human functioning, it would be fruitful to make an especial effort to avoid the oft-implied assumptions (a) that "motivating" is something that is done *to* people, and (b) that the term "motivation" as such is an adequate way of accounting for what people do or not do—or the peculiar qualities of their doing (or not doing) something.

First, it is demonstrably true that we can "trigger" or release our own or others' *intrinsic* motivations (a) by changing our own or their present perceptions or expectations vis-à-vis the environment, (b) through developmental experiences of a crucial sort, or (c) by bringing about changes in our own or others' perceptions of the behavior of other people. But these are not quite the same as "motivating" people. They are ways of doing something about the *relationship* between the individual and his *perceived* environment. We can no more directly "motivate" a person into some orientation to himself or his work which is not already at least a latent part of him than we can directly "communicate" some concept to him which his system is not at least potentially capable of (or susceptible to) comprehending. Motivation and communication are thus ultimately conditions of the individual alone.

Second, to explain that people do what they do "because of" their motivations is not particularly advantageous to either the theorist or the practitioner. To say that a person was "motivated" to do what he did (or was "not motivated" to do what he did not do) doesn't really add much to our understanding of his behavior. We can "define" a person's behavior by saying he was "motivated." But we have not thereby usefully explained why he did what he did.[7]

---

[7] See G. A. Kelly, "Man's Construction of His Alternatives," in G. Lindzey (ed.), *Assessment of Human Motives* (New York: Holt, Rinehart and Winston, 1958).

There are three more or less commonsense characteristics of "motivated" behavior which need to be accounted for in any useful concept of motivation: level of energy investment, control, and direction.

Level of energy investment is determed by: (a) the relative magnitude of the discrepancy between an intended-state-of-affairs and its corresponding apparent-state-of-affairs; (b) the energy resources available to any individual for investment in external behavior;[8] and (c) the period of time over which the cybernetic machines involved are maintained (e.g., the longer their duration, the greater the energy expended).

Behavior control will be a key concept in developing some useful implications of the cybernetic machine. The "machine" can be understood to *control* the behavior of people in the following ways. (a) It is the "felt" or perceived discrepancy between some intended-state-of-affairs and its corresponding apparent-state-of-affairs which energizes the organism. If there were no discrepancy between an I. S. and an A. S., the organism would be dormant—in a state akin to hibernation. (b) Our conscious or nonconscious interpretation of the *nature* of the discrepancy (our identification or naming of it) sets in motion the processes which determine the *direction* behavior will take. (c) It is the logical or *structural necessity* of resolving the machine in some way consistent with one's intentions and expectations which control behavior. When the intended-state-of-affairs is achieved (as interpreted from the feedback available), that machine has done its work. Until that time, or until that machine is resolved or loses its salience, etc., our behavior will be controlled by the increments of negative feedback we acquire—from which we continuously attempt to reassess the changing nature and "size" (as well as the salience) of the discrepancy.

What *controls* behavior is then, in effect, those criteria established in advance (consciously or nonconsciously) for a satisfactory or acceptable resolution or dissolution of a particular machine. Somewhat like the course setting on a compass "controls" the behavior of the helmsman, or like the desired temperature setting on a thermostat "controls" the behavior of the furnace, the criteria to be met in resolving a discrepancy between an I. S. and an A. S. "controls" the behavior of people.

This leaves us with the notion of *direction*. A good way of developing a useful understanding of why behavior takes the direction it does is to reexamine our model from the point of view of two familiar kinds of human behavior—*problem-solving* and *decisioning*.

---

[8] It is always a possibility that a significant amount of energy of the sort required may have been drained off for maintaining the system itself—and hence is not available for more productive behavior. A reasonable hypothesis in view of the empirical data

Problem-Solving

In this book, we will want to view the process of problem-solving in a rather special way. Many writers on problem-solving seem to assume that people apprehend problems more or less as they "actually" exist. But from what we have learned thus far about the nature of communication and the nature of people, we are forced to recognize that this assumption is not a tenable one. People do not apprehend or comprehend *anything* as it "actually" exists. The physical event-data we perceive may be more or less the same for all of those who look at a situation. But what we actually see, what we actually apprehend, and what those events *mean* or *portend*— these are sourced in us, the problem perceivers.

Take another look at the simple model of behavior control we have been exploring in this chapter. Knowing that the apparent-state-of-affairs and the intended-state-of-affairs are each functions or products of the individual of whom they are a part, we can safely and usefully (and logically) conclude that *any discrepancy between an I. S. and an A. S. is also a property—not of the situation being perceived, but of the perceiver.*

Let us refer to any experienced discrepancy between an I.S. and an A.S. as a *problem* for the organism. Any such problem may be either conscious or nonconscious. But it can be worked on by a cybernetic machine only to the extent that it is identified, defined, named, interpreted, characterized, comprehended in some way (whether consciously or nonconsciously).

No *problem situation defines itself. Problem apprehension and definition are products of people.* The event-data of our internal and external environments are *given.* Those data just *are*; they are never of themselves problematical. Like all qualities of all event-data (whether of another person, an object, an idea, etc.), *the problematicalness of any perceived situation is wholly attributed to it by the perceiver.*

Given these facts about people and the nature of being communicated-with, there are four propositions about problem-solving which will be useful when we turn our attention later to certain practical issues in communication. Three of these propositions we will take up here; the fourth must be deferred until after we have considered the process of decisioning. They are:

1. *Problems exist only in people.* Events do occur; situations do exist. But their *import* (their meaning, their significance, their problem-

---

available is that the energy resources available for productive behavior depend upon the integrity of the psychological system: the higher the system integrity, the more usable energy there is available.

maticalness) is a property of people, not of the event or the situation.[9]

2. *Problems exist only in the form in which they are comprehended or conceived.* Nothing comes to us prepackaged in a meaningful form. We put pieces of evidence together in sizing up a situation, and develop thereby a comprehension or conclusion or theory about what that situation means or portends for us. So every problem definition is at best a *personal* interpretation of *selected* evidence about a person or event or situation. Thus the essential characteristics of any problem definition derive from the problem-definer. And the *only* existence the problem has is the shape or form he gives it when he names or identifies it.[10]

3. *The problem we set out to solve is the one we name.* There is no necessary or inherent one-to-one relationship between the problem we "name" and the circumstances which we perceive. So the problem we solve may or may not alter those circumstances satisfactorily. While we can never be sure just how appropriately or adequately we have identified or named a problem, since it is always based upon how we perceive a certain set of circumstances, we can be sure that the problem we try to solve is simply the one we see (and the way we see it). And, from a behavior or communication point of view, there's a rub!

Stress-Resolution and Problem-Solving

As we noted previously, there is seemingly built into the notion of problem-solving the assumption that one somehow apprehends problems

---

[9] Again, the issue here is not a philosophic one. It would be pointless to engage in a debate over whether things "really" exist or not. That's not the point. *The point is simply that the meaning, the significance, the utility, the import of those events is ultimately a property of the people who perceive them.* And the critical factor in behavior is not the existence of things or the occurrence of events, but the *import* of those things and events for the individuals involved. What another person says or doesn't say is real enough. But we react *not* to what he actually says or does, but to the significance or import (*for us*) that we attribute to what he says or does. So it is with problem behavior. The *problematicalness* of anything we see or hear is ultimately a function of our own psychological systems. The event-data are simply givens.

[10] The reader should recall that this naming or identification of problems can occur either consciously or nonconsciously. We react nonconsciously to the lights of an electric traffic signal. But the nonconscious cybernetic machine evoked by a red signal operates in exactly the same functional way as one with which I am consciously concerned. The qualitative differences we have assumed in the past between conscious and nonconscious problem-solving has misled us.

in a ready-made form—more or less as they "actually" exist. But we know from our examination of the process of being communicated-with that the import or meaning of what we are taking-into-account is ultimately a function of us. Therefore the assumption that we deal *directly* with problems that exist "out there" is not only an untenable one, but one which often causes a good many more communication problems than it enables us to solve.

Look again at our basic model. The condition at stake in all of our behavior is some relationship with the environment. But note that we base both our comprehensions and our behavior *not* upon the "actual" relationship, but upon our perceptions of that relationship.

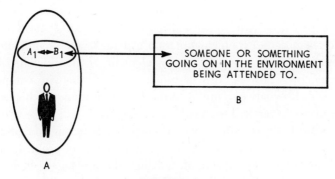

FIGURE 5

Hence we could advantageously conceive of what we ordinarily call problem-solving as internal stress-resolution. The goal is, of course, to be affected by or to affect the environment in such a way that our relationship with it is brought to some intended-state. But we can work on that goal only indirectly—that is, only through our own conceptions of the problem that we see as existing "out there." So the problems which energize, direct, and control our behavior are internal stresses—those "felt" discrepancies between intended-states-of-affairs and the corresponding apparent-states-of-affairs.

It would be awkward to use the term stress-resolution, however. So we will continue to use problem-solving for this basic behavioral process. But we should do so only with the understanding that we are actually referring to the process of internal stress-resolution—with the ultimate practical aim of establishing, maintaining, altering, or exploiting a state-relationship between the organism and some "problematical" circumstance of its environment.

Decisioning

To complete our understanding of what underlies human behavior, we need to develop a useful concept of *decisioning*.

If the reader were to take a close look at the cybernetic machine model, he would notice that—at least as far as human behavior is concerned—something is missing. What is abent from that original diagram, and what can now be added to it to complete our understanding, is a subsystem to be referred to as the *decisioning* process.

When a sensed discrepancy between some intended-state-of-affairs and an apparent-state-of-affairs is *referred* to one's comprehending component, it thereby evokes that comprehension of it which has evolved out of one's previous experiences with similar and related "problems."[11] If an individual tentatively identifies a problem situation as "an X sort of problem," that hypothesis is referred to the decisioning element. If the individual has had some experience with "X sorts of problems" (or otherwise comprehends some possible alternative solutions to the X sort of problem), his definition of the problem is thereby confirmed.

From what has gone before, we can immediately recognize that a person is quite unlikely to define a problem as an X or Y sort of problem unless he feels at least potentially capable of "solving" the problem as defined. This general proposition thus follows: adults characteristically apprehend or identify *only* those sorts of problems for which they have (or believe they could efficiently obtain) workable solutions.

So our last proposition about human problem-solving is this:

4. In a very pragmatic and practical sense, *the solutions people have available* (or think they could get) *determine the sorts of problems which they perceive and the way they classify or name those problems.* In the comprehending component, solutions thus *precede* problem perceptions and identifications.[12]

---

[11] Other elements of the comprehending system are also involved in the problem-definition, decisioning process, of course—e.g., those which enable us to anticipate future events and/or the consequences of our present behavior.

[12] There is an obviousness to this proposition—in spite of the fact that we seem often to ignore our own awareness of it. People with normal sensory equipment don't have to learn to *sense* the world. They arrive equipped to do that. But they do have to learn how to *organize* and *interpret* and *make meaningful* those sensory experiences they have of themselves and of what is going on in their environments. So we simply have to learn certain ways of looking at or comprehending our worlds before we can perceive problems relating ot it. I once overheard a serious discussion between two

If we now add a decisioning element to the cybernetic machine model presented earlier in this chapter, we will have a useful perspective—from the standpoint of communication—on the mechanisms which energize, direct, and control behavior.

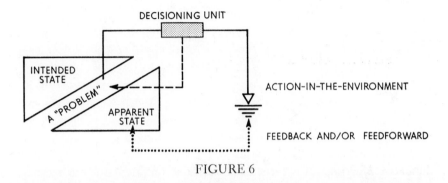

FIGURE 6

Tentatively identified problems are referred to the decisioning unit. If there is a match—that is, if the decisioning unit has "on file" experiences with problems of the sort referred, then some workable alternative solution is selected, and this alternative is converted into action. If, however, there is not a match—that is, if there is nothing appropriate "on file" in the decisioning unit, then the tentative problem-identification is rejected and another hypothesis as to the nature of the problem has to be developed.

The decisioning unit thus serves two purposes: (1) it serves as a sort of accumulated experience "file" to which all problem-definitions are referred; and (2) it serves as a selector mechanism for weighting and evaluating alternative solutions, and for initiating behavior in the direction of the alternative selected.

We should not overlook the extremely crucial role played by the expectations or anticipated consequences of different alternatives generated by the decisioning unit. Kelly's fundamental postulate is that "a person's processes are psychologically channelized by the ways in which he antici-

---

major scientists about why a mirror reverses an image horizontally but not vertically: if, when we look into a mirror, the left side of our heads appears on the right, why (logically) shouldn't we also appear upside down to ourselves? It was an intriguing problem. But it had never been a problem for me before, simply because I hadn't stopped to consider it! The reader can undoubtedly recall similar examples from his own experiences. Since the problems we do apprehend vary directly with the problems we can comprehend, it is likely that those circumstances we consider problematical are only a minute proportion of the problematicalness we might see in the experiences we have of our worlds.

pates events."[13] That is, a critical part of the alternative selection process is some preassessment of the likely consequences (for oneself) of one behavioral alternative as opposed to another.

Similarly, we should not overlook the fact that ways of perceiving the world, and ways of identifying and of dealing with the problems we see, develop their own *functional autonomy.* That is, their "use" facilitates their further use. Once we have perceived a situation in a certain way, once we have identified a certain set of circumstances as problematical in X way, a tendency to see things in similar ways, and to identify similar problems in what seem to be similar circumstances, is almost inevitable. Or, in still other words, we more often force event-data to fit our perceptions than we alter our perceptions to fit the data. The implications for problem-solving and decisioning behavior are manifold and far reaching.

It would not be particularly fruitful to get more deeply involved in how the decisioning process is carried out. Certain conditions such as recency, workability, economy, etc., all play a part in the process. All that is necessary here is this general view of the decisioning process with respect to the problem-solving function in human behavior.

Some Further Implications

There are some further implications of this view of behavior and behavior control which are useful in understanding human and organizational communication.

First, for our purposes in this book, we can advantageously look upon all behavior as a consequence of one particular or some pattern of cybernetic machines in some stage of resolution or of "working themselves out." Whenever we observe someone doing something, we can assume that his behavior is under the direction of one or more "problems" (either conscious or nonconscious).

Second, it is rather important to note that the critical factor in the initiation and persistence of particular behavior patterns is not problem-solving or decisioning as such, but is problem-*apprehension* and problem-*definition.* This fact will become more important as we shift our attention to more applied issues in communication.

Third, it would be careless to overlook the fact that there are both

---

[13] G. A. Kelly, *A Theory of Personality* (New York: W. W. Norton & Co., Inc., 1963), p. 46.

"hazard" and "opportunity" problems. When the problem is one in which the apparent-state-of-affairs is negatively different from an intended-state-of-affairs, the cybernetic machine thereby created is one which "works on" a hazard problem. But it is logically possible, and does indeed occur, for cybernetic machines to evolve which are postively rather than negatively oriented. Consciously, we occasionally set positive goals for ourselves, and set about taking those steps that seem to be necessary to achieve those goals. There are *opportunity* problems. The cybernetic machine that emerges to enerize, direct, and control our behavior in these circumstances functions in precisely the same way, however.

Fourth, we should not fail to understand that *all* behavior necessarily changes the environment, oneself, or both. A central implication of this fact is that the events or circumstances which a person interprets as problematical are never actually solved. The way we perceive any occurrence within our internal or external environments is necessarily a static cross-section of something which is actually a continuous flow of events. Thus we could never solve a situation in the sense of doing away with it (although we might dissolve the way in which we comprehend that situation). The best we can ever do is to alter the flow of events in the environment in a way which is more, or less, satisfactory. What we do when we solve a problem "in" the external environment is to behave in a way designed to alter circumstances in a desired or intended way. What results is not the dissolution of those circumstances, but a transition from a prior set of circumstances to a current set of circumstances. Our solutions don't eradicate circumstances; they just *change* circumstances. Thus we should look upon problem-solving and decisioning as simply *altering* oneself or the environment in some way. The best test, therefore, of the effectiveness and adequacy of any problem-definition, decisioning, problem-solving cycle is not, "Did I eliminate an adverse state-of-affairs?" but "Do I like the present set of circumstances more or less than the circumstances which I considered problematical?"

If the reader will think of a person's comprehending component as the critical nexus in a system which relates the individual to his social and physical environments, and of his behavior control component as the mechanism through which change in himself or in the environment is initiated, directed, and controlled, he will have an adequate model for embarking on the next step in our study of human communication. For in the next chapter, we will turn our attention to some interpersonal factors in human communication.

Suggestions for Further Reading

Concern with matters of the motivation and control (or regulation) of human behavior is as longstanding as man's awareness of himself as an instrument of his own destiny. A wide range of thought at different levels of analysis is reflected in this list of supplemental readings.

BERLYNE, D. E.   *Structure and Direction in Thinking*. New York: John Wiley & Sons, Inc., 1965.

BRUNER, J. S.; GOODNOW, J. J.; and AUSTIN, G. A.   *A Study of Thinking*. New York: John Wiley & Sons, Inc., 1956.

BURKE, KENNETH.   *A Grammar of Motives*. Englewood Cliffs, N.J.: Prentice-Hall, Inc., 1945.

————.   *A Rhetoric of Motives*. Englewood Cliffs, N.J.: Prentice-Hall, Inc., 1950.

CHASE, R. A.   "Sensory Feedback Mechanisms and Speech." Neurocommunications Unit, National Institute of Mental Health, Bethesda, Md., Nov., 1963.

COMBS, ARTHUR W., and SNYGG, DONALD.   *Individual Behavior: A Perceptual Approach to Behavior*. Rev. ed. New York: Harper & Bros., 1959.

DEWEY, JOHN.   *How We Think*. Boston: D. C. Heath & Co., 1911.

GRINKER, ROY R. (ed.).   *Toward a Unified Theory of Human Behavior*. New York: Basic Books, Inc., 1956.

HARVEY, O. J. (ed.).   *Motivation and Social Interaction*. New York: Ronald Press Co., 1963.

JACKSON, JAY M.   "Reference Group Processes in a Formal Organization," *Sociometry*, Vol. 22 (1959), pp. 307–27.

KALMUS, H. (ed.).   *Regulation and Control in Living Systems*. New York: John Wiley & Sons, Inc., 1967.

KELLY, G. A.   *The Psychology of Personal Constructs*. New York: W. W. Norton & Co., Inc., 1955.

LURIA, A. R.   *The Role of Speech in the Regulation of Normal and Abnormal Behavior*. TT66 60821. U.S. Dept. of Commerce, Institute for Applied Technology, 1966.

MARON, M. E.   "On Cybernetics, Information Processing, and Thinking." Paper No. P–2879. Santa Monica, Calif.: The RAND Corp., March, 1964.

MASLOW, ABRAHAM H.   *Motivation and Personality*. New York: Harper & Bros., 1954.

MILLER, G. A.; GALANTER, E.; and PRIBRAM, K. H.   Plans and the Structure of Behavior. New York: Holt, Rinehart & Winston, 1960.

PARSONS, TALCOTT, and SHILS, E. T. (eds.).   Toward a General Theory of Action. Cambridge, Mass.: Harvard University Press, 1952.

PIAGET, JEAN.   Logic and Psychology. New York: Basic Books, Inc., 1957.

POWERS, W. T.; CLARK, R. K.; and McFARLAND, R. I.   "A General Feedback Theory of Human Behavior," General Systems Yearbook, Vol. 5 (1960), pp. 63–73, 75–83.

SARBIN, T. R. "Anxiety: Reification of a Metaphor," Archives of General Psychiatry, Vol. 10 (1964), pp. 630 ff.

SCHREIER, FRED T.   Human Motivation: Probability and Meaning. Glencoe, Ill.: Free Press, 1957.

TAYLOR, D. W.   "Toward an Information-Processing Theory of Motivation," in M. R. JONES (ed.), Nebraska Symposium on Motivation. Lincoln: University of Nebraska Press, 1960.

WASSERMAN, P., and SILANDER, F. S.   Decision-Making: An Annotated Bibliography. Ithaca, N.Y.: Graduate School of Business and Public Administration, Cornell University, 1958.

————, and ————.   Decision-Making: An Annotated Bibliography, Supplement, 1958–1963. Ithaca, N.Y.: Graduate School of Business and Public Administration, Cornell University, 1964.

ZAJONC, R. B., and WOLFE, D. M.   Cognitive Consequences of a Person's Position in a Formal Organization. Tech. Report No. 24. Ann Arbor, Mich.: Institute for Social Research, 1963.

ZIPF, GEORGE K.   Human Behavior and the Principle of Least Effort. Reading, Mass.: Addison-Wesley Publishing Co., Inc., 1949.

6

People, Behavior, and Communication: Some Interpersonal Factors

UP TO THIS POINT, emphasis has been primarily upon certain basic *intraper-sonal* or individual factors relevant to an adequate understanding of the processes of human communication. These preliminaries are an essential prerequisite to any productive interpretation of the practical issues in communication which confront us every day. With the perspectives estab-lished in the preceding chapters as a foundation, it is possible now to turn our attention to some important *interpersonal* factors in human communi-cation. What follows, however, should not be viewed as *alternative* ways of viewing human behavior and the relationships between behavior and communication, but as *additional* factors to be accounted for in any complete understanding of the communication process.

We will look first at what people bring to an encounter which facilitates or impedes their intercommunication, then at how properties of inter-personal relationships emerge and begin to affect intercommunication. Then we will consider the means by which people control and regulate each other via intercommunication, and how these processes relate to the nature of organization.

Some Preconditions of Intercommunication

All of the intrapersonal factors we have given consideration to are, in one way or another, *preconditions* for intercommunication. So it is not a different but an additional set of variables—unique to intercommunication—which we need to consider now. These additional concepts must be superimposed upon, not substituted for, the relevant *intra*personal factors in any communication encounter. The basic phenomenon is ultimately an intrapersonal phenomenon. That process basic to all human communication—the process of attributing meaning or significance or message-ness to raw sensory data—never occurs *between* individuals. It can only occur *within* individuals.

So the practical need to focus upon intercommunication (or communication between people) should not carry with it the illusion that the basic phenomenon shifts to something that happens *between* people. The basic phenomenon is located or sourced only *in* individuals.

There are certain additional concepts which will be useful to us in comprehending intercommunication, however, and in analyzing and understanding how it is that two or more people can—more, or less, effectively—communicate-with each other.

THE FUNDAMENTAL PRECONDITION: A RELATIONSHIP

Just as some way of relating to nonhuman events and objects in the environment is an absolute prerequisite of our dealing with them conceptually (and hence behaviorally), some way of relating to another individual is an absolute prerequisite to dealing with him conceptually—and hence communicatively. Comprehending another person requires me to have a conceptual model of my relationship to him. Thus a basic prerequisite for all intercommunication is that at least one of the persons involved has a conceptual model (conscious or nonconscious) of the assumed relationship.

If each person in a two-person encounter has a different conceptual model of the relationship, it is fairly easy to imagine what an obstacle that would be to their communication. This particular issue has many important implications for the analysis of communication problems that we will undertake in a later section.

What sort of models do people have of their assumed relationship to one another?

Status and prestige are common relationship factors, as are superior-subordinate, expert-novice, etc. If I attribute high status or prestige to another, I then relate to him differently than I would to a person to whom I ascribe low status. If I see another as my superior, or as more expert than

I am in some field, the *structure* of my relationship with him reflects the *distance* I assume exists between us.

There are other conceived relationships, of course—from the most stereotyped (husband-wife) to the most idiosyncratic. It would take us beyond our present purpose to attempt even to categorize them.

The important point here is that *some* conceptual model of one's relationship with another is a basic precondition or prerequisite of any intercommunication with him.

The Second Precondition: Some "Need" or "Appetite," Some Purpose or Intention

It should perhaps be unnecessary to specify this second precondition: that if two or more people are going to engage in intercommunication, at least one of them must have either an intention or purpose vis-à-vis one or more of the others, or an "appetite" to be communicated-with in some way[1] (or perhaps both). But we would be remiss not to be properly aware of the fact that, although talking may not serve any useful purpose, communication always occurs *in the service of* some need of the psychological system—either some "appetite" or some communicative intention.[2]

So unless one or another of the participants has either some particular "appetite" to be communicated-with or some intention to be achieved through communicating-to the other, the necessary preconditions for intercommunication do not exist.

This should not be taken naïvely to mean that the sheer existence of an "appetite" or an intention will assure that the communication one wants to occur is going to occur in the practical sense of $A \rightarrow B = X$. Communication, as we have defined it previously, will indeed occur. But whether the message that a receiver "gets" from an interpersonal encounter is the one intended by the originator is not achieved just by establishing the precon-

---

[1] Perhaps "need" would be a less clumsy term than "appetite." But people often conceive of "need" as necessarily being conscious or mental in some way. Since we can in fact be nonconsciously susceptible to being communicated-with quite apart from our consciously-recognized needs for information to be consumed, "appetite" may therefore be a more meaningful term to use.

[2] This point derives from our understanding of the two basic functions of communication presented earlier. The processes of communication subserve the organism in one of two ways: either as a means of adapting oneself to the perceived environment in some way, or as a means of attempting to affect some aspect of the perceived environment (such as another person) in some way (i.e., by attempting to establish, maintain, alter, or exploit an apparent-state-of-affairs in such a way that it coincides with some intended-state-of-affairs).

ditions. We can say that if the preconditions or prerequisites are *not* met there will be no intercommunication of any consequence. But we cannot say that if these preconditions are met there will be "successful" intercommunication.

ROLES AND RULES: THE THIRD PRECONDITION

There is a further prerequisite or precondition for intercommunication: to the extent the individuals involved in any human encounter (consciously or nonconsciously) do not follow certain minimum *rules* for intercommunication, there will be no intercommunication.

Some of these minimum rules seem so obvious as to be overlooked. For example, the rule that one should be heard by (or his letter read by) the person(s) he wants to communicate-to is a rule we take for granted. Or, the rule that we should speak or write English to an audience trained only in English; the rule that we should speak slowly enough to permit apprehension; or that we should write in keeping with the various grammatical or syntactical conventions of the particular language we are using; or the rule that we should never fail to play the game (of intercommunication) according to all the appropriate rules if we want to stay in contact with our receiver(s): these are all common examples of the sorts of rules we have to be able to follow if we want to engage in intercommunication.

There are rules governing use of the language, rules regarding place and time, rules of protocol, and rules about meeting mutual expectations. There are psychological rules and sociological rules and anthropological rules. There are cultural rules to be learned and abided by: he who hasn't been properly socialized to or who doesn't abide by certain cultural rules will generally suffer the consequences of some kind and some degree of *excommunication* (refusal by others to enter into intercommunication with the non–rule-follower). There are rules of all sorts and of many levels. In sum, they can be roughly compared to the kinds of rules and the levels of the rules one must follow if he is going to play any sophisticated "game" with other people—such as poker or bridge or collective bargaining or managerial politics or intercommunication.[3]

It would take us somewhat afield to attempt to explore in depth the prerequisites and the consequences of rule-following in every sort of cooperative human enterprise—from dating to General Motors to inter-

---

[3] E.g., S. Verba, *Small Groups and Political Behavior* (Princeton, N.J.: Princeton University Press, 1961).

national politics.[4] What we do need to note here is that entering into intercommunication with another person has as a precondition the willingness (or acquiescence) of the individuals involved to submit to a wide range and a number of levels of rule-following.

One particular type of rule which perhaps deserves some additional recognition here is what is usually referred to as role.[5] A person who is "playing" a role, or who is fulfilling the requirements of particular social roles as he comprehends them, is following rules. These rules take the form of "recipes" or guidelines or prescriptions for evaluating (either in advance or in retrospect) the appropriateness of one's own or another's behavior in specific situations[6] according to the role or roles one assumes he (or the other) is supposed to be playing-out in those situations.

Like all rules, however, roles are neither right nor wrong. They may be more (or less) explicit, more (or less) well comprehended by the persons involved, more (or less) crucial, more (or less) general (or specific). Whatever their dimensions or characteristics, their reality is totally *normative* or *social*. They exist and function only to the extent that they are subscribed to by the individuals involved. Thus any "violation" is ultimately a violation of a rule which is assumed by someone to have been the obligation of another person in that situation. To violate a norm or a role is in some way to fail to "play" the game or fulfill the role *others* perceive to be appropriate for an individual under the circumstances. In short, role violations are failures to fulfill the expectations or beliefs of others. They are significant to a person's behavior or his life, therefore, only to the

---

[4] The concept of rule-following is not an uncommon one in the behavioral sciences: e.g., "The 'conclusion' seems to us inescapable that *self-consciously acting in accordance with a rule* (or formulating such rules) is one of the fundamental aspects of social interaction, and any experimental studies which neglect this point simply have nothing to do with that topic," write O. K. Moore and A. R. Anderson, "Some Puzzling Aspects of Social Interaction," in Joan Criswell *et al.*, *Mathematical Methods in Small Groups* (Stanford, Calif.: Stanford University Press, 1962), p. 242. Cf. R. S. Peters, *The Concept of Motivation* (London: Routledge, 1958); T. S. Szasz, *The Myth of Mental Illness: Foundations of a Theory of Human Conduct* (New York: Hoeber-Harper, 1961); E. Goffman, *Encounters: Two Studies in the Sociology of Interaction* (Indianapolis: Bobbs-Merrill Co., Inc., 1963); and E. K. Wilson, *Sociology: Rules, Roles, and Relationships* (Homewood, Ill.: Dorsey Press, 1966).

[5] For recent surveys, see B. J. Biddle and E. J. Thomas, *Role Theory: Concepts and Research* (New York: John Wiley & Sons, Inc., 1966); and E. J. Thomas and R. A. Feldman, *Concepts of Role Theory* (Ann Arbor: University of Michigan Press, 1964).

[6] On the concept of "behavior setting," see R. G. Barker and H. F. Wright, *Midwest and Its Children* (New York: Harper & Bros., 1955). Cf. E. Goffman, *The Presentation of Self in Everyday Life* (New York: Anchor Books, 1959); and E. Goffman, *Behavior in Public Places* (New York: Free Press, 1963).

extent that others are *significant others—i.e.,* are perceived to be one of those with whom one identifies or aspires to identify.

A FOURTH PRECONDITION: A LANGUAGE

A fourth prerequisite of intercommunication is a *language*—the mutual acceptance of communicative "coin," or tokens. These may be words (spoken or written), pictures, musical tones, gestures and/or facial expressions—anything that has been culturally standardized at least by the two persons who want to intercommunicate.

We will want to deal with language at greater length in a later chapter as an aspect of the technology of communication. So we need not dwell upon it here, except to recognize that some tacitly (or explicitly) agreed upon language is a prerequisite to intercommunication.

There are other conditions which underlie intercommunication. But these will be sufficient for our purposes. Having established the major preconditions of intercommunication, we can turn our attention now to some dynamics of the process of intercommunication itself.

The Dynamics of Intercommunication

There are but two ways of affecting or modifying the behavior of others. One could employ physical force. All other attempts to affect others or oneself are necessarily communicational.

Thus, while it would not be accurate to say that intercommunication is the *only* means we have of affecting or influencing each other's behavior, it would be accurate to say that, in our modern world, essentially all of our attempts to change ourselves or others in some way are communicative rather than physical. However else it might be characterized, therefore, *interpersonal behavior* is basically *intercommunication behavior.*[7]

There would be little justification for attempting to catalog here our accumulated knowledge about human behavior and human interaction—

---

[7] I. A. Taylor has written: ". . . much difficulty and confusion may be produced in psychology because the field is defined as the study of behavior of which communication is an aspect, when, essentially, psychology is the study of communication of which behavior is an aspect" in E. Whitney (ed.), *Symbology* (New York: Hastings House, 1961), p. 137. Cf. D. M. MacKay, "Towards an Information-Flow Model of Human Behavior." *British Journal of Psychology*, 1956, 47, 30–43; D. M. MacKay, "Information Theory and Human Information Systems." *Impact of Science on Society*, 1957, 8, 86–101; and G. Vickers, *The Art of Judgment* (New York: Basic Books, Inc., 1965), p. 93 ff.

particularly since surprisingly little of what we presume to know about human behavior has been developed from a point of view which recognizes the essential role of communication in all intra- and inter-human processes.[8] So we will simply attempt to establish four basic perspectives on the dynamics of intercommunication.

Mutuality, Complementarity, Symbiosis

It is unfortunate that we don't have a single term by which to refer to the latent "matching" of the components of two psychological systems at the time they encounter one another. But perhaps a brief explanation of the possibilities will suffice at least to suggest the usefulness of such terms as *mutuality, complementarity,* and *symbiosis* when looking at interpersonal behavior or intercommunication.

The analogy of metabolism was offered earlier as one way of viewing the basic functions of communication. The analogy is most helpful here. To the extent that the communicational "appetites" of one person match or are complementary to the communicational outputs of another, their interaction is greatly facilitated. If the communicational intentions of A match the communicational needs of B, there is a degree of mutuality or complementarity between them which energizes and facilitates their inter-communication. When the intended-states-of-affairs of two people who encounter one another directly or indirectly are mutual or complementary in some way, a condition of symbiosis (or *synergy*) is implicit in their encounter.

---

[8] Seemingly the best-known and most current inventory of knowledge on human behavior is B. Berelson and G. A. Steiner, *Human Behavior: An Inventory of Scientific Findings* (New York: Harcourt, Brace & World, 1964). One chapter is devoted to "mass communication" and there are some allusions to the phenomenon of communication in the chapter on face-to-face relations in small groups. The authors of some current books on psychology, on management, and on organization seem to be able to describe human behavior without referring to communication at all; some others have apparently succumbed to the sheer popularity of the term and devoted a *whole chapter* to communication! Of course, this relative obliviousness to the processes of communication in human behavior is an accident of the manner in which our arbitrary categories of knowledge have evolved. But one might easily infer from the incidental treatment often given communication in books on human behavior that it is somehow possible to interact with other people in ways which are *neither* communicative *nor* physical. No useful or practical conception of human behavior can be developed without some specific reference to what goes on when people "interact." *Something* happens when we transact with our environments and with other people. That "something" is the process of intercommunication, and that process is fundamental to all human behavior—and hence to any useful understanding of human behavior (or of the dynamics of inter-action between and among people).

Such conditions establish the possibilities, and determine the nature and the effectiveness of any human encounter. *The basic dynamics of all human communication encounters derive from the mutuality (or the complementarity or the symbiosis) of the take-into-account-abilities, the take-into-account-susceptibilities, and the dominant expectations of two people when they encounter one another communicatively.* To the extent that the needs and functions of their internal comprehending and behavior components "match" in some way, the success of the encounter is greatly facilitated. To the extent there is some crucial mismatch, there will be difficulties and obstacles, sometimes to the extent of making successful intercommunication impossible.[9]

POWER

Schachter characterizes what is probably a fairly universal conception of the relation between communication and power when he writes ". . . communication is the mechanism by which power is exerted."[10] Communication is conventionally viewed as a means or mechanism of accomplishing other ends.

But a somewhat different conception of the relation between communication and power would be more consistent with the overall frame of reference for comprehending human communication being developed in this book—and would perhaps be a more useful conception.

To develop that concept of power, we need to recall a basic fact: that there are but two ways of affecting others or of attempting to change others or oneself. One is physical force, the other is communication. One of the implications of this fact is that one person may literally overpower another, or may, by controlling the physical environment or the physical metabolism of another, directly or indirectly coerce another person.[11]

Another implication is that one person may, by controlling or affecting

---

[9] For example, if any success you might have in your intention to affect another person communicatively would consequent (as he sees it) in some crucially negative state-of-affairs for him, then your respective behavior control systems ("cybernetic machines") are in fact discomplementary or nonmutual. In that event, you will find intercommunication with him difficult, if not impossible.

[10] S. Schachter, "Deviation, Rejection, and Communication." *Journal of Abnormal and Social Psychology*, Vol. 46 (1951), p. 191.

[11] Certain types of so-called "brain-washing" or "thought control" might serve as examples, although the intent is not just to exercise control, but to reshape the victim's psychological structure. See R. J. Lifton, *Thought Reform and the Psychology of Totalism*. New York: W. W. Norton & Co., Inc., 1961.

the *communication* metabolism of another person in some way, gain some degree of power over another person. For example, one of the "appetites" most of us have in common is for information relevant to our present or future conditions vis-à-vis what we believe to be the significant aspects of our environments. We need that information in order to confirm or disconfirm our hypotheses about the present and the future conditions of our existences (e.g., our state-relationships with our environments). Under certain circumstances, for example, we need to know how another person feels about us, whether or not he approves of us, etc.[12] Or we may feel a need for information from a superior, or from some other person who is in a position to affect our destinies in some way.

When another person has some relatively exclusive prerogative to determine our future destinies in some way, he can exercise *power* over us.[13] So a useful concept of power that we can employ in the study or the application of human communication is this one: *one person has potential power over another person to the extent that he has certain exclusive prerogatives (however gained) for fulfilling specific communicative needs of the other.* Thus power often accrues to us by accident. One's lack of awareness of another's communicative needs gives us a certain degree of power over the other just as surely as if we were intentionally to refuse to fulfill the other's communicative needs. (We should never overlook the fact that most of our getting and giving, most of our communication metabolism, is *nonconscious.* So we may not and probably often do not realize the ebb and flow of power in our interactions with others.)

To clarify a question that this concept of power might give rise to:

---

[12] For some empirical studies, see D. P. Crowne and D. Marlowe, *The Approval Motive* (New York: John Wiley & Sons, Inc., 1964). The experience of seeking or giving approval—or of seeking or giving other information which fulfills some orientational (or other) communicative need or "appetite"—is a common one.

[13] The reader may wish to compare this concept of power with others. French and Raven, for example, have identified five bases of power: *attraction power* (based on B's liking for A); *expert power* (based on B's perception that A has superior knowledge and information); *reward power* (based on A's ability to mediate rewards for B); *coercive power* (based on A's ability to mediate punishments for B); and *legitimate power* (based on B's belief that A has a right to prescribe his behavior or opinions) . . . quoted by J. R. P. French, Jr., in "A Formal Theory of Social Power," *Psychological Review*, Vol. 63 (1956), pp. 183–84. Cf. D. Cartwright (ed.), *Studies in Social Power* (Ann Arbor: Research Center for Group Dynamics, University of Michigan, 1959); and P. M. Blau, *Exchange and Power in Social Life* (New York: John Wiley & Sons, Inc., 1964). These various views are not necessarily incompatible. For example, if we look upon French and Raven's "attraction power" as part of our metacommunicative metabolism (i.e., of feeding a relationship by maintaining it), then all five of their "bases" of power fit nicely into the present analysis.

authority is normative and is *given* in a formal or institutional relationship. It is institutionalized or "legitimate" power. Authority does not accrue from the interaction of people; power does.[14] Another has a certain range of authority to direct our behavior to the extent we give him that authority because of his position or role, his status, etc. Authority is thus a property of the social roles or institutional positions involved, while power is a property of the dynamics of particular situations and particular relationships.

CONTROL AND REGULATION

The concept of *control* has been at issue in much of the previous discussion. There is, as we have seen, more than one level at which behavior is controlled and regulated. Our (conscious and nonconscious) cybernetic machines control and regulate our behavior. At the same time, our expectations regarding another's likely reaction to our behavior may have a preregulative effect on our behavior. Similarly, some people "draw" certain behaviors out of other people through subtle characteristics of their own behavior. For example, psychologically dependent people evoke protective behavior on the part of others—often without either person's conscious realization that it is happening.

Various loci of control and regulation have been considered previously. But there are at least three kinds of control which are unique to the interpersonal level of analysis.

First, any interpersonal encounter which persists or recurs becomes—in a generic sense—an organization. In order to enable themselves to achieve their communicative intentions and to fulfill their communicative needs beyond the level made possible by the cultural (and reference group) orientations which they might have in common, the parties to any interpersonal relationship will gradually *institutionalize* each other. That is, they will gradually develop certain expectations, certain standardized interpretations, and certain rules for their intercommunication peculiar to their own relationship. Each evolves a *psychological contract* with the other, a set of constraints or expectations for mutually regulating their behavior vis-à-vis one another.

---

14 Note, however, that power can be exerted through indirect communication channels. Thus, even though A may not have a face-to-face relationship with B, B may know something that A expects will affect his present or future existence in some way. The President of the United States, for example, may know something which we don't know but have a need to know. Thus he has a certain power over us.

Their institutionalization of each other is not consciously pursued; it just happens. Most of us are probably not even aware of the "constraints" on us which obtain in our relationships with others, for those constraints emerge over time and out of awareness. They are no less real or effective for all of our lack of awareness of them, however.

An interpersonal relationship can therefore be considered a subculture. The particular norms which are generated during the interaction of any two people function in the same manner as any other cultural norm in controlling and regulating the behavior of each person vis-à-vis the other.

Second, in *interpersonal* behavior, we interpret our own behavior in the context of what we assume to be the other persons's intentions, orientations, expectations, values and beliefs, etc. In other words, in interpersonal behavior, the other person's intentions, expectations, etc. (as I conceive of them) become a part of the situation or apparent-state-of-affairs for me. We can be relatively sure that a tree or a dollar bill will not react negatively or disapprovingly toward us. But when the target of our behavior is another person, a new dimension of control enters in. Now one must evaluate not only the adequacy of his own behavior, but he must take-into-account the other's likely evaluation of his behavior (as he "sees" it), and so on.

In this way, the parties to any interpersonal relationship unwittingly contribute one to several additional levels of control and regulation of each other's behavior.[15]

Third (and perhaps this is no more than a different way of looking at the same conditions), what is involved in any interpersonal encounter is not the physical objects themselves. Pragmatically, a person is neither more nor less than his own or another's conception of him. That people exist as objects and as biological organisms is undeniable. But all of their human attributes are purely and totally human conceptions. And it is always the *attributed* human characteristics of people which are involved in interpersonal relations—not the physical objects as such.

What person A brings to an encounter with person B is (minimally): (1) his conception of himself—let us call that concept A_1; and (2) his conception of the other person—which we can refer to as B_1. Person B, in

---

[15] If the reader will pause to contemplate the thinking behind and some of the implications of the following statement, he will begin to develop a "feel" for the kind of control that people exert over each other:

"Writers seldom write the things they think.
They simply write the things they think
other folks think they think." (Elbert Hubbard)

turn, brings to the encounter: (1) his conception of himself—B_2; and (2) his conception of the other person—A_2.

What therefore *interacts* is not A and B as such, but what is for A his subsystem $A_1 \leftrightarrow B_1$, and what is for B his subsystem $A_2 \leftrightarrow B_2$. Perhaps a crude diagram will help the reader to visualize this, the basis of all interpersonal encounters:

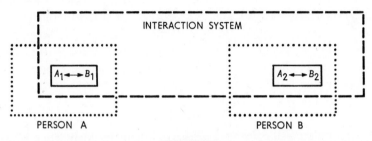

FIGURE 7

$A_1 \leftrightarrow B_1$ and $B_2 \leftrightarrow A_2$ each has its own properties.[16] When the two separate subsystems are involved in a transaction, they become the elements of a higher order *interaction* system. That higher order interaction system might be characterized in the following manner:

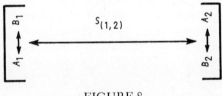

FIGURE 8

The details of this higher order interaction system are not crucial. The points to be made are: (1) the basic dynamic in interpersonal transactions is the systemic interaction between $A_1 \leftrightarrow B_1$ and $B_2 \leftrightarrow A_2$; (2) a new functional system—$S_{1,2}$—is formed; —and (3) the newly formed system has emergent properties of its own which are determined neither by $A_1 \leftrightarrow B_1$ nor by $A_2 \leftrightarrow B_2$, *but by both.* It is these emergent properties of the higher order interaction system which now becomes the loci of certain kinds and degrees of control and regulation of the participants' behavior vis-à-vis each other.

---

[16] We have little or nothing in the way of a language to describe those properties, but our knowledge of systems provides a substantial theoretical basis for this proposition.

This is admittedly a somewhat difficult or awkward concept to grasp. So perhaps a pertinent example or two would be in order.

A man once had a cat who, for no apparent reason, behaved toward him in a way which could be interpreted as fear. Because the man interpreted the cat as being afraid of him, he behaved toward that cat differently than he did toward other cats (which he didn't perceive as being afraid of him). So there developed between them a relationship which was neither man→cats nor cat→people. The same cat exhibited less of the same fear behavior in the presence of other people. So the relationship between *that* man and *that* cat developed some peculiar characteristics of its own, apparently not predicatable either from the man's general concept of cats or from the cat's general concept of people.

So it was that the man and the cat unwittingly came to control each other's behavior vis-à-vis the other. They both became victims of a system (a complex relationship) which neither of them could independently or completely determine. This is, of course, a common experience between every parent and child, every superior and subordinate, indeed between any two people who intercommunicate over time.

Another example: Student X is perceived by Teacher Y as potentially superior to most of the other students—a perception which is quite at variance with the perceptions X's other teachers have of him. The other teachers see X as being lazy, or stupid, or both. But Teacher Y extends Student X some special privileges and prerogatives, on the assumption that this will encourage Student X to do his best work. Student X accepts and exploits those special privileges. But he does not perform. What is Teacher Y to do now? Whatever course of action he chooses, it must in some way be a function of the new relationship that has been established between him and Student X, between him and his fellow teachers, etc. Teacher Y is not a completely free agent, and he will likely take-into-account the conditions of the new interpersonal relationships which now develop (and as he sees them). He did not intentionally create the characteristics or consequences of these new relationships with Student X or with the other teachers. But the dynamics of these new relationships will have some control and regulation over his behavior from this point on. And this example can easily be translated into thousands of boss-subordinate, seller-buyer, etc., relationships.

The point is that we can not and do not determine the emergent properties or characteristics of the higher order interaction systems which link and bind us to other people—nor does the other person. Yet what we cannot control will, in some way and in some degree, control us. Our behavior is controlled and regulated by the properties of the interaction systems—the relationships—which emerge from our interactions with others. We cannot unilaterally or even cooperatively determine in total what those properties will be. But they nonetheless function as controllers and regulators of our behavior toward each other.

GAMING

One additional concept which will be valuable to us in comprehending the nature of intercommunication—of interpersonal behavior—is that of gaming.[17] The usefulness of a concept like gaming should not lead us to assume that people relate to each other *only* as "game-players." Interpersonal behavior cannot be understood *only* as a "game." But some of the concepts by which we comprehend game-playing do provide some useful insights into the dynamics of intercommunication.

We have previously considered the importance of rules and rule-following in interpersonal behavior. Certainly rule-following is basic to gaming. But the issues of "the name of the game," and the criteria for determining who wins and how each should play the game—these issues include, but go beyond simply following the rules.

The games that people play vary from the relatively simple and stereo-typed to the extremely complex and idiosyncratic. We follow certain basic rules of etiquette or protocol in order to be thought of as "in" with the people involved. They, in turn, reward us with *in*-ness and we reciprocate[18] to the extent that they follow what we consider to be the minimal

---

[17] For some different but perhaps equally useful views on gaming, see E. Berne, *Games People Play: The Psychology of Human Relationships* (New York: Grove Press, 1964); T. S. Szasz, *The Myth of Mental Illness: Foundations of a Theory of Personal Conduct* (New York: Hoeber-Harper, 1961), esp. Part V; E. Goffman, *Encounters: Two Studies in the Sociology of Interaction* (Indianapolis: Bobbs-Merrill Co., Inc., 1961); A. Rapoport, *Fights, Games and Debates* (Ann Arbor: University of Michigan Press, 1960); S. Potter, *Gamesmanship* (New York: Holt, Rinehart & Winston, 1948); and S. Potter, *One-Upmanship* (New York: Holt, Rinehart & Winston, 1952).

The quantitative analysis of games stems from J. von Neumann and O. Morgenstern, *Theory of Games and Economic Behavior* (Princeton, N.J.: Princeton University Press, 1947). A recent review of quantitative approaches is M. Shubik (ed.), *Game Theory and Related Approaches to Social Behavior* (New York: John Wiley & Sons, Inc., 1964).

For some perspectives on "gaming" at the animal level, see S. A. Altmann, "Social Behavior of Anthropoid Primates: Analysis of Recent Concepts," in E. L. Bliss (ed.), *Roots of Behavior: Genetics, Instinct, and Socialization in Animal Behavior* (New York: Hoeber-Harper, 1962), pp. 277–85.

[18] Cf. J. Bruner's "Primitive Motive to Reciprocate," in his *Toward a Theory of Instruction* (Cambridge, Mass.: Harvard University Press, 1966, p. 125).

rules governing their behavior in that situation. At the other extreme are the unique two-person games which evolve over time from the interaction between the persons involved. Berne gives a number of examples in his book.[19] Albee's "Who's Afraid of Virginia Woolf?" revolves about an extended game between the central characters of the drama.

The games that people play do indeed influence their intercommunication in many ways, and often unwittingly. What we say, to whom, in what manner, etc.—these are issues which are determined in part by the state of the *relationship* between the individuals involved. And a part of those extremely complex ties that bind us to each other (for our normative existences and our communicative sustenance) is always the nature and the state of the interpersonal games we are playing with each other.

Any further treatment of this important concept here would take us too far from our major objectives in this book. But we could not leave this consideration of gaming without noting the overriding game in which we are all involved in our intercommunication with others. It is simply this: our words and our concepts, the tools of our intercommunication, are all essentially arbitrary and normative. When one person nods his head in recognition of another's words, he is "playing the game": if you react *as if* you understand me, I'll react *as if* I understand you. It is impossible for us to experience another's experiences. There is no way for me to experience your toothache, for example—or your ideas or your feelings or your communicative intentions. I can only experience what *I* experience. I can't understand your understandings. I can only understand my understandings.

Intercommunication is a universal, pervasive game, in which statements, arbitrarily representing states of our separate existences, are offered and accepted (or not).[20] Our willingness to accept the conventional meanings of words is our entry fee into the game. If each participant follows the rules of the game, we say they "communicate with" each other. If one or the other doesn't—or can't—follow the rules for intercommunication, then we say communication "broke down."

This is not to imply that intercommunication is not a serious business. We need only to look at the current international situation to see how serious a business it can be. But the dynamics of gaming are a part of what underlies all intercommunication. As a concept for understanding and analysis, it will be useful to us as we continue to develop a more useful

---

[19] E. Berne, *op. cit.*

[20] As J. Wilson writes: ". . . learning to communicate by means of words is rather like learning to play a game . . ." (*Language and the Pursuit of Truth*. [New York: Cambridge University Press, 1956]).

understanding of the exceedingly complex processes of human communication.

SUGGESTIONS FOR FURTHER READING

Probably more has been written about interpersonal aspects than about any other aspect of the processes of human communication. The listing that follows is not an attempt to present a representative cross-section of that body of literature. Rather, the titles have been selected for inclusion here with the expectation that they may complement the substance of this chapter in some useful way.

ARGYRIS, C. *An Introduction to Field Theory and Interaction Theory.* Rev. ed., New Haven, Conn.: Labor and Management Center, Yale University, 1952.

BENNIS, W. G. et al. (eds.). *Interpersonal Dynamics: Essays and Readings on Human Interaction.* Homewood, Ill.: Dorsey Press, 1964.

BERRIEN, F. K., and BASH, W. H. *Human Relations: Comments and Cases.* New York: Harper & Bros., 1957.

BLAU, P. M. *Exchange and Power in Social Life.* New York: John Wiley & Sons, Inc., 1964.

BONNER, HUBERT. *Group Dynamics: Principles and Applications.* New York: Ronald Press Co., 1959.

CANTRIL, HADLEY. "Perception and Interpersonal Relations," *American Journal of Psychiatry,* Vol. 114 (1957), pp. 119–26.

CARTER, RICHARD F. "Communication and Affective Relations," *Journalism Quarterly,* Vol. 42 (1965), pp. 203–12.

COLLINS, B. E., and GUETZKOW, H. "Communication and Interaction," in *A Social Psychology of Group Processes for Decision Making.* New York: John Wiley & Sons, Inc., 1964.

FESTINGER, L., and THIBAUT, J. "Interpersonal Communication in Small Groups," *Journal of Abnormal and Social Psychology,* Vol. 46 (1951), pp. 92–99.

GIBB, J. R. "Defensive Communication," *Journal of Communication,* Vol. 11 (1961), pp. 141–48.

GIFFIN, K. *A Conceptualization of Interpersonal Trust in the Communication Process.* Working Paper #4. Lawrence: Communication Research Center, University of Kansas, 1966.

HEIDER, FRITZ. *The Psychology of Interpersonal Relations.* New York: John Wiley & Sons, Inc., 1958.

HOMANS, G. C.   *The Human Group.* New York: Harcourt, Brace & Co., Inc., 1950.

————.   "Social Behavior as Exchange," *American Journal of Sociology,* Vol. 63 (1958), pp. 597–606.

————.   *Social Behavior: Its Elementary Forms.* New York: Harcourt, Brace & World, 1961.

JACKSON, JAY M.   *Analysis of Interpersonal Relations in a Formal Organization.* Ann Arbor, Mich.: University Microfilms, No. 5050.

JENKINS, D. H.   "Prediction in Interpersonal Communication," *Journal of Communication,* Vol. 11 (1961), pp. 129–66.

KANFER, FREDERICK H.   "Structure of Psychotherapy: Role Playing as a Variable in Dyadic Communication," *Journal of Consulting Psychology,* Vol. 29 (1965), pp. 325–32.

LEARY, TIMOTHY.   "The Theory and Measurement of Interpersonal Communication," *American Journal of Sociology,* Vol. 63 (1958), pp. 497–505.

————.   "The Theory and Measurement of Interpersonal Communication," *Psychiatry,* Vol. 18 (1955), pp. 147–61.

LEE, IRVING J.   *Language Habits in Human Affairs.* New York: Harper & Bros., 1941.

LENNARD, H. L., and BERNSTEIN, A.   *The Anatomy of Psychotherapy: Systems of Communication and Expectation.* New York: Columbia University Press, 1960.

LYLE, J.   "Communication, Group Atmosphere, Productivity, and Morale in Small Task Groups," *Human Relations,* Vol. 14 (1961), pp. 369–79.

McCALL, G. J., and SIMMONS, J. L.   *Identities and Interactions.* New York: Free Press, 1966.

MacMURRAY, JOHN.   *Persons in Relation.* London: Faber & Faber, 1961.

MEERLOO, J. A. M.   *Conversation and Communication: A Psychological Inquiry into Language and Human Relations.* New York: International Universities Press, 1952.

MELLINGER, GLEN D.   "Interpersonal Trust as a Factor in Communication," *Journal of Abnormal and Social Psychology,* Vol. 52 (1956), pp. 304–9.

MILLER, JAMES GRIER.   *Experiments in Social Process.* New York: McGraw-Hill Book Co., 1950.

MULDER, MARK.   "The Power Variable in Communication Experiments," *Human Relations,* Vol. 13 (1960), pp. 241–57.

MULLAHY, PATRICK.   *Study of Interpersonal Relations.* New York: Hermitage House, 1949.

OLMSTED, MICHAEL S.   *The Small Group.* New York: Random House, 1959.

PEAR, T. H. *The Psychology of Conversation*. Toronto: Thomas Nelson & Sons, 1939.

RUNKEL, P. J. "Cognitive Similarity in Facilitating Communication," *Sociometry*, Vol. 19 (1956), pp. 178–91.

SCHACHTER, S. "Deviation, Rejection, and Communication," *Journal of Abnormal and Social Psychology*, Vol. 46 (1951), pp. 190–207.

SCHUTZ, WILLIAM C. *FIRO: A Three-Dimensional Theory of Interpersonal Behavior*. New York: Rinehart & Co., 1958.

———. "The Interpersonal Underworld," *Harvard Business Review*, July–August, 1958.

SHOSTRUM, E. L. *Man, The Manipulator*. Nashville: Abingdon Press, 1967.

STOGDILL, RALPH M. *Individual Behavior and Group Achievement*. New York: Oxford University Press, 1959.

STRAUSS, ANSELM (ed.). *Social Psychology of George H. Mead*. Chicago: University of Chicago Press, 1956.

SULLIVAN, HARRY STACK. *The Interpersonal Theory of Psychiatry* (HELEN S. PERRY and MARY L. GAWEL [eds.]). New York: W. W. Norton & Co., 1953.

SWANSON, GUY E. "On Explanations of Social Interaction," *Sociometry*, Vol. 28 (1965), pp. 101–23.

SZASZ, T. S. *The Myth of Mental Illness: Foundations of a Theory of Personal Conduct*. New York: Hoeber-Harper, 1961.

TAGIURI, RENATO, and PETRULLO, LUIGI (eds.). *Person Perception and Interpersonal Behavior*. Stanford, Calif.: Stanford University Press, 1958.

THELEN, HERBERT A. *Dynamics of Groups at Work*. Chicago: University of Chicago Press, 1954.

THIBAUT, JOHN W., and KELLEY, HAROLD H. *The Social Psychology of Groups*. New York: John Wiley & Sons, Inc., 1959.

TRIANDIS, H. C. "Cognitive Similarity and Communication in a Dyad," *Human Relations*, Vol. 13 (1960), pp. 175–83.

WATZLAWICK, P.; BEAVIN, H. H.; and JACKSON, D. D. *Pragmatics of Human Communication*. New York: W. W. Norton & Co., Inc., 1967.

WEBB, WILSE B. "Elements in Individual-to-Individual Communication," *Journal of Communication*, Autumn, 1957.

WEINSTEIN, E. A., and DEUTSCHBERGER, P. "Tasks, Bargains, and Identities in Social Interaction," *Social Forces*, Vol. 42 (1964), pp. 451–56.

ZALEZNIK, A., and MOMENT, D. *The Dynamics of Interpersonal Behavior*. New York: John Wiley & Sons, Inc., 1964.

ZAJONC, ROBERT B. "The Process of Cognitive Tuning in Communication," *Journal of Abnormal and Social Psychology*, Vol. 61 (1960), pp. 159–67.

7

People, Behavior, and Communication:
Some Organizational and
"Management" Factors

THERE ARE MANY WAYS of viewing organization and management and "organizational behavior." The relative value of any particular point of view depends upon what one is trying to accomplish. Since this book is addressed to an understanding of human communication, our concern is not with theories or concepts of organization or management as such, but with those particular concepts of organization and management which will be most useful in developing an understanding of human communication in organization, and in managing human organizations.

No attempt has been made to present even a selective survey of the literature of organization or management. Nor is what follows in any sense a comprehensive theoretical statement. Rather it is simply an attempt to formulate and present some basic perspectives on organization and management which stem from and which will hopefully contribute to a more useful understanding of the processes of human communication in managing and organization.

On the Nature of Organization and "Managing"

In a very basic and practical sense, all intercommunication occurs in the context of an organization. Two of the preconditions or prerequisites for intercommunication discussed in the preceding chapter were: (1) a rela-tionship, and (2) mutually understood *rules* and/or *roles* for enabling and regulating the transaction. The essence of any organization—"natural" (such as a total society or an informal group) or "contrived" (such as a business enterprise)—is, in fact, the *structure of the relationships* between and among people and/or departments, and the *rules* by which their behavior vis-à-vis one another is regulated.

So every interpersonal relationship is, in this sense, an organization as well as a subculture. The only *significant* difference between the nature of a government agency (or military unit or business enterprise), and the nature of the organization of any interpersonal relationship (or family or informal small group)—other than sheer size and complexity—is that relationships and rules *emerge* from our informal relations with others, whereas rules and relationships are *imposed* upon the constitutents of contrived relationships. In a contrived relationship (such as between fellow-workers on an assembly line), the rules and relations presumed necessary or desirable to the purpose of that relationship are formalized or standard-ized, whether explicitly or implicitly.[1]

In any formal or "contrived organization, there are, of course, both imposed *and* emergent rules and relations. Similarly, it does happen that rules and relations do get formalized and standardized in informal relation-ships. So the distinction between *imposed* and *emergent* rules and relation-ships rarely exists in an exclusively either-or form. But, for our purposes, this is nonetheless a useful distinction to be made.

So it is important to recognize that what gets organized in any organiza-tion are the rules and relations which guide and regulate the behavior of its members. While it is reasonable therefore to conceive of a two-person

[1] A representative cross-section of relevant treatments of formal or contrived organi-zation is: J. G. March (ed.), *Handbook of Organizations* (Chicago: Rand McNally & Co., 1965); H. J. Leavitt (ed.), *The Social Science of Organizations* (Englewood Cliffs, N. J.: Prentice-Hall, Inc., 1963); V. A. Thompson, *Modern Organization* (New York: Alfred A. Knopf, Inc., 1961); J. G. March and H. A. Simon, *Organizations* (New York: John Wiley & Sons, Inc., 1958); W. W. Cooper, H. J. Leavitt, and M. W. Shelly II (eds.), *New Perspectives in Organization Research* (New York: John Wiley & Sons, Inc., 1965); J. A. Litterer, *The Analysis of Organizations* (New York: John Wiley & Sons, Inc., 1965); A. H. Rubenstein and C. J. Haberstroh, *Some Theories of Organization* (Homewood, Ill.: Richard D. Irwin–Dorsey Press, 1960); A. Etzioni, *Complex Organizations* (New York: Holt, Rinehart & Winston, 1961); and P. M. Blau and W. R. Scott, *Formal Organizations* (San Francisco: Chandler Publishing Co., 1962). The literature in organization theory is already massive. But additional pertinent references are available in the bibliographies of the volumes cited above, and in L. Thayer, "Communication and Organization," in F. E. X. Dance (ed.), *Human Communication Theory* (New York: Holt, Rinehart & Winston, 1967).

organization, it is difficult to visualize the changing structure of a two-person organization. Thus it will be somewhat more useful and expedient to channel our thinking at this point toward a minimum basic model of organization comprised of three elements or parts. The purpose in doing so is not to make a theoretical statement, but to create an analytical tool—something to facilitate our thinking and to help clarify some of the subtle issues which are at stake.

A Basic Model of Organization: I

Particularly if we think in terms of a contrived or "on-purpose" human organization, we need to note that the basic philosophy underlying our reliance upon organized human endeavors is this: that a number of people performing certain specialized tasks, the products of which are supposed to "fit together" in some timely or logical way, can accomplish what could not be accomplished by any one of those people were he to try to perform all of the tasks himself. In other words, the purpose of a human organization is to accomplish ends which are otherwise impossible.

So we visualize a product or mission (P or M) which is made possible (1) by dividing the overall task into task-functions ($T_f a$, $T_f b$, etc.) and (2) by *relating* those task-functions to each other through *rules* in such a way that P or M will be realized—i.e., in such a way that the organization's goals or purposes are achieved.

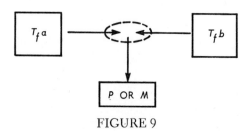

FIGURE 9

Every task function rationally makes its contribution to P or M in such a way and on such a schedule that the desired or necessary timing, quantity, quality, etc., of P or M is achieved. Whether the subtask–functions are carried out side by side, in sequence, or thousands of miles apart (as are many of those carried out in every space mission, for example), the *manner* in which the outputs of the various subtask-functions are integrated to achieve the purpose, product, or mission of the total organization inevitably determines their actual relationship within the context of that organization.

Subtask performance is of course regulated by the rules for task performance in general which people bring to their tasks from their larger cultures, as well as by the rules for performing that specific subtask imposed by the organization and incumbent upon the person who staffs that particular task-function. That is, the rules imposed upon those staffing each task-function of an organization are effective only to the extent that individuals bring with them from their larger cultures inclinations to abide by those rules.

It will be helpful to refer to the rules which do, or are intended to, guide task performance in a formal organization as *constraints*.[2] A constraint is a rule of the following form: under these circumstances, do X; under those circumstances, do Y; and so on. Or, to put it in somewhat different words, the function of constraints is to limit the *degrees of freedom* (or the prerogatives of personally choosing, judging, etc.) relative to any particular task-function which an individual might otherwise exercise.

The intangible "dues" that one "pays" to belong to any organization are, basically, his abdication of certain degrees of freedom to choose, to determine more or less independently when and how to behave, etc. To belong to any organization, an individual must give up certain choices that he might make about the what, the when, the how, the how much, etc., of his task—or of his role-related behavior. This is his *organizational contract*, similar to the *psychological contract* we make with others in order to organize and regulate our interpersonal behavior with them.

The assumed or imposed rules regarding any member's task-related behavior can then be thought of as *constraints*. Internal control of the members of a formal organization, then, is achieved through a system of constraints which in effect limit the personal judgments which the person performing any given task function can exercise about the what, the when, the how, and the where of his task or his performance of that task.

---

[2] Buck's use of *constraint* is somewhat different from mine. He assumes that things like goals, costs, and capacity rationally exist as "constraints" apart from some manager's information about, or conception of, them. I see the "rules" by which managers acquire and consume information in the service of their perceived problems as constraints on human performance in or out of formal enterprises. Cf. V. E. Buck, "A Model for Viewing an Organization as a System of Constraints," in J. D. Thompson (ed.), *Approaches to Organizational Design* (Pittsburgh: University of Pittsburgh Press, 1966).

On the Function of Managing

If it were possible to design a perfect human organization, and *if* humans were perfectly reliable and predictable organization elements, and *if* conditions both within and without the organization which might affect its goal achievement in some way did not change from time to time, no further structuring of an organization would be required. But *because* it is not possible to design a perfect human organizaton, *because* humans are not perfectly reliable and predictable organization elements, and *because* conditions within and without the organization are constantly changing, there is at least a logical need for an additional element in organizations to perform a special task-function.[3] This is the function of *managing*.

Managing functions are provided by those who directly or indirectly exercise managing functions—in organizations—regardless of their formal titles or positions. So it would be misleading to think of managing as that which someone with a managerial title does. In fact, if the managing necessary to the functioning of the organization is not directly provided by those who have that responsibility, it will quite often be provided indirectly by someone else, or through some aggregative effect of the individual behaviors of a number of the organization's other members.

An organization continues to function as an organization only to the extent that its system of constraints is appropriate and adequate to the needs of that organization (in achieving its mission or goals) at some point in time. (Whether those contraints are imposed upon the members, brought by the members to the organization, or simply emerge from the members' interactions over time is immaterial to the present point.)

So the ultimate functions of managing—functions as basic to human organizations as is task specialization—are those of (1) *defining* the *task*(s) of the unit to be managed, and defining in detail the subtask-functions and the subtask-structure necessary to achieve those tasks; and (2) *designing* the most effective regulation of the performance of those subtasks. Such managerial functions are never completed, of course. Changes both within and without the organization require continuous managing in this sense.

But the point is that *managing*, thus understood, is not an arbitrary or superficial function, but a necessary and natural function to be carried out, in one way or another, in all human organizations.

---

[3] Cf. the similar perspectives of A. K. Rice, *Productivity and Social Organizations,* and *The Enterprise and Its Environment* (London: Tavistock, 1958 and 1963).

Managers undeniably do many things and engage in all sorts of behavior which may bear little resemblance to the basic managing functions described above. However, what we want to establish here is not a scheme for classifying what it is managers *do* on the job, but a concept of *managing* which is generic enough to be useful in analyzing the functioning or malfunctioning of organizations of all types, of all sizes, and of all purposes.

As we will want to examine later, people (including managers) *manage* their lives and their endeavors more (or less) well. To a much larger extent than generally assumed to be possible, we can effectively define and design the communication systems within which we are in-formed and within which we are communicatively maintained. That is, we can effectively manage the communicative determinants of our own existences perhaps much more than previously thought possible.

In addition, people do attempt to manage each other in their interpersonal behavior. And every committee gets managed in some way—either by one member in his way, or by some members in their way, or by all in some way. The directions in which the larger society is moving are indeed managed—albeit in a very abstruse and diffuse sense. The point is that there is a specific managing function necessary to the movement and the integrated operations of any organization—a function crucial to contrived human organizations.[4]

Without denying the validity or the necessity of what practicing managers do on their jobs, it is the concept of the *managing function* which we need to establish here. It will be a most helpful conceptual tool.

A Basic Model of Organization: II

Thus we need to add a third element to our basic model of organization—the managing function. That model—the simplest model of organization we could formulate for our purposes here—would now appear something like this:

---

[4] Yet a great many so-called managerial "problems," the occasions for so many of a manager's interpersonal contacts—indeed, much of what engages the energies and attention of practicing managers in their everyday affairs are a consequence of the extent to which they default the intrinsic managing functions for which they are responsible. It is an enigma that the better a manager performs his basic managing functions, the less "fire-fighting" he has to do. But it is an enigma which can be easily understood from the point of view taken here.

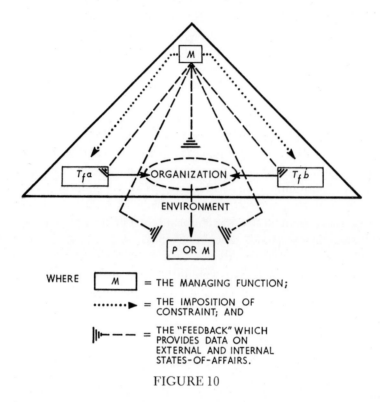

WHERE

M = THE MANAGING FUNCTION;

●●●●●●●▶ = THE IMPOSITION OF CONSTRAINT; AND

⫲───── = THE "FEEDBACK" WHICH PROVIDES DATA ON EXTERNAL AND INTERNAL STATES-OF-AFFAIRS.

FIGURE 10

If the appropriate system of constraints has been designed into the organization, if the appropriate (for the adaptive and goal-seeking needs of that organization) task structure has been defined, and if the product or mission is such that organizational goals vis-à-vis that organization's environment can be adequately met, then the whole system functions smoothly, and internal changes are not required. If, however, there is some problem sensed by a manager and attributed by him to a discrepancy between an intended-state-of-affairs and an apparent-state-of-affairs at any one of the four feedback points (or relevant data generation centers), then he will undoubtedly act to "solve" the problem he has perceived and identified. He modifies the system of constraints in a way he expects will bring the apparent-state-of-affairs into line with the intended-state-of-affairs at the problem point. (He may, of course, behave in many different ways. But any long-term change must come from some modification of goal [I. S.], of task structure, or of task-function constraints.)

Other implications of this basic model of organization and its managing function will be considered as they arise. For the present, we must consider some additional concepts of organization and managing, and how they relate to our understanding of communication.

THE ORGANIZATION AS A SYSTEM

Since our primary concern in this book is with formal or contrived human organizations, it will be helpful to recall that organizations are living systems. As such, they can be characterized by the two basic processes which sustain them and determine the condition of their state-relationships with their environments, and hence the direction of their movement, growth, and so forth.

The basic processes of an organization, which are the basic processes of all open living systems, are:

1. *Importing* from the environment certain raw materials and resources for conversion into products or services which are *exported* for consumption by the same or other parts of its environment;[5] and

2. *Acquiring* data from the environment, and from its internal parts, to be "consumed" in *problem-definition* and *decisioning* in the service of its attempts to alter its intended-states-of-affairs, its internal structure or functioning, or some aspect or domain of its environment.

The significance of the latter process for the managing of organizations is unscored by the fact that it is ultimately not the *things* of the world with which managers deal. They deal primarily with information or data *about* the things of the world.[6] While it is true that in some organizations raw materials are physically converted into some other form, it is information *about* that material flow and *about* those conversion processes which is the vital element in the managing function,[7] and hence the vital element in the performance of that organization. *It is the communication which*

---

[5] Cf. this particular description with A. K. Rice, *The Enterprise and Its Environment* (London, Tavistock, 1963).

[6] Cf. D. W. Miller and M. K. Starr, *Executive Decisions and Operations Research* (Englewood Cliffs, N. J.: Prentice-Hall, Inc., 1960); and A. O. Putnam, E. R. Barlow, and G. N. Stillian, *Unified Operations Management* (New York: McGraw-Hill Book Co., 1963).

[7] "It is axiomatic that a man's judgment is no better than his information." From the Introduction to *Information for Administrators* (Ithaca, N. Y.: Cornell University Press, 1956), by P. Wasserman. Regardless of what is going on that is relevant to his judgments, a manager bases his judgments and decisions only on the information he has, and even then only in a manner consistent with his own interpretations of that information.

occurs *within it,* and *the communication which occurs between the organization and its environment, which both defines the organization and determines the conditions of its existence and the direction of its movement.*[8]

The functions of any organization *qua* system are thus those of establishing, maintaining, exploiting, or altering some *state-relationship* between it and its environment. This objective can be achieved only through communication to and amongst its internal parts, and through communication to and with certain parts of its environent.

Every subsystem or organizational division (such as a production or research department) is determined ultimately by the communication system within which and through which it exists and maintains itself. That communication system is composed of people, of rules for "communicating," and of the resulting structure. Thus the communication processes which ultimately determine the efficacy of any organization are these:

a) *who* acquires or transmits *what* "information,"[9]

b) *from* or *to whom,*

---

[8] This point of view has been espoused by a great many writers, in one way or another, from Confucius to Wiener, Barnard, and Simon. Thus little in the way of further documentation would seem to be necessary here. Simon has written: "It is obvious that without communication there can be no organization" (H. A. Simon, *Administrative Behavior,* 2d ed. [New York: Macmillan Co., 1957]). Writes Colin Cherry, ". . . communication means organization" (*On Human Communication* [New York: John Wiley & Sons, Inc., 1957]). And Barnard: ". . . the structure, extensiveness, and scope of the organization are almost entirely determined by communication techniques" (C. I. Barnard, *The Functions of the Executive* [Cambridge, Mass.: Harvard University Press, 1938]). Other similar perspectives are widely available, but for the interested reader, one or more of the following may be particularly useful: K. W. Deutsch, "On Communication Models in the Social Sciences," *Public Opinion Quarterly,* 1952, 16, 365–80; R. A. Johnson, F. E. Kast, and J. E. Rosenzweig, *The Theory and Management of Systems* (New York: McGraw-Hill Book Co., 1963); S. Beer, *Cybernetics and Management* (New York: John Wiley & Sons, Inc., 1959); and W. R. Dill, "The Impact of Environment on Organizational Development," in S. Mailick and E. H. Van Ness (eds.), *Concepts and Issues in Administrative Behavior* (Englewood Cliffs, N.J.: Prentice-Hall, Inc., 1962). A discussion of this issue and a more extensive bibliography may be found in L. Thayer, "Communication and Organization," in F. E. X. Dance (ed.), *Human Communication Theory* (New York: Holt, Rinehart & Winston, 1967). Cf. N. Wiener, *The Human Use of Human Beings* (Boston: Houghton Mifflin, 1950, p. 124): "Control is nothing but the sending of messages which effectively change the behavior of the recipient."

[9] "Information" is used here, even though the reader will realize that what is actually acquired or transmitted are *data,* not information. Information is a property of people, not of the messages which people send and receive. What a person acquires, consumes, and transmits is *information* for him, but that is a characteristic of him and not of the data from which he or his target receiver have educed that information.

c) *when*, and

d) with *what consequences?*

The implications of these criteria for the efficacy of any organization will probably be apparent.

Managerial Communication

What has been called managerial communication is therefore that communication system which does, or could, serve those who provide managing functions for any organization. It is that *system* of communication which, on the input side, begins at the point of the generation and/or dissemination of any data which a manager does or should acquire and consume in the performance of his task. On the output side, it is that communication system which begins at the point of any manager's generation or dissemination of data which is intended for acquisition and consumption by other members of the organization in the performance of their tasks.

By managerial communication we will not want to mean all of the intercommunication which managers engage in on the job, but only that communication which is related to the managing functions of that organization. Or, in other words, it is that communication which does (or could) alter, exploit, create, or maintain the state-relationship(s) between or among any of the task-functions for which he is responsible, or between his subunit and any other subunit of the larger organization.

Organizational Communication

Like all living systems, organizations establish and maintain themselves through communication with their environments and amongst their parts. Thus by organizational communication we will want to mean all of those data-flows that subserve the organization's communication and intercommunication processes in some way.

It might be helpful to consider that every organization's communicational needs and functions are fulfilled through three basic communication systems:

1. The *operational communication* system, which "conveys" data about *task-related* activities and operations within the organization from the

generation and dissemination of that data through any of its intermediate processing to its acquisition and ultimate consumption by some organization member(s).

2. The *regulatory communication system*, which "conveys" to the organization's members those orders, rules, and instructions which are intended to regulate their material- and/or information-processing functions. The inputs to the organization's managers, who initiate regulatory messages, are sourced both outside and inside the organization, and are acquired and consumed by them for the ends of a) establishing intended states-of-affairs (goals); and/or b) determining apparent states-of-affairs. Regulatory messages are thus the natural consequence of the problem-definition/decisioning behaviors of the organization's managers.

3. Given that it is people who ultimately determine the operating effectiveness and efficiency of any human organization—and to a large extent the conditions of the organization's environment as well—the *maintenance and development communication system* serves (on the input side) the purposes of providing feedback as to the condition of the people or the communication channels upon which the organization is dependent for the inflow of resources or information from the environment, its internal functioning, and its relationships with various constituencies in its environment. On the output side (in and through the organization's managers), the maintenance and development communication system provides "preventive maintenance" or remedial information of one sort or another. Public and employee relations, advertising, training, and so on, fall into this category. The maintenance data an organization *inputs* are data relevant to the *relations* which obtain between and among the organization and its several constituencies (including its market, the government, suppliers, etc.), and between and among the parts of the organization itself. On the *output* side, the messages of the maintenance and development system are those intended to maintain or improve those relations, or to maintain or develop the task-related conditions of any of the organization's members or their internal relations.[10]

---

[10] A small group is, from the point of view we have taken here, an organization. As an organization, two-person or *n*-person groups have the same generic organizational characteristics and the same generic communication system functions as other organizations. An interesting parallel is to be found in J. R. Gibb, Grace N. Platts, and Lorraine F. Miller, *Dynamics of Participative Groups,* © 1951. Litho available from the senior author, National Training Laboratories, Washington, D. C.

Two New Factors

At the organizational level of analysis, two new factors emerge and need to be taken into account.

"The Law of Large Numbers"

Actually an extrapolation from the so-called law of large numbers, we need to be cognizant of the fact that generalizing from the characteristics of the *individuals* we know will not reliably characterize for us the properties of large numbers of people. We need to understand the behavior of large numbers of people differently than we would understand the behavior of individuals who might comprise those larger numbers. We need a concept of *mass*—one which does not derive from adding individuals together.

For example, everyone a given manager knows may seem to him completely trustworthy. But in a given population of people-at-large, there will be a certain (relatively invariant) proportion who are not "trustworthy" in that same sense.

So communicating-to large numbers of people (e.g., employees, the public, etc.), requires a different orientation based upon the properties of *that* aggregate—which may or may not be discernible properties of any individual in that aggregate.

The Implications of "On-behalf-of . . ."

There can be, and often is, considerable difference between intercommunication which involves two people personally, and that which involves them on-behalf-of . . . the organization of which they are both members.

We needn't jump to conclusions. There isn't any definitive evidence that the one condition is any more effective or easier than the other.

But we do need to recognize that, in contrived organizations at least, people engage in intercommunication of both types—on-behalf-of . . . themselves, and on-behalf-of . . . the organization. It is a useful distinction with a great many suggestive implications for dealing with communication in organizations.

A Recapitulation: People, Behavior, Communication

A number of basic concepts pertinent to a useful way of viewing the relation between people, their behavior, and their communication have been presented and discussed in the last four chapters. There are other, perhaps equally valid, concepts. A great many more pages could be devoted to the development of those few concepts we have looked at, and a great many pages more than that to a fuller description of their far-ranging implications. But our purpose here has been simply to formulate a useful foundation upon which to build an understanding of communication in human affairs. Therefore many of the practical ramifications of these elementary concepts must await the concerns of later chapters, or become an immediate target of the reader's own conceptual "thinking-through."

We have seen that *it is the processes of communication which ultimately determine the nature of people, their behavior, and their organizations.* One could hardly wish for a more basic, a more difficult, or a more promising area to which to devote his thinking—whatever his interest in human behavior or human affairs.

SUGGESTIONS FOR FURTHER READING

Any comprehensive list of publications relating to management and organizational aspects of communication would be many times longer than this book. So I have made no attempt to provide either a comprehensive or even a representative listing here. I have simply selected these few suggested readings on the basis of the value they have had for me in developing the ideas in this chapter. Perhaps the reader can find similar value in them as a supplement to the concepts presented.

APPLEWHITE, P. B.   *Organizational Behavior.* Englewood Cliffs, N.J.: Prentice-Hall, Inc., 1965.

ARENSBERG, C.   "Behavior and Organization," in J. H. ROHRER and M. SHERIF (eds.), *Social Psychology at the Crossroads.* New York: Harper & Bros., 1951.

ARGYRIS, C.   *Personality and Organization.* New York: Harper & Bros., 1957.

BAKKE, E. W.   *Bonds of Organization: An Appraisal of Corporate Human Relations.* New York: Harper & Bros., 1950.

————, and ARGYRIS, C.   *Organizational Structure and Dynamics.* New Haven, Conn.: Labor and Management Center, Yale University, 1954.

BARNARD, C. I.   *The Functions of the Executive.* Cambridge, Mass.: Harvard University Press, 1938.

BASS, B. M.   *Leadership, Psychology, and Organizational Behavior.* New York: Harper & Bros., 1960.

————.   *Organizational Psychology.* Boston: Allyn and Bacon, Inc., 1965.

BEER, S. *Cybernetics and Management.* New York: John Wiley & Sons, Inc., 1959.

———. *Decision and Control.* New York: John Wiley & Sons, Inc., 1966.

BLAU, P. M. *The Dynamics of Bureaucracy.* Chicago: University of Chicago Press, 1955.

———. "Formal Organization: Dimensions of Analysis," *American Journal of Sociology,* Vol. 63 (1957), pp. 58–69.

BOULDING, K. E. *The Organizational Revolution.* New York: Harper & Bros., 1953.

BURNS, T. "The Directions of Activity and Communication in a Departmental Executive Group," *Human Relations,* Vol. 7 (1954), pp. 73–97.

———, and STALKER, G. M. *The Management of Innovation.* London: Tavistock, 1961.

CADWALLADER, M. L. "The Cybernetic Analysis of Change in Complex Social Organizations," *American Journal of Sociology,* Vol. 65 (1959), pp. 154–57.

CAPLOW, T. *Principles of Organization.* New York: Harcourt, Brace & World, 1964.

CHAPLINE, J. D. (ed.). *The Manager's Role in Organizational Communications.* Proceedings of the 1963 IEEE/MSU Colloquium. New York: Institute of Electrical and Electronic Engineers, 1964.

CHISHOLM, C. (ed.). *Communication in Industry.* London: B. T. Batsford, 1955.

COOK, P. H. "An Examination of the Notion of Communication in Industry," *Occupational Psychology,* Vol. 25 (1951), pp. 1–14.

CORSON, JOHN J. "The Role of Communication in the Process of Administration," *Public Administration Review,* Vol. 4 (1944), pp. 7–15.

CRANE, EDGAR. "Communication within Organizations," Ch. 9 in *Marketing Communications.* New York: John Wiley & Sons, Inc., 1965.

CROZIER, M. *The Bureaucratic Phenomenon.* Chicago: University of Chicago Press, 1964.

DAVIS, KEITH A. "Communication within Management," *Personnel,* Vol. 31 (1954), pp. 212–18.

———. *What You Should Know about Administrative Communication.* Bloomington: Business Information Bulletin #20, Bureau of Business Research, School of Business, Indiana University, 1954.

DYER, F. C., and DYER, J. M. *Bureaucracy vs. Creativity.* Coral Gables, Fla.: University of Miami Press, 1965.

EVAN, W. M. "The Organization-Set: Toward a Theory of Interpersonal Relations," in J. D. Thompson (ed.), *Approaches to Organizational Design.* Pittsburgh: Univ. of Pittsburgh Press, 1966.

Fischer, Frank E. "A New Look at Management Communication," *Personnel*, Vol. 31 (1954), pp. 487–95.

Foundation for Research on Human Behavior. *Communication in Organizations: Some New Research Findings.* Ann Arbor, Mich.: The Foundation, 1959.

Glover, John D., and Hower, Ralph M. *The Administrator: Cases on Human Relations in Business.* 3rd ed. Homewood, Ill.: Richard D. Irwin, Inc., 1957.

Guetzkow, H. "Relations among Organizations," Ch. 2. in Bowers, R. V. (ed.), *Studies on Behavior in Organizations.* Athens: University of Georgia Press, 1966.

Haire, Mason (ed.). *Modern Organization Theory: A Symposium of the Foundation for Research on Human Behavior.* New York: John Wiley & Sons, Inc., 1959.

————. *Psychology in Management.* New York: McGraw-Hill Book Co., 1956.

Haney, Wm. V. "A Comparative Study of Unilateral and Bilateral Communication," *Academy of Management Journal*, Vol. 7 (1964), pp. 128–36.

Hinds, George L. "The Communicative Behavior of the Executive," *Journal of Communication*, Spring, 1957, p. 7 ff.

Hugh-Jones, E. M. (ed.). *Human Relations and Modern Management.* Amsterdam: North Holland Publishing Co., 1958.

Inkeles, A., and Levinson, D. J. "The Personal System and the Sociocultural System in Large-Scale Organizations," *Sociometry*, Vol. 26 (1963), pp. 217–29.

Jacques, Elliott. *The Changing Culture of a Factory.* New York: Dryden Press, 1952.

Janis, J. H. (ed.). *Business Communication Reader.* New York: Harper & Bros., 1959.

Jones, M. H. *Executive Decision Making.* Homewood, Ill.: Richard D. Irwin, Inc., 1957.

Kahn, R. L., and Boulding, Elise (eds.). *Power and Conflict in Organizations.* New York: Basic Books, Inc., 1964.

Katz, D., and Kahn, R. L. *The Social Psychology of Organizations.* New York: John Wiley & Sons, Inc., 1966.

Keane, M. et al. "Communication in Administration," *Public Management*, Vol. 37 (1955), pp. 218–22.

Koontz, H. (ed.). *Toward a Unified Theory of Management.* New York: McGraw-Hill Book Co., 1964.

LEAVITT, HAROLD J. *Managerial Psychology*. Chicago: University of Chicago Press, 1958.

LEVINSON, H. "Reciprocation: The Relationship between Man and Organization." Address before the American Psychological Association, Sept. 3, 1963.

LIKERT, R. *New Patterns of Management*. New York: McGraw-Hill Book Co., 1961.

LITTERER, J. A. *The Analysis of Organizations*. New York: John Wiley & Sons, Inc., 1965.

LOOMIS, C. P. *Social Systems*. New York: D. Van Nostrand, 1960.

LULL, P. E.; FUNK, F. E.; and PIERSOL, D. T. "What Communications Mean to the Corporation President," *Advanced Management*, Vol. 20 (1955), pp. 17–20.

McGUIRE, J. W. *Theories of Business Behavior*. Englewood Cliffs, N.J.: Prentice-Hall, Inc., 1964.

McMURRY, R. N. "Clear Communications for Chief Executives," *Harvard Business Review*, March–April (1965), pp. 131–47.

MARCH, J. G. (ed.) *Handbook of Organizations*. Chicago: Rand McNally & Co., 1965.

―――――, and SIMON, H. A. *Organizations*. New York: John Wiley & Sons, Inc., 1958.

MASLOW, A. H. *Eupsychian Management*. Homewood, Ill.: Richard D. Irwin, Inc., & The Dorsey Press, 1965.

NAGESWARAN, S. "Communication in Industry," *Industrial Relations* (Calcutta), Vol. 7 (1955), pp. 50–54.

PEABODY, R. L. *Organizational Authority*. New York: Atherton Press, 1964.

PETERS, R. W. *Communication within Industry*. New York: Harper & Bros., 1949.

READ, WILLIAM H. "Upward Communication in Industrial Hierarchies," *Human Relations*, Vol. 15 (1962), pp. 3–15.

REDDING, W. C., and SANBORN, G. A. (eds.). *Business and Industrial Communication: A Source Book*. New York: Harper & Row, 1964.

REDFIELD, CHARLES E. *Communication in Management*. Rev. ed. Chicago: University of Chicago Press, 1958.

ROETHLISBERGER, F. J. "The Administrator's Skill: Communication," *Harvard Business Review*, Vol. 31, Nov.–Dec. (1953), pp. 55–62.

SAYLES, LEONARD R., and STRAUSS, GEORGE. *Human Behavior in Organizations*. Englewood Cliffs, N.J.: Prentice-Hall, Inc., 1966.

SCOTT, W. G. *Organization Theory: A Behavioral Analysis for Management*. Homewood, Ill.: Richard D. Irwin, Inc., 1967.

SEILER, J. A.   *Systems Analysis in Organizational Behavior.* Homewood, Ill.: Richard D. Irwin, Inc., & The Dorsey Press, 1967.

SELZNICK, PHILIP.   *Leadership in Administration: A Sociological Interpretation.* Evanston, Ill.: Row, Peterson & Co., 1957.

SHIFF, ROBERT A.   "Presidents and Paperwork," *Dun's Review and Modern Industry,* April, 1959.

SIMON, HERBERT A.   *Administrative Behavior: A Study of Decision-Making Processes in Administrative Organization.* 2d ed. New York: Macmillan Co., 1957.

TEAD, ORDWAY.   *Administration: Its Purpose and Performance.* New York: Harper & Bros., 1959.

THAYER, L.   "Communication and Organization," in F. E. X. DANCE (ed.), *Human Communication Theory.* New York: Holt, Rinehart & Winston, 1967.

UDY, S. H., JR.   "The Comparative Analysis of Organizations," in JAMES G. MARCH (ed.), *Handbook of Organizations.* Chicago: Rand McNally & Co., 1965.

URWICK, LYNDALL F.   *The Pattern of Management.* Minneapolis: University of Minnesota Press, 1956.

VICKERS, SIR G.   *The Art of Judgment.* New York: Basic Books, Inc., 1965.

WEISS, R. S.   *Processes of Organization.* Ann Arbor: Survey Research Center, Institute for Social Research, University of Michigan, 1956.

WHYTE, WILLIAM H., JR.   *The Organization Man.* New York: Simon and Schuster, Inc., 1956.

YOUNG, S.   *Management: A Systems Analysis.* Glenview, Ill.: Scott, Foresman & Co., 1966.

8

On the Nature of
Communication: II

BASED UPON the conceptual framework developed in the preceding chapters, it would be appropriate now to reformulate some basic concepts of the communication process, and to set the stage for the following chapters. Those are the two purposes of this chapter.

Communication: Levels of Analysis

THE INTRAPERSONAL LEVEL

The one process basic to all human communication, whenever and wherever it occurs, is the *intrapersonal* process of organizing and converting sensory data into meaningful units ("messages") having some relevance or utility for that individual's past, present, or future behavior. Because the psychological system is constantly engaged in making sense of its environment in the service of that organism's adaptive and goal-seeking needs, the question is not *whether* communication is going to occur, but *what* communication and with what *consequence*. Communication is a continuous, on-going process, determined by an individual's take-into account-abilities and his take-into-account-susceptibilities. The process is rarely ever limited to another's communicative intentions vis-à-vis a given individual.

Apart from purely physiological swamping or deprivation, one's take-into-account-*abilities* are a function of the *capacities* of his conceptual system to ascribe meaning or significance to certain patterns and sequences of that event-data being continuously generated by what is going on in his internal and external environments. One's take-into-account-*susceptibilities* are a function of (1) the interpreted demands of the situation, (2) the temporary "appetites" of the system, and (3) the informational requirements of that individual's conscious information-processing behavior—all balanced by the cost to the individual of acquiring and converting raw sensory data into consumable units or "messages" about itself and its environment.

Every take-into-account-ability is its own disability, in the same way that every way of seeing is a way of not seeing. Because we can or do structure and interpret our worlds in certain ways, we are prevented from structuring and interpreting them in other ways. In the service of the basic functions of communication—adaptation and goal-seeking—our take-into-account-abilities are simultaneously both our strengths and our weaknesses. It isn't true that we see only what we "want" to see; we see and hear only part of that which we have learned to see or hear, and almost nothing of that for which we don't have the appropriate or necessary take-into-account-abilities. *We comprehend nothing of our worlds which is not a part of us.*[1]

Communication is therefore ultimately a co-function of the individual and of what is going on in his world(s) that has immediate relevance for him. The world and our conceptions of it co-determine each other. All that we perceive, all that we comprehend, must be perceived and comprehended in and through ourselves. Our comprehend-abilities structure and energize our existences, and determine both the possibilities and the limitations of our being communicated with by our world(s)—including other people.

---

[1] The French mechanist Condillac wrote: "Though we should soar into the heavens, though we should sink into the abyss, we never go out of ourselves; it is always our own thought that we perceive." Cf. E. Knight: ". . . if the world is not identifiable apart from our intentions in respect to it, then that intention constitutes us, as well as the world . . ." (*The Objective Society* [New York: George Braziller, Inc., 1960]); J. J. Gibson: "The . . . world is an unlearned experience . . . meaningless when seen for the first time, and . . . what one learns is to see the meanings of things" (*The Perception of the Visual World* [Boston: Houghton Mifflin Co., 1950], p. 200); and B. Whorf: ". . . the world is presented to us in a kaleidoscopic flux of impressions which has to be organized by our minds . . . we cut nature up, organize it into concepts, ascribe significance to it, largely because we are parties to an agreement to do it in this way" ("Science and Linguistics," *The Technology Review*, 1940, 42, p. 231).

The phenomenon basic to all human communication is the intra-personal process of "relevanting" or "messaging" the raw, unstructured event-data of our inner and outer worlds, of organizing and translating event-data into comprehendable, consumable functional units or "messages."

INTERCOMMUNICATION: THE INTERPERSONAL LEVEL

Given this empirically-unavoidable perspective on the basic human processes underlying all communication, we need a working concept of interpersonal communication which adequately accommodates the facts. Many of our communication difficulties stem from the very widespread assumption that we communicate *to* each other. We do talk to each other; we do write to one another. But communication always occurs *in* the receiver.

Thus *intercommunication* should be understood as we understand interpersonal behavior. We behave toward others. Our behavior toward them is essentially communicative behavior. We talk or write; we behave communicatively *toward* others. We produce event-data—about ourselves and about the things we are referring to—which others can or cannot, do or do not, take-into-account.

Intercommunication is thus not a different phenomenon, but the same phenomenon viewed from a different *level of analysis.* The basic functions and processes of communication at the level of intercommunication are not different. The basic phenomena are the same. Communication occurs *in* the participants, not *between* them. There are additional variables that can and should be taken into account, however—variables which are properties of the new, more complex system created when we behave toward each other communicatively.

People are a part of our environment, a part of our environment which we are very susceptible to—communicatively. But the functional processes by which non-human objects of our environment communicate-to us are exactly the same as those by which people communicate-to us. The differences are that we *can* affect other people communicatively, and thus alter our human environment in nonphysical ways. And other people *can* intentionally affect us communicatively, to the extent that our take-into-account-abilities and -susceptibilities enable them to do so.

People bring expectations to their interpersonal encounters. And they bring expectations about the other's expectations. These expectations continuously influence their communication behavior toward each other and their responses to each other. Intercommunication might thus be viewed as a process of mutual regulation and control.

Whenever we communicate toward others, we inevitably generate and disseminate data about ourselves as well as about what we are talking about. For example, the source of a message is always a part of our comprehension of it.

Just as we can comprehend only in terms of relationships, we can communicate only in terms of relationships. The minimum relationship for intercommunication is the relationship the receiver perceives between himself and the originator.

Intercommunication is thus an attempt on the part of at least one of the participants to establish, maintain, exploit, or alter some state-relationship vis-à-vis the other (or another) either by adapting himself to the other or by attempting to adapt the other to him in some way. But the immediate and ultimate consequences are determined by the communication processes which occur *within* each participant, not by what goes on between them.

ORGANIZATIONAL COMMUNICATION: THE THIRD LEVEL

Organizational communication is the third level of analysis. Although all intercommunication occurs in an organized context, a formal organization is characterized by some *rational* attempt to structure the transportation of data among the operating and decisioning parts of the organization, and between the organization and its several constituencies. The organization's actual structure is thus characterized by the pattern or networks of information-decision flows within the organization and by the channels and networks which describe its communication with its environment. Special information systems can be established for certain of the organization's departments, or to serve as management information systems."[2] But these are often no more than special cases of the interface between organizational communication and data technology. They do not materially alter (and have sometimes even intensified), *communication* problems within an organization.

---

[2] See, for example, T. R. Prince, *Information Systems for Management Planning and Control* (Homewood, Ill.: Richard D. Irwin, Inc., 1966); A. M. McDonough and L. J. Garret, *Management Systems* (Homewood, Ill.: Richard D. Irwin, Inc., 1965); and J. D. Gallagher, *Management Information Systems and the Computer* (New York: American Management Association, 1961). Cf. J. W. Widing, Jr. and C. G. Diamond, "Buy by Computer," *Harvard Business Review*, 1964, 42 (No. 2), 109–20.

Even though such systems and their associated equipment are usually referred to as "information" systems, they are actually *data transportation* and *data-processing* systems. Their *informational* value is determined by how, when, and where their data outputs are converted into information consumable by members of the organization.

Even the most elaborate data systems do not guarantee that the intended communication will occur, any more than the best delivered speech thereby guarantees that the intended impact will occur. There is no data-handling procedure or electronic equipment which can obviate the fact that communication occurs only in people, not in the transportation or in the mechanical or electronic processing of data.

There are mass communication aspects of organizational communication. The mass production and mass distribution of messages for mass consumption offers some efficiencies in the transmission of potentially useful data to all or some part of an organization's members. But, again, communication does not occur in the formulation, the transmission, or the transportation of data. Communication is a process which occurs *within* a consumer of the system's outputs, not in the system which transports data to him. Nor, to repeat, is there any significance or meaning or utility in the data itself. That communication which occurs is a property of the consumer and the data flow combined—not of the data flow itself.

INTERORGANIZATIONAL COMMUNICATION

The data systems presently available, and those which can be expected in the future, have given rise to a further level of analysis—what might be called the interorganizational level.[3]

Even though some new problems have thereby arisen, interorganization communication, like interdepartment communication, is better thought of as data transportation (with or without data-processing of one sort or another). Communication is a process unique to living (biological) systems. When one machine, or one part of one machine, takes-into-account the data products of another, what occurs may be enticingly analogous to what occurs when one human takes-into-account something said by another. But the similarity ends there. The capacity of the human system to process information (to be communicated-with) is of such a superior magnitude as to imply a distinct *qualitative* difference between human and

---

[3] E.g., F. Kaufman, "Data Systems That Cross Company Boundaries," *Harvard Business Review*, 1966, 44, 141–55.

machine take-into-account-abilities. Further, the human comprehending component evolves biologically as well as functionally. Nonbiological machines which "evolve" their data-processing capabilities in some fashion are evolving only *programs*; the equipment itself is not in the process of evolving through use. Even if machines could evolve themselves structurally, it would necessarily have to be in some way comprehendible to their designers. And this may be some time off, for we have no substantial way yet of fully comprehending the evolution of *human* comprehend-abilities!

Departments and organizations as such do not intercommunicate. Only people do. It will be to our advantage to conceive of interorganizational communication as interorganization data-transportation linkages. Certainly communication does not occur between organizations any more than it occurs between people. Communication, as contrasted with the *data* generation, dissemination, and acquisition processes of intercommunication, always occurs *within* some individual.

Communication Systems and Data Systems

There are at least two useful distinctions to be made between data systems and communication systems. Data systems map the flow of *data* to or from humans or machines from the point at which that data is generated or disseminated, to the point of its intended destination.[4] Data systems are rational systems designed by people, deduced from some set of rational criteria of system efficacy.

Communication systems, by contrast, are defined by the data acquisition-consumption practices (rational or not) of the consumers of the output of that system whether by intention or by accident. Thus, in communication systems the source(s) of the data transported is a function of the actual communicative behavior of the person who is the locus of consumption.[5]

Communication systems are, in other words, natural or emergent systems. They emerge, are utilized, atrophy, etc., as a function of the

---

[4] See, for example, C. P. Bonini, *Simulation of Information and Decision Systems in the Firm* (Englewood Cliffs, N.J.: Prentice-Hall, Inc., 1963).

[5] This distinction accounts for what E. Walton has termed a "Magnetic Theory of Organizational Communication" (China Lake, Calif.: U.S. Naval Ordnance Test Station, 1962). Data systems are rationally deductive; communication systems are behaviorally inductive. The distinction is more than "just semantic." It is a distinction crucial to our understanding of communication and communication systems.

information acquisition-consumption patterns and practices of a given individual at a given point in time. Through careful analysis, an observer would be able to detect certain regularities in the sources, frequency, and categories of data that a given individual consumes. If he were to formalize those patterns and establish some rational data system based upon them, then for a period of time that individual's communication system and the rationally designed data system would be congruent. But communication systems are continuously evolving—and in ways that are not predictable. Evolving a *data* system (as contrasted with rationally designing it) would require predicating its "evolution" either upon *some comprehendible* evolutionary pattern or upon complete indeterminacy. Neither of these is a likely analog for the evolution over time (and through use) of human consume-abilities and information appetites, and hence would not likely be adequate substitutes for the *communication* systems that subserve that individual.

There is another distinction: people may be *informed* by the data systems which serve them. But people are *in-formed* within their communication systems. Data systems may or may not alter the future communicate-abilities of its users. Communication systems, by definition, always affect the communicate-abilities of the consumer in some way, however minor. Whether they gain or lose, people are always changed by their communication systems. The impact of rationally-designed *data* systems depends upon the type, degree, and extent of communication which occurs as a result of consuming its outputs.

A person is inevitably some consequence of what has been communicated-to him, and of the reactions of those who have been subject to being communicated-to by him. These consequences hold for data systems only to the extent they serve simultaneously as communication systems for specific individuals.

The latter distinction is not always a significant one, nor is it always a detectable one in practice. But it is useful to be aware of the fact that what are often called "information" or data-processing systems are not always, or necessarily ever, *communication* systems for those who are linked or exposed to them in some way.

Control Systems

All communication systems are control systems. Conventionally, control systems are those rational data systems which are designed to control their own outputs in some way, or to channel in some intended way the problem-solving-decisioning behavior of those persons who are linked to it. But data systems do not and cannot control human behavior beyond the *communication* which occurs as a consequence of their outputs.

The pertinent distinction to be made is that the control and regulation of behavior in communication systems is a consequence (1) of the people involved, and (2) of the communication which occurs. The controls of data systems are rationally built into them before any communication occurs, in anticipation of the communication which should occur. Machines can quite readily be designed and interlocked in such a way that they control each other. The automation of routine decisions[6] may seem to be a mere substitute for human decisioning, and something analogous to human communication may seem to be involved. But the similarity is limited to the analogy.

Metacommunication

"Metacommunication" is a term which is useful to refer to anything which a person takes-into-account as a help in interpreting what another is saying, the import of a situation, how to comprehend what is going on, etc. Metacommunication is therefore any clue or evidence which a person uses in "relevanting" or "messaging" his comprehension of something or someone.

We must necessarily take-into-account a great deal more than the "content" of what another is saying if we want to comprehend him as he expects or intends us to. There is the matter of who he is and what we see as the purpose of his attempt to communicate-to us, and of how we orient ourselves to those conditions. There is the place, the time, and the manner. There are his inflections, his tempo, his pitch, his gestures, his countenance and facial expressions (if we can see him). There is our understanding of and our feeling about the history of previous encounters with him and the personal consequences of those encounters. There is always the mood, and the kind and the state of the "game." There are the roles which we enact and expect, and the rules by which we attempt mutually to regulate the encounter. Anything which *can* be taken-into-account as relevant to our interpretation of what another is saying or doing beyond the manifest "content" of what he is saying or doing—can be referred to as *metacommunication*.

"Noise" in the information theoretic sense is often assumed to be deleterious to communication. But, as Berne writes, "In interpersonal

---

[6] See H. A. Simon, *The New Science of Management Decision* (New York: Harper & Row, 1960).

communication, 'noise' is of more value than 'information,' since in such cases it is of more value to the communicants to know about each other's states than to give 'information' to each other. 'Noise' carries latent communications from the communicant."[7]

The issue is not, however, whether or not there is "noise" in human communication. The issue is simply that what is often called noise actually serves as metacommunication.

The Occasions of Communication

The occasions of our being communicated-with are largely determined by our take-into-account-abilities and -susceptibilities. We considered the occasions and the conditions of being communicated-with in Chapter 4. We can be communicated-with to the extent that we have the necessary take-into-account-abilities and to the extent that the message we "get" has relevance, and some past, present, or future *utility* for us—whether we were specifically seeking that message or not.[8]

Or, we can communicate-to another (others) to the extent *he* has the necessary take-into-account-abilities (and that we have the ability to adapt to them), and to the extent that the message he "gets" from what we are saying has some relevance, and some anticipated past, present, or future utility for him. Thus, while we often think of the occasions of communication as those instances when some person is attempting to communicate-to others or when some person is attempting to be communicated-with by another (others), we must recognize that the *communication* sought by the one or intended by the other may or may not occur. We affect others (communicatively) precisely as we wish *only* when and if they have the appropriate take-into-account-abilities and only when and if the message they get has some relevance, is valid, and has some utility for them. Conversely, we can be affected by others (communicatively) precisely as

---

[7] E. Berne, "Concerning the Nature of Communication," *Psychiatric Quarterly*, 1953, 27, p. 197. Cf. J. Ruesch: "In the theory of human communication, noise has no place. Anything that Wiener, in his machine systems, calls noise, we call metacommunication. Anything that enters, regardless of what it is, will shape the content and will not, as in the telephone system, merely reduce intelligibility" ("The Observer and the Observed: Human Communication Theory," in R. R. Grinker (ed.), *Toward a Unified Theory of Human Behavior.* [New York, Basic Books, Inc., 1956], p. 49).

[8] Throughout this exploration of the occasions of communication, no distinction is made (or is necessary) between indirect communication (via letters, books, telegrams, etc.) and direct communication (face-to-face). Nor is the difference in time between origination and reception of messages of any special consequence in this context. It is still possible for us to be communicated-with by Aristotle, even though direct inter-communication is impossible.

we wish only (1) when the data which we need or have an "appetite" for is physically available, (2) when we have the appropriate take-into-account-abilities,[9] and (3) when what they say has some relevance, validity, and some past, present, or future utility for us.

So we need to understand that the most ideal occasion for communication is when the receiver wants or needs what the originator intends to communicate-to him (and when he has the necessary take-into-account-abilities and the appropriate take-into-account-susceptibilities—and conversely).

All other communication situations are less than ideal, even though they are probably far more common. Typically, there is rarely a perfect match between the needs and appetites of the receiver and the intentions of the originator.[10] Some degree of mutuality and/or complementarity between the needs and appetites of the one and the intentions or objectives of the other is necessary if they are to communicate-to each other at all. But that mutuality or complementarity of need and intention is typically less than ideal.

To summarize, then. An individual will enter into a communicative encounter with another (others):

1. As an originator, when he intends to achieve some purpose vis-à-vis some receiver(s).
2. As a receiver or recipient, when he has a need or his system has an "appetite" for what the other could or might communicate-to him.

Too, it often happens that we accidentally, or in the process of fulfilling personal or institutional roles, come across some unexpected or unsought-after data which has some utility for us. And it happens that our communicative intentions vis-à-vis another change during the encounter itself. But the criteria for determining whether the intended or hoped-for communication occurred or not must obviously be the same in such situations as these.

Physical proximity may increase, just as "psychological distance" may

---

[9] Our take-into-account-susceptibilities are given in our communicative needs and appetites. And, of course, our susceptibilities will change all during the time we expose ourselves to another's attempts to communicate-to us. Our initial susceptibilities may shift to resistance, or vice versa. Our take-into-account-susceptibilities are continuously changing and shifting.

[10] "Originator" and "receiver" are being used here as if each role were fixed for the duration of any communicative encounter. But we have all observed that the functional roles of originator and receiver frequently shift from one to the other person in an extended conversation. So it is the *functional role*—originator or receiver—that we are concerned with, not the person as such.

decrease, the likelihood of a communicative encounter.[11] But the crucial factor is the implicit or potential matching of the receiver's communicative appetites and the originator's communicative intentions.

The Consequences of Communication

The degree of mutuality or complementarity (or matching) which obtains between the intentions of an originator and the appetites of a receiver at any point in time predicts to one of four possible categories of consequence:

1. The receiver's communicative needs complement the originator's communicative intentions (and conversely) in such a positive way that the outcome of the encounter is *inevitable*, or "given" by the circumstances. That is, the competencies of both are only minimally required to bring about the satisfaction of both.
2. The receiver's needs are incompatible with the originator's intentions (and conversely) in such a way and to such a degree that success is *impossible*. That is, the communicative competencies of both, optimally brought to bear, could not bring about the needed or intended communication.
3. The needs of the receiver and the intentions of the originator are neither particularly complementary nor particularly incompatible; a limited range of situational consequences is thus *possible*, but whether or not the intended and/or the needed communication occurs depends essentially upon the communicative competence of one or both participants.[12]
4. No particular consequence could be predicted from the initial complementarity or mutuality of the originator's intentions and the receiver's needs, and the communicative competencies of the participants could not logically be expected to influence the outcome one way or the other. The consequences of the encounter (if it ensues) would therefore be purely *serendipitous*.

---

[11] A highly readable account of proxemics is E. T. Hall, *The Hidden Dimension* (Garden City, N. Y.: Doubleday & Co., Inc., 1966). Cf. E. S. Bogardus, *Social Distance* (Yellow Springs, Ohio: Antioch Press, 1959).

[12] Again, although the terminology here would seem to imply a face-to-face encounter, the basic points apply equally to mass communication, to written "communication," and to any originator and receiver widely separated in time and/or space, assuming the originator's statements are available to the receiver in some immediate and "consumable" form.

Perhaps this sketch will help:

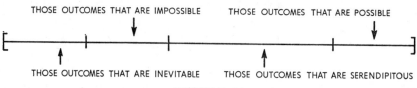

FIGURE 11

This view of the categories of consequence inherent in the initial complementarity of the needs and intentions of those involved can be very useful in understanding the potential and the limitations of communication competence and control.

The Communication Event

Because this book is devoted largely to *purposive* or instrumental communication, one unit of analysis could be the *communication event*. The simplest communication event has these components:

a) (An *originator* or *source*[13]—which may be removed in space and/or in time from the receiver).

b) A *receiver* (who could be in lieu of or in addition to the intended receiver).

c) A *situation* or *circumstance* (which purposefully or accidentally relates originator to receiver in some way, as perceived by either or both).

d) An *intention*, *purpose*, or *need* (on the part of the originator, the receiver, or both).

e) A *medium* or *"channel"* (which may be part of the *metacommunication* of the communication event as well as the means of data transportation); and

---

[13] We should be quite careful to avoid over-rationalizing the role of the originator. Receivers do make meaningful messages out of another's silence, out of another's unintended comments or actions, or even out of those general conditions which he illogically attributes to another's behavior (or lack of behavior). In other words, an originator purposefully transmitting some set of statements directly to an intended receiver is not an absolute requirement of a communication event in the same way that a receiver is an absolute requirement of a communication event. If there is something going on inside or outside him which a person makes a meaningful message out of, that is sufficient to establish a communication event. If that something includes an originator purposefully trying to affect that receiver communicatively, then there is clearly an originator. But if it does not, a receiver is still communicated-with by that something he has taken-into-account. So an originator as such may or may not be an element of a communication event.

f) A *statement* or a *question*—i.e., a "message" (transmit-able by an originator and/or acquire-able by a receiver), having some relevance and some utility or anticipated import for the receiver's past, present, or future behavior.

The message which a receiver "gets" is almost always comprised of factors which are well beyond the sheer informational "content" of the originator's statements or questions. Of necessity, the receiver must often take-into-account what he perceives to be the originator's intention (or lack of intention), the situation, the past history of his communicative encounters with that originator, his own intentions or needs, the expected consequences for him of comprehending and/or agreeing with what he perceives the originator to be saying, the anticipated consequences (for him) of complying with the originator's intentions, etc. In other words, the *metacommunicative* aspects of every communication event play a large part in determining the message that a given receiver "gets."

So it is helpful to think of a communication event as actually having its origin at the moment of the relevant communication occurrence *in* some receiver, and of then moving backward in time to incorporate the originator (if any), and forward in time to incorporate the consequences anticipated by that receiver.

A crude sketch may help us visualize the communication event:

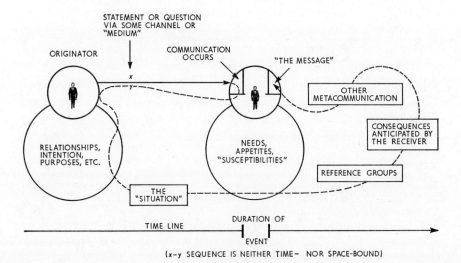

FIGURE 12

The Communication Sequence

Another, perhaps more rationalized, way to view communication events is the communication sequence, based on the "Lasswell formula":[14]

1. Who says . . .
2. (or does not say) . . .
3. what . . .
4. to whom . . .
5. when . . .
6. in what manner . . .
7. under what circumstances . . .
8. with what effect.[15]

These should not be thought of as discrete steps, because a communication event is but a single event—a functional whole. But analytically, this view can be useful.

It makes a difference *who* the originator is. His status, his position, his credibility, his reputation, one's past communication experiences with him: all of these make a difference in the way the receiver interprets what is being said. People learn to expect certain qualities and motives from certain other people they come into contact with either directly or indirectly. If they do not perceive these qualities and motives in what the originator says or does, or if they "see" other motives, the originator's effectiveness is thereby lessened, and perhaps minimized. This is the reason why so many attempts at producing employee goodwill are wasted effort and money; how the employees perceive the company and their working conditions simply may not validate the propaganda. People look to an originator's actions (or for some other external evidence) for validation of his utterances if they seem immediately contrary to one's own beliefs and perceptions. If there is a discrepancy, they will normally rely upon what they believe to be true, *not* upon what he says.

---

[14] H. Lasswell, in L. Bryson (ed.), *The Communication of Ideas* (New York: Harper & Bros., 1948). Cf. a review of several models of the communication process in R. L. Smith, "General Models of Communication." Dittoed report, Purdue University, Communication Research Center, 1962.

[15] One useful sourcebook which either describes or refers to a broad range of research and speculation regarding the elements of this sequence is W. C. Redding & G. A. Sanborn, *Business and Industrial Communication* (New York: Harper & Row, 1964). The continuing program of research at Purdue's Communication Research Center and other research centers is also pertinent to this scheme.

It makes a difference when an originator either says nothing, or says something other than what was expected or "needed" by the receiver.[16] Silence can be as interpretable and as meaningful to others as anything we might purposefully say or write to them—if they are expecting something from us.

What is said (or not said) is codetermined by the originator's utterance *and* by the receiver, not alone by the originator. A document or a conversation has "content" only to the extent that we agree upon its content. What is meaningful to one may not be meaningful to another. It never happens that any two people will interpret the same statement or event in exactly the same way. The fact that we do successfully intercommunicate is based upon our willingness to disregard the *differences* between what the originator's statement means to him and what it means to each receiver.

But how many communication breakdowns and disagreements revolve around a dispute over *what* was said! There may be many justifications for analyzing what the originator "said" from some special point of view. But the *receiver's* behavior will inevitably be based upon how *he* interprets what was said, not how the originator or some other person interprets that same statement.

The *to whom* it is said (or not said) makes an obvious difference. People conceptually relate themselves to other people in specific situations in different ways—some of which are predictable (in a conventional sense), and some of which are not. The receiver's past experiences with the originator make a difference. The way people classify and categorize what is going on about them makes a difference. Every person has typical and habitual ways of thinking and behaving and believing. A person organizes his behavior around certain stereotypes which serve to categorize and classify the world in a way that simplifies his perception and judgment-making processes.

For example, even though an administrator may know that there are wide individual differences among employees, he may think of employees as a group, and assign to them general traits and characteristics such as loyalty, laziness, ignorance, and so forth. And the employees may classify all bosses as thoughtless tyrants who arbitrarily make decisions disadvantageous to them. Or to a secretary, every executive whose income is above a certain level may be thought of as a potential husband. She may "misin-

---

16 See, for example, C. J. Dover, "Silence—An Employee Relations Pitfall," *Advanced Management*, September, 1957. An anonymous quotation from the last century reads: "Truth may not only be violated by falsehood, it may be equally outraged by silence."

terpret" things he says to mean that he thinks of her as a potential wife, when he does not "mean" that at all. Employees who classify all bosses as thoughtless tyrants will misinterpret what those bosses say in such a way as to ascribe the source of those statements to thoughtless tyrants.

Thus the way people classify and stereotype other people has a definite influence on the outcome of their attempts to communicate effectively with each other. What is of concern to the potential receiver at any given time makes a difference. For example, if an employee did not get a raise when he thought he deserved one, and an administrator makes a written statement directed to the employees about wages, that subject itself will likely have emotional overtones for that employee, and he may thereby unfavorably "distort" what the administrator says (and conversely of course).

When we say or do not say something has a part in determining the effectiveness and the efficiency of our intercommunication. There are two considerations here. One of these is *timing*, and the other is *appropriateness*.[17]

Leaving a letter unanswered, for example, gives the person waiting for the answer reason to doubt our interest in his problems. Then if we do give him a positive answer, the "edge" may likely be off our statement, and we may have lost an opportunity. If, on the other hand, we must answer negatively, the receiver might say to himself: "Well, I figured it would turn out this way, anyhow. Why did he have to fool around so long telling me?" A sense of *timing* is valuable. Communication about company difficulties when employees have their own important problems will fall on deaf ears. There are likely to be negative reactions. Waiting until you want to ask a new favor before thanking someone for a past service is another example of poor timing. Or, as Charlie Brown says: "I hate writing 'Thank you' letters for toys that I've already broken!"

Closely related to the idea of timeliness is that of *appropriateness*. Just as people dress appropriately for weather conditions and for social functions, we must also adapt our intercommunication attempts to the time, the situation, the subject, and the people involved. A humorous report would likely not be the most appropriate tone for an investment analysis involving several million dollars. At the same time, making a twenty-six page report analyzing the problem of who should empty the pencil sharpeners is perhaps no more appropriate. At another time, or under

---

[17] In some situations, these may, of course, be synonymous.

different conditions, either might be appropriate. The *propriety* of inter-communication is thus often an important metacommunication factor.

How a message is presented may make the difference between its acceptance and rejection. There are, in this respect, at least two factors which may greatly affect response.

The first of these is the *means* used. Varying with the type of material, the situation, the communicator, and the audience, different means may lead to different degrees of effectiveness. Frequently, when time is the most important consideration, oral communication is the most effective. If I must know the answer to a question in five minutes, I can probably "get on the telephone" and get it. This emergency kind of communication has the disadvantage of not producing a recorded account of the exchange of information. On the other hand, written records may be useless simply because they are too late or too poorly written. Yet an unclear, ambiguous, confused report may be worse than no report at all. So the solution to the problem of *means* has many inherent complexities. Showing a movie or slides may be the best means of communicating-to others in certain circumstances. Using a public address system may be more or less effective than bulletin boards, given certain conditions. Putting an important message in an employee's pay envelope may be one reliable way of getting it looked at. And so on.

The second factor which may affect the response to a message is that of the *manner* in which the message is presented. Was it hurried? Curt? Dictatorial? Too pleading? Too "nice"? Too cautious? Not friendly? Was the "tone" inappropriate? These are but some of the multitude of criteria by which receivers judge the manner behind another's attempt to com-municate-to them.

As we have seen, the *circumstances* under which communication occurs also make a difference. Even a slight change in circumstances may alter a situation from one that is "impossible" to one that is "inevitably" success-ful. For example, any attempt to persuade union employees of the "fact" that the company has only *their* welfare at heart—when those employees are out on strike against the company—is likely to fail. Timing is always a part of the circumstances, as is the setting, other receivers, the general mood of the intended receiver, etc. But it is always the circumstances-as-perceived by the receiver which makes the difference in the way a message will be interpreted by the receiver—not the circumstances as perceived by the originator, not the circumstances as they "really" are.

There are other factors that go into making a difference in the outcome of any communicative encounter, of course. But this perspective on the communication sequence is one useful way of reminding ourselves of some of the obvious difficulties and pitfalls involved.

The Basic Facilitators and Barriers in Human Communication

Whatever the other variables that might be considered relevant in predicting or assessing the effectiveness of human communication, the basic facilitators and barriers remain the same for all communication situations. To summarize, these are:

COMMUNICATIVE FACILITATORS AND BARRIERS

To the extent that a receiver needs or has an "appetite" for what is communicatively available to him from any originator, communicating-to that receiver will be facilitated. To the extent that an originator attempts to communicate-to any receiver something which that receiver can take-into-account (and has a need or an appetite to take-into-account), the intended intercommunication will be facilitated. *To the extent that these conditions do not hold*, there will be "barriers" or obstacles to intercommunication, and intercommunication will be impeded.

METACOMMUNICATIVE FACILITATION

To the extent that the relationship, the situation or circumstances, the nonverbal clues, or any other metacommunicative elements serve to enhance the take-into-account-susceptibilities of the receiver, intercommunication will be facilitated. *To the extent that metacommunicative factors diminish the receiver's take-into-account-susceptibilities*, there will be "barriers" or obstacles to intercommunication, and intercommunication will be impeded.

The Role of Intention and Expectation

Communication behavior, like all human behavior, is energized and channeled (a) by the sorts of intended-states-of-affairs that concern us broadly and momentarily, (b) by our perceptions and conceptions of current and anticipated states-of-affairs, (c) by the way we name and identify the problems posed by discrepancies between the I. S.'s and A. S.'s, and (d) by the state-of-affairs expected if we behave in a given way. Communicative *intentions* are thus of the form, "I want (or need) to affect X in such-and-such a way (or the converse: I want (or need) to be affected by X in such-and-such a way)." Communicative *expectations*, by contrast, are of the form, "Given the other's intentions, if I do so-and-so (or behave communicatively in such-and-such a way) the consequences for me (him, us) will be Z." Or, from a receiver's perspective: "Given the other's intentions, if I comprehend him or react to him in such-and-such a way, the consequences for me (him, us) will likely be Z."

People do quite characteristically take-into-account both what they perceive to be the originator's (receiver's) intentions with regard to the encounter, *and* their own and their conceptions of the other's *expectations* about the consequences if one or another of various alternative consequences occurs. In other words, we take-into-account both the other's intentions and his expectations (as we perceive them), *and* we take-into-account the anticipated consequences for each of us depending upon what action we might take or reaction we might give.

A simple illustration of how we thus "play the game" communicatively, and how we take-into-account the other's expectations as well as various alternative consequences, is a game like checkers or poker. If the reader will reflect carefully upon what the players take-into-account in these games, the whole range of implications of this point for communication and intercommunication should begin to come into focus. That so much of our typical communication behavior is nonconscious (or perhaps not rational) does not alter the functions of our "gaming." The functions and processes are the same whether conscious or nonconscious.

And certainly we should never overlook this fact: that the conceptions we have of our own and the other's *intentions*, and of our own and the other's *expectations*, are taken-into-account in formulating our communicative behavior vis-à-vis any others whom we might communicate-to or by whom we might wish to be communicated-with.

Two Modes of Intercommunication

It is sometimes useful to think of intercommunication as occurring in one of two "modes"—the *synchronic* and the *diachronic*. The words here are significant. One could think of the difference between these modes as the difference between *monologue* and *dialogue*. But the less familiar terms fit much better the conceptual framework previously established—and will thus perhaps be more suggestive of the difference between them.

In the synchronic mode, the consequence sought or realized is the "synchronization" of the participants. It is the sort of encounter in which one of the participants, Y, has as his objective either (a) bringing the psychological state of another person, Z, from its present apparent-state-of-affairs to the state-of-affairs desired or intended by Y, or (b) achieving some intended-state-of-affairs through the actions or behavior of Z. In both cases, Z is the "sink" for Y's "message." And the situation is resolved (the "problem" solved) when Z is brought into some satisfactory state of synchronization with Y, or when Z's action brings about a satisfactory state-of-affairs with respect to an intended state-of-affairs between Y and some aspect of his environment.

The other mode of intercommunication is the diachronic mode. The end sought or realized from a communicative encounter in the diachronic mode is either (a) a new state-of-affairs between Y and Z, or (b) a new state-of-affairs between Y and Z and their respective environments. But, unlike the synchronic mode, the diachronic mode does not hinge upon the resolution of one or the other's intended-state-of-affairs, but upon a joint or cooperative effort to achieve *whatever* result comes from the encounter.

One might call a conference, for example, simply to apprise the participants of a new policy or problem. That ensuing intercommunication would therefore be in the synchronic mode—and the attempt would be to synchronize the participants' knowledge about the new policy or problem with the conference leader's knowledge of the same thing. Or, one might call a conference for the purpose of mutually exploring a common problem and some of the alternative solutions that might occur to the different participants. That communication would be more in the diachronic mode, and the end sought would be the production of some new or previously unspecified ideas or perspectives, etc., through open-ended (nonsynchronic) intercommunication.

The product or the output of a synchronic communication encounter is one of "tuning" another to one's thinking or intentions, or of changing some aspect of the environment *through* the behavior of the other. The product or the output of a diachronic communication encounter is typically some new insight or comprehend-ability on the part of one or all participants. In the synchronic mode, the objective is the achievement of one or the other's intended-state-of-affairs. In the diachronic mode, the objective is the achievement of some mutually advantageous consequence not known in advance by either participant.

It is probably obvious that these modes of intercommunication rarely, if ever, occur in pure form. Most encounters have characteristics of both modes. But one or the other mode is typically dominant in every communication encounter. So the distinction will be useful as a thinking tool.

Media and Channels of Communication

It will also be useful to make a distinction between *media* and *channels* of communication.

In this book, we shall use *media* to refer to the technological medium "over" or "through" which messages are disseminated. The telephone, the television, the daily newspaper, the postal system, a loudspeaker, a flashing-light signaling system—are examples of media. We will also include speaking, writing, reading, and listening as media, since the hardware and skills involved are indeed part of the technology of communication.

This concept of media permits us to use the term *channel* to refer to any specialized, functional communicative link and/or chain between and among people—whether those linkages have evolved through use or have been formally established for task-related data flows through an organization or an enterprise. Media will thus refer to the *technological* aspects of generating, disseminating, acquiring, and consuming messages, whereas channels will refer to the *functional* communication policies, rules, and/or practices that link individuals together in common communication systems.

Communication Competence and Communication Control

There are two basic communication competencies—one we might call *strategic* competence, and the other, *tactical* competence.

Strategic competence in communication refers to an individual's ability veridically (or accurately) to perceive or intuit or comprehend the state-relationship between himself and some aspect of his environment (e.g., between himself and the other(s) whom he wishes to communicate-to or by whom he wishes to be communicated-with). In other words: in every communication encounter, what "gets communicated" is dependent upon the complex state of the relationship between originator and receiver(s)—and conversely. An originator's (or receiver's) competence in comprehending the state of that relationship at any point during the encounter is thus his strategic competence.

Only in addition to one's strategic competence would we consider the sum of his skills and abilities to successfully communicate-to or be-communicated-with by others—his *tactical* competence.

Every person is constantly attempting to adapt himself communicatively to others, or others to himself. When two or more such adaptive and adapting systems encounter each other, a superordinate communication system is formed, with each participant being an element of that system. As elements of this larger system, they are continuously evolving some state relationship vis-à-vis each other in that particular system. The better we are at sensing or intuiting those state relationships with others in our communicative encounters, the more strategic competence we exhibit. Strategic competence is also, in part, one's ability veridically to perceive when certain communicative consequences are possible, and when they are impossible, for then he can devote his tactical competencies to achieving that which is possible and avoid investing them fruitlessly in attempting to achieve consequences which are communicatively impossible (at that time and in that place, etc.).

But our abilities to "size up" a communication situation accurately are not to our advantage unless we can implement that advantage effectively through our tactical competencies—e.g., through our abilities to deliver the message in the right form at the right time, through the right medium, with the proper skills, and so on.

Communication control can usefully be understood in the following way:

1. There is no such thing as "perfect communication."
2. Thus our communicative intentions vis-à-vis others are never completely attained.
3. Therefore our *control* of communicative encounters to our own and the other's advantage should not be geared to perfection but to minimum error or variation-from-intention over a large range of communication challenges of varying degrees of difficulty.
4. We achieve control not just through study and the accumulation of "recipes" for success (although these might be useful as hypotheses), but through practice.
5. The "practice" of communication for the purpose of increasing control can be fruitful only to the extent that we attempt to communicate-to or be communicated-with with respect to some very specific end or purpose.[18] By measuring the distance and the dimension of our errors or limited failures, and by having an understanding of the process (which permits us to understand *why* we might not have achieved our intended purposes as fully as might have been possible), we can sharpen both our strategic and tactical competencies.

---

[18] Compare this to learning how to be an expert marksman or bowman. One does not improve his control simply by shooting arrows. He does so only by shooting arrows at a very specific target, so that he can measure the kind and the degree of the miss. Only then can he helpfully set about refining his strategic and his tactical competencies.

People do not, and can not, control each other communicatively in any absolute sense, even though all communicative encounters are mutually regulatory to some degree. Each gains more control only by achieving more effective means of controlling and developing *his own* strategic and tactical competencies. Only in that way can he exercise maximum control over his attempts to communicate-to others and be communicated-with by them.

This concludes our brief study of some of the necessary conceptual foundations for understanding human communication—and for its practice in human affairs. But we need to take these considerations with us as we turn now to some other aspects of communication in management, organization, and human relationships.

SUGGESTIONS FOR FURTHER READING

The specific references for this chapter would of course include most of those suggested readings listed at the end of the other chapters of this book. Those selected for this list are those which, taken together, seem to me to have especial relevance to the *scope* of the concept of communication presented in this chapter. However, the readings suggested at the end of Chapters 1, 2, 3, and 4 should also be consulted.

AMERICAN MANAGEMENT ASSOCIATION, INC. "Building a Balanced Communications Program," *General Management Series*, No. 170. New York, 1954.

AYER, A. J. et al. *Studies in Communication*. London: Martin Secker and Warburg, 1955.

BERLO, DAVID K. *The Process of Communication*. New York: Holt, Rinehart & Winston, Inc., 1960.

BRAM, JOSEPH. *Language and Society*. Garden City, N.Y.: Doubleday & Co., Inc., 1955.

CHERRY, E. COLIN. *On Human Communication*. Rev. ed. Cambridge, Mass.: MIT Press, 1966.

DE FLEUR, M. L. *Theories of Mass Communication*. New York: David Mc-Kay & Co., Inc., 1966.

DEUTSCH, KARL W. "On Communication Models in the Social Sciences," *Public Opinion Quarterly*, Vol. 16 (1952), pp. 356–80.

FESTINGER, L. "Informal Social Communication," *Psychological Review*, Vol. 57 (1950), pp. 271–82.

GUETZKOW, HAROLD, and SIMON, H. A. "The Impact of Certain Communication Nets upon Organization and Performance in Task-Oriented Groups," *Management Science*, Vol. 1 (1955), pp. 233–50.

HALL, EDWARD T.   *The Silent Language.* Garden City, N.Y.: Doubleday & Co., Inc., 1959.

HOCH, PAUL H., and ZUBIN, JOSEPH (eds.).   *Psychopathology of Communication.* New York: Grune and Stratton, Inc., 1958.

MANDELBAUM, DAVID G. (ed.).   *Selected Writings of Edward Sapir in Language, Culture, and Personality.* Berkeley: University of California Press, 1949.

ROTHSTEIN, JEROME.   *Communication, Organization, and Science.* Indian Hills, Colo.: Falcon's Wing Press, 1958.

RUESCH, JURGEN.   *Disturbed Communication.* New York: W. W. Norton & Co., 1957.

———, and BATESON, GREGORY.   *Communication: The Social Matrix of Psychiatry.* New York: W. W. Norton & Co., 1951.

———, and KEES, WELDON.   *Nonverbal Communication.* Berkeley: University of California Press, 1956.

SCHRAMM, WILBUR (ed.).   *The Process and Effects of Mass Communication.* Urbana: University of Illinois Press, 1954.

SHANDS, H. C.   "Outline of a General Theory of Human Communication . . . ," in L. THAYER (ed.), *Communication: Concepts and Perspectives.* Washington, D.C.: Spartan Books, Inc., 1967.

SONDEL, BESS.   *Communication: A Field Theory.* Chicago: University of Chicago Press, 1958.

WERNER, H. (ed.).   *On Expressive Language.* Worcester, Mass.: Clark University Press, 1955.

———, and KAPLAN, B.   *Symbol Formation.* New York: John Wiley & Sons, Inc., 1963.

PART II

Communication, Messages,
and Communication Systems:
Qualities and
Characteristics

9

Communication: Effectiveness

EVEN COMMUNICATION EXPERTS "miscommunicate" because they assume that we all have a similar understanding of what characterizes effective vs. ineffective communication. There is considerable confusion about this point simply because the criteria we use to judge effectiveness are often very vague and elusive.

So it will be our purpose in this chapter to clarify some of the issues at stake. Certainly how one measures communication effectiveness will largely determine what he attempts to communicate—and how he goes about it. So this clarification of the issues involved in assessing effectiveness is a crucial one.

The Sources of Confusion

The two factors that have probably contributed most to the present confusion are these:

1. We have failed to distinguish the effectiveness of the communication *performance* from the effectiveness of the communication *encounter*; and
2. We have slighted the difference between sheer *comprehension* of a message and the receiver's *subsequent behavior* with respect to the originator's intentions.

Because our conventional models or concepts of communication are of the simple cause→effect (S→R) sort, we have quite logically looked to the communicator, "the message," and the communicator's performance as the crucial determinants of communication effectiveness. For example, we have been led to believe that there are good and bad ways to compose letters or reports or speeches, quite apart from any consideration of the audience or their reactions. It is easy for many people to believe—on the basis of how they understand the communication process—that if the originator does everything "right" but he doesn't achieve his purpose, then the fault must somehow lie with the receiver(s).[1]

Similarly, faulty conceptions of the process of communication itself have led us to describe as communication "breakdowns" those situations in which another person didn't behave as we expected him to behave following the communication encounter. As we have seen earlier, it is perfectly possible for a receiver to have a clear understanding (his own comprehension, of course) of the originator's message, but still not do what the originator wanted him to do. Why? Because, like any other two people, the originator and the receiver can only interpret the originator's message as each individually perceives it (and the import of its consequences for them). Yet—except for the implications of the originator's authority or power over the receiver—the originator's interpretation of the message is not necessarily any more "accurate" than the receiver's. The originator may or may not have clearly in mind what he *intends* to accomplish, but his interpretation of his message is not, simply because he is the originator, necessarily any more accurate than the receiver's interpretation of that same message. Indeed, the originator may have more reason to "distort" the meaning of his message than the receiver has!

Also, we have probably all had the experience of agreeing about the meaning of a message, only to find that people subsequently behave differently in spite of their similar interpretations.

So let us attempt to clarify this basic point of confusion. *First*, "the message" (i.e., the originator's product), the originator's performance in planning or presenting his message, and the originator himself—all are certainly elements of the communication process. But so is the situation, so is the intended receiver, so is the message the *receiver* "gets" so are the receiver's skills and comprehend-abilities, etc. All are important elements of the process. While it is possible and sometimes profitable to

---

[1] It is interesting to note how the empirical fact that the audience is a factor in communication gets "discovered" from time to time by people who become interested in communication from the perspective of other disciplines. See, e. g., as recently as 1965: *The Obstinate Audience*, Ann Arbor, Mich.: Foundation for Research on Human Behavior.

look at these separate factors in isolation—apart from each other—we are likely to be making a mistake if we try to attribute communication effectiveness to any one of these elements.

For, as a matter of empirical fact, the effectiveness of any communication encounter is partly determined by all of these elements. We *could* say that the effectiveness of any communication encounter is totally determined by the receiver's skills, in the same way that we often want to attribute effectiveness wholly to the originator's skills. Both play some part—as does every other element in the process.

Our inclination to look for single causes and single effects is the fallacy of the single cause. In complex systems and processes such as we are dealing with when we consider intercommunication, the consequences of an originator's attempts to communicate-to someone else are determined by a multiplicity of factors. The "stimulus" of the originator's message is but one of these factors.

Second, the difference between a receiver's sheer ability to *comprehend* an originator's message satisfactorily and that same receiver's ability or willingness to do what the originator intends him to do as a consequence— is often a significant one. The difference between "communicating" someone into *understanding* something as we want him to, and communicating him into *doing* something we want him to do is a difference which often goes far beyond the communicate-abilities of either the originator or the receiver. For example, a receiver may read and fully understand a letter asking him to take some specific action. But let us assume that—as it frequently happens—this particular receiver cannot carry out the requested action at that particular time, for reasons which have nothing to do with the letter, or with his relationship with the originator, etc. Was the letter effective or not? Was the originator's intent achieved or not? A communication failure?

Clarification of the first misconception—that the determinants of effectiveness in communication are located primarily in the originator or the message or the originator's performance—is a matter of accepting the unavoidable fact that the results of any communication encounter are determined by many factors, only one of which is the message or the performance of the communicator.[2]

There are differences in the quality of messages and communication performances which do contribute to the effectiveness or ineffective-

---

[2] On this, and other difficulties that stem from conventional views of the communication process, see L. Thayer, "On Theory-Building in Communication: I. Some Conceptual Problems." *Journal of Communication*, 1963, 13, 217–35.

ness of the encounter. But the criteria for judging these particular factors as good or bad are not intrinsic to the message or the performance. What determines their qualities lies in the positive or negative contribution they make to the overall success of the encounter. What we want to achieve is a very pragmatic point of view: what is effective is what works, not how nicely constructed the message or how articulate the performance.[3] Situational factors over which the originator has no or little control will always establish limits to what can be accomplished communicatively. The effective communicator is not one who works at trying to alter those limits, but one whose competence and control enable him generally to achieve his communicative intentions to the full extent of those limits, however small or large they may be.

Clarification of the second misconception—that there is or should be some necessary correlation between the receiver's comprehension of the originator's message and the appropriateness of his subsequent behavior—will be a matter to be taken up in further detail in this and the succeeding two chapters. Perhaps it will suffice here to remind the reader once again that whether a receiver *understands* a message and whether he subsequently *behaves as intended* by the originator—must be viewed as two separate operations, either one of which could be effective (from the originator's point of view) independent of the other.

One-Person and Two-Person Communication Effectiveness

A further point of confusion stems from our failure to clearly distinguish the level at which we want to assess effectiveness—intrapersonal, interpersonal, technological, or organizational. It makes considerable difference.

For example, the measure of the effectiveness of any individual's total communication behavior would be some measure of how satisfactorily he acquires and consumes the information he needs or has an "appetite" for, plus some measure of how satisfactorily he achieves his communicative intentions vis-à-vis himself and others in his environment. That's straightforward enough.

But when two people encounter each other communicatively, and they individually have needs and intentions which are not totally mutual or complementary, then one of those individuals must in a sense succeed at

---

[3] On this and related issues, see L. Thayer, "Some Theoretical Approaches to Business Communication," *Journal of Business Communication*, 1963, 1, 15–21.

the cost of the other, or vice versa. In the synchronic mode, one of the participants will be the "sink" for the other's message, and that other participant often expects to fulfill his communicative intentions in or through the other. So we can measure the effectiveness of two-person communication encounters—at least in the synchronic mode—simply by determining whether or not the intentions of the originator were adequately achieved either in or through the receiver.

Of course, one could ask: how effective was the *intra*personal communication for each of the participants? Suppose, for example, a manager asks for certain data to be supplied to him. The receiver of the request complies. So that encounter was effective, in that sense. But suppose also that the data he requested either was not the best data he could have obtained for his purposes, or was of a magnitude or complexity far beyond his ability to assimilate. Given these consequences for his own input side, was the encounter effective or not? In other words, if the ultimate consequences of one's successfully communicating-to another are detrimental to him in some way, was the original encounter effective or not (for him)? We tend to ignore the consequences for the communication systems of the individual participants when assessing the effectiveness of their communication performances in an encounter. But there may be situations in which we need to take *intra*personal consequences into account when assessing the effectiveness of any intercommunication.

Difficulties in assessing *effectiveness* also begin to arise (1) when any two-person communication encounter is purposefully or accidentally *dia-chronic*, or (2) when the organization or the communication net involves more than two persons. Let us look at the two-person diachronic situation here and the organizational situation in the following section.

In a diachronic communication encounter,[4] the two (or more) participants commit their intellectual and communicative resources to a cooperative endeavor, the objective of which is simply the best consequence that can be mutually produced. Under the circumstances, effectiveness could not be determined from the "needs" or the objectives of any one participant. Rather, effectiveness in diachronic communication encounters must be determined by:

---

[4] A reminder: neither diachronic nor synchronic communication encounters ever occur in the "pure" form in which we are discussing them here. There are perhaps always some of each mode in every encounter. But one or the other mode is usually dominant, so the propositions being raised here have universal relevance, with whatever qualification seems necessary in view of the relative *degree* of each mode implicit in any encounter.

a) the value or utility of the resources each participant brings to the encounter—intellectual, attitudinal, communicational, etc.—for the other participant(s); and

b) the relative commitment to the cooperative enterprise each participant makes—with no specific objective vis-à-vis the other(s) except that of cooperating with him in the achievement of some mutually advantageous communication experience.

In other words, the *criteria* by which we must judge the effectiveness of any diachronic encounter are not in the consequences as such, but in the relative contributions of the participants. A diachronic encounter in which individual A has nothing of value to contribute to individual B is thereby doomed to a large degree of ineffectiveness.

Determining the Effectiveness of Organizational Communication

Determining the effectiveness of organizational communication presents a still different set of circumstances.

Recall that communication in organizations inevitably takes place within people, and that the members of an organization are linked together by both formal and informal channels into networks of task-related communication of one sort or another. Recall, too, that there is, in all organizations which are larger than face-to-face, a need for some physical system of data *transportation,* and that in some organizations certain data-processing functions (with associated equipment) have been inserted into those data transportation systems.

So when we ask about the effectiveness of organizational communication, we need to ask three questions (although they would likely vary in relative importance in any particular situation):

1. How effective was the communication that occurred from an *intrapersonal* point of view?
2. How effective was the communication that occurred from an *intercommunication* (diachronic and/or synchronic) point of view?
3. How effective was the communication that occurred from the point of view of the internal well-being (maintenance), or the external adaptation or goal-achieving (operational and regulatory) conditions of the organization as a whole?"[5]

---

[5] Note too, that what is relatively effective communication for any individual member of the organization could be relatively *ineffective* from an intercommunication point of view, relatively *effective* from the point of view of the organization's relations with one of its constituencies, and so on.

Further, in all organizations one can, and should, ask about the effi-cacy[6] of the media and the channels employed in task-related communica-tion, intercommunication, and mass communication within the organiza-tion. And, in those larger organizations having data transportation and/or data-processing systems, the efficacy of those technological networks and the equipment integrated into them is often a factor contributing to the effectiveness or ineffectiveness of communication within that organization.

How communication effectiveness in organizations is to be determined thus depends upon which of the four levels of analysis—*intrapersonal, interpersonal, organizational,* or *technological*—is the most pertinent to the reason for wanting to determine effectiveness in any situation. If effec-tiveness at all four levels is important, one should be prepared to recognize that what is effective at one level may be detrimental or ineffective at another level, and conversely. Then we are forced to think in terms of effectiveness *on balance*—i.e., after taking into account negative effects at certain levels which might offset some positive effects at other levels, or conversely.

That is why, in large formal organizations, it is probably appropriate to think of communication effectiveness in general as that which satisfices or suboptimizes[7] the relevant variables at the different levels of analysis. That is, communication effectiveness in organizations is not a unidimensional quality or characteristic. It may be that immediate organizational goals must be sacrificed (or delayed) in the interest of employee relations. Or the converse may occur. The point is that one cannot, in organizations, think of *maximizing* effectiveness across all levels. Given the hierarchy of needs and goals with which every manager has to operate, he may need to think of communication effectiveness as some satisfactory suboptimization of effectivenesses at the various levels at which it could be assessed—i.e., some satisfactory degree of effectiveness *on balance*.

Communication Satisfaction

Communication satisfaction is occasionally mistaken for communica-tion effectiveness—and conversely.

---

[6] The term, "efficacy," is useful here to distinguish between the effectiveness of human communication encounters and the efficacy of the communication systems within which people, and organizations, are in-formed and maintained as living systems.

[7] I have borrowed the first of these useful terms from March and Simon (J. G. March and H. A. Simon, *Organizations* [New York: John Wiley & Sons, Inc., 1958]), and the second from Hitch and McKean (C. Hitch and R. McKean, "Suboptimization in Operations Problems," in J. F. McCloskey and Flora F. Trefethen [eds.], *Operations Research for Management* [Baltimore: Johns Hopkins University Press, 1954]).

There are those situations when the intended or accidental consequence of a communication encounter is indeed the communication *satisfaction* of one or all of the participants. There is, of course, some personal satisfaction inherent in successfully communicating-to someone or in successfully being communicated-with (whether in fulfillment of conscious need or a nonconscious "appetite"). And there is inevitably some feeling of dissatisfaction when our needs or expectations (whether inputting or outputting) are not fulfilled in our communicative encounters.

But it would not be accurate to assume—especially in synchronic communication encounters—that what provides communicative satisfaction is therefore effective. Or if a particular communication encounter is personally satisfying in some way to the originator, he should not assume that it was therefore effective. Nor should he try to "package" his message in a way that will be satisfying to the receiver, unless the receiver's communicative satisfaction is his specific intent. Synchronic communication is not necessarily satisfying to the receiver, nor is it always pleasurable for the originator.

In *diachronic* communication, logically enough, effectiveness and satisfaction are more congruent. But in synchronic communication, the pleasantness or satisfactoriness of the encounter should not automatically be taken as a reliable measure of its effectiveness.

The Role of Purpose

One of the most troublesome factors to deal with in assessing communication effectiveness is *purpose.*

First, we can safely hypothesize that the ineffectiveness (and/or inefficiency) of a large proportion of intercommunication in organizations is traceable to the originator's failure to establish a clear-cut purpose before initiating the communication encounter. Without a clear-cut and very specific purpose either for communicating-to or being communicated-with, the assessment of effectiveness is not even relevant. One can be effective communicatively only in terms of his specific purpose—whether intending to communicate-to someone to some specific end, or to be communicated-with to some specific end.

Second, as we have seen, our communicative behavior is generally energized and directed by the discrepancy between one or more *intended-states-of-affairs* and their respective *apparent-states-of-affairs.* The resolution of those inconsistencies or dissonances is behind all of our attempts to communicate-to or be communicated-with in some way. But when we are

communicating on-behalf-of . . . our organizations, when we are performing as members of human organizations, we can often establish rational
"oughts" and/or "shoulds" as appropriate purposes or intentions. But,
whether "naturally" (in the service of the individual's own needs, intentions, "appetites," etc.) or "rationally" (in the service of some on-purpose
organization) derived, we always have some conscious or nonconscious
purpose for attempting to affect ourselves or others communicatively, and
it is in terms of those purposes that effectiveness must be measured.

As noted previously, effectiveness is a measure of goal- or intention- or
purpose-fulfillment. If the single goal of a football team is to win a
particular game, then its effectiveness in that game is simply a measure of
whether the game was won or lost. But, if the purpose was to play with
good team spirit as well as to win, then its effectiveness is some aggregate
measure of the achievement of the two goals combined. In other words, in
organizational life, there are rarely single or exclusive goals or purposes to
be achieved. Intercommunicatively, we must frequently attempt to influence another in the direction of our own interests, but we need to do so
without damaging the relationship, and so on.

In personal or organizational life, there are usually long-range goals. But
the effectiveness of any specific communicative encounter can be measured
only with respect to the specific intentions of those specific participants in
that specific encounter. Whether the achievement of those situational
intentions contributes to or detracts from the achievement of long-range
goals is another order of effectiveness. And there may be n-order measures
of effectiveness for a great many communication encounters within organizations.

Third, whether our point of view be of communication, intercommunication, or of organizational communication, we need to remember that
there are but three generic purposes in human communication:

1. To affect one's own or another's knowledge of or thinking about
   something in some way—by attempting to alter a present conception,
   to add to it, to establish a new concept, etc.
2. To affect one's own or another's attitudes or orientations toward himself, others, or some aspect of his (or one's own) environment in
   some way; or
3. To affect or influence one's own or another's behavior in some way.

In other words, what a person is attempting to do when he seeks to
communicate-to or be communicated-with is to affect in some way his or
another's thinking, attitudes, or behavior—to the end of bringing some

apparent-state-of-affairs into congruence with its related intended-state-of-affairs. How the consequences of that encounter simultaneously satisfy or dissatisfy other intended-states-of-affairs (either one's own, another's, or the organization's) greatly complicates the question of communication effectiveness.

But hopefully it will be clear that a specific purpose or intention is indispensable to the assessment of the effectiveness of any specific communication encounter.

Communication Effectiveness and Behavior

In an earlier chapter, we raised this question: if a receiver adequately comprehends an originator's message, but subsequently behaves contrary to the originator's intentions, was that attempt to communicate-to the receiver effective? If an organizational superior directs a subordinate to do X, and the subordinate comprehends what the superior said, yet behaves contrary to the originator's intent, was that communication encounter effective or not?

There are at least three factors at issue:

First, there is the fact that the receiver inevitably bases his interpretation of what the originator says, and his subsequent behavior, upon *his* comprehending and behavior systems—not upon the originator's or upon any "objective" assessment of what was said or what behavior was supposed to ensue.

Second, there is the fact that the meaning, and/or the implications of the meaning of an originator's message, are constantly undergoing change within each of the participants *subsequent* to their communicative encounter. As a result of reflecting upon what was said, or as a result of communicative encounters with others which occur *after* the initial message but *before* the receiver is supposed to carry out the action specified by the originator, the continuously self-organizing systems of both the originator and the receiver continuously reformulate their individual interpretations of the message, and/or the import of that interpretation (for each of them). In other words, either the receiver or the originator, or both, could nonconsciously and unintentionally reinterpret what was said.

Third, we must also remember that the way the originator extrapolates from his message to the behavior desired of the receiver may not be the way a receiver would extrapolate from *his* interpretation of a message to *his* understanding of what he is expected to do.

For these and the other reasons discussed in the preceding section, message effectiveness does not always parallel subsequent *behavior* effectiveness. There may be many factors quite beyond the control of the originator or the receiver (and quite beyond either one's ability to predict) which could and do intervene between the original message and the receiver's behavior. Behavior effectiveness thus requires the establishment and manipulation of conditions prior to, during, and subsequent to any attempt to communicate-to or be communicated-with.[8]

Thus, to measure the effectiveness of any message which has as its purpose some *later* impact upon a receiver's thinking, orientation, or behavior, a number of factors other than the immediate effectiveness of the communication encounter have to be taken into account. To insure a particular interpretation of a particular message, certan conditions surrounding and following its reception may have to be controlled—or compensated for in some way.

Message Validity, Utility, and Consequence

A message will not be effective if it is not attended to. And it will likely not be attended to unless the receiver can validate it in some way—in terms of its relevance, its "credibility," its appropriateness, its "truth," and so on.

A message will not be effective unless it is consumed by the receiver. And it will be consumed only to the extent it has some utility for that receiver, that is, only to the extent it has some usefulness to him in terms of his own (or his on-behalf-of . . .) communicative needs, "appetites," etc.[9]

---

[8] The participants' interpretations of these conditions are themselves established, maintained, etc., through intercommunication. We do exploit these conditions intuitively; for example, the formalized and standardized penalties for failure to obey an order contribute to more efficient (not necessarily more effective) communication of orders in military organizations than in many civilian organizations. If failure to behave as intended carried with it severe punishment, behavior effectiveness (as opposed to message or communication effectiveness) is greatly enhanced. Or, if subsequent to hearing a leader's call for a greater effort on everyone's part, a worker hears favorable comments from his fellow-workers (and actually observes them working more diligently) that leader's appeal will have quite a different impact on this worker than it would have if the fellow-worker's reactions had been negative—i.e., if he had perceived them actually slowing down on the job, etc. Again, conditions quite apart from the "content" of a message contribute to the way it is understood and acted upon.

[9] "Communicated" data may have some utility for a receiver either in terms of establishing intended-states (goals) or in terms of assessing apparent-states-of-affairs (feedback and/or feedforward).

Finally, a message will be *ineffective* to the extent that the receiver's expectations relative to the *consequences* of "accurately" comprehending it or behaving appropriately subsequent to it would be disadvantageous to him in some way. (Or, conversely, a message will likely be ineffective to the extent that the receiver anticipates that his understanding or his behavior would be unduly *advantageous* to that particular originator in some way.) Considerably over-simplified, we might illustrate some of the implications of the latter point as shown in Figure 13.

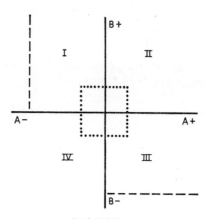

FIGURE 13

Experiment with Figure 13 in the following way: If the pay-off[10] in terms of achieving his intentions and/or expectations vis-à-vis B is high (+) for A, but the pay-off for B if A achieves his intentions is negative (−), then a point representing the intersection of those combined pay-offs would be plotted in quadrant III. The reader will recognize that quadrants I and III are the domains of alternate monologue: where people talk at each other, but neither is really *listening* to the other, but simply waiting his turn to say something more.

If the pay-off (or the consequences of B's behaving as intended by A) for B is *neither* especially positive nor especially negative, then synchronization is possible—given that A has the appropriate tactical competencies.

---

10 Since this illustration is greatly oversimplified, it does not graphically reflect the fact that A may take-into-account the expected pay-off for B and therefore unconsciously *disunderstand* what B is saying. But B may take into account A's expectation, and devise some way to communicate-to A successfully in spite of this barrier. And so on, through many levels of complexity (of the "gaming" sort) not portrayed by this one-dimensional graph.

If the anticipated consequences for both A and B are negative, however, then the encounter will normally not be initiated or, if it is initiated, will be abandoned as quickly as one or the other can properly terminate it.

Quadrant II is, by contrast, the dialogue or diachronic communication area. When the pay-off for both participants is positive, then their intercommunication will be effective—even though it may not be efficient.

The dashed lines in Quadrants I and III are intended to indicate that, in synchronic communication (or alternate monologue), there are those communicative situations in which A's intentions vis-à-vis B (or conversely) are *impossible* to achieve. For example, if B's full comprehension of what A is saying would be excessively "costly" or otherwise disadvantageous to B, B might either abandon the encounter—or, if he can't abandon it, might *disunderstand* what A is saying. These are the cases in which B *comprehends* what A is saying, but can't "afford" to understand fully what A *means* by what he is saying, or exactly what A wants him to do, etc. Or, the behavior expected of B by A may be so negative in some way (in B's anticipation) that B simply cannot comply, and consequently may have to "distort" A's message regardless of how A presents it. A committed Democrat, for example, can *fully* comprehend what a committed Republican is saying only at the cost of eventually voting contrary to his political beliefs. Or, a thorough-going laborite can *fully* comprehend what management is saying only at the "cost" of agreeing with management's position on certain contract issues. And so on.

There are *organizational imperatives*, of course, such as those which operate in the military. If the consequences of *not* comprehending or *not* behaving as intended by the originator are anticipated by the receiver as clearly more negative than doing so, then there is a degree of willingness to comprehend and behave appropriately that exceeds the "content" of the message, its "motivating" power, etc. These organizational imperatives, as we will see later, may be either advantageous or disadvantageous or simultaneously both advantageous and disadvantageous to the organization.

Finally—although these few examples do not exhaust the usefulness of this simple diagram—there is an area near the center point where the pay off is neither very positive nor very negative for either of the participants involved. People will engage in communication encounters with near-zero individual pay-offs only to the extent that they assume their commitments to their organizational or institutional roles "require" them to do so. This is the domain of communicating-on-behalf-of. . . . The indifference which people bring to many such on-behalf-of . . . encounters is the point we need to note here.

Effectiveness in Being Communicated-With

The emphasis to this point on the effectiveness of communicating-to may unduly obscure the equal importance of one's effectiveness in being communicated-with.

Purposive inputting—that is, in acquiring and consuming relevant and utilizable information from within and without—is just as important to the effectiveness of an individual as are his abilities to affect others (communicatively) as he intends. So what has been said of effectiveness in communicating-to is equally true of effectiveness in being communicated-with. For example, our ability, as receivers, to seek out and acquire (to educe) data of value to our own purposes and functioning—to induce originators to communicate-to us consistent with our needs and "appetites" and intentions—is a communicate-ability as important as any ability we may have (or desire) as originators (communicators-to).

On Communicating Effectively

One's communication effectiveness is ultimately limited by the full set of circumstances within which he must communicate.

Three examples may help to emphasize this point—and it needs to be emphasized.

1. A person cannot be communicated-with beyond his individual communicate-abilities (his personal take-into-account-abilities and -susceptibilities). What this means is that we cannot communicate-to another beyond his abilities to comprehend nor beyond the consequences he sees for himself if he (a) comprehends and behaves accordingly, (b) comprehends but doesn't (or "can't") behave accordingly, (c) disunderstands and therefore doesn't initiate the behavior intended by the originator—and so on. We are inclined to think only of the problem in which an individual may be faced with a difficult situation of communicating-to someone else—the outcome of which he feels may greatly affect him or his organization in some way. But it is just as important to realize that the same person has limitations on his own abilities and susceptibilities to be communicated-with.

So a person's overall communication effectiveness must be assessed in two ways: his record and potential for affecting others communicatively in keeping with his own intentions, and his record and potential for being affected *by* others in ways which are or might be advantageous to him and/or his organization. Developing one's abilities to be communicated-with is just as important as developing one's abilities to communicate-to.[11]

2. A basic source of effectiveness/ineffectiveness *in* the communicator is thus his *strategic* competence, particularly the consistency with which he is able to discern which consequences are "possible" in which situations, and which situations are "impossible," given his communicative intentions. (When certain consequences are temporarily impossible, he can and usually should, of course, compensate for this obstacle in some way, or set about altering the conditions until they are conducive to his intentions at some other time.)

When situations are difficult, but possible, then the originator needs to be able to muster the *tactical* competencies which would enhance his communicative effectiveness in those situations.

So one's effectiveness as a communicator depends first upon the implicit facilitators and inhibitors (the "circumstances") which establish consequences as possible, inevitable, or impossible; *then* and only then upon his competence accurately to discern which type of situation he is in; and *then* and only then (a) upon his ability to *compensate* for those situations in which certain communicative intentions or goals are impossible, and (b) upon his tactical competence to succeed in those situations in which it is possible to achieve his purposes to some degree.

3. Thus one's effectiveness depends only thirdly upon his *techniques* (which are part of his tactical competencies).

It is important to realize that one may succeed or fail in difficult (but possible) situations depending upon whether or not he has the appropriate and adequate techniques. But—to emphasize once again—it is just as important to realize that one's techniques can be effective only to the degree that the situation has been fully and accurately perceived. The way one comprehends the communication process—in the context of the

---

[11] It would seem that we commonly take for granted our sufficient effectiveness in acquiring (or educing) and "consuming" information. We place unwarranted emphasis on the "output" side of communication. One is just as important as the other. It may be possible that one's effectiveness in *outputting*—communicating-to others—can be no greater than his effectiveness in *inputting*—being communicated-with.

situation he is faced with—is a much more basic determinant of his general communication effectiveness than are his techniques.

This concludes our examination of the notion of *effectiveness* in communication. Some implications of these concepts will be taken up in later chapters, but those chapters should not be consulted before the reader has a firm understanding of the conceptual issues at stake in assessing, or attempting to achieve, communication effectiveness.

SUGGESTIONS FOR FURTHER READING

The effectiveness of intercommunication is all too often assumed away. There is no single set of criteria for measuring effectiveness subscribed to by all writers on communication. Thus what I have suggested in this list is a set of readings which reflect the *levels of analysis* problem in evaluating communication effectiveness—rather than suggesting readings which would offer various normative guides to "communicating effectively." Those will be found at the end of Chapter 18.

AMERICAN MANAGEMENT ASSOCIATION, INC.   *Checking the Effectiveness of Employee Communications*, Personnel Series, No. 108. New York, 1947.

BARLOW, WALTER G.   *Measuring the Effectiveness of Communication.* General Management Series, No. 181. New York: American Management Association, 1956.

FEATHER, N. T.   "A Structural Balance Model of Communication Effects," *Psychological Review*, Vol. 71 (1964), pp. 291–313.

FUNK, H. B., and BECKER, R. G. "Measuring the Effectiveness of Industrial Communications," *Personnel*, November, 1952.

Human Performance in Information Transmission. Coordinated Science Laboratory, University of Illinois, Sept. 1962.

KLAPPER, J. T.   *The Effects of Mass Communication.* New York: Free Press, 1960.

McCASLIN, D.   *Reaching Other Minds.* New York: F. S. Crofts & Co., 1931.

RANDALL, C. B.   "The Myth of Communications," *Dun's Review*, Vol. 75 (1960), pp. 37–39.

RANEY, E. T.   "A Method for Evaluating Employee Communications Media," *American Psychologist*, Vol. 4 (1949), p. 286.

SARTAIN, A. Q.   "Effective Communications," *Advanced Management*, Vol. 16 (1951), pp. 20–21.

SHEPHERD, C., and WESCHLER, I. R. "The Relation between Three Interpersonal Variables and Communication Effectiveness: A Pilot Study," *Sociometry*, Vol. 18 (1955), pp. 103–10.

WILLIS, I. L. "Basic Principles for Effective Communications," *Advanced Management*, Vol. 15 (1950), pp. 8–10.

ZELKO, H. P. "How Effective Are Your Company Communications?" *Advanced Management*, February, 1956.

10

Communication: Economy

THERE IS ALWAYS some kind of investment or expenditure whenever communication occurs. At the intrapersonal level, there is inevitably the investment of an individual's attention and information-processing capacities—which precludes his investing those capacities in some other way.

At the interpersonal level, there is, in addition to that investment of capacity, the "cost" to each participant of the loss of certain degrees of freedom, the "cost" of fulfilling the demands and expectations (of the other) even when these may run counter to one's own immediate self-interests, and so on.

At the organizational level, there are inevitably the dollar costs of data-transportation and/or processing, of all sorts of communication activities and programs, of white-collar salaries (most of which gets invested in communication of one sort or another), or committee meetings, telephone conversations, mail boys and messengers, paper, and of the supplies and equipment which support task-related communication, data transportation and communication systems, etc.

There are hardware costs, and software costs, in addition to the operational time invested in communication of one sort or another.

So there is always some economic factor in communication. And since no measure of communication *effectiveness* can be fully meaningful apart from the cost of achieving that effectiveness, some way of comprehending the *economy* of communication is a necessary part of any comprehensive view of communication.

154

Intrapersonal Factors

On the input side, the "cost" of acquiring and consuming information has two facets.

First, we must all "pay the price" of investing time and energy in either seeking out or in ingesting data expected to have some utility for our past, present, or future behavior.

Second, a hidden cost of acquiring and consuming a particular kind of information is that we cannot acquire and consume other kinds of potentially relevant information at the same time, since our information-acquisition/consumption capacities are extremely limited. Certainly we do not—and can not—consume all of the event-data that we acquire, so there are certain losses involved in the selective conversion (of sense-data to functional information) process. Further, the patterns of information-acquisition/consumption a person engages in today serve to determine the patterns of information-acquisition/consumption that are *possible* for him tomorrow. That represents an additional hidden cost of intrapersonal communication behavior.

On the output side, there are obvious investments of time and energy. It takes time to produce consumable messages for others, and some expenditure of energy in preparing and transmitting them is inevitable. When one is communicating-to someone or some audience about X, he cannot be communicating-to another person or a different audience about Y (or about X for that matter). There is always some relative cost involved in investing limited resources in one way rather than another—especially in view of the long-range goals that may be at stake.

Finally, at the central information-processing level, there is always a significant investment of limited capacity, and a significant expenditure of energy. The human brain uses a disproportionately large amount of the body's energy. Functionally, our information-processing capacity is limited, particularly our capacity for short-term storage.[1] Thus the utilization of

---

[1] See H. A. Simon, *The New Science of Management Decision* (New York: Harper & Row, 1960); G. A. Miller, "The Magical Number Seven, Plus or Minus Two: Some Limits on Our Capacity for Processing Information," *Psychological Review*, 1956, 63, 81–97; D. W. Taylor, "Toward an Information-Processing Theory of Motivation," in *Nebraska Symposium on Motivation* (Lincoln: University of Nebraska Press, 1960); and J. G. Miller, "The Individual as an Information Processing System," in W. S. Fields and W. Abbott (eds.), *Information Storage and Neural Control* (Springfield, Ill.: Charles C Thomas, 1963).

human information-processing capacities for one purpose precludes the use of those same capacities for another purpose, and therefore represents both a relative and an absolute cost to the individual.

There are other aspects of communication economy at the individual level. But perhaps these major ones will be sufficient to suggest the range of "costs" within a given individual when he engages in communication.

Interpersonal Factors

At the interpersonal level, there are costs of intercommunication which are *in addition to* those incurred by each of the participants. And they are of a somewhat different order or quality.

Perhaps some examples will be suggestive.

Entering into a communicative relationship with another always involves giving up certain individual degrees-of-freedom—i.e., certain privileges to choose the what, the when, the where, the how, etc., of the encounter itself. Those issues now become collective issues, and such decisions or choices now become aggregative, not exclusively individual, prerogatives.

Second, those with whom we have established some normal communication channel—i.e., those who form our personal communication networks—may become more or less difficult to communicate-with. But, given our psychological contracts with them, we must pay whatever "price" they demand or expect, at least up to the extent of the value to us of continuing that relationship. For only by paying that price can we maintain communication with them and keep that channel open to and from them. These circumstances often give rise to costs of considerable magnitude.[2]

Third, there is more than just information give-and-take in interpersonal encounters. Feelings are involved, as by-products of the effectiveness *and* the satisfaction we derive from those encounters. When our intentions, needs, appetites, or communicative satisfactions are frustrated, great quantities of energy and misplaced attention may be diverted to fuel those feelings. There is thus some reduction of energy available to expend on other communication needs and intentions. In addition, as frustrations increase and feelings begin to dominate one's psychological system, the

---

[2] The penalty for not paying one's "dues" to the others who comprise his personal and/or occupational communication networks is often *excommunication*—an extreme cost not many of us are willing to pay. So we overlook the cost of the dues we have to pay to remain members in good standing in every useful or satisfactory communicative relationship we have with other people.

cost of communicating-to and being communicated-with increases exponentially.

Fourth, the difficulty a person experiences in communicating-to another may not be totally attributable to the immediate encounter itself. It often happens that the difficulty one has in "getting through to" another is really a function of the low pay-off or high cost the other anticipates as a result of understanding and/or undertaking the behavior the originator intends subsequent to the encounter. We should never overlook the fact that one's present take-into-account-susceptibilities may be determined in large part either by his expectations about the future or by his recollections of the past—or both—as well as by what's going on at the moment. The remembered past, the perceived present, the anticipated future—all can play a part in determining the cost (e.g., in time and/or effort) as well as the effectiveness of any communication encounter.

Organizational and Technological Factors

There are inevitable dollar costs for communication at the organization level of analysis. Because the structure and functioning of an enterprise are determined by its communication systems, it is understandable that a large proportion of the dollar costs of running a formal organization[3] are costs for communication (and, of course, for large quantities of miscommunication).

In an on-purpose organization, there are payroll (and hidden) dollar costs for generating, disseminating, acquiring, and consuming event-data presumed relevant to the goals, the current operations, and the conditions of the organization, its state-relationships with various organizational con-

---

[3] A. M. McDonough says that "at least 50 percent of the cost of running our economy is information costs." (*Information Economics and Management Systems* [New York, McGraw-Hill, 1963]). But, if we consider that white-collar workers are engaged essentially in processing information and communicating information and decisions about the operation of an enterprise, and that the ratio of white- to blue-collar workers has been rapidly increasing (in some industries as high as 6:1), then this estimate is probably low. Whatever task-related activity does not *directly* (i.e., physically) contribute to the product in some way is communication (or data) *about* the product and the enterprise's operations, control, goals, etc. Such task-related activity constitutes a fundamental cost of running organizations. Cf. F. Machlup, *The Production and Distribution of Knowledge in the United States* (Princeton, N.J.: Princeton University Press, 1962), for a somewhat different view. A further interesting comparison that might be useful is R. L. Meier, "Information Input Overload: Features of Growth in Communication-Oriented Institutions," *Libri*, 1963, 13, 1–44.

stituencies in the environment, and so on. All of these costs are in addition to the costs at the individual and the interpersonal levels.

The *technology* of communication represents either a relative cost, an absolute cost, or both.

As part of our communication technology, our eyes and their associated equipment (and our language) introduce relative costs of one sort or another. Because we are, in our culture, primarily visual creatures, a large proportion of all the event-data we acquire for consumption comes to us through our visual equipment. Given what it is we are seeking, visual acquisition may be more (or less) costly than acquisition through another sensory modality—or through some combination of sensory modalities (e.g., visual and tactile, one complementing the other in some way).

Or consider our languages: for certain purposes, one language (e.g., mathematics, French) may be relatively more (or less) costly to use than another language, given a targeted level of effectiveness to be achieved.

Man-made equipment to facilitate, amplify, or extend man's own communication equipment represents both an absolute and a relative cost. For example, one sort of hearing aid or telephone or computer requires a dollar expenditure, but, depending upon the uses to which they are put, these devices may be relatively more (or less) costly than another piece of equipment of the same type, or than some completely different kind of device. Closed circuit TV might be less costly in some instances than an elaborate telephone network.

The equipment and media employed in any communication linkage or system, then, are more (or less) *efficacious* (to use an earlier concept) than some alternative way of accomplishing the same level of effectiveness relative to cost.

Communication Efficiency[4]

In all of the preceding, we may have come close to confusing two closely-related concepts: economy and efficiency.

The economy of communication relates to its *cost*—the required investment, expenditure, time, etc. The efficiency of communication, by contrast, is its *cost effectiveness*. Diagrammatically:

$$\text{Efficiency} = \frac{\text{Effectiveness}}{\text{Cost}}$$

---

[4] Throughout this discussion of efficiency, we will avoid raising specific details. All we need to do here is to develop some useful concepts and perspectives of the various types of efficiencies pertinent to communication.

where the efficiency of communication is viewed as the ratio of its effectiveness to its cost.

From an individual point of view, efficiency would be a simple measure of how efficiently one achieves a specific purpose (on the input side), or how efficiently he achieves an intention vis-à-vis another (on the output side).

At the interpersonal level, there are necessarily three different measures of efficiency: the efficiency with which A communicates-to and is communicated-with by B; the efficiency with which B communicates-to and is communicated-with by A; and the efficiency of the encounter itself. The efficiency of a communication encounter (as contrasted with the efficiency of the participants) may not be of major concern to the participants at the time, but it can be of considerable importance when the communication efficiency of the larger organization (on whose behalf they have encountered one another) is to be assessed. A task-related communication encounter represents a cost to the organization, and an organization's internal efficiency depends ultimately upon some composite of the efficiency of all of the communication encounters that occur within it.

MESSAGE EFFICIENCY

We should be aware that the sheer effort expended by an originator in preparing a message, or the sheer effort expended by a receiver in trying to comprehend a message, cannot be taken as a measure of efficiency. Nor can the efficiency of an encounter be determined simply from the length or the brevity of a message. These are not reliable measures of message efficiency. Message efficiency cannot be determined apart from the individual costs to the originator and the receiver. The relative utility of the message to the receiver must also be taken into account in addition to the relative ease or difficulty of the receiver's comprehension of the message (even assuming that the receiver comprehends the message in a way adequate to the originator's intentions).

The efficiency of any message is thus encounter-specific; it depends upon the participants, the situation, the timing, etc.—upon all of the conditions of any specific communication encounter. This is so because the effectiveness and the cost of any communication encounter depend upon that same array of conditions, as we have seen.

CHANNEL EFFICIENCY

A channel is efficient to the extent that it enables effective communication at minimum cost. Communication channels are thus more (or less) efficient, given their special functions. *The efficiency of communication channels therefore predicts to their use and creation in the emergence of communication systems between and among people.*

Media Efficiency

Given the purpose, the audience, and all of the other conditions of any communication encounter, the medium employed will be more (or less) efficient. There are certain relative costs involved in the use of one medium rather than another in the pursuit of specific communicative intentions or purposes. Communicative purposes will be fulfilled at greater or lesser cost, therefore, as a consequence of the medium employed.

System Efficiency

In the same way, a communication system is more (or less) efficient, given the degree of communication effectiveness it permits or facilitates, relative to the cost involved in running it or maintaining it. There is inevitably some cost involved in generating, disseminating, acquiring, and consuming information. The ratio of the overall effectiveness of any communication system to the composite cost of generating, disseminating, acquiring, and consuming information within it—is one rough measure of its efficiency.

Economy and Effectiveness: Two Further Issues

The criteria for assessing costs are fairly clearcut. We can count dollars or hours or units of energy expended, etc. But, as pointed out in the preceding chapter, the assessment of effectiveness is difficult, at best. The units by which communication effectiveness should be measured are not as obvious as those by which we measure cost.

As a result, we often substitute some measure of economy (or efficiency) as a measure of effectiveness. Unwittingly, we often incline toward—both personally and organizationally—communicative relationships and encounters which are easy and comfortable (and therefore seemingly efficient). It is all too easy to assume that the *convenience* of communication encounters is an adequate measure of their effectiveness. As a result, our anticipations of how difficult or uncomfortable a particular encounter might be often (unwittingly) divert us to those encounters which promise more ease or satisfaction.

There is an important issue at stake here. It is this: *some communication objectives are worth achieving (or must necessarily be achieved) whatever the cost.* The efficiency of a communication encounter cannot be taken as evidence of the necessity of that encounter—to either the participants or to the organization on whose behalf they may have initiated the encounter.

For example: dialogues (diachronic encounters) are typically quite inefficient. But, by and large, they are often extremely worthwhile or potentially valuable. Or, as another example: modifying employee attitudes in a direction which might enhance the quality of their workmanship on the job would likely be a long-term and very inefficient undertaking. But the consequences, if achieved, could offset the difficulty and the inefficiency of the mission.

A final example: the effectiveness with which people work productively together is a very desirable goal to strive for. But the vagaries of human nature are such that attaining some optimally productive relationship may be (communicatively) a very inefficient process. Yet to substitute an immediate efficiency for a later capability would be to substitute immediate successes for later and larger weaknesses or incapabilities.

Thus the second issue at stake in assessing the effectiveness and efficiency of communication is this: that *long-range advantages to people or to their organizations do not inevitably accrue from the effectiveness of specific and immediate communication encounters.* In fact, the effectiveness of any specific encounter could have long-range *disadvantages* for the participants or the organization.

We considered this dilemma in the preceding chapter as one to be faced in the assessment of effectiveness. But it deserves reemphasis here. Not only do we occasionally (or often) accept the efficiency of an encounter as evidence of its effectiveness. but we rarely consider more than the immediate consequences of those encounters when assessing their effectiveness. Our near-sightedness in assesssing communication effectiveness and efficiency may have to be paid for many times over in other ways. For example, obtaining satisfactory short-range agreements with employees may (and has) cost management a constant decline in individual productivity.[5]

By clearly differentiating comunication effectiveness and efficiency in

---

[5] An historical phenomenon made obvious by merely holding power constant. The continuing contribution of capital equipment (as physical and now "mental" augmentation of human capabilities) has, of course, more than offset—and has perhaps obscured—this regular decline.

our own thinking, we can avoid the first error—of assuming that what can be efficiently "communicated" thereby attests to the value or the effectiveness of doing so. But how we can avoid the second pitfall—of unwittingly trading immediate effectiveness for long-term disadvantages—is not so obvious.

SUGGESTIONS FOR FURTHER READING

Those involved in some way with business writing or paperwork management have long been aware of the significant direct and indirect costs of preparing letters and reports, of filing, of providing adequate equipment and facilities for internal communication, and so on. But it has been only recently that the more intangible costs of communication in and between organizations have begun to be identified. Some aspects of both the tangible and intangible costs of communication are described in the following documents.

GRIFFEN, MARVIN A. "The Cost and Value of Reports—A Case Study in a Telephone Company," Ch. 27 in CHARLES FLOGLE et al. (eds.), *Operations Research and Systems Engineering.* Baltimore: Johns Hopkins Press, 1960.

JANIS, J. H. "Writing Skills Cut Management Waste," *Nation's Business,* April, 1958.

LANZETTA, JOHN T., and KAVAREFF, V. T. "Information Cost, Amount of Payoff, and Level of Aspiration as Determinants of Information Seeking in Decision Making," *Behavioral Science,* Vol. 7 (1962), pp. 459–73.

McDONOUGH, A. M. *Information Economics and Management Systems.* New York: McGraw-Hill Book Co., 1963.

MACHLUP, F. *The Production and Distribution of Knowledge in the United States.* Princeton, N.J.: Princeton University Press, 1962.

MacKAY, D. M. "The Informational Analysis of Questions and Commands," in C. CHERRY (ed.), *Information Theory.* London: Butterworths, 1961.

MARSCHAK, J. "Towards an Economic Theory of Organization and Information," in R. M. Thrall, et al. (eds.), *Decision Processes.* New York: John Wiley & Sons, Inc., 1954.

———. "Economics of Language," *Behavioral Science,* Vol. 10 (1965), pp. 135–140.

SPENCE, LEWIS H. "Dollars and Sense of Employee Communications," *Advanced Management,* February, 1957.

SZASZ, T. A. "Entropy, Organization, and the Problems of the Economy of Human Relationships," *International Journal of Psychoanalysis,* Vol. 36 (1955), pp. 289–97.

11

Messages: Comprehensibility, Validity, and Utility

THERE ARE THREE basic qualities of purposive or instrumental messages (message-receiver interactions) which determine the extent to which the desired communication is likely to occur. They are *comprehensibility*, *validity*, and *utility*.

Let us consider briefly each of these three consequential characteristics of messages.

Comprehensibility

Probably the most common of all of the "recipes" for good communication that turns up again and again is the simple precept: "Be clear."

But people do communicate-to each other for many reasons beyond the sheer exchange of information. As one civil servant once quipped, "To be clear would be to be found out!" This applies to all of us from time to time. It is sometimes the very obscurity of one's language which others use as evidence of his intelligence or profundity. Or, if a nuclear physicist were put upon to explain *clearly* to a vacuum cleaner salesman exactly what it is he does in his work, no other nuclear physicist would be able to recognize his colleague by what was said! And vice versa.

We need to accept first the fact that "clearness" as such is not *always* a desired quality of communication. But, given that the receiver's understanding is often a prerequisite to achieving one's communicative purposes, we need to accept a second fact: that clearness is not a characteristic of messages alone, but of particular messages vis-à-vis particular receivers.

The term *comprehensibility* might therefore be a better tool for thinking about and talking about this important characteristic of message-receiver interaction. One advantage, suggested above, is that thinking in terms of the comprehensibility of messages might prevent us from assuming that clearness is a quality which inheres in the way messages are prepared, quite independent of the receiver, the conditions of its apprehension, etc. A letter or a speech or a memo might in some abstract sense be clear—but only to specific receivers or audiences, and then only under specific circumstances, etc. Only people can comprehend. The *comprehensibility* of a message thus implies the crucial question: comprehensible (i.e., "clear") *to whom?*

A second potential advantage of the term comprehensibility is that it permits us to take account of those purposive communication encounters in which the originator intends something other than simple informational synchronization of himself and the receiver(s). People often want to "convey" feelings or to get someone else to see some point which is not (or perhaps cannot be) a part of the "content" of the message. For example, people occasionally try to put some evidence of their attitudes or feelings into a message directed to another. These are often vague feelings which are not even clear to the originator. We often say, "Do you get me?" when we want someone else to get what we mean when we either can't or don't want to spell out clearly what we mean. Or, it may simply be impossible to spell out completely what we want to get across to another. Organization superiors frequently have occasion to communicate-by-indirection to their subordinates—and vice versa.[1]

Under these circumstances, we want the message to be *comprehensible* to the receiver, even though we cannot (or feel we should not) make our meaning totally "clear" to him.

A third potential advantage of the term comprehensibility is that it helps us to think in terms of *receiver* processes rather than in terms of the composition of messages. It is the former and not the latter which

---

[1] See, for example, P. B. Hammond, "The Functions of Indirection in Communication," in J. D. Thompson *et al.*, *Comparative Studies in Administration* (Pittsburgh: University of Pittsburgh Press, 1959); cf. D. Mechanic, "The Sources of Power of Lower Participants in Complex Organizations." *Administrative Science Quarterly*, 1962, 7, 349–64; and R. L. Simpson, "Vertical and Horizontal Communication in Formal Organizations." *Administrative Science Quarterly*, 1959, 4, 188–96.

determine the message the receiver "gets."[2] For example, we might expect a grammatical error or an awkward phrase to reduce the "clearness" of a message. But it may not reduce the comprehensibility of the message the reader "gets" at all. Not only might the receiver be perfectly unaware of the error, but it may have been particularly useful to his "getting the message."

At the same time, the source of a message, or the circumstances, could provide quite a different "set" within a receiver for interpreting a particular message. The receiver comprehends a message by taking-into-account considerably more than the sheer "content" of that message. Metacommunication is not always clear, but it is either taken-into-account, or not, by a receiver. The setting, the relationship, the circumstances—any aspect of a communication encounter which *could* be taken-into-account by a receiver in order to comprehend another's message plays a part in the message the receiver "gets." And these factors go far beyond the "clearness" of the originator's message. What makes the difference is what the receiver takes-into-account—whether that be such circumstances as time or place or past experiences or future expectations—in addition to what the originator is saying. These can all be components of the message the receiver "gets."

The critical factors in difficult communication situations are whether or not things add up to the receiver—not whether the originator's statement is clear. The receiver has certain expectations about how the various elements that he takes-into-account in forming usable messages about the world should "add up." These are based upon his present conceptions of his world—his normative realities, the way he understands and explains to himself certain happenings. If those elements that he takes-into-account don't jibe with his conceptions and expectations in some way, then that communication encounter is to that extent incomprehensible to him.

Thus a term like comprehensibility will perhaps serve us better than "clearness," particularly in assessing and coping with difficult communication objectives.

Finally, we need to recall that an originator who wants to affect some specific receiver(s) in some specific way can do nothing more than set up some potential event-data accessible to that receiver with the hope or the expectation that the receiver will take those event-data into account and create out of them a message for himself which is (as inferred from his response) adequate to the originator's intentions or purposes. Thus the

---

[2] For a further discussion of this distinction between the structure and function of messages, see L. Thayer, "Some Theoretical Approaches to Business Communication." *Journal of Business Communication*, 1963, 1, 15–21.

crucial factor is not the clearness of the originator's message but the receiver's comprehend-abilities.

COMPREHENSIBILITY AND AMBIGUITY

It is sometimes helpful to look upon the process of making sense of one's world—being communicated-with—as a process of *disambiguating* the complex patterns of raw event-data which impinge upon the body's senses. Einstein referred to the impact of the world's event-data upon us as "the rabble of our senses." We begin with a never-ending flow of sensory experiences of ourselves and our environments, and engage in a continuous process of *disambiguating* those raw sensory experiences—of "making sense" out of them.

From the point of view of the $A \rightarrow B = X$ model of purposive communication, there are three kinds of ambiguity which may adversely affect the message which the receiver creates out of the event-data of an originator's attempt to communicate-to him.

There is first and most obviously *ambiguity of meaning*. Assuming that the receiver is both able and susceptible to being communicated-to by the originator, he will try to create for himself a meaning satisfactory to himself. In the process of creating that message out of the event-data of a particular communication encounter, the receiver will be trying to understand what the originator means by what he is saying. The receiver asks himself: "What does the originator *mean* by what he is saying (writing, etc.)?" Depending upon how comprehensible the originator's message is *to that receiver*, the receiver can more or less successfully *disambiguate* the event-data provided by the originator. He shapes and structures it, and selectively attributes significance and/or meaning to it—according to the comprehend-abilities he has for doing so. To the extent the receiver cannot readily and efficiently disambiguate the originator's message—*in terms of what he interprets the originator meant by what he said*—the originator's message must remain ambiguous to him, and hence (to that extent) incomprehensible (to him).[3]

There is second the *ambiguity of intention*. In most communication

---

[3] It will perhaps be obvious to the reader at this point that a considerable part of our education and socialization is devoted to building into us fairly standardized comprehend-abilities. This accounts for the fact that certain standardized "recipes" for successful communication can indeed produce the predicted results in certain situations. The members of every culture, and of every subculture, have a number of comprehend-abilities in common. That is, they hold in common certain standardized conceptual structures for apprehending and comprehending messages, for attributing the proper or "correct" meaning and significance to others' attempts to communicate-to them. Thus

encounters, a vital part of the message that any receiver "gets" is his own answer to the question: "Why is this particular person saying this particular thing to me at this particular time in this particular way, etc.?" To the extent that the receiver cannot interpret (or disambiguate) the metacommunicative clues available to him, the originator's intentions will be ambiguous to him.

If the occasion doesn't jibe with the topic or the timing—in terms of the receiver's expectations about how such things *should* fit together communicatively—then the originator's intentions will likely seem ambiguous to that receiver. Or, if an originator's statements seem inconsistent with a particular receiver's expectations regarding what the originator could or should be saying, then, again, the originator's intentions will seem ambiguous to the receiver.

A third form of ambiguity is what might be called *ambiguity of consequence*. Part of what a receiver takes-into-account when making messages out of the originator's attempts to communicate-to him are his own expectations with regard to the *consequences* of comprehending the originator's message one way rather than another. A receiver may accurately perceive an originator's meaning *and* his intentions, but still feel some ambiguity about the *consequences* (especially for himself) of understanding or comprehending the originator's intentions in that particular way. Given his special comprehend-abilities, a receiver may not have sufficient evidence, or may have conflicting evidence, about the conse-

---

any standardized recipe for communicating-to others will—if accurately devised, and if directed toward properly equipped and "programmed" receivers—produce the results promised. Every subculture has its standardized recipes for communication. Using those recipes correctly is a "template" for successful communication. Thus certain recipes can work in certain situations.

A large proportion of Americans share a number of such standardized comprehend-abilities. To the extent one follows accurate "recipes" for communicating-to those who have the appropriate take-into-account-susceptibilities, he will be able to communicate-to them successfully. But it is not the recipes which "cause" the communication that occurs, but the fact that the recipes employed were based upon the standardized take-into-account-susceptibilities which the members of that particular culture or subculture hold in common. If one designs a lock, and then designs a key that will open that lock, he could not say that the key "caused" the lock to work any more than that the lock "caused" the key to work. (Cf. D. M. MacKay, "Communication and Meaning—A Functional Approach," in F. S. C. Northrop and Helen H. Livingston (eds.), *Cross-Cultural Understanding: Epistemology in Anthropology* [New York: Harper & Row, 1964].) If all of the locks in the world were standardized then one could quite easily determine a design for a key that would operate all of the locks equally well. In the same way, if all of our take-into-account-susceptibilities were completely standardized, then all intercommunication could be reduced to recipes. But they are not. So "recipes" for successful communication will not work beyond the lowest common denominator of the comprehend-abilities which the members of any audience hold in common.

quences of interpreting the originator's utterances in one way rather than another way. If so, he will be unable to disambiguate the situation—and the communication encounter will therefore be to that degree ambiguous to him.

The originator's communication competencies thus serve either to facilitate or to impede the receiver's efforts to disambiguate a communication encounter and create an appropriate message. If there remains any ambiguity for the receiver regarding the originator's utterances, intentions, or consequences, the message the receiver "gets" will be ambiguous and to that degree incomprehensible to him.[4]

In general, then, any attempt to communicate-to another is *comprehensible* only to the extent that the receiver has and can exercise the necessary and appropriate take-into-account-abilities.

Validity

A message may be comprehensible to a particular receiver, yet not affect him as intended by the originator. If an originator's message is not perceived as *valid* by the receiver, then its impact on him will be slight or insignificant, or even contrary to what was intended. A message must obviously be comprehended before it can be validated. But its comprehensibility does not insure its validity for a particular receiver in a particular situation.

There are at least three process of "validating" messages which a receiver might employ in a given situation.

There is first what might be termed *consonance* validation. The validity of any externally-originated message is lessened to the extent that there is lack of consonance between the originator's message and his behavior, the message and the occasion, situation, time and place, the channel, the medium, the manner, other related factors or events, etc. In other words, to the extent that all of the metacommunicative clues which a receiver

---

[4] It may have occurred to the reader that there are some interesting parallels between what is referred to here as the process of disambiguation and some current applications of information theory (and particularly uncertainty reduction) to human perception and cognition. But I would emphasize that uncertainty reduction is not sufficient to account for the total process of communication. Such intriguing analogies are pertinent, but only to certain aspects of being communicated-with. See, for examples, W. R. Reitman, *Cognition and Thought: An Information Processing Approach* (New York: John Wiley & Sons, Inc., 1965); E. B. Hunt, *Concept Learning: An Information Processing Problem* (New York: John Wiley & Sons, Inc., 1962); and W. R. Garner, *Uncertainty and Structure as Psychological Concepts* (New York: John Wiley & Sons, Inc., 1962). Cf. J. L. Owen, "The Effect of 'Uncertainty' on the Retention of Messages Presented in an Informative Speech." Unpublished doctoral dissertation, University of Denver, 1967.

takes-into-account are consonant with the originator's message (as compre-hended by the receiver)—to that extent the message can be validated. Or, a message may or may not be consonant with what an individual believes to be his responsibilities and obligations organizationally. Superiors can "consonantly" issue orders to subordinates under specified conditions understood by both, but the reverse is not true. The channel, then, is one source of validating the consonance of potential messages. In other words, what is perceived as legitimate is also perceived as consonant.

In sum, a message is valid only to the extent it is perceived as consonant with all of the other conditions and factors surrounding the encounter which the receiver takes-into-account.

There is second what could perhaps best be understood as *credibility* validation. That is, receivers come to weight or to judge the validity of certain kinds of messages emanating from certain sources in terms of their credibility.[5]

Media as well as sources come to be looked upon by receivers as having more (or less) credibility for certain kinds of messages. Comparative media studies have gained considerable momentum in recent years, both in mass communication and in organizational communication studies.[6] But it remains an area in which very little in the way of systematic knowledge has been built up.

What we can be sensitive to, however, is the fact that receivers can and do *validate* messages on the basis of their perceptions of the credibility of the source and/or the medium.

There is a third process of validating messages which serves to determine

---

[5] See, e.g., C. I. Hovland *et al.*, *Personality and Persuasibility*, and *Communication and Persuasion* (New Haven, Conn.: Yale University Press, 1953, 1959); cf. R. P. Abelson and D. E. Kanouse, "Subjective Acceptance of Verbal Generalizations," in *Cognitive Consistency* (New York: Academic Press, 1966).

[6] E.g., R. O. Nafziger and D. M. White, *Introduction to Mass Communications Research* (Baton Rouge: Louisiana State University Press, 1963); C. I. Hovland *et al.*, *Experiments on Mass Communication* (New York: John Wiley & Sons, Inc. [Science Editions], 1949); D. B. Judd and G. Wyszecki, *Color in Business, Science, and Industry.* 2nd ed. (New York: John Wiley & Sons, Inc., 1963); and M. McLuhan, *Understanding Media* (New York: McGraw-Hill Book Co., 1964). One should not overlook the relevance of the research being done on educational technology, or perti-nent sources such as the Purdue Communication Research Center or the Industrial Communications Council. Cf. also R. Newcomb and Marg Sammons, *Employee Communications in Action* (New York: Harper & Row, 1961); W. C. Redding and G. A. Sanborn, *Business and Industrial Communication: A Source Book* (New York: Harper & Row, 1964); the July, 1967, issue of *Communication Reports*; and the work of G. Patrick Meredith: e.g., "Where Oral, Where Visual," *Look and Listen* (English), February, 1950, and *Instruments of Communication* (London: Pergamon, 1967).

the message the receiver "gets." It is what could be called *congruity validation*. In addition to the consonance and credibility tests of externally-originated messages, a receiver will usually test a particular message against his own realities, values, beliefs, prejudices, attitudes, expectations, etc.[7] In doing so, he is testing an originator's message for its perceived congruity with his own psychological system and his own intentions and expectations.

In certain cases of critical incongruity a receiver may, of course, "refer" the originator's utterance to one or more of the sources of his own social reality—his peers, reference groups "endorsers," etc. A message may in fact be invalidated not by the receiver but by those to whom he "refers" it for validation.

In addition to these three validation processes, we must be aware of a further important fact. Although externally-originated messages cannot be valid unless they are at least minimally comprehensible, the validity of any message, as perceived by the receiver, will reflect back upon the comprehensibility of the message. This works both ways. If another's utterance is not totally comprehensible, but appears to have high validity for a receiver, he is likely to work harder at disambiguating the message—at making it more comprehensible to himself. On the other hand, a fully comprehensible message may later be miscomprehended (*disunderstood*) because on reflection it seemed to be seriously lacking in validity for that particular receiver.

Utility

A further characteristic or quality of messages is their *utility*. There may be those occasions when the validity of another's message is also its utility. But there are also those (more frequent) occasions when the utility of a message is determined separately from its validity. To comprehend and increase one's competencies in those occasions, the concept of utility can be useful.

Externally-originated messages are more (or less) "consumable." That is, they are more (or less) useful to the receiver's psychological system in carrying out its basic communication functions of establishing, maintaining, exploiting, or altering some state-relationship between the organism and its environment, or vice versa. For example, data which confirm our models of the world (particularly those aspects of our model that might

---

[7] E.g., M. Sherif and C. I. Hovland, *Social Judgment* (New Haven, Conn.: Yale University Press, 1961); and C. W. and M. Sherif, and R. E. Nebergall, *Attitude and Attitude Change* (Philadelphia: W. B. Saunders Co., 1965).

recently have been brought into question) not only seem valid but have considerable utility. At the same time, data which clearly contradict our beliefs, values, etc., not only seem invalid, but thereby have *disutility*. Data which can be consumed in the process of establishing intended- or desired-states-of-affairs, or which can be consumed in the process of identifying problems, of assessing apparent-states-of-affairs or the feedback from some action-in-the-environment, likewise have utility.

A person may have a low threshold for particular kinds of data as a consequence of some nonconscious appetite of the psychological system itself. He may, at the same time, be seeking certain data to resolve a particular problem concerning him at the moment. Should he then happen upon some data which might satisfy his system's "appetite," but which are irrelevant to his conscious information-acquisition efforts, that data could have both conscious utility and nonconscious disutility. Whether or not that message will be "consumed" would then depend upon the strength of any opposing needs or appetites.

Utility, then, is a measure of the relevance and the consume-ability of messages. The more relevant and useful another's message is to our central information-processing, to the maintenance and dynamics of our information-processing systems, to our needs and purposes, the more utility it has.

The *relevance* of messages is obviously a factor determining their utility. In terms of our needs, appetites, take-into-account-abilities and -susceptibilities, and our immediate expectations and intentions, the data that comes into our purview will have some relevance for us. Messages are also relevant to the extent that they are consume-able in the service of our roles, task-functions in organizations, psychological contracts with others, and so on.

Again, however, we should note an important point. An externally-originated message which is not comprehensible may therefore not be valid, and will therefore have little or no utility. But any message which is perceived as having potentially high utility may be retroactively "endowed" with more validity, and we might therefore make a considerable investment to disambiguate it—to increase its comprehensibility to us. Additionally, since a message may have *past* or *present* or *future* utility for a receiver, the fact that such qualities as utility inhere not in the message alone, but in the receiver-message interaction, is underscored.

It is difficult, but necessary, to conceptualize such processes as these which operate in both directions. The ultimate process of being communicated-with is not unidirectional. It operates in several directions simultaneously. What is comprehensible to us largely determines what we consume (or process). But we can't afford to overlook the fact that what has high potential utility or validity for us makes a difference to what is comprehensible to us.

Thus the originator's competencies do not lie in his being able to follow a recipe for successful communication. Rather, they begin with his ability to comprehend the *dynamic interdependence* between himself and a specific message and a specific receiver in a specific situation.

Hopefully the present chapter has provided some useful conceptual tools for comprehending this complex, multidimensional process.

SUGGESTIONS FOR FURTHER READING

The issues of message comprehensibility, validity, and utility are usually approached from the originator's point of view. Thus many useful readings relevant to this chapter will be found at the end of Chapters 15 and 18. But an intriguing array of insights with many far-reaching implications for receiver behavior could also be gained from the following references.

BENNETT, E. et al. (eds.).   *Military Information Systems.* New York: Frederick A. Praeger, Inc., 1964.

BROWN, R.   *Words and Things.* New York: Free Press, 1958.

BRUNER, J. S.   *Toward a Theory of Instruction.* Cambridge, Mass.: Harvard University Press, 1966.

GOLDMAN, A. S.   "Information Flow and Worker Productivity," *Management Science,* Vol. 5 (1959).

HUNT, E. B.; MARIN, J.; and STONE, P. J.   *Experiments in Induction.* New York: Academic Press Inc., 1966.

HARRAH, D.   "A Model for Applying Information and Utility Functions," *Philosophy of Science,* Vol. 30 (1963), pp. 267–73.

OGDEN, C. K., and RICHARDS, I. A.   *The Meaning of Meaning.* New York: Harcourt, Brace & World, 1945.

UPTON, A.   *Design for Thinking.*   Stanford, Calif.: Stanford University Press, 1961.

WERTHEIMER, M.   *Productive Thinking.* Enl. ed. New York: Harper & Row, 1959.

YOUNG, J. Z.   *Doubt and Certainty in Science.* New York: Oxford University Press, 1960.

ZIPF, G. K.   "Some Determinants of the Circulation of Information," *American Journal of Psychology,* Vol. 59 (1946), pp. 401–21.

12

Communication Systems: Efficacy

As SUGGESTED in an earlier chapter, it is advantageous to think of communication as being more (or less) *effective*, but to think of communication systems[1] in terms of *efficacy*. The communication that occurs as a consequence of the outputs of a communication system can be determined to be relatively more or less effective, given the originator's purpose. But the system itself should be thought of as being efficacious or not, given the relationship and the organization or enterprise it serves.

There's more at stake than just the words, as we shall see. Our purpose in this chapter will be to develop a concept of communication systems in terms of their efficacy—that is, as having or not having the kinds of qualities and characteristics that would enable and facilitate effective communication by their users.[2]

---

[1] Given the distinction made earlier between data and communication systems, the reader could rightfully assume that the characteristics by which data systems are evaluated may be different from those by which communication systems are to be evaluated. For this reason, we will focus our attention primarily upon communication systems. Some contrasts are presented later in this chapter.

[2] Throughout this chapter, when the reference is to multiperson organizations, the reader should understand that what is said applies equally to the operational, the regulatory, and the maintenance/development systems within the organization.

Basic Processes

Regardless of size or use, all communication systems are characterized by the same four basic processes:[3]

1. *Data acquisition.* Whether the system is limited to a single individual or links thousands together in some collective effort, data for its user(s) must be acquired or collected or educed in some way. Data must be brought into the system at certain points, with certain selectivities, and on some sort of planned or fortuitous schedule.

2. *Data transportation.* Once in the system, data must be transported, distributed, or routed to designated terminals, "sinks," or processing centers.

3. *Data processing.* Whether data or communication system, there are but two kinds of internal elements: processing centers or "nodes" where something is done to the data received, and the "links" over which the data are routed or distributed. The kinds of processing which might be carried out by these nodes or processing centers range from simple storage and reproduction to rearrangement, recombination, reduction, amplification and extrapolation, to mechanical analysis or synthesis and mechanical "decisioning,"[4] to packaging and rerouting.

4. *Data display.* Wherever data are routed throughout a communication (or data) system to some node or terminal or sink, those data must be displayed in some way. These displays are the system's basic output.

The question to be asked, therefore, if we want to evaluate communication systems, is this: How *efficacious* are *these* processes in any particular communication system, given the needs, intentions, organizational function, potential, capacities, etc., of the user(s) of that system? It might be useful to take a closer look at how one might pursue such an evaluation.

---

[3] Cf. J. G. Miller, "The Individual as an Information Processing System," in W. S. Fields and Abbott (eds.), *Information Storage and Neural Control* (Springfield, Ill.: Charles C. Thomas, 1963).

[4] We have all sorts of devices which mechanically or electronically perform "analytic" or "decisioning" operations on data. For example, a simple bathroom scale could be said to "decide" how much we weigh by the process of translating pressure into an instrument reading. In a similar way, computers could be said to make "decisions" through the mechanistic processes they are designed and programmed to carry out in translating or converting one set or pattern of data into another set or pattern of data—all according to the man-made scheme by which the data input and data output are to be related.

Acquisition

Are the data wanted or needed (in the larger sense of the consequences for the individual or the organization) being "imported"—that is, being acquired and brought into the system?[5]

Conversely, are irrelevant data *not* being imported—that is, being selected out at the point of acquisition (or elsewhere in the system)? Are the acquisition schedules, orders of priority, etc., such that the wants and the needs of individual users and the larger organization (vis-à-vis its environment) are being efficaciously met? Are the quantity and the quality of the data acquired efficacious for the system and its users, given whatever criteria of sufficiency and utility might be applied?

Transportation/Distribution

The fact that data are transported, transmitted, distributed, diffused, etc., within a communication system implies (a) that a structure pre-exists, or (b) that a structure is being created in the process. About this structure (i.e., channels and interconnected sets of channels), and about the patterns of distribution of data through that structure, we can ask a further set of questions:

Do those who want or need data available somewhere in the system receive those data when wanted or needed? Conversely, are data *not* distributed to those who do not want or need those data?

Are the data required in the performance of all of the organization's task-functions available when required? In the quantity and of the quality required?

Are the transportation/distribution processes and patterns flexible enough to accommodate unusual requests for data, or unusual users? Are those processes quickly responsive to changes, to crises, to special circumstances—at no sacrifice of reliability, fidelity, etc.?

Is the fidelity of dissemination adequate to the purposes and functions being served? Is there the kind of stability and validity that permits an efficacious, evolving *symbiosis* with users?

---

[5] The questions raised in this and the following subsections are meant to be only suggestive of the sorts of questions that might be asked in determining the efficacy of these four processes. I would not want to imply that these few parameters are in any way definitive.

Are the transportation/distribution processes reliable? Even under great time or load pressures?

Is there the sort of noise or "impedance" which would block the movement of irrelevant or unusable data to the various terminals and users of the system—at least under normal circumstances? Conversely, is there the sort of discrimination in the system that reliably identifies currently needed data and speeds it through without delay? Are there priorities which realistically and dependably accommodate most exigencies?

PROCESSING

Every element in every communication system which receives and ingests data, whether a cell, an individual, a computer, a department, or a giant government or industrial enterprise, processes the "consumable" data it receives in some way. Whether that processing takes the form of storage, redistribution (with or without reproduction, amplification, or reduction), analysis, synthesis, or "decisioning," it can be thought of functionally as of the same order—as "doing something to" or "processing" the received data in some way.

When a communication system involves more than one individual, determining the efficacy of the data processing which goes on within it requires a different order of questioning. Not only must we ask about the efficacy of the basic processes; we must ask about the composite processing efficacy of the total system. An individual can determine the efficacy of his own communication system. But in a large formal organization, the efficacy of the composite of all of the processing which goes on within it is an extremely complex and difficult measure to come by. It is nonetheless a most important one.

With this order-of-magnitude difficulty in mind, we can pose some of the questions which could help reveal the efficacy of a communication system's processing function:

Are the processing elements designed, equipped, and programmed in such a way that they can and do induce from the system those data which they need to fulfill their task-functions? For example, are individual members of an organization structured and oriented in such a way that they can and do induce from the system the data they need to perform their task-functions in a superior manner? How effective are the system's processors? How efficient?

Do the processors have the scope and the kinds of capacities which they need in order to make their full contribution to the system? How timely are the functions which they perform?

How reliably do they perform? How adaptable are they to changing conditions—to the absence of needed data, to inadequate or unreliable data, etc.?

How adequate are the system's processors to their function in the system?

DISPLAY/PRESENTATION

The output of the processing elements or nodes of a communication system must be in some form and pattern and sequence. Additionally, each of these processing elements or nodes is designed, structured, and programmed or equipped to acquire and process data only in certain forms, patterns, and sequences.

Thus determining the efficacy of display or presentation of data in a communication system can be approached from either direction—generation-dissemination or acquisition-consumption.[6] Obviously, however, data which are not generated within the system or imported from outside the system cannot be consumed. And if the form or pattern of presentation of data is not one which is acquire-able or consume-able by the receiving element, no further evaluation need be conducted.

But if these two basic conditions have been minimally satisfied, we can begin to ask questions that will lead us to an assessment of the efficacy of the system's data-presentation/display.

For example, we can ask, as indicated above, how acquire-able or consume-able the system's various outputs are with respect to their timeliness, form, pattern, sequence, etc. For what a given manager needs to know at a given moment, for example, a brief oral summary may be considerably more expedient than a comprehensive written report. A graph may be a much more meaningful way of presenting data about the relationship of two interacting conditions than any other form in which the data might be presented. On the other hand, the sheer volume of consume-able data imported or generated within the system may create a condition of overload.[7] And so on.

---

[6] Cf. J. D. Baker, "From the Diet of Worms to the Bucket of Worms: A Protest Concerning Existing Display Dogma for Information Systems," in J. Spiegel and D. E. Walker, *Information System Sciences: Proceedings of the Second Congress* (Washington D.C.: Spartan Books, Inc., 1965); and F. Muckler and R. Obermayer, "Information Display," *International Science and Technology*, 1965 (Aug.) 44, 34–40.

[7] Cf. J. G. Miller, "Information Input Overload," in M. C. Yovits et al. (eds.), *Self-Organizing Systems—1962* (Washington D.C.: Spartan Books, Inc., 1962); and R. L. Meier, "Information Input Overload: Features of Growth in Communications-Oriented Institutions," *Libri*, 1963, 13, 1–44.

We can ask not only how adequate the system's data presentation/display may be in a general sense, but in addition how adaptable these processes are to the idiosyncrasies of individual users. Or, how available are the same data in *different* forms, sequences, patterns, etc., according to the needs or requests of individual users? When two people are engaged in a dialogue, for example, they are communicatively linked to each other in a "synergistic" way—suggesting that each could and would "package" his statements and questions in the form or manner needed or requested by the other. This is the sort of presentation adaptability or flexibility that could be taken as a major determinant of this component of a communication system's overall efficacy.

These few illustrations and examples do not by any means exhaust the possibilities of describing the parameters of communication systems. But they will serve our immediate purposes.

Some Further Dimensions of System Efficacy

Various attempts have been made to establish a definitive set of characteristics or dimensions common to all systems.[8] What follows is not intended to be definitive or even competitive with other statements about the characteristics of systems.

Rather, it is intended only to add some further conceptual dimensions to the framework outlined in this and previous chapters. The focus is exclusively upon *communication* systems and how they might be better understood and perhaps therefore more efficaciously designed.

Adequacy

Implicit in much of the preceding discussion is the general question of the *adequacy* of the system *qua* system. That is, how adequate is the system to its tasks—given the goals, the constraints, the environmental adversities, the opportunities, etc., that do (or might otherwise) exist?

As discussed in the chapter on communication effectiveness, there are both short- and long-range considerations. What is adequate for the short-range may prove to reduce the adequacy of the system over the long range.

What is adequate in one set of circumstances may not be adequate in

---

[8] See, e.g., the annual *Yearbook* of the Society for General Systems Research, published by the Society since 1955 (Vol. I).

another. Conditions both within and without organizations (and individuals) are constantly changing, continuously evolving. If the communication system serving that organization (or individual) is not likewise continuously evolving its own adequacy vis-á-vis those changing conditions, goals, etc., it may and often does become inadequate by default.

Inevitable factors are time and place. If those persons or elements who want and/or need given data in consume-able forms do not get it at the right time[9] and the right place in a useful form, the system is to that extent inadequate to its task.

ADAPTABILITY

To be fully adaptable, a communication system must not only accommodate the *generic* requirements of the task-functions or positions it must serve, but the *idiosyncratic* requirements of the particular users of the system. For example, two persons engaged in a conversation need not only observe the general requirements for intercommunication in their particular culture, but the *particular* demands and requirements of the other participant. Or, at the level of a formal organization, not only must the communication system subserving that organization satisfy the task-function requirements of the members of that organization, but—to be fully adaptable—it must be capable of at least minimally satisfying the idiosyncratic needs and requirements of the individuals who are staffing those positions.

To be efficacious, the linking channels of any communication system must also exhibit "variable impedances"—that is, the capacity to variously impede or facilitate the passage of data according to its priority, its consume-ability, its relevance, its timeliness, etc. In closed systems, data demands and reactions are either totally predictable or are simply designed in. But an open system—whether a single human or a formal organization—presents a different order of challenge. Crises, hazards, opportunities, and multiple interactions and interdependencies of all sorts give rise to conditions requiring the continuous adaptation, flexibility, evolution, and resiliency of their communication systems.

Probably the optimum system adaptability is a consequence, once

---

[9] However, we should note that "real-time" systems are not by any means the whole answer to the issues of time and place adequacy. Data received too soon, or received at various points in an arbitrary or an inappropriate sequence, can be detrimental to an organization's functioning. Speed and *timeliness* are different criteria. It is *timeliness* which makes a difference in system adequacy, not mere *speed*.

system adequacy is achieved and maintained, of the degree of symbiosis[10] which evolves between each element or member or user in the system, and the input-output subsystems which serve those individual elements or members. At least some part of that evolved symbiosis must be compensatory. Both the system and the user have peculiar strengths and peculiar weaknesses.[11] To the extent that the strengths and the weaknesses of the user and his system are adaptively *compensated for* in some way by the other, the resulting symbiotic relationships will enhance the efficacy of the system. To the extent they are not symbiotic and do not adaptively compensate for mutual strengths and weaknesses, the total system is less efficacious.

RELIABILITY

Perhaps, like adequacy and adaptability, the dimension of *reliability* is fully implied in the preceding discussion. But, to the extent it is not, it should be brought forward as a major factor in system efficacy.

A reliable system is one which can be and is fully relied upon under all conditions by its users. If we see members of an organization by-passing the established channels of communication to get or give task- or self-maintenance-related data, we have some evidence that the communication system serving them is not adequate, not sufficiently adaptable, or not *reliable*.

Reliability lends a quality to the atmosphere of the system in much the same way that credibility and dependability contribute to the qualities of particular communication encounters. An unreliable system becomes generally less relied-upon in the same way that people give less and less notice to what is for them a fallible or questionable source of information.

---

[10] See e.g., J. C. R. Licklider, "Man-Computer Symbiosis," *IRE Transactions on Human Factors in Electronics*, HFE–1, 1960, 4–11; and Ruth M. Davis, "Man-Machine Communication," in C. A. Cuadra (ed.), *Annual Review of Information Science and Technology* (New York: Interscience Publishers, Inc., 1966).

[11] Cf. D. T. Campbell, "Systematic Error on the Part of Human Links in Communication Systems," *Information and Control*, 1958, 1, 334–69; M. Glanzer and R. Glaser, "Techniques for the Study of Group Structure and Behavior: II. Empirical Studies of the Effects of Structure in Small Groups," *Psychological Bulletin*, 1961, 58, 1–27; A. M. Cohen, "A Model of Group Adaptation to Organizational Change in Communication Networks," in L. Thayer (ed.), *Communication: Theory and Research* (Springfield, Ill.: Charles C Thomas, 1967); C. P. Bonini, *Simulation of Information and Decision Systems in the Firm* (Englewood Cliffs, N.J.: Prentice-Hall, Inc., 1963); and H. C. Triandis, "Notes on the Design of Organizations," in J. D. Thompson (ed.), *Approaches to Organizational Design* (Pittsburgh: University of Pittsburgh Press, 1966).

A reliable system is one that can be relied upon to supply relevant and timely data of the appropriate quantity and quality, when or where needed in the system. Conversely, a reliable system is one that can be relied upon to protect consumers or processors from irrelevant or untimely data, or from data of an inappropriate quantity or quality.

Compatibility

As the rapidly advancing technology of "information systems" is increasingly deployed in the future, the issue of *compatibility* will likely gain in importance. Whether intraorganizational or interorganizational,[12] the efficacy of any communication system or subsystem may depend upon its compatibility with other systems to which it becomes linked.

There are analogies across levels of analysis. For example, bringing the language of the user and the language of a computer into compatibility with each other is a necessary condition of the efficacy of that particular man-machine relationship. Interpersonally, no matter how crucial a message to the receiver, it isn't going to be acquired and consumed by him unless he is equipped physiologically, linguistically, conceptually, and technologically to acquire and consume it. (The reader can perhaps think of myriads of examples: if a person we are calling by telephone doesn't have a telephone receiver which is compatible with the transmitter we are using, he won't be able technologically to receive our message, and hence certainly will not consume it. And so on and on.)

If two organizations want to link one's purchasing function into the other's supply function through their respective automated equipment, that equipment and its associated languages will have to be compatible.

If for any other reason the output of one organization or organism is not compatible with the input mechanisms of another organization or organism, that lack of compatibility will likely preclude their interaction.

If one man is blind and another one deaf, they are going to have to agree upon some common—and mutually compatible—means of communicating-with each other. If I speak English but you know only French, that part of our system is incompatible.

And so on, over the whole range of analogic illustrations at the various levels of analysis. But perhaps these few will suffice to suggest the importance of compatibility to system and inter-system efficacy.

---

12 For a discussion of some nontechnological factors, see H. Guetzkow, "Relations Among Organizations," in R. V. Bowers (ed.), *Studies on Behavior in Organizations*. Athens: University of Georgia Press, 1966.

Viability and Efficacy

A biological term used with increasing frequency to suggest the relative health and grow-ability of a living system at some point in time is *viability*. It is usually intended to connote something like "capable of surviving," but is often intended to include such conditions as the organization's or the organism's creativity or innovativity, its ultrastability—i.e., its ability to maintain an advantageous state-relationship with its environment despite continuous internal and external changes—its abilities to achieve its goals, its flexibility and resiliency, and so forth.

So it may be an appropriate note on which to conclude this chapter to suggest that the efficacy of an organization's communication system is an ultimate determinant of that organization's viability—whether that organization is a single individual or a large corporation.

SUGGESTIONS FOR FURTHER READING

Most of the accumulated literature on communication deals with the messages or the people involved in single communication encounters. Although there is a rapidly growing body of literature addressed to data systems, there is as yet surprisingly little which is addressed to communication systems. While not many of the following documents were written from the point of view of communication systems as such, each has a particular and a unique contribution to make to our formative thinking about communication systems.

BARNLUND, D. C., and HARLAND, C. "Propinquity and Prestige as Determinants of Communication Networks," *Sociometry*, Vol. 26 (1963), pp. 467–79.

BEER, S. *Decision and Control*. New York: John Wiley & Sons, Inc., 1966.

BENNETT, E. et al. (eds.). *Military Information Systems*. New York: Frederick A. Praeger, Inc., 1964.

BOGUSLAW, R. *The New Utopians: A Study of System Design and Social Change*. Englewood Cliffs, N.J.: Prentice-Hall, Inc., 1965.

BONINI, C. P. *Simulation of Information and Decision Systems in the Firm*. Englewood Cliffs, N.J.: Prentice-Hall, Inc., 1963.

CAMPBELL, D. T. "Systematic Error on the Part of Human Links in Communication Systems," *Information & Control*, Vol. 1 (1958), pp. 334–69.

CAREY, J. W. "Communication Systems and Social Systems: Two Economic Postulates Applied to a Theory of Communication Systems." Unpublished doctoral dissertation, University of Illinois, 1963.

DEARDEN, J., and McFARLAN, F. W. *Management Information Systems.* Homewood, Ill.: Richard D. Irwin, Inc., 1966.

DEUTSCH, KARL W. "Communication in Self-Governing Organizations," in LYMAN BRYSON et al. (eds.), *Freedom and Authority in Our Time.* New York: Harper & Bros., 1953.

————. *The Nerves of Government: Models of Political Communication and Control.* New York: Free Press, 1963.

EASTON, D. *A Systems Analysis of Political Life.* New York: John Wiley & Sons, Inc., 1965, esp. Ch. 8.

FORRESTER, JAY W. "A New Corporate Design," *Industrial Management Review,* Vol. 7 (1965), pp. 5–18.

GAGNÉ, R. M. *Psychological Principles in System Development.* New York: Holt, Rinehart & Winston, 1962.

HEISE, G. C., and MILLER, G. A. "Problem-Solving by Small Groups Using Various Communication Networks," *Journal of Abnormal and Social Psychology,* Vol. 46 (1951), pp. 327–35.

JOHNSON, R. A.; KAST, F. E.; and ROSENZWEIG, J. E. *The Theory and Management of Systems.* New York: McGraw-Hill Book Co., 1963.

JONES, W. M. *On Decision Making in Large Organizations.* Memorandum RM–3968–PR. Santa Monica: The RAND Corp., 1964.

KLEMMER, E. T. "Communication and Human Performance," *Human Factors,* Vol. 4 (1962), pp. 75–79.

LASSWELL, H. D. "The Structure and Function of Communication in Society," in LYMAN BRYSON (ed.), *The Communication of Ideas.* New York: Harper & Bros., 1948, pp. 37–51.

LEAVITT, H. J. "Some Effects of Certain Communication Patterns on Group Performance," *Journal of Abnormal and Social Psychology,* Vol. 46 (1951), pp.38–50.

LICKLIDER, J. C. R. "The System System," Ch. 39 in E. BENNETT, J. DEGAN, and J. SPIEGEL (eds.), *Human Factors in Technology.* New York: McGraw-Hill Book Co., 1963.

McNULTY, J. E., JR. "Information, Human Behavior, and Organization Structure in Business," in G. FISK (ed.), *The Frontiers of Management Psychology.* New York: Harper & Row, 1964.

MESAROVIC, M. D. "Multi-Level Systems and Information Problems." Mitre Corp., 1st Congress on the Information Sciences, Nov., 1962.

Rome, S., and Rome, B.   Communication and Large Organizations. SP–1690. Santa Monica: System Development Corp., 1964.

Rothstein, J.   Entropy Concepts for Complex Systems. Boston: Laboratory for Electronics, 1966.

———.   Communication, Organization, and Science. Indian Hills, Colo.: Falcon's Wing Press, 1958.

Smith, C., and Brown, M. A.   "Communication Structure and Control Structure in a Voluntary Association," Sociometry, Vol. 27 (1964), pp. 449–68.

Stahl, N.   "Information Networking," Mechanical Engineering, Vol. 86 (1964), pp. 34–37.

Thayer, L.   "Communication and Organization," in F. E. X. Dance (ed.), Human Communication Theory. New York: Holt, Rinehart & Winston, 1967.

Toda, M., and Shuford, E. H., Jr.   Logic of Systems: Introduction to the Formal Theory of Structure. Tech. Doc. Rep. No. ESD–TDR–64–193. Bedford, Mass.: Decision Sciences Lab., AF Systems Command, L. G. Hanscom Field, U.S.A.F., 1964.

Walker, C. C.   A Study of a Family of Complex Systems: An Approach to the Investigation of Organisms' Behavior. Tech. Rep. No. 5. Electrical Engineering Research Laboratory, University of Illinois, 1965.

Walton, E.   A Magnetic Theory of Organizational Communication. China Lake, Calif.: U.S. Naval Ordinance Test Station, Jan. 1962.

Watt, Kenneth E. F. (ed.).   Systems Analysis in Ecology. New York: Academic Press, Inc., 1966.

PART III

The Functions of
Communication

13

The Information Function

IN CHAPTER 4, we examined the *basic functions* of instrumental communication—those of adapting oneself to the environment in some way, and/or of adapting the environment to oneself in some way. Quite obviously, the basic element of both functions is *information*. We must have some information about something going on in our environments to concern ourselves about it. And we must have some information about ourselves, our intentions, goals, etc., in order to have something to be concerned about. So *the getting or giving of information thus underlies all communication encounters*—either directly or indirectly.

But, because there are other applied functions of instrumental communication[1]—instructive and command functions, influence and persuasive functions, and integrative functions—it will be helpful to think of the informative function of communication as one of four applied functions. Certainly communication is not going to occur unless *someone* is acquiring and consuming *some* information about himself or his environment. So information is basic to all of the other applied functions of communication. But in human organizations we often want, or need, to inform someone else, either because there is some rule which requires that we do so, or because we see some problem or opportunity which we believe (on-behalf-of the organization) he should know about. Similarly, we personally often need, or want, to be informed of something, either because we anticipate its relevance for our own tasks or as having some usefulness for

---

[1] There are, of course, a number of other functions of noninstrumental or consummatory communication. Those will not be considered here.

the regulation of the tasks of others which are subordinate to or interdependent with our own.

So, on a number of counts, the *information function* of communication
deserves our further attention here.

Importance of the Information Function

Perhaps we need first to recall that living systems—people and organizations alike—can achieve some viability in their environments only to the
extent that they have some appropriate means of acquiring and processing
information about themselves and their environments. This information is
"used" as the basis for orientation to those environments and for determining behavior. Thus the ingestion of potentially informative data about the
internal conditions of oneself or one's organization, and about the conditions of one's environment, is a process as basic to living systems as the
ingestion of food and fuel for keeping energy resources up to necessary
levels.

In this respect, a man—or an organization—is like every other living
system. But the technology of *human* communication (including man's
symbol-handling capabilities) has greatly enhanced man's information-
generating capacities. It is our ability to affect each other communicatively
which has so greatly increased the importance of the information-giving
and -getting aspect of our existences. As a consequence, we can create on-
purpose organizations[2] of people variously committed to some common
endeavor. Because we have technologically sophisticated ways of affecting
each other communicatively (which plants do not have, and which animals
have only at the most elementary and crude levels), we can establish complex human organizations designed with our own ends in mind.

It is particularly the existence of such on-purpose organizations which
gives rise to the importance of information giving and getting as an applied
function, although information is basic to all of our intra- and interpersonal processes as well. No organization can exist without internal and
internal/external communication. No organization can fulfill its purpose or
its charter except to the extent that its communication processes further its
movement toward its specified goals in some way.[3] And because any living

---

[2] On-purpose, contrasted with one that simply *evolves*, or one whose sheer existence
is its only apparent purpose.

[3] An *evolved* organization might be looked upon somewhat differently. We would
assume that a "naturally" evolving organism (such as American society, for example)
would "naturally" seek out and ingest the information it "needed" to survive and to

system and its environment co-determine each other to a greater or lesser degree, the intentional "giving" of information (of communicating-to within organizations, and between and among organizations and their various external constituencies) is as vital to their existence as the intentional "getting" of relevant or needed information.

On the Nature of Information

There is apparently something irresistible about "Information Theory" for some psychologists and students of human communication. But Shannon[4] specifically disavowed any pertinence of his mathematical communication theory (and Wiener of Information Theory) for human communication. The notion that what is informative is what reduces "uncertainty" has nonetheless captured the imagination of many current writers in communication and related fields.

But getting involved in a discussion of the issues involved would take us too far afield here. Without attempting in any way to resolve those issues, a somewhat less sophisticated notion of when messages are informative will serve us quite well.

Everything is potentially informative. Whatever an individual could take into account—in attempting to make his experiences of what is going on meaningful to himself—is potentially informative to him. But if we restrict our attention to those messages that are intended by a specific originator to be informative to a specific receiver, then we can say that those messages are informative which

a) Are physically within the receiver's purview.
b) Are comprehensible to that receiver.
c) Can be validated by that receiver; and
d) Have some utility for that receiver.

Even the information we seek is "informative" only if those conditions are met to some necessary degree. If one is looking through his files for a certain report, that report itself is not informative, even though it exists

---

continue to evolve. As soon as we begin to manipulate its purposes or goals or structures or communication processes, however, it ceases to be a "natural" organization. This is not to say that the structures of formal or contrived organizations do not evolve. They do. But, theoretically, at least, they are "evolved" in an imposed direction. This distinction could make considerable difference in the way we establish and assess the internal and internal/external information functions of an organization.

[4] C. E. Shannon & W. Weaver, *The Mathematical Theory of Communication* (Urbana: University of Illinois Press, 1949).

somewhere. Yet the fact that it cannot be located where it was supposed to be *is* informative, for that bit of data fits all four of the conditions listed above.

The message which an originator transmits to another may have some particular informational value to the *originator*. But the crucial factor is the informational value that same message has for the *receiver*.[5] Any message is informative only to the extent that the four preceding conditions are met. (It follows, therefore, that any message can be more [or less] informative—that "informativeness" is not an all-or-none situation.)

Individual and Organizational Information

If organizations evolve "naturally," their communication systems evolve with them, consistent with their needs, whatever those may be. But when organizations are contrived or created on-purpose, then some rational attempts must necessarily be made to design into them those communication and data transportation systems deemed *by someone* to be advantageous and appropriate for that organization. As individuals, we concern ourselves very little with the internal data transportation and biological communication which occurs within us, and which keeps us alive and viable as organisms. But there are no more important concerns for the managers of formal organizations than those relating to the design and operation of the organization's communication systems—internal and external. But, like individuals, managers often don't concern themselves with their organization's communication systems until something appears to be "going wrong." Even then, his concern is more likely to be with data transportation than with communication systems.

It is necessary that data be transported, of course, so that it falls within the intended receiver's purview. Reports are *sent* to certain people simply because they could not be communicated-to by those reports if the reports were not physically available in some form to those intended receivers. But exposure to a message is only one condition of informativeness.

As we have seen, informativeness is a function of the receiver as well as of the message. The receiver's taking-into-account is indispensable. Hence

---

[5] The reader will recall that data which are irrelevant or which have some specific disutility for a receiver will thereby be to some degree incomprehensible to him, even though he understands all of the words used, etc. Cf. E. Cooper & M. Jahoda, "The Evasion of Propaganda: How Prejudiced People Respond to Anti-Prejudice Propaganda," *Journal of Psychology*, 1947, 23, 15–25. The results of this particular study are probably generalizable to a good many organizational situations. People who come into contact with statements which do not fit their own basic beliefs will probably evade the issue by *disunderstanding* the originator's message, or his intentions.

whatever is informative within an organization must be informative to some *individual* in that organization.

Again, data are not necessarily informative. Task-related messages which are transported from place to place within an organization are informative only to the extent the four conditions of informativeness described above are satisfied.

Information and Information Systems

We attempt to design and establish, on-behalf-of the organization, those data generation-dissemination, and acquisition-consumption systems which will insure that communication occurs which is needed to keep the organization running and viable. But, if perhaps it should be emphasized again: "information" systems do not carry *information*, they transport, process, distribute, etc., *data*.

The potential effectiveness of an organization cannot be determined by looking only at its data systems. Every organization has needs for certain information at a certain time in a certain form at a certain place. But the process of getting the data there at the right time in the right form is at least three-stage: first, we must be clever enough to design a data system which will either generate or acquire the needed data in a timely way; second, we must be ingenious enough to bring into that system those persons and/or equipment which will properly filter, organize, and present that data in a form which is potentially informative to those to whom it is to be addressed; and third, the recipient of that data must have the kind of take-into-account-abilities and -susceptibilities which would enable him to acquire and consume the data thus made available to him.

We can see from this that the issues at stake in organizational communication are essentially the same as those at stake in any purposive human encounter. The complex and often intricate geography of the communication channels, and the sophistication of our communication technology, should not obscure the fact that if we want a message to be informative to the intended receiver(s), we must therefore communicate-to him effectively. The intervening space, time, and equipment does not change the *basic* phenomenon of communication within organizations— that of some receiver taking-something-into-account.

Needs for and Uses of Information

Outside of the differences which stem from communicating on-behalf-of some organization (as contrasted with communicating on-behalf-of oneself), the basic needs for and uses of information within organizations are the same as those which occur outside of organizations. But it would perhaps be appropriate here to describe these needs and uses in the form they take within the organizations.

First, information is necessary to every manager as a basis for determining goals and objectives, and for detecting and defining problem areas. A well-designed operational data system will provide for the latter need, and a well-designed regulatory and maintenance system will provide the data he needs for determining or adjusting goals and objectives. If we follow the previously suggested procedure of working backward from consumer to source, then we could establish the sources and the channels through which these data should normally be transported. Further, if we fit the data supply system to the man, rather than vice versa, then we could determine the necessary processing, the timing, the form and quantity, etc., in such a way as to establish an effective and efficient symbiosis between a particular manager and the particular data system designed to serve his needs.

Second, information is necessary to the manager for the purpose of assessing performance—both individual and collective. Data for these purposes will be supplied by well-designed operational and maintenance data systems.

Third, those members of an organization whose tasks are functionally interdependent need information:

a) Which will permit them to make on-the-spot coordinative adjustments; and

b) Which would specify the limits to which those members are privileged to exercise their own judgments in determining and carrying out their assigned task functions.

The data which might permit members of an organization to make such adjustments and judgments are often not available to them (even though their needs indicate that they should be linked to each other's operational data systems in some appropriate way). Organizations would typically gain in both effectiveness and efficiency when data of both types are available to those who need that data—when they need it.

Fourth, every member of an organization needs information about what is expected of him in the way of performance and product, about who has surveillance over him and what the evaluative criteria are, about his own output and various means of assessing it, about what his obligations and privileges are with regard to exercising his own judgment in carrying out his assigned tasks, about what the consequences of varying levels of output and quality of performance may be, and so on. Every member of an organization should logically be one of the recipients of data about his own performance and operations. The other information he needs should be available to him through the established channels of well-designed regulatory and maintenance data systems.

Every need and use for information by the members of organizations could not be anticipated in advance. Thus the effectiveness and the efficiency with which members inform one another depends upon the versatility of the communication channels that are normally employed in the getting and giving of information by the members involved. For example, if the communication channel linking a supervisor and a particular worker has never been used for anything but orders transmitted from the superior to the subordinate, there is little likelihood that the subordinate will use that channel to inform his superior of some ideas that have occurred to him for improving productivity, reducing costs, etc. Unless the channels which link management to labor, as another example, have in the past been used for "levelling" with employees about the company's conditions, what is expected of them, etc., it will be very difficult, if not impossible, to inform them of such things via those channels. Employees may talk freely with fellow-workers about those same topics, however, if the communication channels which link them to their fellow-workers have been established and function for such purposes.

Thus we can design a set of rational data systems which link task-functions within an organization, but the members of the organization thus linked are going to be informed within those systems according to their needs and their actual consumption of the data available—not according to the speed or the quantity of the data made available to them. If anything, the problems of management-employee communication may be increasing as a result of the advent and spread of high speed information systems throughout modern organizations.

The Concept of "Eduction"

People exhibit differences in their abilities to acquire and consume the information they need or want. To refer to these differences, the term *eduction*—in the sense of drawing out, drawing forth, eliciting, abstracting, etc.—can be quite useful.

For example, people vary with respect to their abilities to "retrieve" even from themselves the data they have a need for at any given moment.[6] Second, people vary with respect to their abilities to "mine" effectively the existing sources of of information in libraries, reference documents, etc. Third, people vary with respect to their abilities to *educe* useful information from other people and the environment, their abilities to question and to observe and to listen effectively. Finally, people vary with respect to their ability to *deduce* from their observations what is pertinent and what is not, what is significant and what is not.

Thus, whether the focus is upon the manager himself or upon the organization as a whole, the organization's communication systems can be no more effective or efficient than the eductive and deductive capabilities of those it serves. People are more—or less—*informable*. Even if all of the data needed to make a perfect decision were available, the efficacy of the decision would still hinge upon the abilities of the individual involved to educe information from the data available to him, and to deduce its import advantageously.

So, while we often think of our difficulties as inhering in the problems of communicating-to others, there are inevitably those barriers we present to others in the form of our unique "*un-inform-abilities.*" From an organizational point of view, one member's take-into-account-abilities (and concomitant inabilities) are not, as such, either more or less detrimental to the overall functioning of the organization than another's. For example, a manager's superior position often provides him with some artificial immunity from being effectively and/or efficiently *informable* by his own subordinates, a fact for which many organizations have suffered detrimental consequences.

The ability to *educe* information and to deduce its import is, then, as important as the ability to communicate-to others informatively.

Intentional and Unintentional Information

It is helpful to recognize and keep in mind the distinction between intentional and unintentional communication. Usually, when we speak of informative communication, we are referring to *intentional* communication; that is, we are referring to the consequences or reactions *intended* or sought by the originator. But the receiver may not distinguish (it may not

---

[6] For a further discussion of this particular process, see D. W. Taylor, "Toward an Information-Processing Theory of Motivation," in *Nebraska Symposium on Motivation* (Lincoln: University of Nebraska Press, 1960).

even be possible for him to do so) between what the originator intended and how he (the receiver) actually comprehends the originator's message.

All information which is not intended by some originator to be consumed by some intended receiver(s) we may refer to as *unintentional information*. The significance of this particular distinction is simply this: *The originator of a message may think and behave on the basis of his intentions regarding his utterances. The receiver is never so restricted. The receiver may think and behave on the basis of any data he takes-into-account, intended or not.*

Some Further Obstacles to Informative Communication

In the preceding pages and in the preceding chapters, we have frequently touched upon the most fundamental and most pervasive "barrier" to communication—the fact that the meaning, the significance, the utility of any and all data available to any receiver are a function both of the receiver *and* of the message. If one looks upon this condition as a barrier, rather than as a simple *given* in all human communication, then of course we must look upon this particular obstacle as basic to ever other obstacle to communication we might conceive of—whether in or out of formal organizations. But for the purposes of expanding the implications of the issue at stake, we could specify five additional types of barriers to the effective communication of information in organizations:[7]

a) Organizational.
b) Interpersonal.
c) Individual.
d) Economic, geographic, and temporal.
e) Channel and media.

Let us briefly examine each of these in turn.

ORGANIZATIONAL BARRIERS

The structure and conventional procedures of the organization itself may be the source of significant barriers to the effective or efficient dissemination of information. These barriers may stem from one or more of four conditions:

---

[7] Insofar as other kinds of communication are also informative, the same "barriers" would of course apply.

1. The simple *physical distance* between members of an organization, both in terms of activity locus and organization structure, may present obstacles to intercommunication. Two people working side by side on a mutual task present a physical accessibility that may greatly facilitate information exchange. But if two department heads who can achieve their task-functions only with the cooperation of the other are inaccessible to one another, their intercommunication may be impeded. They might have to rely upon some indirect means of coordinating their activities. Thus proximity may facilitate, distance impede, informative and timely inter-communication—although it would be naïve to assume that such conditions as physical distance necessarily produce those effects.

2. The *specialization* of task-functions, fundamental to all organizations, has the effect of complicating and thus perplexing the exchange of information in organizations.

When one man performs task A and another man task B, they may have less to communicate about than if they were both performing task A—or they may have more. Being separated by their range of activities, they must communicate through channels. More emphasis may thus be put upon "formal" communication, and less upon "informal" communication, although misinterpretation and misunderstanding are likely to occur more frequently as one consequence of this increased reliance upon "formal" channels.

Task specialization is fundamental to organization. So some of the communication problems which arise are inevitable. The challenge is to create those communication systems which efficaciously compensate for the communicative obstacles inherent in task specialization.

3. *Power, authority, and status relationships* may impede the proper flow of information in an organization. The superior-subordinate relationship has a direct effect upon communication. Numerous studies can be interpreted to suggest that the subordinate tends to "filter out" of his "upward" communication to the boss that information which the boss "doesn't want to hear." At the same time, subordinates may "slant" information so it will seem "good news" to the boss. In this sense, as has been pointed out in *Fortune*, the managerial hierarchy is increasingly isolated.[8] Managers and executives operate in an informational environment provided largely by other people; they don't often (and probably shouldn't often) get the raw event-data. They get someone's *interpretation* of what is going on.

The manager or executive does some information filtering himself, both

---

[8] "Problem for the Front Office, *Fortune*, 1951, 43, pp. 78ff.

wittingly and unwittingly. Here's how one observer describes the loss of information in "downward" communication: "When the board of directors sends a message down through the levels of management, the vice presidents understand 67 percent of what is said. At the general supervisory level, 56 percent is understood; at the plant manager level, 40 percent is understood; at the foreman level, 30 percent; at the worker level, only 20 percent."[9] While this example is intended to reflect typically poor listening and transmitting techniques in organizational hierarchies, it serves to illustrate how the downward flow of information may be unwittingly distorted.

Supervisors are affected by their hierarchical relationships, too. For example, although the superior's organizational authority and status are institutionalized, he is not likely to communicate-to his subordinates the kind of information that might be interpreted as reflecting his incompetence or unimportance, a mistake, etc.

In addition, there are inevitably certain power relationships between and among people in organizations. These often result in various forms of information manipulation to the advantage of one or the other individual or group.

4. Closely related is another barrier which derives from the very nature of human organizations—that of information "ownership."[10] Whether "information ownership" becomes an obstacle probably depends upon the intensity of the aspirations of the persons involved, and upon their modes of achievement. As long as greater value is placed upon achievement via position rather than achievement via performance, it will appear to many people that the organization somehow sanctions the power that accrues to those who possess information needed by others.

Duplicating information sources among personnel assigned to the same general tasks, and *dissanctioning* such illicit power in an organization, are two methods of neutralizing information ownership.

INTERPERSONAL BARRIERS

While the barriers just discussed are in a sense also interpersonal barriers to communication, they arise from the nature and functions of the organization. There are additional barriers which arise from interpersonal

---

[9] R. G. Nichols, "Listening, What Price Inefficiency?" *Office Executive*, April, 1959. Cf. M. D. Feld, "Information and Authority," *American Sociological Review*, 1959, 24, 15–22.

[10] Cf. J. W. Forrester, "A New Corporate Design," *Industrial Management Review*, 1965, 7, 5–17, esp. p. 11ff.: "To possess information is to possess power."

contacts within the organization, but which are attributable to the people involved rather than to the organization as such.

1. The first of these we might refer to as the *climate* of the interpersonal contact or relationship. A good example of climate, in this context, might be this one: Imagine how the changing climate of the relationship between a male and a female facilitates or impedes certain kinds and modes of intercommunication, as they interact from the first possibly awkward meeting through courtship, marriage, raising a family, sickness or tragedy, and on into the fears or insecurities or joys of old age. The total complex of feelings and sentiments that obtains between them at any point in their relationship serves to limit or encourage what *can* be communicated between them, as well as the manner in which they attempt to communicate-to each other. This total complex of feelings and sentiments and orientations may be referred to as the *climate* of an interpersonal relationship.

In the context of organizational life, a supervisor may avoid seeming "bossy" on his first days as boss. Typically, long-term employees and new employees "warm up" to each other rather slowly, even though lasting friendships may ensue. The climate of every interpersonal relationship is constantly changing, and with it change the possibilities—the needs and the opportunities—for effective and efficient informative communication.

Climate depends largely upon actions and intentions, not upon words as such. A positive and advantageous relationship cannot be built out of words or from the principles of human relations. It derives ultimately from the treatment each has at the hands of the other, and from the way their behavior toward each other is interpreted and evaluated by each. The most facilitating climate comes from the most mutually advantageous intentions and actions.[11]

2. People obtain their *values* and *standards of conduct* from the norms of the groups to which they belong, or to which they aspire to be identified. So when the values of the receiver and of the originator conflict—i.e., when they identify themselves with sources of belief and value which are significantly different—exchange of information between them without distortion, misinterpretation, misunderstanding or disunderstanding, will be difficult, occasionally impossible.

3. Closely related is the barrier which may arise from the conflicting or antagonistic attitudes of the persons involved. A negative attitude toward the communicator, or toward the content of his message, will likely cause

[11] Cf. C. Argyris, "Interpersonal Barriers to Decision Making," *Harvard Business Review*, 1966, 44, 84–97.

the intended receiver to misunderstand, to disunderstand, or perhaps to ignore the originator's message. Even at the interpersonal level, there is evidence from research in mental health that one's attitude toward himself has a great deal to do with how accurately he is able to educe information and how competently he is able to transmit it.[12]

4. One other potential interpersonal barrier to communication to which little attention has been given is that of the *effect of mass communication* on our communicate-abilities. Since little unequivocal research has been done in this area,[13] we could at this point do little more than speculate on the ways in which our addictions to mass means of communication have affected our abilities to communicate-to and -with each other. But there is some justification for assuming that, as the mass media increase in coverage and influence, our ability to communicate successfully and effectively with each other may diminish somewhat. Exposure for long periods of time to television, for example, leaves the person with what might be called "communication fatigue." His own abilities to communicate, along with his own needs for doing so, can be numbed.

There is some danger of a similar consequence for the executive who is bombarded every day and from all sides by great quantities of data directed to him. It is possible that some executives do suffer from time to time from "information overload,"[14] and this may undoubtedly have some effect on their interpersonal communicate-abilities, although that effect cannot as yet be clearly specified.

Some obvious *advantages* of mass communication include the potential for enlarging the range of our information-gathering, and of increasing those experiences, however vicarious, which we may draw upon in future relations with others. Mass communication has also become a basic means of communicating-to large number of employees.

INDIVIDUAL BARRIERS

There are two barriers to informative communication which are sourced "in" the individual. These are his individual competencies to think and to

---

[12] See particularly J. Reusch, *Disturbed Communication* (New York: W. W. Norton & Co., Inc., 1957); and P. H. Hoch & J. Zubin (eds.), *Psychopathology of Communication* (New York: Grune & Stratton, 1958).

[13] But for some controversial speculations, see M. McLuhan, *The Gutenberg Galaxy* (Toronto: University of Toronto Press, 1964); and *Understanding Media: The Extensions of Man* (New York: McGraw-Hill Book Co., 1964).

[14] Cf. J. G. Miller, "Coping with Administrators' Information Overload." Mimeoed preprint (No. 119), Ann Arbor: Mental Health Research Institute, University of Michigan, 1963.

act (strategic competencies), and his skills in receiving and transmitting information (tactical competencies).

1. *Individual habits of thought and action*, when obsolete or inappropriate (or incompetent), account for one of the most serious obstacles to effective intercommunication. People vary greatly in their abilities to acquire, and consume or process, information in thinking, problem-solving, decisioning, etc. The abilities we have for conceptualizing, discerning, and manipulating ideas, for perceiving relationships, and for generalizing and extrapolating, are all tools of thinking necessary to adequate human performance. Without going into the reasons for the variances, suffice it to say that all people do not have all of these abilities in the same degree.

There are two specific differences in people's thinking ability we should perhaps distinguish here. If a manager deals with his problems today as if today were 1925, we could say that his habits of thought are obsolete. If a manager consistently makes poor decisions, we might say that his habits of thought are inappropriate or inadequate. His thinking abilities may be sufficient and satisfactory for some kinds of problems, but not for the particular problems he faces as a manager today.

If a person is aware of such weaknesses and of the barriers they could create in his attempts to communicate-to others and to be communicated-with by them, he may of course overcome the weakness and hence eliminate that barrier. But a person's habits of thought and action, as discussed earlier, are modifiable only at great effort, and usually then only in very small steps or stages.

A person may also create a barrier to effective informative communication through his own behavior. Regardless of how accurately and appropriately he thinks, a manager's behavior may imply a *social distance* or create a poor interpersonal climate that could offset the advantage of his thinking ability. Or his actions, following a "correct" decision, may simply be inappropriate. From a communication point of view, the adequacy of an individual's decision making and problem solving is not based alone upon his ability to think, nor alone upon his ability to communicate-to others his decision. The *actions* he does or does not take on the decisions he makes may communicate-to others more or more loudly than his words do.

2. The individual's *inabilities to receive and transmit information*, in terms of his personal communication skills, clearly create barriers which impede his intercommunication with others. Poor habits of listening or speaking, of reading or writing, will almost certainly mean that he cannot handle all of the information directed to him, or that he will be unable to

transmit effectively all of the information that he must, or desires, to communicate-to others.

ECONOMIC, GEOGRAPHIC, AND TEMPORAL BARRIERS

The individual who originates or receives a message may simply not have or take the time (a) to read it (write it, say it, hear it) properly, or (b) to comprehend it, or (c) to act upon it "properly" (i.e., as intended). The attention of key managers in most large organizations is always at a premium. There is competition for their attention both from without and from within the organization. Yet one's undivided attention is often necessary to a full understanding of the information directed to him. So the allocation of one's time and attention presents a potential obstacle to efficient informative communication—both to him and from him.

There are economic barriers. An individual may want to receive or may want to send certain data. But the gathering, or the preparation and presentation of a completely comprehensible, unambiguous message may be too costly. So a compromise may mean that only part of the data will be gathered and prepared, or that it may be done in a hurried or careless manner.

Or, as suggested previously, the physical proximity[15] (or distance) of people who frequently have a need to exchange information with each other is always a potential obstacle to economical, if not effective, informative communication.

CHANNEL AND MEDIA BARRIERS

The channel or the medium employed to transmit data may itself act as a barrier to successful informative communication. Certain kinds of messages are best "communicated" in person, other kinds by memos, other kinds by reports or by telephone or teletype, and so on. Certain kinds of messages are "communicated" most successfully by utilizing formal channels, other kinds through informal channels, etc. For example, the use of the grapevine among executives, says Barnard, promotes the communication of ". . . intangible facts, opinions, suggestions, suspicions, that cannot pass through formal channels without raising issues calling for

---

[15] For a recent treatment of "proxemics," see E. H. Hall, *The Hidden Dimension* (Garden City, N.Y.: Doubleday & Co., Inc., 1966).

decisions, without dissipating dignity and objective authority. . . ."[16] However, as suggested previously, considerable research needs to be done before we could reliably assign specific kinds of informative communication tasks to specific channels.

A BASIC TECHNOLOGICAL BARRIER

The concept of "information overload" was described earlier. But there is more at stake than just the stress of "too much" information.

Consider this dilemma: while our technological abilities to generate and disseminate potentially useful data have increased manyfold in the past few years, man's physical *capacity* to register and to process potentially informative data has probably increased very little, if indeed at all. The sheer volume of data that crosses the typical executive's desk today should serve to spotlight the inadequacies of the education and development of our acquisition strategies and practices. But no gain in *ability* could offset the widening gap between the exponentially-increasing quantity of data available for consumption and man's very limited capacity for acquiring and processing useful information.

Consider all of the data available which might be relevant to any given problem or opportunity or decision a manager might be concerned with. Let us call that A. Now consider that small fraction of all of the data available which actually comes within that manager's purview. Let us call that B. Then consider the fraction of B which he actually ingests: we can refer to that quantity as C. To press the point, consider the small fraction of C which he actually consumes to some useful end. That might be characterized as D. Finally, consider that fraction of all he consumes which eventually brings about some measurable advantage to him or to his organization. We can refer to that quantity as E. A rough sketch of these successive "filtering" or demagnitude factors might look something like Figure 14.

The proportions are not intended to be accurate. But they may serve well enough to emphasize the nature of this one technological obstacle. That data which ultimately has measurable informational utility for an organization is but a minute proportion of that magnitude available to its members at any point in time.

---

[16] Chester I. Barnard, *The Functions of the Executive* (Cambridge, Mass.: Harvard University Press, 1938), p. 225.

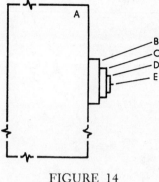

FIGURE 14

This discussion of certain basic obstacles to informative communication is not meant to be exhaustive. There are others. But perhaps these are representative of the most pervasive of the obstacles to informative communication within organizations.

SUGGESTIONS FOR FURTHER READING

Although the information function of communication has usually been implicit in most treatments of communication, specific study of this basic function is of fairly recent origin. Detailing even a representative list of readings in this area would be prohibitive. But the suggested readings below could provide a good overall perspective on the several possible approaches to the analysis of the information function of communication.

BENNETT, W. E. "Communication in Industry," *Journal of Communication*, Vol. 2 (1952), pp. 38–40.

BUREAU OF APPLIED SOCIAL RESEARCH. *The Flow of Information among Scientists: Problems, Opportunities, and Research Questions.* New York, 1958.

CHERRY, E. COLIN. "The Communication of Information (An Historical Review)," *American Scientist*, Vol. 40 (1952), pp. 640 ff.

————. "The Communication of Information," *Endeavour*, Vol. 23 (1964), pp. 13–17.

DAHLE, T. L. "Transmitting Information to Employees: A Study of Five Methods," *Personnel*, Vol. 31 (1954), pp. 243–46.

DEFLEUR, MELVIN L., and LARSEN, OTTO N. *The Flow of Information: An Experiment in Mass Communication.* New York: Harper & Bros., 1958.

EMERY, F. E., and OESER, O. A.   *Information, Decision and Action*. Carlton: Melbourne University Press, 1958.

HILL, M. J.   "The Elgin Information Program," *Personnel Journal*, Vol. 26 (1947), pp. 207–9.

HYMAN, H. H., and SHEATSLEY, P. B.   "Some Reasons Why Information Campaigns Fail," *Public Opinion Quarterly*, Vol. 11 (1947), pp. 412–23.

KAHN, R. L., and CONNELL, C. F.   "Nobody Tells Me Anything: Getting the Facts You Need for Decision," *Dun's Review and Modern Industry*, November, 1957.

KATZ, D., and KAHN, R. L.   "Communication: The Flow of Information," Ch. 9 in *The Social Psychology of Organizations*. New York: John Wiley & Sons, Inc., 1965.

KING, GILBERT W.   "Information," *Scientific American*, Vol. 187 (1952), pp. 132 ff.

MEREDITH, G. P.   "The Flow of Information," *Occupational Psychology*, Vol. 29 (1955), pp. 99–103.

MILLER, J. G.   *Coping with Administrators' Overload*. Ann Arbor: Mental Health Research Institute, University of Michigan, Oct., 1963.

PEAK, HELEN, and MORRISON, H. WILLIAM.   "The Acceptance of Information into Attitude Structure," *Journal of Abnormal and Social Psychology*, Vol. 57 (1958), pp. 127–35.

RIESMAN, DAVID, and BENNEY, MARK.   "Asking and Answering," *Journal of Business*, October, 1956.

ROGERS, E. M.   *Diffusion of Innovations*. New York: Free Press, 1962.

ROTHSTEIN, D. A.   "Psychiatric Implications of Information Theory," *Achives of General Psychiatry*, Vol. 13 (1965), pp. 87–94.

ROTHSTEIN, J.   "An Informational Approach to Organization and System Engineering Design," *Transactions*, Professional group on Engineering Management, Institute of Radio Engineers, Feb., 1954, pp. 25–29.

STANTON, A. H., and SCHWARTZ, M.   "Communication: The Transmission of Information and Misinformation," Ch. 2 in their *The Mental Hospital*. New York: Basic Books, Inc., 1954.

14

Command and Instructive Functions[1]

THOSE WHO are hierarchically superior—whether in family, business, military, civic, or personal life—often initiate communication encounters not only for the purpose of informing their subordinates but often for the purpose of telling them what to do (or how), of directing them, or of *commanding* their behavior in some way.

One of the expectations that properly socialized subordinates bring to their relationships with their superiors is that they are obliged to accept certain kinds of orders from certain superiors to do certain kinds of things. Those are orders which subordinates expect to follow. When the rules about who can order whom to do what things are mutually understood, neither the superior nor the subordinate expects to engage in a dialogue.

---

[1] I have referred to this applied function in earlier writings only as the instructive function—which is exercised whenever a superior tells a subordinate "what to do or how to do it." But I have here acquiesced to numerous thoughtful suggestions made by colleagues and others to use a "stronger" term. Hence "command functions." This term also clarifies an obvious relationship between the command function in human organizations and the "command and control systems" notions of cyberneticists and certain empirically oriented organization theorists (e.g., Beatrice K. Rome and S. C. Rome, "Leviathan: An Experimental Study of Large Organizations with the Aid of Computers," in R. V. Bowers (ed.), *Studies on Behavior in Organizations* [Athens: University of Georgia Press, 1966], pp. 257–311). The combined terminology may also serve to connote the hierarchical nature of so many of our communicative relationships—boss/employee, parent/child, teacher/student—and the rank-ordering of a great many more of our communicative relationships—e.g., policeman/speeder, elder/younger, bigger/smaller, high status/low status, smarter/dumber, high prestige/low prestige, and so on. To all of these and all other vertical relationships, the command and instructive functions are pertinent.

There are those specified occasions, in other words, when hierarchically related individuals expect the encounter to be one in which the subordinate is the "sink" for the originator's orders or instructions. And if the relationship is mutually perceived as a legitimate one, the subordinate expects to accept and carry out his superior's instructions, to the extent he can, to the extent feasible, etc. On those occasions, neither participant expects the mode of the encounter to be anything but clearly synchronic. It is those occasions to which the instructive and command functions[2] of communication are pertinent.

Formal Organizations

The command instructive and functions of communication are more observable in formal organizations than they are in informal organizations. Individuals who are hierarchically (positionally) superior within an organization structure are both privileged and obligated to command (and/or to control) certain task-related behaviors of their subordinates. Those same subordinates have a similar obligation and privilege vis-à-vis *their* subordinates, and so on from the top to the bottom of the organizational hierarchy.

Orders, directives, requests, procedures, even performance appraisals— all function as command (and/or control) messages. They are intended to *constrain the subordinate's freedom to exercise his own judgment* about those parameters of his task specified by those messages.

To this extent, of course, an instructive or command message must be *comprehensible* to the subordinate. It has *validity* to the extent that it falls within the subordinate's expectations about being command-able by *that* superior in respect to the behaviors or performances specified in the message. It has *utility* only to the extent that the receiver perceives some advantage for himself if he complies, or some disadvantage for himself if he does not comply.[3]

---

[2] The command function in military organizations is probably obvious. But, however obscure it may be in other human organizations, or however much it may be eroded, the *function* of command remains the same. In all hierarchical relationships, the superior is organizationally obligated (whether he fully accepts the obligation or not) to command or direct or instruct certain of his subordinates' comprehensions, actions, or intentions. How and when and where (and how effectively) he fulfills this obligation constitutes his exercise of the command and instructive functions of communication.

[3] That advantage, of course, may be nothing more than satisfying the superior in some way. The advantage could inhere in simply doing what one expects he *should* do

Power and Authority

In Chapter 6, a useful distinction between power and authority was made:

a) One person has *power* over another to the extent that he can arbitrarily divulge or withhold information for which the other has some past, present, or future communicative need.

b) *Authority* is formalized, standardized, "poisitionalized" power. E.g., a superior has authority to command a subordinate in certain ways consistent with their tacit (or formalized) agreement about *what* domains that authority to command covers, *when* it can be exercised, *how* it should be exercised, and so on.

Power is thus relationship-specific while authority is hierarchical-position–specific.[4] Or, we can say that authority is legitimized or conventionalized power.[5]

Interpersonal relationships between superiors and subordinates in those organizations having formalized hierarchical structures thus have both power and authority dimensions. But the command function of communication is relevant primarily to the exercise of authority.

The members of formal organizations apply certain general criteria to determine when a command message—an order, directive, etc.—will be accepted as authoritative. Some years ago, Barnard suggested these four criteria:

---

in those circumstances. Or the advantage may be that in complying he can perform his own task with less effort, less danger, etc.

Disadvantages may be some fear of formal or informal reprisals, or some "fracturing" of the relationship with his superior, a relationship upon which the subordinate must depend. But the disadvantage could also be some anticipated extra work or extra effort or psychological discomfort. If so, the intent of the originator's message might then be disunderstood (in the manner described earlier).

[4] Cf. D. Katz and R. L. Kahn, *The Social Psychology of Organizations* (New York: John Wiley & Sons, Inc., 1966), esp. Ch. 8, "Power and Authority"; R. L. Kahn and Elise Boulding, *Power and Conflict in Organizations* (New York: Basic Books, Inc., 1964); and P. M. Blau, *Exchange and Power in Social Life* (New York: John Wiley & Sons, Inc., 1964).

[5] Anthropologist John Honigmann writes that "an administrator possesses authority when the decisions he makes and executes are legitimate in the eyes of the organization in which he acts . . . Basically, it emanates from the explicit or implicit consent of a group to follow a particular administration and to accept its policies because morally they are justified," in *The World of Man* (New York: Harper & Row, 1959), p. 477.

A person can and will accept a communication as authoritative only when four conditions simultaneously obtain: (a) he can and does understand the communication; (b) *at the time of his decision* he believes that it is not inconsistent with the purpose of the organization; (c) *at the time of his decision*, he believes it to be compatible with his personal interest as a whole; and (d) he is able mentally and physically to comply with it.

a) A communication that cannot be understood *can* have no authority. An order issued, for example, in a language not intelligible to the recipient is no order at all—no one would so regard it. Many orders are exceedingly difficult to understand. They are often necessarily stated in terms that are very general, and the persons who issued them could not themselves apply them under many conditions. Until interpreted they have no meaning. The recipient either must disregard them or merely do anything in the hope that it is compliance.

Hence, a considerable part of administrative work consists in the interpretation and reinterpretation or orders in their application to concrete circumstances that were not or could not be taken into account initially.

b) A communication believed by the recipient to be incompatible with the purpose of the organization, as he understands it, could not be accepted. Action would be frustrated by cross purposes. The most common practical example is that involved in conflicts of orders. An intelligent person will deny the authority of that one which contradicts the purpose of the effort as he understands it. In extreme cases many individuals would be virtually paralyzed by conflicting orders. They would be literally unable to comply.

c) If a communication is believed to involve a burden that destroys the net advantage of connection with the organization, there no longer would remain a net inducement to the individual to contribute to it. The existence of a net inducement is the only reason for accepting any order as having authority. Hence, if such an order is received, it must be disobeyed (in the more usual cases evaded) as utterly inconsistent with personal motives that are the basis of accepting any orders at all. Cases of voluntary resignation from all sorts of organizations are common for this sole reason. Malingering and intentional lack of dependability are the more usual methods.

d) If a person is unable to comply with an order, obviously it must be disobeyed, or better, disregarded. To order a man who cannot swim to swim a river is a sufficient case. Such extreme cases are not frequent; but they occur. The more usual case is to order a man to do things only a little beyond his capacity; but a little impossible is still impossible.[6]

All communication occurs *within* a specific receiver, so the acceptance of another's commands is ultimately a function of the person being ordered, directed, or instructed to behave in a certain way or carry out a

[6] C. I. Barnard, *The Functions of the Executive* (Cambridge, Mass.: Harvard University Press, 1938), pp. 165–66.

certain activity. As Barnard has suggested, acceptance of authoritative messages within formal organizations can be generally expected because:

a) Most orders meet the four criteria described above;

b) There is usually a range of instructions or orders which subordinates will accept without question; and

c) Pressures exerted by other members of the organization insure a certain degree or range of acceptance (through conformity).[7]

Those individuals who carry out managerial functions within formal organizations often find themselves in the position of having to communicate-to others outside their own organizations. Often these must take the form of commanding or instructing others what to do, how to do it., etc. Telling suppliers, distributors, and/or customers what to do or how to do it has become a common communicative necessity for most business and industrial enterprises. But, for different reasons, the four criteria specified above still apply. The receiver cannot accept and comply unless the message directed to him is *comprehensible*. Nor will he be likely to accept and comply with the directive (or set of instructions) unless it seems to him to be consistent with the nature and the purpose of the relationship that he perceives to exist between himself and the originator.[8] Further, he will likely accept and comply with the directive or instructive message to the extent that the anticipated behavior on his part *seems to him* potentially beneficial in some way (or at least not specifically disadvantageous to his personal or institutional needs, wishes, better judgment, etc.). And certainly no person or organization will comply with a command or a directive unless it is *possible* for him to do so. For example, a manufacturer may send you a set of instructions for adjusting your dishwasher. But if you are incapable of carrying out the actions called for, you can't comply.

At least theoretically, managers are interested in the effectiveness of their subordinates' performances on the job. This is (at least theoretically) the rationale and the occasion for all command or instructive communication. Glover has suggested that the more a person knows of *what* to do, of *when* and *where* it is supposed to be done, and of *how* to do it, the more

---

[7] *Ibid.*, pp. 167–70 (paraphrased).

[8] For example, manufacturers instruct purchasers how to set up or maintain their products. Most purchasers would consider this perfectly legitimate. Food manufacturers include a set of directions for preparing everything from soup to cake mixes. That's perceived as legitimate, too. For, in both cases, this is information we need, and have come to expect. But if we receive a flyer from a merchant saying, "Buy product X today!" the same legitimacy does not exist.

effective—and efficient—that person's performance will be (assuming that adequate tools are available and that the individual has an appropriate motivation for the task.).[9] But, as discussed in the chapter on effectiveness, the origination of orders and directives in no way assures an advantage to the enterprise, even if they are carried out exactly as intended.

ORDERS AND DIRECTIVES

On the basis of information he has educed from within and without the organization, each manager is concerned with the control and regulation of his organization in the direction of the goals and objectives which have been set for it (or for his department within that organization). At his command is the regulatory communication system, which "transports" orders and directives from some legitimated hierarchical superior to those who institutionally attribute to him the prerogative of commanding their task-related behavior or activities in some way.

On the basis of the messages he has from the operational and maintenance communication systems by which he is served, the manager must determine first *what* orders and directives are needed in order to bring the performance of his organization up to the level expected. Then he must determine *who* is to receive the intended regulatory directive. He must then determine, on the basis of his understanding of the receiver(s) and the conditions, how he is to formulate his orders or directive in such a manner (*when* and *how*) that its acceptance, and compliance, will be optimized. (Ultimately, of course, he must also establish some means of "feedback" so that he may judge the effectiveness of his message.)[10]

Three of the most relevant questions which arise in the order-giving, directing, or instructing process are those regarding *content, manner,* and *intent.*

Content. While it would seem to be insignificant when compared to a manager's daily run of problem-solving and decisioning, deciding what to put in an order or directive (and what to leave out) is of real concern to most conscientious managers. The question is always: how much detail?

To this question, there is no absolute answer. But a little reflection on the communication situation as it occurs will help.

---

[9] J. G. Glover, *Fundamentals of Professional Management* (New York: Republic Books, 1954), p. 288.

[10] Cf. the American Management Association's Executive Communication Course, in which seven steps in order-giving are recommended: (1) plan, (2) prepare, (3) present, (4) verify reception, (5) act, (6) check, and (7) evaluate.

People differ markedly in their working habits, particularly in their desire and abilities to plan their own work. Some people want to be told not only what to do, but how to do it. Others prefer being told only what the objective is. They prefer to decide for themselves how to accomplish a specified objective. The problem to be solved is the difficult one of balancing constraint and freedom in such a way as to encourage initiative and responsibility on the part of the subordinate without at the same time promoting inefficiencies or organization ineffectiveness.[11]

At the same time, there are managers who perhaps feel insecure and as a result may insist upon work being carried out exactly as they specify.[12] Other managers seem to be unable to deal with details at all, and leave all detail to subordinates—sometimes indiscriminately.

Order-giving relates one or more subordinates to the originating manager through the order and its implications. To say that there is a best way of deciding upon "content" would be as misleading as saying there is one "best" way of receiving and carrying out every order.

How much detail should be included depends, obviously, upon how much detail is needed. To arrive at some decision about how much detail is needed, one needs to consider—beyond the individual differences of the people concerned—the *consequences* of the alternatives. Too much detail, over time, has a tendency to discourage independence and initiative and to encourage dependence on authority. In many instances, such consequences are undesirable. Too little detail may contribute to inefficiency and, ultimately, to the ineffectiveness of the organization. In some instances, too little detail may endanger the lives of employees; combat training, heavy production, and the handling of radioactive materials may serve as examples of such instances.

Ideally, then, the superior needs to include that amount of detail which will insure compliance adequate to the purpose of the order, consistent with safety, cost, and efficiency, *and with other related orders.*

In general, it would seem to be useful to consider these three basic guides to order formulation:

---

11 See F. Herzberg, *Work and the Nature of Man* (Cleveland: World Pub. Co., 1966); V. H. Vroom, *Work and Motivation* (New York: John Wiley & Sons, Inc., 1964); C. Argyris, *Integrating the Individual and the Organization* (New York: John Wiley & Sons, Inc., 1964); and L. R. Sayles, *Individualism and Big Business* (New York: McGraw-Hill Book Co., 1963).

12 See, e.g., H. Sherman, "How Much Should You Delegate?" *Supervisory Management Magazine*, October, 1966, as an example of this issue.

1. The order or directive should describe only the minimum *actions* necessary. Fanfares, embellishments, and long-winded justifications[13] usually detract from the order itself.
2. The order or directive should, when appropriate—and it usually is—specify the beginning and end of the actions to be taken, and their timing (consistent with related activities).
3. The applicability of the order or directive should be specified. That is, the order should specify who and when and to what kinds of circumstances and/or behavior it applies.

Manner. The importance of the *manner* of giving orders has perhaps been overemphasized in the past. Considerateness, for example, is not always the best manner for giving orders.

The manner of order-giving has been studied and reported by the Glenn L. Martin Company.[14] In this analysis, four kinds of orders were distinguished: (1) the call for volunteers, (2) the implied order, (3) the request, and (4) the direct order. Our concern here, however, is focused primarily upon the fourth type of order—the direct order. Other means of securing cooperation and channeling behavior are dealt with in the next chapter on the influence and persuasive functions of communication.

Some pointers to be followed in giving orders and instructing have been offered by the Louisiana Power and Light Company:

1. Know and understand thoroughly the job to be done.
2. Assign work to the proper employee. Some workers are more skilled or adept at certain jobs than others and should be called on to do those things in which they are proficient. It is particularly important to assign hazardous work to thoroughly trained and capable men. Be impartial, however, in the distribution of work. Don't overload the willing worker and permit the uncooperative one to carry too light a load.
3. Give orders clearly, concisely, and distinctly.
4. Don't assume that orders are understood. Be sure they are understood. Repeat them if necessary. It is usually good practice to ask if the orders are understood.

---

[13] A justification would seem to be called for only when the order, or the receiver's compliance with it, might violate certain values or beliefs of the people involved, or when it might be clearly inconsistent with organizational or personal goals.

[14] "Ask Them or Tell Them?" in M. Joseph Dooher and Vivienne Marquis (eds.), *Effective Communication on the Job.* (New York: American Management Association, Inc., 1956), pp. 102–3.

5. Keep orders on a high level; avoid sarcasm or other forms of antagonism.

6. If necessary, demonstrate. This is an excellent aid to clear appreciation of the problem.

7. Do not give too many orders at one time. This can be very confusing. Confusion leads to accident and waste.

8. Allow a reasonable time for work to be done.

9. If a worker is capable, do not nag or stand over him.

10. Give orders through proper channels. Intermediate supervisors should never be bypassed or ignored in getting word to a worker to perform a task. The worker should be made to realize that his immediate supervisor not only has the responsibility of getting the job done, but has authority to a comparable degree. This functional procedure and line of authority should not be disrupted. It is demoralizing to a group and to the immediate supervisor for a higher supervisor to go directly to a member of the group with instructions without clearing through the immediate supervisor.

11. Give adequate details, but do not confuse. Detailed orders are desirable when hazards exist, where the work is of a special or infrequent nature, when the men have limited experience, where a standard procedure is desired, or in a teaching situation.

12. Follow through. It may be desirable after a reasonable time to check back and be sure that the worker has understood and that he is performing his job satisfactorily.[15]

The circumstances as well as the "content" of orders are of some concern in deciding upon *manner* of presentation. There is no single best guide, because circumstances differ, as do people. There is some agreement, however, on the following basics (considering only direct order-giving):

1. The order or directive should be direct and unequivocal. There should be no question in the receiver's mind as to exactly what is intended.

2. The order or directive must be so phrased as to obviate any potential ambiguity. Any possibility of misinterpretation should be minimized. It should be phrased not so the receiver can understand it, but so he cannot misunderstand it.

3. The order or directive, when possible, should be timed to coincide with maximum receptiveness. When in the midst of labor-management strife, for example, even the best manner of presentation might be inadequate to overcome the disfacilitation likely to be encountered

---

15 "Pointers on Order Giving," in Dooher and Marquis, *op. cit.*, pp. 100–101.

in all but the most clear-cut situations between supervisor and subordinate.

It should be emphasized that, in practice, manner cannot be separated from content. The receiver considers the order as a whole. If he reacts negatively to the manner of presentation, he will likely be reluctant to accept the order or carry it out. Conversely, if he objects to carrying out the actions called for, he may perceive the manner as irritating.

Nor can manner be considered, in practice, apart from channel and medium. Sending a messenger boy to deliver orally an important order may consequent in poor reception of that order. Some organizations reserve a special channel for the transmission of orders (i.e., those channels which comprise the regulatory communication system). The most that we can say about the relationship of channel and manner at the present time, however, is that the command channel should be a formal one. Using informal channels for order-giving would likely give rise to some ambiguity about either the intent or the legitimacy (validity) of the order.

Intent. As he does with most messages, a receiver will need some understanding of the originator's intentions if he is to understand the message itself. Inadequate or inaccurate comprehension of the intentions of the originator of command or instructive messages may have more detrimental consequences than miscomprehension of other kinds of messages, however—for all of the obvious reasons.

The most significant point to be made in this regard is one that is frequently overlooked. In addition to asking himself, "Why did the originator put out this order?" the receiver usually asks himself, "Does he *mean* it?" If some orders and directives are intended to be strictly complied with, while others are intended only as general guides to behavior, and still others are generally ignored, it is left to the receiver to decide the extent of his own compliance.

To avoid being looked upon as naïve by one's peers, one must accurately perceive the intentions of the order giver as far as expected compliance is concerned—as those intentions are revealed by his *subsequent* behavior.[16] People interpret an order or a command in terms of its validity *for them*. Thus, consistent intentions make for the least ambiguous situations: "He

---

[16] One way of "testing" the originator's intentions is to determine what action the originator would take if the order were not complied with as specified in the order. It is safe to assume that this calculated validity of the order guides the subordinate in his interpretations, for it is only by such determinations that he can fully comprehend orders.

always means just what he says," or "He doesn't mean it; just ignore it." Inconsistent validity induces frustration, dissatisfaction, and insecurity.

As indicated earlier, if the originator leaves to the receiver's judgment when and under what circumstances the order is to be implemented, the receiver must also determine the order giver's intentions in this regard.

If the receiver does actually misperceive the originator's intentions as to expected compliance or implementation, and is admonished or punished as a result, he can (and does) hold the vagueness or ambiguity of the order to blame. Thus, in formal organizations, responsibility for comprehending the *intentions* of the originator (as well as the order itself and its implementation) could advantageously be imposed upon the receiver.

INSTRUCTIONS AND PROCEDURES

What has been said about the content, manner, and intention of orders holds for instructions and procedures as well. While orders are often limited to descriptions of *what* to do (and occasionally *when*), instructions and procedures are employed to describe in more detail *how* to carry out the order, directive, policy, etc.[17] The need for standard procedures (SOP's) is a function of size, task specialization, and work-flow boundaries in formal organizations. To implement a plan, certain activities must occur in a certain sequence.[18] Thus the need for *prescribing* the format or routine of certain activities.

When two or more people are performing the same task, standard procedures may be desirable simply for reasons of economy. Ross has enumerated some other reasons for standardization:

1. Assuring compliance with company policy.
2. Providing uniformity in practice.
3. Reducing operational errors.
4. Shortening training period for new employees.
5. Expediting interchange of employees between various jobs.

---

[17] H. John Ross defines a procedure as "a formal instruction which controls the mechanics by which . . . routines are performed; including equipment, forms and forms flow, sequence of operations and working conditions." In *How to Make a Procedure Manual.* 4th ed. (Miami: Office Research Institute, 1956), p. 1.

[18] In recent years, departmentally separated but functionally related work, material, people, and other flows have been conceptually reintegrated by a variety of schemes often referred to collectively as "operations research." See, e.g., Abe Shuchman (ed.), *Scientific Decision Making in Business* (New York: Holt, Rinehart & Winston, 1963).

6. Eliminating snap decisions about important systems changes.
7. Assisting in maintaining good organization.[19]

Procedures are ordinarily thought of as command imperatives which apply to highly repetitive or widely duplicated activities within the organization, while *instructions* may be more often looked upon as guidelines to be followed in learning how to carry out a new or nonrepetitive task. The most important qualities of both procedures and instructions, if they are to be effective, are these: They should be

1. Unambiguous.
2. Unequivocal.
3. Detailed only to the extent of precluding any unnecessary ambiguity —of content, situation, or intention.
4. Specific as to time and place, both beginning and ending.
5. Consistent with the functions, the capabilities, and the judgment-abilities of the receiver.
6. Consistent with other procedures and instructions.
7. Consistent with the goals and objectives of the organization.

Policies.   Policies are obviously a relevant form of command in organizations. Sir Geoffrey Vickers summarizes some of the issues to be considered when he writes: "People can only carry out a policy if they can recognize the kind of situation to which it is intended to apply. This is most difficult to convey in words; hence the difficulty of writing policy directives and the fatal ease with which they degenerate into formulae; hence, in consequence, the formalism which tends to infect all large organizations."[20] What is implied in this statement, it would seem, is that unthinking reliance upon formulae in bureaucracies—whether public or private—may ultimately be detrimental to the capacities and capabilities of the organization.

If we assume that policies are for a purpose—the purpose of *guiding* the task-related judgments and decisions of organizational members—then they must continuously be adapted to both external and internal conditions. They cannot be immutable and remain valid. Policies will be interpreted as perceived by the organization's members. Their usefulness thus lies in their function as guides to judgment, decision, planning, etc., and not as behavior specifications. Hence they differ in this respect from instructions and procedures. But all three are forms of command and control.

---

[19] Ross, *op. cit.*, pp. 2–3.

[20] Sir Geoffrey Vickers, "Communication in Economic Systems," in *Studies in Communication.* (London: Martin Secker and Warburg, 1955), p. 85.

Education and Training. Task-related training and education in formal organizations serves the purpose of either (a) *obviating* certain policies, orders, instructions, etc., or (b) *facilitating* the command function in some way.

Mary Parker Follett some years ago emphasized that "it has been hard for many old-fashioned employers to understand that *orders will not take the place of training.*"[21] An order, a policy, or an instruction which is intended to "tell" a subordinate what to do or how or when to do it will not be effective—no matter how valid and legitimate it may be perceived—unless that subordinate is both capable and prepared to comprehend it, and to implement it as intended. There may be other reasons why a particular subordinate might be reluctant or unwilling to carry out an order, of course. But unless the subordinate is capable of *comprehending* the order, and unless he is *capable of implementing* that order, he will not carry out the originator's intentions simply because he can not do so. It is appropriate training and education which prepares organizational members both to comprehend and to implement commands, policies, etc.

Thus training and education are logically a part of the command and instructive functions of communication. A few writers have insisted that managers have an inherent responsibility to train and develop subordinates; e.g., ". . . the manager's function is to assist others to develop themselves in carrying out their assigned tasks in the organization."[22]

Any attempt to deal with the details of training and education in formal organizations would take us too far from our major concerns in this book. But it should perhaps be emphasized, if the point is not obvious, that all training and education activities are basically communication encounters, and that the effectiveness of all development, education, and/or training efforts depends ultimately upon the effectiveness of the communication that occurs therein.[23] Yet surprisingly few documents on education and training have more than a cursory reference to issues of communication and intercommunication.

Further, it should be made clear that the comprehend-abilities and the

---

21 *Dynamic Administration: The Collected Papers of Mary Parker Follett* (H. C. Metcalf and L. Urwick, eds. New York: Harper & Row, n.d.), p. 53.

22 N. Cantor, *The Learning Process for Managers* (New York: Harper & Bros., 1958) p. 28. Cf. G. C. Houston, *Manager Development: Principles and Perspectives* (Homewood, Ill.: Richard D. Irwin, Inc., 1961); and W. McGehee and P. W. Thayer, *Training in Business and Industry* (New York: John Wiley & Sons, Inc., 1961).

23 The effectiveness of training and education programs depends upon many other factors, such as timing, sequencing, appropriateness of objectives and content, utility to the trainee, his "motivation," and so on. But, ultimately, no training or education program can be any more effective than the communication which occurs within it or as

task-abilities of subordinates have far-reaching implications both for what is necessary and what is possible in carrying out the command function of communication within formal organizations. For example, the more capable subordinates are to carry out their tasks effectively, the less day-to-day involvement is required of superiors in directing or regulating those subordinates' performances. Moreover, the *less* capable the subordinate is to perform his assigned task, the *more* difficult (or less possible) it is to direct his behavior communicatively. The relationship between task-abilities (achieved through training and education) and the aggregative effectiveness of the command function in organizations is thus an inseparable one.

Even this very brief excursion into the role of communication in training and in command and control should serve to underscore the fact that it is *not* the eloquence or the form of an order or an instruction as such which ultimately account for its success or failure. Rather, we should ask: Is it *comprehend-able* (to the receiver)? Is it *valid* (for the receiver)? Has the receiver the necessary *implement-abilities?* These are the factors which basically account for the success or failure of command and instructive messages—whether order, instruction, policy, or procedure.

Informal Organizations

The command function of communication is as pertinent to informal relations as it is to formal relations, although in ways which are probably not as apparent.

Informal relations which persist over time—particularly two-person or *n*-person face-to-face encounters—are founded upon mutually-understood relationships, and upon mutually-understood rules prescribing certain behaviors vis-à-vis one another. Even when relationships are not hierarchical, their participants continuously exercise some permanent or momentary prerogative they have in order to *command* the behavior of another. For example, we may say, "Listen carefully!" or "Would you repeat that?" or "I want you to make a note of this," etc.

Whenever we exercise such a prerogative to order or direct another's behavior in some way (and to the extent he acquiesces to it), the communication which occurs is serving the command function.

Interpersonal power (as contrasted with formalized authority) contributes to command prerogatives in two ways:

---

a consequence of its existence. There is no generally accepted single notion of what constitutes effective training. But whatever criteria one applies, the requisite of effective communication in conducting or implementing a training or education program is inescapable.

a) If another person has a "need" for me to behave communicatively toward him in a particular way, then I have some measure of power vis-à-vis that person.

b) But if *I* have a "need" to get another person to behave in a certain way (to some end which may involve a third person), then *his* prerogative to fulfill or not to fulfill that need, and *his* doing so or not doing so, give him that degree of power over me.

Given this moment-by-moment ebb and flow of power in face-to-face encounters, prerogatives to command the other(s) shift frequently from person to person. But, whether being exercised by one person or by an aggregate in some collective way, the command function inevitably underlies much human interaction. Whenever one person assumes or is extended even a temporary prerogative to tell another what to do or how to do it, he is commanding or directing the other's behavior.

Given that the authority of superiors in hierarchical relationships has perhaps eroded over the past several decades, they have had to rely more and more upon informal relations, upon interpersonal power and influence. At this point, the line between command and influence functions becomes a very tenuous one. So it is appropriate that we turn our attention next to the influence and persuasion functions of communication.

SUGGESTIONS FOR FURTHER READING

Documents which pertain to the techniques of order-giving and of instructing are a part of the reading list which follows Chapter 18. Here are listed a very limited number of references which might be useful in achieving a fuller perspective on the concepts dealt with in this chapter.

DALKEY, N. C.   *Command and Control—A Glance at the Future.* Mitre Corp., 1st Congress on the Information System Sciences, Nov., 1962.

DIMOCK, M. E.   *A Philosophy of Administration.* New York: Harper & Bros., 1958, esp. ch. 12.

FELD, M. D.   "Information and Authority: The Structure of Military Organization," *American Sociological Review,* Vol. 24 (1959), pp. 15–22.

FRENCH, J. R. P., JR.   "A Formal Theory of Social Power," *Psychological Review,* Vol. 63 (1956), pp. 181–94.

PIGORS, PAUL, and PIGORS, FAITH.   *Understanding as a Condition for Success in Order-Giving.* Cambridge, Mass.: Industrial Relations Associates, 1945.

VICKERS, SIR GEOFFREY.   "Positive and Negative Controls in Business" *The Journal of Industrial Economics,* Vol. 6 (1958), pp. 173–79.

15

Influence and Persuasive Functions

OF ALL that has been written about communication over the years—and that has been considerable—perhaps more has been written about persuasion than about any other single topic. There are reasons why this is so.

From the beginning of man's social existence, the need to sway or influence the thoughts or attitudes or behavior of others has been of concern to those who would lead—whatever the arena: politics, religion, intellect, aesthetics. Aristotle addressed himself to the elements of mass persuasion three and one-half centuries before the birth of Christ. Communicating effectively to a mass audience, Aristotle suggested, depends upon three factors:

a) The personal character of the speaker;

b) Putting the audience into a certain frame of mind; and

c) The apparent proof provided by the words of the speech itself.[1]

The reader may recognize an immediate similarity between Aristotle's three conditions of persuasion and the position taken here regarding the relative importance of the three factors which contribute to the effectiveness of any communication situation: the originator's competencies, his attitudes, and then his techniques.[2]

---

[1] In his *Rhetoric*, Book I, Ch. 2. *The Works of Aristotle*, Vol. XI (Oxford: Clarendon Press, 1924).

[2] Given our present state of knowledge regarding the processes of communication, however, we have been forced to recognize that many factors which contribute to the effectiveness and the efficiency of any communicative encounter lie outside the control of the originator. For example, the *receiver's* comprehend-abilities must ultimately be reckoned with, as must the *receiver's* attitudes and the *receiver's* communicative skills.

There are those who take the position that *all* communication is persuasive in character.[3] But is is obvious that we have not followed that position here.

The position we are taking here is that influence and persuasion taken together represent but *one* of the applied functions of communication—alongside the other functions: information functions, command and instructive functions, and integrative functions. Therefore, no special attempt will be made here to review the literature on influence and persuasion. A number of books which provide this sort of overview are suggested in the reading list following this chapter.

Rather, our purpose here will be to examine the communicative functions of influence and persuasion—as those functions fit into the particular frame of reference being developed in this book. That is, we will be asking not "What has been said or written *about* persuasion?" as such, but "How can we come to a better understanding of influence and persuasion by looking at the communication processes which underlie those phenomena?" —and conversely.

We can begin by noting that our interest in the persuasive and influence functions of communication is twofold: *First,* we may assume that one could advantageously be more aware of the attempts of others to persuade or influence him—so as to be better qualified to evaluate and interpret those attempts to persuade or influence him; and, *second,* we may assume that one must frequently engage in attempts to influence or persuade others to think or behave in intended ways. (Throughout this chapter, however, the reader should not forget that his abilities to be influenced by others, to his own or his organization's advantage, are just as important and valuable to him as are his abilities to influence or persuade others.)

"Influence" and "persuasion" are not just techniques. They are basic communicate-abilities that one has (or does not have) in some degree. These abililties are basically conceptual, secondarily attitudinal, and only thirdly matters of technique. Whether one is momentarily originator or

---

But, if we consider "persuasion" only from the point of view of the originator, Aristotle's perspectives are as relevant for us today as they were hundreds of years ago.

[3] E.g., J. H. Campbell and H. W. Hepler, *Dimensions in Communication: Readings* (Belmont, Calif.: Wadsworth Publishing Co., Inc., 1965). Cf. H. R. Huse: "Language is mainly a means to bring others to think, feel, and act as we desire: it is a medium for interpsychological or social activity. The primary function is to influence: hardly anything would be said if there were no interest in others' beliefs and actions." In *The Illiteracy of the Literate: A Guide to the Art of Intelligent Reading* (New York: Appleton-Century, 1933).

receiver, his techniques are generally of less significance in determining the value and the effectiveness of his communication encounters than are his conceptual capabilities and his attitudes.

To emphasize again: the ability to be persuaded or influenced when it is in one's own best interests (or in the interests of the enterprise for which one is responsible) is altogether as important as one's ability to affect other people as he intends (in the same way that one's comprehend-abilities determine the extent to which he is informable by others).

Persuasion and Influence

It may seem awkward that this particular applied function of communication is described by both words: influence and persuasion.

Popularly, "persuasion" is often thought of as the process of affecting receiver thinking or behavior (or attitude) in a way which is presumed to be in the best interests of the *originator*, and at the same time likely contrary to the receiver's own immediate interests. "Influence," on the other hand, is more commonly thought of as a typically longer-range attempt to affect the receiver(s) in a way presumed to be more in the receiver's best interests (or at least not inimical to them.) Persuasion also seems to be understood as being more overt and intentional (as in propaganda), whereas influence is perhaps more often thought of as being covert, sometimes unintentional, and typically more indirect. For example, we would think of an individual as being influenced (not persuaded) by the culture in which he is raised. Persuasion is more typically thought of as having rather specific psychological or behavioral objectives, whereas influence is commonly thought of as having broader, more general, or less specific aims. Finally, influence is often thought of as being interpersonal, whereas persuasion is the term more often used when masses of people are involved.

The reason for the use of both terms to characterize the particular applied function of communication to be explored in this chapter is a practical one. We are concerned primarily in this book with *intentional* or *purposive* communication behavior (both inputting and outputting) within both formal and informal organization contexts. Thus we need something of the connotation of each term: from the notion of persuasion we will take the implications of conscious intention and specificity of objective; from the notion of influence the implications of communicating-to another in ways which are not intended to be disadvantageous to him (in terms of his role or position vis-à-vis the originator). And from influence we will take the notion of indirectness; from persuasion the implication of planning a strategy whenever necessary to achieve the goal or objective set.

But to emphasize once again: being influence-able or persuade-able, when in one's own best interests, is as vital and important a communicate-ability as one's abilities to influence or persuade others. And it is often more difficult to develop one's abilities to be advantageously influenced than it is to develop one's abilities to influence others.

For convenience, our focus will seem to be restricted to the common perspective of originator→influencing→receiver; but everything that will be said has relevance for the perspective of receiver←seeking←to←be←influenced←by←originator. Also, it will be less awkward now to use the one term—*influence*—with the understanding that what we are referring to is the influence/persuasion amalgam described above.

On the Nature of Influence

To develop a useful concept of influence, we need to reconsider some basic points made earlier.

First, you will recall that there are but two means of affecting others: physically (coercively) and communicatively. Thus, if people are to be influenced, it must be communicatively.

Second, since communication is a process which occurs *within* people (not *between* people), the outcome of any attempt to influence another[4] is ultimately determined by that other. If the intended receiver cannot *comprehend* what is said to him, or if his understanding or acceptance of what is said would disconfirm his comprehending system in some way (including "dissonance"), he is not likely to be affected as the originator intended (i.e., in the direction desired). If what is said hasn't adequate past, present, or future *validity* for him, its effect on him (in the direction desired) will be slight. If the state-of-affairs intended by the originator has

---

[4] As indicated above, it would be clumsy to try to detail the conditions of both one's ability to influence and one's influence-ability at every step. The reader will understand that the *conditions* of a person's influence-abilities are like a mirror-image of the originator's abilities to influence him, and that being capable of being influenced (to one's advantage) is a more difficult achievement than being capable of influencing others—although the barriers and impediments in one direction are the converse of what they may be in the other direction (for any individual).

little or no *utility* for the receiver, or if the receiver anticipates negative consequences of being influenced (in the direction intended), then the originator's efforts will not likely be effective.[5]

Third, we should recall the four general categories of consequence of any communication encounter—those that are inevitable, those that are impossible, those that are serendipitous, and those that are possible. Any attempt to influence or be influenced must therefore be some attempt either (a) to alter the *relative likelihood* of one or another of these consequences in any given relationship (e. g., to alter the extent or range of the *metacommunicative facilitation* that obtains in a given relationship); or (b) to capitalize on, and/or to manipulate to achieve the optimum *possible* consequences of the encounter (in the direction desired). In other words, the only two feasible choices the originator has open to him are those (a) of strategically altering the relationship in some way expected to be advantageous to him at some time in the future, or (b) of comporting himself tactically in such a way as to optimize those consequences which are currently "possible."

Fourth, because so many of our day-to-day relations with others are "institutionalized"—that is, they institutionally endow one or the other participant with certain legitimized power or authority over the other—we have a tendency to confuse influence with authority and/or power. For example, if a parent implicitly threatens to withhold affection, or if a superior implicitly threatens to dismiss or downgrade or disapprove of a subordinate *if* he does not do what is intended—this should not be thought of as influence. It is helpful to think of the first as a case of "authority," and the second as "power." Whatever role influence plays in the examples cited is either insignificant or irrelevant to the consequences.

It will be helpful, therefore, to think of influence as the impact or effect of one person on another *above and beyond the impact* (or *effect*) one has on the other given his power (or institutionalized authority) over him. In other words, influence should be thought of as any impact or effect one person has on another exclusive of the consequences of any authority or power he exercises over that other person.

To assess influence, consider first the power or authority one has over another. Given the mutually-recognized power or authority one has over another, certain communicative consequences are inevitable. Only when a

---

[5] Or, if the anticipated consequences of "being influenced" (as intended by another) have *disutility* for the receiver, that attempt to influence him will be to that extent effective.

consequence occurs which could not be attributed to the power or authority dimensions of the relationship should it be attributed to influence.

Degree or amount of influence cannot be determined, therefore, until after the fact. It would be logically (and in this sense empirically) impossible to assess influence prior to a communicative encounter; *potential* influence, yes, actual influence, no. To say that a man is "influential" can therefore be understood to mean that he has established relationships with others which have, as a noticeable aspect, their mutual expectations of his influence.

Also, like all communication, the measurable impact or consequence is not limited to that-which-was-intended by some originator. In fact, influence often occurs quite apart from the intentions of *any* originator. We are influenced by the *ecologies*[6] within which we live and work—whether physical, cultural, or interpersonal—in ways no particular person ever intended. We are influenced when, consciously or nonconsciously, we take-something-into-account which (sooner or later) affects us or changes us in some way.

So a useful concept of influence, it should be understood—like a useful concept of communication—must accommodate empirical subtleties that go far beyond our casual notions of "influencing" people. Nonetheless, it is that purposive aspect of the influencing function we are most concerned with in this book, so it is to that aspect we shall now turn out attention.

Two Types of Influence

It will be useful, in developing a sound perspective on the influence function of purposive communication, to distinguish between two types of influence. Although the process is the same for both types, the "target" is different.

In short, we may wish to influence another's (others') *behavior*, as such; or we may wish to influence another's (others') *comprehension* system(s),

---

[6] E.g., J. H. van den Berg, *The Phenomenological Approach to Psychiatry* (Springfield, Ill.: Charles C Thomas, 1955); R. G. Barker and H. F. Wright, "Psychological Ecology and the Problem of Psychosocial Development," *Child Development,* 1949, 20, 131–43; and G. A. Theodorson (ed.), *Studies in Human Ecology* (Evanston, Ill.: Row, Peterson, 1961). The influence of man's ecology often has scopic consequences—e.g., E. Huntington, *Civilization and Climate* (New Haven, Conn.: Yale University Press, 1924)—as well as very specific consequences: e.g., H. J. Jerison, "Effects of Noise on Human Performance," *Journal of Applied Psychology,* 1959, 43, 96–101.

as such.[7] The distinction may be made clear by drawing upon the basic conceptual tools developed in an earlier chapter.

Greatly oversimplified, the purpose of influencing another's comprehending system in some way would be to alter that receiver's general beliefs, understandings, values, orientations, etc., in some desired way (i.e., in the direction of the originator's intended-state-of-affairs). Influencing the receiver's *comprehending system* is thus relatively nonspecific as far as his subsequent behavior is concerned. The ultimate effect would be that of modifying or exploiting that receiver's take-into-account-susceptibilities, or his problem-perceiving and adaptation priorites.

By contrast, influencing another's *behavior* is typically more action-specific and situational. One might attempt to influence another's behavior in one or more of four different ways. It will help to call upon an earlier model as an aid to visualizing how these four ways differ.

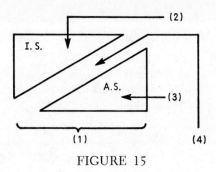

FIGURE 15

(1) We might attempt to incite the emergence of (or enhance the importance of) a "problem" or "cybernetic machine" for that receiver.

(2) We might attempt to *modify* one or more of his intended-states-of-affairs in some way.

(3) We might attempt to create or modify the apparent-state-of-affairs (or influence his perception of the apparent-state-of-affairs) in some way deemed consistent with our purposes.

---

[7] While it is true that the way we comprehend something determines our behavior toward that something, another's attempts to influence us may be purposefully satisfied with changes in our comprehending systems, quite without regard to any subsequent behavior. On the other hand, it would be unlikely that we would attempt to influence another's behavior without assuming the necessity of first impacting his comprehending system in some way (even though it is possible to do so). Thus, to influence another's behavior we would generally assume the prior step of influencing his comprehending system in some way—and so it shall be understood here.

(4) Or, we might attempt to influence the other's interpretation or identification of the discrepancy between an I. S. and an A. S., in a way intended to preclude any but the desired behavior on his part.

There are other ways of conceptualizing the influence process, of course. But the main value of this particular point of view is that it is consistent with the conceptual framework developed here for understanding the processes and the functions of human communication.

INFLUENCE, REALITY, AND IDENTITY

People can be communicated-to, and can structure their behavior only in terms of their own models of the world, their own social realities, their own values, beliefs, orientations, etc. What this fact implies is that it is relatively easier or more possible to influence others to believe or to understand or to take action in a direction toward which they are already oriented. But it is relatively difficult—and sometimes impossible—to influence them to think or behave in ways which are contrary to their basic orientations, values, and beliefs (i.e., the *anchorages* by which they maintain their identity).[8]

In others words, as we scan the continuum of self- and group-identity anchorages (beliefs, norms, etc.) from the superficial toward those more central to an individual's identity, we cross a point beyond which it would be *impossible* to communicate-to him messages which are not consonant with those anchorages. A crude diagram (Figure 16) may help to visualize this relationship.

Without a grasp of such factors as this, our understanding of the process of influence would be inadequate. For example, being aware of the fact that we are individually much less influence-able when our own identity anchorages are jeopardized[9] would enable us to compensate for this potential barrier when it is to our advantage to be influenced.

---

[8] The concept of "anchorages," which derives from the earlier notion of "frame of reference," was introduced in M. Sherif and H. Cantril, *The Psychology of Ego-Involvements: Social Attitudes and Identifications* (New York: John Wiley & Sons, Inc., 1947). It is my opinion that this concept logically belongs to the concept of *identity*, as dealt with by such writers as E. Goffman, *The Presentation of Self in Everyday Life* (New York: Doubleday & Co., Inc., 1959); T. Shibutani, *Society and Personality* (Englewood Cliffs, N.J.: Prentice-Hall, Inc., 1961); and G. J. McCall and J. L. Simmons, *Identities and Interactions* (New York: Free Press, 1966).

[9] Cf. C. W. Sherif, M. Sherif, and R. E. Nebergall, *Attitude and Attitude Change* (Philadelphia: W. B. Saunders Co., 1965), esp. Ch. 3.

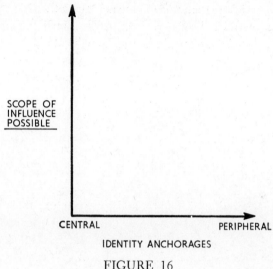

FIGURE 16

The way receivers forecast or project the consequences of various alternative reactions to messages directed to them likewise affects their influence-ability. A receiver may *understand* what an originator intends, but if he anticipates some disutility or negative consequence (for him) of behaving *as if* he understood, he may react by *disunderstanding* (or by some other nonconscious mechanism that gets him "off the hook"). In other words, when a receiver takes-into-account his own expectations regarding the consequences (for him) of reacting to the originator's message as intended by the originator, then his expectations become a key factor in determining the effectiveness of that attempt to influence him.

INFLUENCE AND LEADERSHIP

This perspective on influence brings us close to another concept—that of leadership. Rightfully so.

By leadership, we will want to mean more than "charisma." Those who "lead" by intent depend upon a great deal more than the serendipity of charisma. They develop both strategic and tactical competencies to affect others in intended ways. These competencies may consequent or evidence themselves in the form of mutually-positive interpersonal relationships, of attention to the impact of setting or timing, of "impression management," of satisfying identification needs, and so on. Since the message the receiver "gets" may depend upon all of these conditions, we can readily see how such factors may establish favorable *preconditions for influence*, and hence how they bear upon the outcome of any attempt to influence others.

However, we need to remind ourselves that we should not mistake the impact of a leader's power or authority as being influence. Leaders exercise both, but this must not obscure the fact that the two processes are different.

A leader's role is that of "leading" his followers from one state of affairs into another state of affairs. Depending upon the leader's institutionalized position (his authority) and his power, he may be able to bring these changes about without exercising any influence whatever. But, at least in democratic situations, a leader's susceptibility to influence by his less authoritative constituents may ultimately determine the success and the length of his leadership.[10]

In the same way, successful leadership in all but the most authoritarian organizations is as much a function of the leader's susceptibility *to* influence by his subordinates as it is of his competence to influence them. This is especially true of leadership in interpersonal relationships.

INFLUENCE AND CONTROL

How, then, can we comprehend the relationship between influence and control?

What influences people will sooner or later (and more or less) channel or affect their behavior in some way. There can be little doubt about that. In this respect, influence and control are coincidental.

But it is also important to note that it is one's communication networks within which he is basically *in-formed* and maintained (in terms of his psychosocial equilibrium), and that *those* influences are far more potent and pervasive than any specific attempts made to influence him in his adult life. In other words, it is those influences which we are unaware of that generally determine our thinking and our behavior—far more so than those we are aware of. Those attempts to influence us which we are aware of simply pose additional (and often conscious) alternatives, and hence the occasion for choice. Those we are not aware of serve to limit the scope of the alternatives we might perceive, and they therefore determine or control our thought and behavior in more basic and more pervasive ways. For these reasons we are far less susceptible to the entreaties of mass advertising, for example, than we are to the day-to-day endorsement of our

---

[10] Cf. Chapters 11 and 12 of L. W. Milbrath, *The Washington Lobbyist* (Chicago: Rand McNally & Co., 1963).

identities and our "realities." And these are endorsements which we solicit from our families, friends, colleagues and co-workers, reference others, and so on.

Such influences are so subtle as to be imperceptible. So we could profitably raise the issue of the ethics or "morality" of *purposive* influence (as opposed to incidental or nonintended influences).

The Ethics of Purposive Influence

Purposive influence is one of the applied functions of purposive communication. As such, it is subject to the same conditions that every other function of communication is subject to.

The most pertinent condition of communication (relevant to this issue) is the basic one: what *can* be communicated-to someone depends ultimately upon that person's take-into-account-susceptibilities. People are influence-able therefore *only* within the range of possibilities which exists within the structure of their particular psychological systems at that point in time.

Our fear of adverse influence at the hands of others through communication stems from a common (but faulty) concept of communication held by many people—that there is some "magic" in communication that can basically affect the thinking or behavior of a receiver in spite of his will or efforts to fend off those influences. As we have seen, this cannot be so. What an individual *can* comprehend is ultimately determined by his own take-into-account-abilities. And how he will react as a consequence of "getting the message" depends upon him and upon his values and beliefs, not upon the "content" of the utterances directed at him.

Thus it is *impossible* (except serendipitously) to influence another person communicatively beyond the susceptibilities of that receiver's own comprehending systems. The "ethics" of purposive influence is therefore intrinsic to the conditions by which communication occurs. What can't be, communicatively, won't be, behaviorally. What won't be, behaviorally, can't be, communicatively.[11]

The same intrinsic check-and-balance does not hold true for the exercise

---

[11] Cf. Chapters 8 and 11 for a review of these limitations. The reader may be reminded here of the furor about "subliminal communication" some years ago. Most of our communicative functioning *is* necessarily subliminal or nonconscious. One's take-into-account-susceptibilities derive from a comprehending system, whether we are consciously aware of what is going on or not. The conclusion forced here is that it isn't possible to influence another "subliminally" any *more* than we could influence him "directly."

of authority or power, however. No parent has to present any affidavit of qualifications for exercising his or her institutionalized power. Television broadcasters are not only policed by government agencies; most subscribe to their own professional code of ethics. Yet parents and teachers and bosses, who are privileged to exercise institutionalized power over subordinates, affect our attitudes and beliefs and actions far more pervasively in the long run than television programs do.

We could always ask whether or not the ends sought through influence are consistent with those valued or sanctioned in the larger society. We might thereby determine that the ends sought are unethical. But there could be nothing unethical about the process itself.

Role Prescription and Influence

We learn to perform certain roles in certain settings[12] in ways which permit us to have mutual expectations regarding each other. Thus a proportion of all so-called interpersonal influence has as its object or end the mutual determination by the participants of their appropriate roles in a particular situation. In other words, in nonhierarchical encounters, it is usually not the other's behavior which we wish to influence directly, but his *perception or conception of his appropriate role in that situation.*

The strategies and tactics we employ to produce this sort of influence vary from finishing schools to situational embarrassment through a disapproving glance.[13] "Candid Camera" has, over the years, captured a wide range of examples of the consequences of sometimes subtle, sometimes overt, attempts to influence others by situationally ascribing roles to them.

On Mass Communication and Mass Persuasion

It is probably apparent to the reader that on-purpose attempts to influence large numbers of people are usually referred to as "persuasion" or

---

[12] See B. J. Biddle and E. J. Thomas, *Role Theory: Concepts and Research* (New York: John Wiley & Sons, Inc., 1966) for a recent survey and assessment of role theory. Cf. R. G. Barker and H. F. Wright, *Midwest and Its Children* (New York: Harper & Bros., 1955), for a description of *behavior setting.* Cf. E. Goffman, *Encounters: Two Studies in the Sociology of Interaction* (Indianapolis: Bobbs-Merrill Co., Inc., 1961).

[13] Cf. E. Goffman, "Embarrassment and Social Organization," *American Journal of Sociology,* 1956, 62, p. 267; E. Goffman, "On Face-Work," *Psychiatry,* 1955, 18, 213–31; E. Berne, *Games People Play* (New York: Grove Press, 1964); and S. S. Feldman, *Mannerisms of Speech and Gestures in Everyday Life* (New York: International Universities Press, 1959).

"propaganda" rather than as influence. As noted earlier, when we think at the level of the mass, we are likely to use the term "persuasion" rather than the term "influence."

It would be pointless to argue the appropriateness or relative merits of these terms in this usage. The phenomenon we want to focus upon is the same whether we use one term or the other.

There can be little doubt that "mass communication" methods and techniques are applied, and are pertinent, in large organizations. So whatever the terms used, there are some keys to understanding the process of mass communication in organizations which can be isolated for purposes of our analysis.

BASIC CONSIDERATIONS

The body of literature relating in some way to the issues of mass communication and persuasion is massive.[14] It would not be possible to summarize that literature here. Nor would it be particularly fruitful to attempt to do so. We can, however, usefully abstract from that literature a few key factors that will help to extend our understanding of this particular function of communication.

1. We need to recall that what can be communicated-to large numbers of people is limited to the comprehend-abilities (and -susceptibilities) that are culturally common to the members of that particular audience. There

---

[14] In one way or another, a tremendously wide range of approaches and perspectives has some relevance to the issues involved. A representative sampling will illustrate the diversity of this range: e.g., A. R. Cohen, *Attitude Change and Social Influence* (New York: Basic Books, Inc., 1964); L. W. Pye, *Communications and Political Development* (Princeton, N.J.: Princeton University Press, 1963); W. P. Davison, *International Political Communication* (New York: Frederick A. Praeger, Inc., 1965); R. Newcomb and M. Sammons, *Employee Communications in Action* (New York: Harper & Row, 1961); American Management Association, *Effective Communication on the Job* (New York: The Association, 1963); J. Ellul, *Propaganda: The Formation of Men's Attitudes* (New York: Alfred A. Knopf, Inc., 1965); E. Crane, *Marketing Communications* (New York: John Wiley & Sons, Inc., 1965); M. Sherif & C. I. Hovland, *Social Judgment* (New Haven, Conn.: Yale University Press, 1961); W. C. Minnick, *The Art of Persuasion* (Boston: Houghton Mifflin Co., 1957); J. T. Klapper, *The Effects of Mass Communication* (New York: Free Press, 1960); C. I. Hovland et al., *Communication and Persuasion* (New Haven, Conn.: Yale University Press, 1953); and H. I. Abelson, *Persuasion: How Opinions and Attitudes Are Changed* (New York: Springer Publishing Co., Inc., 1959). Cf. H. Guetzkow, "Communications in Organizations," in J. G. March (ed.), *Handbook of Organizations* (Chicago: Rand McNally & Co., 1965); and L. Thayer, "Communication and Organization," in F. E. X. Dance (ed.), *Human Communication Theory* (New York: Holt, Rinehart & Winston, 1967). Others are listed in the selected bibliography at the end of this chapter.

are two very practical but inevitable alternatives: one can, if possible, adapt his message to the take-into-account-susceptibilities of a particular target audience or, alternatively, he can look for and segregate out an audience which already has in common the kinds of comprehend-abilities and -susceptibilities that he deems necessary to the success of his endeavor.

Persuasion (or influence) has to occur, as noted earlier, within the domain of what is *possible*. And what is possible varies as a consequence of either (a) adapting the elements of communication to a given audience, or (b) selecting an audience communicatively adapted to the "givens" of the other elements.

2. Whenever we look at the processes of intercommunication or mass communication, we need to keep in mind the sources of people's take-into-account-abilities and -susceptibilities. What is "good," "true," "appropriate," "satisfactory," "status-endowing," "right," etc., is an aspect of social reality. Thus, whether or not individual X is persuade-able may depend ultimately upon the acceptability of that intended change in him *to those* from whom he gets or seeks personal endorsement.

There is nothing simple or certain about making such judgments in advance. Beliefs, opinions, attitudes, and the like are always relative— relative to some standard which itself varies over time, both within individuals and within their mutually-endorsing cultures and subcultures. The reason hourly workers don't think "like managers" is that their reality-sources for certain of their basic orientations and values are not managers, but their fellow-workers. It is therefore relatively impossible to "persuade" worker X to believe or behave in ways which he anticipates would be significantly at odds with those from whom he wants and seeks regular endorsement.

So whether or not a message has the appropriate degree of perceived relevance or validity (beyond its comprehensibility), and whether or not it has perceived utility for a given individual, may depend as much upon what he assumes to be the validity and utility of that message for his endorsers as it does upon its perceived validity and utility for himself.

3. Given these prior considerations, it may be useful to restate the applicable measurement criteria. If the target audience is given, then the primary measure is *effectiveness*, and cost is secondary. When the intent is to reach every individual in an audience "persuasively," then the matter of primary concern is how successful the attempt was—not the cost efficiency of that attempt.

However, when the message is adapted to a particular audience (as is true in some advertising), then the primary criterion is cost efficiency and

234   *Communication and Communication Systems*

not effectiveness. This is so for the simple reason that the degree of effectiveness has supposedly been built-into the encounter by selecting a preadapted audience.

This particular distinction may not always be applicable. But certainly the assessment criteria to be applied must vary with the "givens" of any attempt to persuade at the mass level.

4. Timing is important. Timing is critical strategically; messages may be effective or not depending upon how propitious the originator's timing is.

Perhaps even more important, however, is the issue of when to measure the results. The developing body of literature dealing with "diffusion"[15] should give us cause for reconsidering the simplistic bases for determining the timetable for measuring mass communication effectiveness.

As we move from the level of what's easy toward what's difficult (across the domain of what's *possible* communicatively), the time required to achieve a specific purpose increases rapidly. For example, it has taken many years even for small numbers of people to realize that management and labor are not natural enemies, in spite of the fact that both "sides" have been trying for several years to communicate that point of view to each other.

Also, what was communicatively impossible at one point in time may later become possible (and conversely).

5. A final consideration stems from the same studies on diffusion, and from sociological studies on opinion leaders and "gatekeepers."[16] It is this: that affecting large groups or aggregates of people hinges upon the immediate reactions of those who function as change agents (or leaders) in those groups or aggregates. Their role or function in bringing about changes in opinion, attitude, belief, etc., becomes more crucial as the issue at stake becomes more central to the norms, beliefs, orientations (i.e., the basic anchorages) of those groups or aggregates.

In other words, if the end to be gained involves (or otherwise engages) a norm central to the individual's personal identity[17] (or his state-relation-

---

[15] There is a considerable lineage of such studies. A recent specific study is J. S. Coleman, E. Katz, and H. Menzel, *Medical Innovation: A Diffusion Study* (Indianapolis: Bobbs-Merrill Co., Inc., 1966). An excellent assessment of work in this field is E. M. Rogers, *Diffusion of Innovations* (New York: Free Press, 1962).

[16] E.g., P. F. Lazarsfeld, B. Berelson, & H. Gaudet, *The People's Choice* (New York: Columbia University Press, 1948); E. Katz & P. F. Lazarsfeld, *Personal Influence: The Part Played by People in the Flow of Mass Communications* (New York: Free Press, 1955); et seqq.

[17] Cf. M. and Carolyn W. Sherif, *An Outline of Social Psychology.* Rev. ed. (New York: Harper & Bros., 1956), esp. Part III; E. P. Hollander, *Leaders, Groups, and Influ-*

ships with his endorsers), then any change of attitude or opinion will likely have to be mediated by the cognizant leaders of those reference groups or aggregates.

"Mass persuasion" may therefore depend ultimately more upon interpersonal influence than upon any other factor.

ON PERSUADE-ABILITY

Given that a manager's (or an administrator's) effectiveness in fulfilling his function in organizations depends upon his susceptibility to advantageous persuasion as much as upon his competence in persuading others, reversing the direction of all of the preceding points would be a useful exercise. For example, as a manager the unlikelihood of one's accepting as valid any statement which does not jibe with his conceptions of the world should be compensated for in some way—if accepting that statement as valid were in his own (or his organization's) best interest.

What serves to protect us from being disadvantageously persuaded by others also serves to bar us from accepting ideas or beliefs that could be advantageous. The issue here is not that of being "right," but of setting aside our negative inclinations long enough to examine the potential advantages (to ourselves) of being persuaded in directions intended by others.

Perhaps this is a good point at which to turn our attention to the most ubiquitous of all of the applied functions of communication—the *integrative function*.

SUGGESTIONS FOR FURTHER READING

The literature on persuasion and influence (and related topics) is undoubtedly the most extensive in the field. While no claim could be made either to the comprehensiveness or the representativeness of the following list of suggested readings, it is intended to provide a useful cross-section of that literature. It could particularly be used to examine the various approaches that are taken to the study of persuasion and/or influence.

ABELSON, H. I. *Persuasion: How Opinions and Attitudes Are Changed.* New York: Springer Publishing Co., Inc., 1959.

ence (New York: Oxford University Press, 1964); and S. H. Britt (ed.), *Consumer Behavior and the Behavioral Sciences: Theories and Applications* (New York: John Wiley & Sons, Inc., 1966).

ARGYLE, M. "Social Pressure in Public and Private Situations," *Journal of Abnormal and Social Psychology*, Vol. 54 (1957), pp. 172–75.

ASCH, SOLOMON E. "The Doctrine of Suggestion, Prestige, and Imitation in Social Psychology," *Psychological Review*, Vol. 55 (1948), pp. 250–76.

BACK, K. "Influence through Social Communication," *Journal of Abnormal and Social Psychology*, Vol. 46 (1951), pp. 9–23.

BARNOUW, ERIK. *Mass Communication*. New York: Holt, Rinehart & Winston, 1956.

BAUER, R. A. "Limits of Persuasion," *Harvard Business Review*, Vol. 36 (1948), pp. 105–10.

———. "The Obstinate Audience: The Influence Process from the Point of View of Social Communications," revision of a paper delivered to the Western Psychological Association, April 20, 1963.

BILLS, BENJAMIN FRANKLIN. *Persuasion in Business*. Chicago: Gilbert Publishers, 1937.

BREMBECK, WINSTON L., and HOWELL, WILLIAM S. *Persuasion: A Means of Social Control*. Englewood Cliffs, N.J.: Prentice-Hall, Inc., 1952.

CALHOON, R. P., and KIRKPATRICK, C. A. *Influencing Employee Behavior*. New York: McGraw-Hill Book Co., 1956.

CARTWRIGHT, D. "Achieving Change in People: Some Applications of Group Dynamics Theory," *Human Relations*, Vol. 4 (1951), pp. 381–92.

———. "Some Principles of Mass Persuasion," *Human Relations*, Vol. 2 (1949), pp. 253–67.

CHASE, STUART. *Power of Words*. New York: Harcourt, Brace & Co., Inc., 1953.

———. *The Tyranny of Words*. New York: Harcourt, Brace & Co., Inc., 1938.

———, and CHASE, MARIAN T. *Roads to Agreement*. New York: Harper & Bros., 1951.

COCH, L., and FRENCH, J. R. P., JR. "Overcoming Resistance to Change," *Human Relations*, Vol. 1 (1948), pp. 512–32.

COHEN, A. R. *Attitude Change and Social Influence*. New York: Basic Books, Inc., 1964.

CRANE, E. *Marketing Communications*. New York: John Wiley & Sons, Inc., 1965.

DEUTSCH, M., and GERARD, H. B. "A Study of Normative and Informational Social Influences upon Individual Judgment," *Journal of Abnormal and Social Psychology*, Vol. 51 (1955), pp. 629–36.

DOOB, LEONARD W. *Public Opinion and Propaganda*. New York: Henry Holt & Co., 1948.

Dovring, Karin. *Road of Propaganda: The Semantics of Biased Communication.* New York: Philosophical Library, 1959.

Festinger, L., and Kelley, H. H. *Changing Attitudes through Social Contact.* Ann Arbor: Research Center for Group Dynamics, University of Michigan, 1951.

Harvey, Ian. *The Technique of Persuasion.* London: Falcon Press, 1951.

Hopkins, T. K. *The Exercise of Influence in Small Groups.* Totowa, N.J.: Bedminster Press, Inc., 1964.

Hovland, Carl I. (ed.). *The Order of Presentation in Persuasion.* New Haven, Conn.: Yale University Press, 1957.

————, and Janis, Irving L. (eds.). *Personality and Persuasibility.* New Haven, Conn.: Yale University Pess, 1959.

————; Janis, Irving L.; and Kelley, Harold H. *Communication and Persuasion: Psychological Studies of Opinion Change.* New Haven, Conn.: Yale University Press, 1953.

Katz, Elihu, and Lazarsfeld, P. F. *Personal Influence.* New York: Free Press, 1955.

Kelley, H. H., and Lamb, T. W. "Certainty of Judgment and Resistance to Social Influence," *Journal of Abnormal and Social Psychology,* Vol. 55 (1957), pp. 137–39.

Kirk, John R. "Communication Theory and Methods of Fixing Belief," *ETC: A Review of General Semantics,* Vol. 10 (1953).

Lasswell, H. D. *Language and Politics.* New York: E. W. Stewart, 1949.

Lerbinger, O., and Sullivan, A. J. (eds.). *Information, Influence, and Communication.* New York: Basic Books, Inc., 1965.

Lewis, G. W. (ed). *Resolving Social Conflicts: Selected Papers on Group Dynamics.* New York: Harper & Bros., 1948.

Minnick, W. C. *The Art of Persuasion.* Boston: Houghton Mifflin Co., 1957.

Milbrath, L. W. "Lobbying as a Communication Process," *Public Opinion Quarterly,* Vol. 24 (1960), pp. 32–53.

Miller, Clyde R. *The Process of Persuasion.* New York: Crown Publishers, Inc., 1946.

Muehl, William. *The Road to Persuasion.* New York: Oxford University Press, 1956.

Oliver, R. T. *The Psychology of Persuasive Speech.* New York: Longmans, Green & Co., 1942.

Raven, B. H. "Social Influence on Opinions and the Communications of Related Content," *Journal of Abnormal and Social Psychology,* Vol. 58 (1959), pp. 119–28.

ROBINSON, C.   "The Gentle Art of Persuasion," Public Relations Journal, June, 1956.

ROBINSON, E. J.   Communication and Public Relations. Columbus, Ohio: Charles E. Merrill Books, Inc., 1966.

ROSENBERG, M. J. et al.   Attitude Organization and Change. Yale Studies in Attitude and Communication, Vol. 3. New Haven, Conn.: Yale University Press, 1960.

SARNOFF, I., and KATZ, D.   "The Motivational Bases of Attitude Change," Journal of Abnormal and Social Psychology, Vol. 49 (1954), pp. 115–24.

SHERIF, C. W.; SHERIF, M.; and NEBERGALL, R. E.   Attitude and Attitude Change. Philadelphia: W. B. Saunders Co., 1965.

SMITH, B. L.; LASSWELL, H. D.; and CASEY, R. D.   Propaganda, Communication and Public Opinion. Princeton, N.J.: Princeton University Press, 1946.

SMITH, GEORGE HORSLEY.   Motivation Research in Advertising and Marketing. New York: McGraw-Hill Book Co., 1954.

SMITH, M. BREWSTER et al.   Opinions and Personality. New York: John Wiley & Sons, Inc., 1956.

WALTER, B.   Bureaucratic Communications: A Statistical Analysis of Influence. Chapel Hill: Institute for Research in Social Science, University of North Carolina, 1963.

WHYTE, W. H., JR., and THE EDITORS OF Fortune.   Is Anybody Listening? How and Why U.S. Business Fumbles When It Talks with Human Beings. New York: Simon & Schuster, Inc., 1952.

WINDLESHAM, LORD.   Communication and Political Power. London: Jonathan Cape, 1966.

WRIGHT, CHARLES R.   Mass Communication. New York: Random House, Inc., 1959.

16

Integrative Functions

WHEN WE THINK of purposive or instrumental communication, we most likely think of it in terms of informing someone, of ordering or commanding someone, or of trying to persuade or influence someone. But there is a conglomerate of other functions of purposive or instrumental communication which we need to be aware of. Collectively, we will refer to these as the *integrative* functions of communication.

To gain some insight into the importance and the universality of the integrative functions,[1] we need particularly to bring back into focus one of the basic concepts outlined in the first part of this book.

Toward a Basic Understanding

As discussed in an earlier chapter, the communication that occurs has the consequence of energizing, organizing, and channelizing the behavior

---

[1] ". . . (the) passage of new information (in communication) is no more important than what we call the integrational aspect of the communication process. In the broadest sense, the integrational aspect includes all behavioral operations which:
1. Serve to keep the system in operation.
2. Serve to regulate the interactional process.
3. Cross-reference particular messages to comprehensibility in a particular context.
4. Relate the particular context to the larger contexts of which the particular interaction is but a special situation." Ray Birdwhistell, quoted in T. A. Sebeok, A. S. Hayes, and Mary C. Bateson (eds.), *Approaches to Semiotics* (The Hague: Mouton, 1964), pp. 161–62.

The notion of integration within an enterprise is occasionally used with a slightly different, but complementary meaning. Cf. J. W. Lorsch, *Product Innovation and Organization* (New York: Macmillan, 1965).

of living systems. However, if the messages we create in order to comprehend our environments were not cumulative and self-organizing in some
way, it would be impossible to gain or to maintain the necessary degree of
equilibrium or stable state-relations vis-à-vis those various aspects of our
environment we concern ourselves with (the human, the physical, the
ideational, the aesthetic, and so on).

Always in terms of how we have previously been in-formed by our
communication experiences, our psychological structures evolve. Those
psychological structures (or systems) then provide for their own continuity
by establishing adaptive mechanisms which, as we have seen, become
functionally autonomous. The consequence is a very complex and intricate
set of *state-relationships* between and among various aspects of one's
environment and the corresponding functional subsystems of his own
psychological structure.

If the adaptive mechanism for a given state-relationship is confirmed or
endorsed by significant others (or other aspects of one's environment)
confirmation serves to maintain, integrate, and perpetuate that part of
one's psychological structure.

Even though we seem to be dichotomizing "internal" and "external"
here, the reader will recall that all of our understandings of the world are
ultimately "internal." The state-relationship we attempt to stabilize is the
one between our concept of ourselves and *our concept* of someone or
something happening "out there," not the "out there" happening itself.
But the level at which we comprehend and the level at which we take
some action-in-the-environment are two different levels of phenomena.
One confirms his conceptual models of the world by feedback from his
actions vis-à-vis the "external" target—and vice versa.

So much for the basics. We need pursue this abstract level no further.
It is the implications we are after.

For our purposes, the central (and perhaps rather gross but nonetheless
valid) implications of the communicative process (in which all living
systems engage) are these:

1. A substantial proportion of our informational needs is for that
information which *confirms* established (or desired) state-relationships
with pertinent aspects of our physical and human environments. The
functional consequence of such confirmation for the individual is the
integration and perpetuation of his psychological system. The functional
consequence of *disconfirmation* of established (or desired) state-relationships in any critical magnitude is the gradual (or rapid—depending upon
the centrality of the state-relationships involved) *disintegration* of the

psychological structure of the individual involved. So one major function of communication at the *intrapersonal* level is that of self-integration (or, to put it conversely, of continuously offsetting any disintegration [i.e., entropy] that might otherwise occur).[2]

2. *Interpersonally,* relationships ranging from two-person interactions to the full matrix of an individual's communicative acquaintances become structured as complex state-relationships; and, as structures or organizations, they persist and are maintained only to the extent that the participants reaffirm their organization-ness in some mutually acceptable way.[3] One's failure to behave in a friendly fashion toward another with whom he shares a friendship relation could erode or deteriorate that relationship in some way. Certainly it would alert the other to that potential disconfirmation of their relationship which he detects in his friend's behavior.[4]

3. At the level of larger than face-to-face human groups, the same inherent "need" of the system structure for continuous integration holds true. At this level, the level of formal organizations, integrative functions are provided in part by bureaucratization, proceduralization, institutionalization, etc. When a social system exceeds the integrative limits of face-to-face encounters, the necessary integrative mechanisms become imbedded in that social system's literature, art, folklore, mythology, beliefs, mores, orientations, "small talk," etiquette, and institutional practices.[5] Whatever

---

[2] The perceptive reader may note immediately the similarity of this function to the concept of *negentropy.* That similarity is not accidental. See, e.g., W. R. Ashby, *Design for a Brain* (London: Chapman and Hall, 1954); and S. Beer, *Cybernetics and Management* (New York: John Wiley & Sons, Inc., 1959). Cf. D. E. Berlyne, *Structure and Direction in Thinking* (New York: John Wiley & Sons, Inc., 1965); and O. J. Harvey (ed.), *Experience, Structure, and Adaptability* (New York: Springer Publishing Co., Inc., 1966).

[3] The reader may see some parallels between this and what has been referred to as "phatic communication" (e.g., Malinowski, et seqq.).

[4] Cf. P. M. Blau, *Exchange and Power in Social Life* (New York: John Wiley & Sons, Inc., 1964); G. C. Homans, *Social Behavior: Its Elementary Forms* (New York: Harcourt, Brace & World, 1961); E. Goffman, *Encounters: Two Studies in the Sociology of Interaction* (Indianapolis: Bobbs-Merrill Co., Inc., 1961); A. Zaleznik and D. Moment, *The Dynamics of Interpersonal Behavior* (New York: John Wiley & Sons, Inc., 1964); and W. G. Bennis et al. (eds.), *Interpersonal Dynamics* (Homewood, Ill.: Dorsey Press, 1964).

[5] It would hardly be feasible to document these points in any definitive way, for they have long been familiar to comparative sociologists and cultural anthropologists. However, some recent treatments may be of interest to the serious student of communication: e.g., Hugh Dalziel Duncan, *Communication and Social Order* (New York: Bedminster Press, Inc., 1962), and "The Symbolic Act: Basic Propositions on the Relationship between Symbols and Society—A Theory that *How* We Communicate

it is that the members of large social systems separately partake of in common is a potential vehicle for the integrative functions of communication, which in turn link them together culturally.

For those who would manage or study human organizations, there are thus a great many implications of the integrative functions of communication. These are but representative of the kinds of concerns that might be advantageously thought through:[6]

a) To the extent there do not emerge, accidentally or on-purpose, exclusive means by which members of an organization can identify and relate to each other as members of that organization, they are not likely to become personally involved with the goals of that organization.[7]

b) To the extent that the integrative functions of an organization and those of the larger society are incompatible, the members of the organization must ultimately either choose a preferred allegiance, or suffer the consequences of the psychological conflict that ensues.

c) An organization's maintenance information system, to be effective, must be based upon the integrative conventions and practices common to the members of that organization.

d) At the interpersonal level, the crucial integrative processes function horizontally and not vertically. For example, the source of a particular member's social realities concerning those organizations of which he is a member is typically his own peers—his own work group—and not his superiors or subordinates. In other words, we might say that horizontal or lateral relationships are more (or less) "symbiotic," while vertical relationships are more (or less) "synergistic."

e) Horizontal and vertical integration (in a task-relevant sense only) are the major sources of the integrity of any organization qua organization.

f) The increasing magnitude of man-machine partnerships raises some interesting questions about the need for, the changing sources of, and the

---

Determines How We Relate as Human Beings," in L. Thayer (ed.), *Communication: Theory and Research* (Springfield, Ill.: Charles C Thomas, 1967); J. O. Hertzler, *A Sociology of Language* (New York: Random House, 1965); and A. Kuhn, *The Study of Society: A Unified Approach* (Homewood, Ill.: Richard D. Irwin & The Dorsey Press, 1963). Cf. M. R. Cohen, "Fictions," and R. Dubin, "Organization Fictions," in R. Dubin, *Human Relations in Administration.* 2d ed. (Englewood Cliffs, N.J.: Prentice-Hall, Inc., 1961).

[6] Since these few examples are intended to be only suggestive, they should not be construed as systematically bounding the full range of implications in any way.

[7] The reader may want to examine M. Sherif et al., *Intergroup Conflict and Co-operation* (Norman, Oklahoma: Institute of Group Relations, 1961) as an empirical demonstration of how such phenomena occur. Cf. I. A. Berg and B. M. Bass (eds.), *Conformity and Deviation* (New York: Harper & Row, 1961).

changing nature of the integrative functions of communication for those involved.

g) At the intrapersonal level, it can be seen that those who occupy successively higher positions in a managerial (or leadership) hierarchy must have—if they are to be effective in those positions—increasingly more personal autonomy (i.e., must be integratively more self-sufficient). The "higher-up" the leader or manager in the hierarchy, the fewer "needs" he must have for integrative communication from his peers, subordinates, and superiors.

h) Finally, and this doesn't exhaust the list of implications by any means, one's own integrative "needs," and the nature of the communication channels which link him to other members of an organization, often make it extremely difficult for him to distinguish between what has *informative* and what has simply *integrative* utility. "Telling the boss what he wants to hear" is primarily integrative. It takes a perceptive superior to understand his own integrative needs and the peculiar nature of the communication networks in which he is continuously integrated in such a way that he can successfully bias himself against the pitfall of mistaking what is merely integrative as having some utility as operating information.

Some Ends and Means of Integrative Communication[8]

The integrative functions of communication underlie much of our interpersonal behavior. A look at some of the ends and means of integrative communication may help to further suggest the pervasiveness of this function.

RELATING, ORIENTING, AND IDENTITY PROCESSES

The ways in which we communicate-to others and are communicated-with by them determine how we relate ourselves to others, how we relate others to ourselves, and how we come to relate the people, things, events, conditions, ideas, etc., of the world to each other. Without communication as we know it, we could relate ourselves to our worlds, and the elements of our worlds to each other, only in very crude and elementary ways. Communication is thus both the means and the end of the manner in which we adapt to and seek our goals in our environments—particularly our social environments.

---

[8] The reader may find it interesting to compare this perspective with those of J. O. Hertzler, *op. cit.*; and Hugh Dalziel Duncan, *op. cit.*

It is thus apparent that all of the orientations we have to ourselves, to others, and to the things and happenings of the world "out there" are communicatively derived and maintained.

Given that our models of the world are largely in-formed through communication with others, it follows that the ways in which we define and identify ourselves reflexively are created, maintained, exploited, or altered via the integrative functions of intercommunication. It is in the nature of the psychological system to require continuous reaffirmation and confirmation. It is only by being treated by others in a way that seems consistent with the view we have of ourselves that our identities perpetuate and sustain themselves. Ultimately, the answers to questions such as "Who am I?" "What is this all about?" and so forth—can come only from other people. Once in-formed within our personal communication systems, we are linked to others who at least endorse us, who variously confirm our models of the world, who to some greater or lesser degree reaffirm our values and beliefs—in short, who provide the continuous integration required by our psychological systems.[9] In the process, of course, the structures or organizations defined by those communication networks are themselves maintained and integrated.

Social Structure

Social structure is both the cause and the consequence of intercommunication. Every organization has a structure.[10] That structure is, at any point in time, a consequence of the intercommunication which has occurred, which is a consequence of the structure within which it occurred, and so on. But, like all living systems, human organization structures are

---

[9] This may raise the general semanticist's concern about *extensional* vs. *intentional* orientations. See, e.g., Wm. V. Haney, *Communication: Patterns and Incidents* (Homewood, Ill.: Richard D. Irwin, Inc., 1960), esp. chapters IX–XII. It seems to me, however, that the extensional-intentional distinction is useful only to the extent that we bear in mind the fact that the "territory" ("reality") often exists *only* in the "maps" (the "subjective" models-of-the-world held by people). This possibility of the reversal of the locus of the ultimate "reality" of our maps would seem to be especially likely when we look at the integrative functions. For example, whether this is *"in fact"* a good company to work for can be measured only against the "maps" or beliefs people have about it. Sometimes the only way to understand the "territory" is to be aware of all of the different "maps" which constitute its only existence.

[10] Throughout this book, except where specifically noted, *structure* refers to the matrix or network of intercommunication channels by which the functions of an organization are actually carried out. By structure I do not refer to "organization charts"; they may bear little relation to the actual communicative structure of a given organization. Cf. S. F. Nadel, *The Theory of Social Structure*. New York: Free Press, 1957.

constantly evolving. Thus the intercommunication which occurs today within an organization has its impact in creating and recreating the structure by which the organization is defined tomorrow, which in turn enables and limits intercommunication, and so on and on.

Two-person relationships, as well as small groups, also have structures. These structures, just as the structures of larger organizations, are best characterized by the pattern and the nature of the communication channels via which the members or participatants relate and intercommunicate.

Whether large or small, formal or informal, the structures of organizations are perpetuated only to the extent that the individuals involved *mutually* subscribe to the constraints which these communication channels place upon them, and only to the extent that they mutually reaffirm each other in that channel in terms of their respective identities, etc.

CEREMONY, RITUAL, ETIQUETTE, PROTOCOL

Indirectly, social structures are reinforced or integrated through mutually obligatory rituals, ceremonies, etiquette and protocol.[11] Such prescribed communication behaviors serve the purpose of integrating the participants and the social structures within which they are performed.

When relationships are widely institutionalized, the type of deference to be shown hierarchical superiors is a part of protocol of those relationships.[12] Typically, for example, it is appropriate "etiquette" for a subordinate to telephone in advance and request an audience with his superior, although the superior is presumed to be operating within prescribed bounds if he decides to "drop in" on the subordinate without announcing his intentions.

People always bring such behavior "prescriptions" with them to any gathering, and to the organizations which they become members of. But prescriptions peculiar to any particular organization or to any face-to-face encounter also emerge from the intercommunication of the people involved. Whether general to a total human society, or peculiar to a single

---

11 These means of fulfilling the integrative function of communication have received treatment in a wide variety of sources. See, for example, Hugh Dalziel Duncan, *op. cit.*; E. Goffman, *op. cit.*; and E. Goffman, *Behavior in Public Places* (New York: Free Press, 1963). Cf., for various other implications, E. Berne, *Games People Play* (New York: Grove Press, 1964); and J. A. M. Meerloo, "Greeting as Trial Approval," *Archives of General Psychiatry*, 1966, 15, 256–59.

12 Cf. E. Goffman, "The Nature of Deference and Demeanor," *American Anthropologist*, 1956, 58, 473–502; Tom Burns, "The Forms of Conduct," *American Journal of Sociology*, 1958, 64, 142–43; and E. K. Wilson, *Sociology: Rules, Roles, and Relationships* (Homewood, Ill.: Dorsey Press, 1966), esp. Ch. 9.

interpersonal relationship, such prescriptions serve the same purpose—of maintaining (or not) or integrating (or not) the existing relationship (and the orientations of each of the participants to each other and hence to the relationship itself).

EXPRESSIVE AND EVOCATIVE FUNCTIONS

Certain expressive uses of language are also integrative—either for the individual utterer or for the social gathering in which they occur. Dramatic gestures or expressions such as "Ouch!" or "Well, I'll be a son of a gun!" are illustrative.

From time to time, we all use certain expressions intended to communicate-to others not information as such, but a sign of recognition, a willingness to order the relationship in a certain way, etc. An utterance which has purely expressive functions serves only the end of integrating oneself in some way. But an expressive utterance may serve indirectly to integrate a relationship or a social gathering through the response of the receiver(s).

Communication is also used to evoke feelings or feeling-states—to amuse or to entertain. Art, music, sculpture, poetry, etc., can all have as their function that of affecting the reader or viewer in some "aesthetic" way—which response might thereby contribute to the receiver's integration, and further to the integration (or disintegration) of the larger society.

VERBAL FENCING AND GAMING

There is often some pleasure in the sheer exercise of our abilities to conceptualize and verbalize vis-à-vis a worthy opponent. If these encounters take the form of verbal fencing or "gaming," their latent function (whatever their manifest purpose) is usually that of integrating or reaffirming each participant in some way. Arguments occasionally are not intended to bring the other person around to one's own point of view, but are for the purpose of "working something through" in one's own mind. In this way, verbal fencing serves an integrative function.

Norbert Wiener once said, "How do I know what I think until I've heard what I have to say." He was describing the manner in which our own utterances are often used to create or maintain our own psychological systems; in these instances, we are not primarily concerned with the reactions of others.

While such encounters are therefore consummatory rather than instrumental, it is nonetheless useful to take account of them. If we mistakenly believe that another is being "informative" when in fact his behavior is intended to be simply self-integrative, we may frustrate ourselves and him too. And, if nothing else, that would likely consequent in some disintegration of our relationship with him.

LOGIC AND THINKING

It is probably apparent that the intercommunication which subserves the function of integrating the participants' psychological systems serves also the function of perpetuating the peculiar logic of their knowledges and the means by which they gain and maintain these knowledges. Communicating via any language serves to perpetuate the logic of that language itself.

For example, even though a common language provides a certain degree and a certain kind of integration of a society or a professional group (through its argot), that same language may stand as a barrier to perceiving the world in different (but perhaps extremely advantageous) ways. Einstein reported that he had to break through the barrier of the logic of the English language (and hence his own thinking) in order to perceive and describe the physical processes of the world in the more advantageous ways he has given us.

The "Amorality" of the Integrative Functions

It is important to realize that the integrative functions of communication (as is true of all the functions of communication) are "amoral." That is, there is nothing inherent in the process which predicts to the value or to the advantage or disadvantage of the process. Undoubtedly there is some advantage both to the individual and to the organization in the relative *integrity* of their respective structures. But this advantage would hold only if the competencies or capabilities thus created have some value or usefulness to the adaptive or the goal-pursuing capabilities of the individual and/or the organization. Integrity is of course advantageous to an organization *qua* organization, but that leaves open the question of whether the products or the services (or other uses) of that organization are, or can be, valued by the larger society.

In the same way, a well-integrated psychological structure is advantageous sheerly in terms of its strength, but this leaves open the further question of the value of that individual in some larger (societal) sense. Or, to take the point one step further, the fact that a relationship between people is "solid" is not in and of itself a guarantee that their relationship is a particularly good or healthy one—either for the individuals involved or for the organizations to which they belong, or the larger society.

It's easy to fall into the trap of assuming that those processes which serve to bring cohesion to human organizations, and equilibrium to individuals and their relationships, are thereby worthwhile and desirable. The measurement of communication effectiveness is at best a complex and tricky task. But beyond this is the question of the value of the goals being intercommunicatively sought. These are value judgments which can only be made by people. They are never inherent in the communication process itself.

The Integrative Functions and Metacommunication

There are both similarities and distinctions to be noted between metacommunication and the integrative functions of communication.

First, it is probably obvious that the state of integration (disintegration) of any communication encounter is an aspect of metacommunication. People do (or might) take-into-account the implications of any message or other aspects of a communicative encounter to assess their own psychological systems, to evaluate their present relationship with the originator or any other relationship which might be affected, and so on. So in this respect, integrative-disintegrative factors serve also as metacommunication.

Second, all metacommunication is either integrative or disintegrative in consequence. The cues and clues that people take-into-account as an aid to interpreting another's message or intentions inevitably serve the structure of the receiver (and hence of the relationship) either integratively or disintegratively.

Strategically, a competent communicator strives for harmony or consistency between what is communicative and what is metacommunicative to the receiver. But there may be occasions when he must bring about some new (or some additional degree of) integration between himself and another, even though he may be metacommunicatively disadvantaged. For example, a boss may appear to a subordinate to be arbitrarily exercising his authority, when in fact he may have the subordinate's personal interests in mind. Here he must communicatively compensate for what is a metacommunicative disadvantage.

At this point, we conclude our analysis of the four applied functions of communication, and of the development of a conceptual scaffolding for understanding the elements and the dynamics of human communication. In the following sections, we will concern ourselves with the implications of this conceptual framework for an understanding of communication technology, methods and techniques, and current research, problems, and issues.

SUGGESTIONS FOR FURTHER READING

As indicated in the text, there have been very few studies of the integrative functions of communication, as such. Nonetheless, there is a broad array of literature which has one or another kind of relevance for the perspectives developed in this chapter. A representative few have been selected as suggested additional readings.

ALLPORT, GORDON W., and POSTMAN, L. *The Psychology of Rumor*. New York: Henry Holt & Co., 1947.

BRYSON, LYMAN *et al.* (eds.). *Symbols and Society*. New York: Harper & Bros., 1955.

COHEN, A. M. "A Model of Group Adaptation to Organizational Change in Communication Networks," in L. THAYER (ed.). *Communication: Theory and Research*. Springfield, Ill.: Charles C Thomas, 1967.

CROWNE, D. P., and MARLOWE, D. *The Approval Motive*. New York: John Wiley & Sons, Inc., 1964.

DAVISON, W. P. *International Political Communication*. New York: Frederick A. Praeger, Inc., 1965.

DEFLEUR, M. L. "Mass Communication and Social Change," *Social Forces*, Vol. 44 (1966), pp. 314–26.

DEUTSCH, KARL W. *Nationalism and Social Communication*. New York: Technology Press of Massachusetts Institute of Technology and John Wiley & Sons, Inc., 1953.

DOOB, L. *Communication in Africa: A Search for Boundaries*. New Haven, Conn.: Yale University Press, 1961.

DUNCAN, H. D. *Communication and Social Order*. New York: Bedminster Press, Inc., 1962.

EISENSTADT, S. N. "Communication and Transformation of Symbolic Systems —Some Problems of Communication in Developing Societies," in L. THAYER (ed.). *Communication: Theory and Research*. Springfield, Ill.: Charles C Thomas, 1967.

FESTINGER, L.; SCHACHTER, S.; and BACK, K. *Social Pressure in Informal Groups*. New York: Harper & Bros., 1950.

Foa, U. G.   "Differentiation in Cross-Cultural Communication," in L. Thayer (ed.). *Communication: Concepts and Perspectives.* Washington, D.C.: Spartan Books, Inc., 1967.

Glanzer, M., and Glaser, R.   "Techniques for the Study of Group Structure and Behavior: II. Empirical Studies of the Effects of Structure in Small Groups," *Psychological Bulletin,* Vol. 58 (1961), pp. 1–27.

Goffman, E.   "On Face-Work: An Analysis of Ritual Elements in Social Interaction," *Psychiatry,* Vol. 18 (1955), pp. 213–31.

———.   "The Nature of Deference and Demeanor," *American Anthropologist,* Vol. 58 (1956), pp. 473–502.

———.   *Behavior in Public Places.* New York: Free Press, 1963.

Hall, D. M.   *Dynamics of Group Action.* Danville, Ill.: Interstate Printers & Publishers, 1957.

Hayakawa, S. I.   *Symbol, Status, and Personality.* New York: Harcourt, Brace & World, 1963.

Hertzler, J. O.   *A Sociology of Language.* New York: Random House, 1965.

Hymes, D.   *Language in Culture and Society: A Reader in Linguistics and Anthropology.* New York: Harper & Row, 1964.

Innis, Harold A.   *The Bias of Communication.* Toronto: University of Toronto Press, 1951.

Lyle, J.   "Communication, Group Atmosphere, Productivity, and Morale in Small Task Groups," *Human Relations,* Vol. 14 (1961), pp. 369–79.

Merton, Robert K. (ed.).   *Social Theory and Social Structure.* Rev. ed. New York: Free Press, 1957.

Newcomb, J. M.   *The Acquaintance Process.* New York: Holt, Rinehart & Winston, 1961.

Northrop, F. S. C.   "The Neurological and Behavioristic Psychological Basis of the Ordering of Society by Means of Ideas," *Science,* Vol. 107 (1948), pp. 411–17.

Packard, Vance.   *The Status Seekers.* New York: David McKay Co., Inc., 1959.

Ronken, H. O.   "Communication in the Work Group," *Harvard Business Review,* Vol. 29 (1951), pp. 108–14.

Ruesch, J.   "Technology and Social Communication," in L. Thayer (ed.), *Communication: Theory and Research.* Springfield, Ill.: Charles C Thomas, 1967.

Schatzman, L., and Strauss, A.   "Social Class and Modes of Communication," *American Journal of Sociology,* Vol. 60 (1955), pp. 329–38.

Smith, A. G.   *Communication and Status: The Dynamics of a Research Center.* Eugene: University of Oregon Press, 1966.

PART IV

Technology
and
Techniques

17

The Technology of Communication

THE TECHNOLOGY of communication encompasses *all of the means* by which the functions and ends of communication are served or carried out. It encompasses all of the devices, procedures, and equipment which have been created to amplify, augment, enable, or otherwise facilitate man's communication with himself and his fellows. In sum, the technology of communication encompasses all of the tools of communication which have been created (or have evolved)—and which therefore have served both to enhance and to limit man's communicate-abilities.

A look at the major categories of communication technology may help to clarify some of these often misconstrued elements of communication in human affairs.

The "Software" of Communication Technology: Languages

The most basic and by far the most significant of all communication technology has been the evolution and use of languages. A review of the history of language inventions and uses would take us too far afield, and such reviews are available elsewhere.[1]

What we need to develop here is a full appreciation of the fact that languages are a basic aspect of the technology of communication.

To do so, let us consider three kinds of languages that we all use, and ask how their invention and widespread use have both enhanced our

---

[1] E.g., M. Pei, *The Story of Language* (Philadelphia: J. B. Lippincott Co., 1949); and C. Laird, *The Miracle of Language* (New York: World, 1953).

communicate-abilities—(intra- and interpersonal)—and placed limits upon those same communicate-abilities.

Consider first the language(s) by which we customarily speak and write. For most of us, that would be English—although there may be a number of readers who use other languages to speak and to write (e.g., French or Spanish). Such languages are *tools*—tools which were invented and are constantly evolving, with and through which we can communicate with ourselves and with each other. The language(s) that we use to communicate with ourselves and with each other is thus a part of the "software" of the technology of communication.

Consider another language that we all use—the "language" of gesture.[2] It has been estimated that, while our English language dictionaries might contain up to 600,000 entries, a comparable "dictionary" of gestures, facial expressions, etc., would list more than 700,000 discriminable units. The language of gesture, expression, posture, etc., is indeed a "language" that greatly enhances and augments our abilities to be communicated-with and to communicate-to others.

Or consider a third language in common use—the "language" of numbers. It is the language of mathematics that has so greatly facilitated the inquiries and the achievements of the physical (and now the social) sciences. Without the language of numbers, our everyday transactions at the grocery store might be still as cumbersome and awkward as physically trading a cow for a bag of ground meal and other supplies. In fact, such transactions would be extremely awkward and limited were it not for the fact that we have a language of weights and measures—by which to determine how the exchange is to be carried out. Our modern way of life would be impossible without the language of numbers.

These are but three examples. There are many other languages, both specialized and general-purpose. But perhaps these examples will serve to emphasize the crucial role of language(s) in the evolution of our contemporary communicate-abilities. Just as important is our recognition that languages are inventions. They are but one category of tools or means by which we communicate with ourselves and with each other. As such, they are best viewed as part of the technology of communication—as a part of the "software" of that technology.

---

[2] Charlotte Wolff, *A Psychology of Gesture* (London: Methuen, 1948); cf. R. L. Birdwhistell, *Introduction to Kinesics: An Annotation System for Analysis of Body Motion and Gesture* (Washington, D.C.: Foreign Service Institute, 1952); and E. T. Hall, *The Silent Language* (Garden City, N.Y.: Doubleday & Co., Inc., 1959).

Further, we should be aware that the language(s) we learn to use enable and limit us communicatively in two fundamental ways.

THINKING—ADAPTATION AND ORIENTATION TO THE ENVIRONMENT

First, a language facilitates and enriches our abilities to adapt and to orient ourselves to our environments. How? In a very simple way. Because we can name or identify the things and events of our environments (and talk to ourselves and others about them), we are freed from the necessity of re-establishing some satisfactory relationship with the things and events of our environment each time we come across them. In short, a language makes it possible to *accumulate experience* and hence successively to structure more and more complex anticipations and expectations. Because we have tools for talking to ourselves, we can successfully avoid recurrent victimization by the things and the processes of our environments. Because we can say to ourselves, "Since the weather is likely to be as hot tomorrow as it was today, I'm going to plan my day quite differently"—we can thereby achieve successively more complex and advantageous adaptations and orientations to our environments.

Language, Thought, and Reality. It is, therefore, obvious that there is an inextricable relationship between our language(s) and our thinking. Without becoming entangled in the continuing controversy over the specific nature of this relationship,[3] we should be cognizant of the apparent facts that sophisticated thinking abilities appear and develop concurrent with the acquisition of language(s); that people seem to conceive of themselves and their worlds largely in terms of their language(s); and that our *comprehensions* of ourselves and the physical and social processes of our environments are limited by the sorts of cognitive

---

[3] B. L. Whorf, *Language, Thought and Reality* (New York: John Wiley & Sons, Inc., 1956), p. 252: ". . . the forms of a person's thoughts are controlled by inexorable laws the pattern of which is unconscious. These patterns are the unperceived intricate systematizations of his own language . . ."; S. Chase, *Power of Words* (New York: Harcourt, Brace & World, 1953), pp. 181 and 104; "Each language shapes the reasoning of its speakers. Thus English forces either-or thinking, while Chinese does not . . . Indo-European languages lead to subject-predicate relationships, yet the whole trend of modern physics is away from them"; *et seqq.* Cf. H. J. Chaytor, "Reading and Writing," in E. Carpenter and M. McLuhan (eds.), *Explorations in Communication* (Boston: Beacon Press, 1960). The current search for "semantic universals" gives substance to the opposing argument: e.g., J. Greenberg (ed.), *Universals of Language* (Cambridge, Mass.: MIT Press, 1963).

structures our particular languages make possible.[4] Whatever the specific nature of the language-thought interdependency, the point to be made is this: that languages are most advantageously thought of as fundamental aspects of the technology of communication. As such they produce certain possibilities and certain limits on our abilities (and capacities) for being communicated-with by our environments. We *comprehend* the nature of our environments in and through the languages we have learned for doing so. And—at this stage of our evolution—we think about the things and the events of our environments largely in and through the use of those languages. For example, we typically conceive of and think about our worlds *verbally*—i.e., in the terms of the languages with and through which we have learned to do so.

Language, Feeling, and Behavior.   Because languages are learned, and because our uses of language are inseparable from our internal experiences of ourselves, there are always feeling-tones of some sort associated with our orientations to, and use of, the tools of language. Sometimes these are so vague as to be unnoticeable. At other times, they dominate. We are vexed when another mispronounces our name; there are some words (tools of communication) to which we react so emotionally they are omitted from our dictionaries. We have all had the experience of saying something to another in the spirit of simply informing him, only to have him react as if we had "struck a nerve." The emotional overtones that accompany all of our communication experiences are not always so obvious.

In the same way that our languages both enable and limit the conceptual part of our existences, they structure the possibilities and the limits of our feelings, of our emotional and aesthetic adaptations and orientations to our worlds.

Our languages similarly create and bound much of our behavior. The grammars of the languages with which we think and feel have their counterparts in the "grammar" of our actions and inactions.[5] For example,

---

[4] Cf. P. Meredith, *Instruments of Communication* (London: Pergamon, 1966); J. Piaget, *The Language and Thought of the Child* (New York: Humanities Press, 1932); and a Nobel-prize winning physicist's reflections on the same issue: P. W. Bridgman, *The Way Things Are* (Cambridge, Mass.: Harvard University Press, 1959). Early scientists sought "heat" as one of the elements primarily because "heat" is a noun— hence a grammatical substantive like oxygen or mercury (e.g., J. S. Bois, *Explorations in Awareness* [New York: Harper & Row, 1957], pp. 56–58). At the sociological level, cf. H. A. Innis, *The Bias of Communication* (Toronto: University of Toronto Press, 1951).

[5] Cf. K. A. Burke, *A Grammar of Motives* and *A Rhetoric of Motives* (Englewood Cliffs, N.J.: Prentice-Hall, Inc., 1945 & 1950), for a slightly different perspective on the same issue; and Meredith, *op. cit.*

what it is possible for an individual to express verbally will likely set the upper and lower limits on his aspirations and endeavors.

Probably we have carried this far enough to fix two major conclusions in mind:

1. That the languages we learn and use are significant determinants of—and place upper and lower limits upon—our thinking, our feeling, and our behavior (just as all technology enables and restricts its user); and

2. That, most importantly for our purposes in this book, languages and their components (words, grammars, etc.) are neither more nor less than one aspect of the "software" of the technology of communication.

INTERCOMMUNICATION—MUTUAL ADAPTATION AND SOCIAL EVOLUTION

It is the technology of human communication which has made possible man's adaptation to himself and his fellows (as contrasted with his adaptation to his nonhuman environment[6]), and hence the evolution of social organizations—from the pristine organization of man and wife to the great cultures which have influenced the lives and actions of millions of people over hundreds of years. It is our languages, in common, that have made possible the level and the scope of the intercommunication which seems so commonplace to us today.

Individually, men could have successfully adapted to their physical environments in any number of idiosyncratic ways. But to adapt to each other, various kinds of technological hardware had to be invented, accommodated to, and used by each. Thus while any arbitrary language could adequately serve a single human in his adaptation and orientation to his nonhuman environment, *it is only through mutual subscription to a common means of intercommunication* that the evolution of larger social units became possible. Today, with the kinds of communication technology rapidly becoming available, a single, world-wide society will ultimately be possible.[7]

---

[6] E.g., H. F. Searles, *The Nonhuman Environment* (New York: International Universities Press, 1960).

[7] Not that such a possibility appeals to each of us in the same way, of course. Some representative prophecies and points of view are: W. Schramm, *Mass Media and National Development* (Stanford, Calif.: Stanford University Press, 1964); C. Cherry, "Communication, Politics and People," in L. Thayer (ed.), *Communication: Theory and Research* (Springfield, Ill.: Charles C Thomas, 1967); E. B. Weiss, "The Communications Revolution" (Chicago: Advertising Publications, Inc., 1966); and W. Schramm & D. Lerner, *Communication and Change in the Developing Countries* (Honolulu: East-West Center Press, 1966).

Such concerns, once noted, are beyond our immediate interest, however. The points to be made are that:

1. The achievement of our present communicate-abilities has required the invention and the continuous evolution of useful languages; and

2. The achievement of viable two- to n-person social organizations has required mutual subscription to languages held in common, and mutual deference to the grammar or the rules for language behavior vis-à-vis one another.

The "Hardware" of Communication Technology: Media

Languages and their grammars, and the rules and protocols for their use, have their consequences on the *generation* and on the *consumption* of data. Media, by contrast, have their consequences for the *dissemination* and *acquisition* of data. Thus the "hardware" of communication technology has to do with the transportation (or amplification or deamplification of data), while the "software" of communication technology has to do with our individual abilities to communicate-to and to be communicated-with.

As social organizations grew in size and complexity, the need to augment human means of disseminating and acquiring potentially useful data led to the invention and adoption of the wide range of media and materials which we now take for granted. For example, the invention of paper offered a new means of intercommunication which was, and still is, crucial to the development and maintenance of both formal organizations and other social structures. The paperwork required to create a modern aircraft weighs more than does the vehicle itself. The invention of paper forever onward altered intercommunication—and ourselves and our capabilities in the process. The development of other materials, like the invention of ink, has similarly revolutionized our intercommunication.

But it has been the combined impact of materials and devices which has altered our communicative existences, problems, and possibilities most strikingly. For example, given the existence of paper and ink, it was the invention of the movable printing press which altered the course of history perhaps as much as any other event in history.[8]

These and like details of the technology of communication are fascinating in and of themselves. But they take us a bit afield. Our concern is with the processes of communication, not just the technology of communication.

What we need to focus upon here is the fact that the sequence of

---

[8] See M. McLuhan, *The Gutenberg Galaxy* (Toronto: University of Toronto Press, 1962).

inventions of *material*, and of *devices* or *equipment*, have given birth to a succession of new *media* of communication. And with the birth of each new *medium* of communication have come increased possibilities for cooperative or collective endeavor. For example, the medium of written communication has made possible the maintenance of relationships at great distances. The television: common ways of thinking and believing across large numbers of people. Our "communication" satellites: the dissemination (and hence potential acquisition) of consumable event-data throughout the world—*as those events occur*. And so on.

The media of communication—the intersection of materials and devices, the "hardware" of communication technology—have therefore amplified and extended the reaches of man's own equipment (his eyes and vocal cords, etc.) for disseminating and acquiring useful data about the world in which he lives. In the same way that the microscope has enabled us to look into the micro-universes which exist around us, and that the telescope has increased our awareness of the macro-universes which surround us, trans-Atlantic and trans-Pacific television satellites now serve us as a technologically unique means of acquiring those event-data which are occurring beyond the range of our own sensory apparatus. Thus the means of *data transportation* (*media*) subserve integrative as well as informative functions. This is a fact having far-reaching implications for the design of communication systems in formal organizations.

Of primary importance here is an understanding that combinations and recombinations of materials and devices (technologically evolved) have created new media of communication, from the chisel and stone tablet, to the germanium diode, to the use of laser beams to produce three-dimensional TV (holography). Further, the adoption and exploitation of the various media within human organizations—given the distinct impact of each separate medium on our intercommunication and mass communication—has inevitable consequences for the way organizations get structured, and the way they function. That is, an available medium is a *tool* of intercommunication or mass communication), and its use (or not), plus the manner in which it is used, will have inevitable consequences for the very nature of the organization which ensues, whether that organization consists of one, two, or thousands of people.

ON CLASSIFYING MEDIA

It would be possible to classify communication media in organizations in a number of different ways. We could classify media as being either aural or visual, or both. Such a classification would have the disadvantage, however, of lumping together media as different as films and lectures and closed circuit television(CCTV). All are aural and visual, but each has unique characteristics which could greatly vary its efficacy for a particular task or purpose.

We seem to have a tendency to assume that newer media are therein more advantageous. This is clearly not so.[9] An old-fashioned face-to-face talk still has some advantages over the same encounter via CCTV. On the other hand, the adoption and use of the picturephone in large organizations will undoubtedly bring some advantages which are not possible when people must physically transport themselves to some common meeting place for a face-to-face encounter.

In short, classifying media as to their relative efficacy *qua media* would have little or no usefulness—and certainly questionable validity. We can usefully determine the efficacy of media *only in the context of the communication system(s) which they serve*, and only then in terms of the ends or purposes to be fulfilled.

We are not communicated-to *by* media, for they are simply data transportation technology. However, the medium employed can make a difference in the message we "get," for the consistent use of certain media link them functionally to the channels involved—and hence they do have communicative consequences.

MEDIA VERSUS CHANNELS

The advent of new media and new combinations of media do create the possibilities for new *channels* of communication. But the media are not themselves channels of communication. They are primarily means of transporting data, and of converting data in particular ways which serve to

---

[9] Interesting in itself is the fact that most media research, to date, has been carried out in the interests of advertising and education; what little research has been done on media in formal organizations is often equivocal. E.g., P. H. Rossi & B. J. Biddle (eds.), *The New Media in Education* (Chicago: Aldine Publishing Co., 1966); C. W. Taylor & F. E. Williams, *Instructional Media and Creativity* (New York: John Wiley & Sons, Inc., 1966); C. S. Steinberg (ed.), *Mass Media and Communication* (New York: Hastings House, 1966); Chap. 7 in E. Crane, *Marketing Communications* (New York: John Wiley & Sons, Inc., 1965); T. Peterson, J. W. Jensen, & W. L. Rivers, *The Mass Media and Modern Society* (New York: Holt, Rinehart & Winston, 1965); W. C. Redding, "The Empirical Study of Human Communication in Business and Industry," in P. E. Ried (ed.), *The Frontiers in Experimental Speech-Communication Research* (Syracuse, N.Y.: Syracuse University Press, 1966); and T. L. Dahle, "Transmitting Information to Employees: A Study of Five Methods," *Personnel*, 1954, 31, 243–46; et seqq. Cf. M. McLuhan, *Understanding Media* (New York: McGraw-Hill Book Co., 1964).

enlarge the scope of man's abilities to acquire and disseminate consumable data.

As was proposed in an earlier chapter, it will be especially useful to think of channels of communication as *functional* links between and among people which they do in fact utilize in communication and inter-communication. Media, by contrast, can be better understood in terms of the *hardware* by which they are uniquely characterized. For example, television is a single medium. But commercial television and CCTV are, for most people, distinctly different *channels* of communication. Or, to consider an additional example: an internal public address system would probably be considered a single medium of communication. But if that medium is utilized on one occasion to broadcast music, and on another occasion to announce a previously-unscheduled holiday for the members of that organization, it should be clear that functionally different *channels* of communication are established by those different uses of the same medium, and that one would therefore anticipate varying degrees of efficacy for the different channels of communication possible via the same medium.

It will be useful to keep this distinction in mind.

Forms and Conventions

Media which subtend man's unaugmented reaches (for acquisition and dissemination) therefore emerge from the coincidence of a common language and some (at least tacitly) common need or purpose. Reaching large numbers of people all over the world via television is possible only as the technological means of transmission and broadcast become available, but even then only to the extent that the intended receivers (a) have the appropriate technological acquisition equipment, and (b) have a language in common with the originator, with all that implies about complex comprehend-abilities held in common, sources of validation, etc.

Given all of these conditions, however, the use of a medium will create new *channels* of communication. But at this unique intersection of common language, common medium, and now common channel, there is a new derivative. Through use over time, *forms* and *conventions* for both "sending" and "receiving" via these channels begin to emerge. These are the rules which serve to govern the manner in which a particular medium is to be used, and the rules regarding the forms of communication which are possible and/or appropriate for those channels. If widely adopted and institutionalized, these forms and conventions seem, to those of us who simply learn them (as contrasted with *creating* them), to be intrinsic or inherent qualities of the medium. But they are not.

There is no *inherent* reason why television, for example, could not be used as a means of simultaneous transmission of letters. But, as a matter of convention, it is not. The conventions of the theater are a good example. A further example: there is nothing intrinsic to either the medium or its users which would predict to the forms that our letters, memos, and reports normally take. The *form* in which we present *messages* via certain media are thus matters of convention. Those forms are in part imposed by the technical limits of the equipment or material used, in part a property of their users.

We "package" or display (for acquisition and consumption) messages which are *conventionally* formed. Forms and conventions are thus a part of the "software" of technology of communication.

Communication Systems: Technological Efficacy

Communication systems, as described in an earlier chapter, can be understood as the pattern (or network) of channels (or links) which an individual (or a human organization) actually utilizes for purposes of acquiring information from, or disseminating information to, other individuals (or organizations). Complex communication systems, of the sort we find commonplace in most human organizations today, have been made possible by the advent of the kinds of technology which link people together beyond their natural ranges for acquiring and disseminating information, and by the emergence of mutually comprehendable forms and conventions for use by those who share particular *channels* of communication. Communication *systems* are thus inclusive of all of the technological hardware and software which makes their existence possible.

It can be advantageous to have some cognizance of the *interdependence* of these three constituents of communication channels and complex communication systems—language, form, and medium. For example, it would hardly be feasible to determine the efficacy of language apart from form and medium, or of form apart from medium and language. Their subtle interrelationships in communication systems make it necessary to take into account the particular conditions and consequences of their interdependence in determining the efficacy of any communication system.

The possible variations defy cataloging here. In formal organizations, when is an intercom more efficacious than a dial phone between offices? When would it be more efficacious to produce a particular report as a film rather than as a document of static prose and graphics? When are pay envelope inserts more efficacious than an employee newspaper for getting certain messages across to organization members? When are meetings more efficacious than trying to accomplish the same thing in a series of written exchanges? And so on. The list is long and is daily growing longer, as new devices and new forms (and, indeed, new languages) are created.

There are few if any reliable principles or "recipes" for making such decisions and, as we have seen, substantive research on technological and system efficacy is just beginning.

There are always costs involved. The formally-attributable costs of getting the job done communicatively in human organizations are, however, only a part of the total costs involved. How much time do two members of an organization spend talking to each other about something which they might have been satisfactorily informed of via some routine, formal medium of communication in the organization? How much time is invested unprofitably in conferences simply because of the conventions and forms that they take? How much do "call-backs" or "call-agains" cost, relative to the cost of a back-up transcriber for messages when a line is busy?

One conclusion to be reached regarding technological efficacy is this: the technology employed in any communication system can be properly evaluated only as an integral part of that communication system, and only in the context of the efficacy of *that* system in terms of its specific purposes and functions and, ultimately, only in view of the effectiveness and the efficiency of the communication which occurs through the use of that system. In other words, the efficacy of the technology employed in any communication system can be no greater than the efficacy of the system itself.

On Computers as an Aspect of Communication Technology

It would perhaps be remiss not to clarify the role of computers as components of communication systems.

Computers are technologically unique. But not in the ways often assumed.

Prior to the inclusion of computers as a component of communication systems, the technology of communication had pertinence primarily for the dissemination-acquisition phases of communication. That is, most of our technological hardware served the purpose of extending or amplifying our own sensory capacities for acquiring and disseminating potentially consumable data. But computers are unique in the fundamental respect that they are utilized to augment and extend man's *information-processing* and *information-generating* capacities. Computers do not transport data from place to place—as is characteristic of much of our previous technological innovations; they *process* data. They are designed and programmed to reduce, analyze, synthesize, reorganize, and variously to display or "print-out" forms or patterns of data that either (*a*) might not otherwise be available to us, or (*b*) might require considerably more time to generate or process.

The point is that computers (when deployed as components of communication systems) are a part of the evolutionary stream of communication technology—involving both software elements (language and form and convention) and hardware elements (media and devices). As such, computers are tools—tools which have begun to alter, for good or ill (as a consequence of the ways in which they are used in communication systems) human communicate-abilities and -susceptibilities. They will continue to determine many of the possibilities and limits for communication systems now and in the future.

SUGGESTIONS FOR FURTHER READING

Our typical conceptions of the technology of communication often do not extend to the "software"—i.e., languages, rules for use of those languages, culturally determined modes of thinking and of conceptualizing, etc. In this list of selected readings, therefore, I have tried to achieve some appropriate balance between the "hardware" and the "software" aspects of the technology of communication.

ALEXANDER, H. G.   *Language and Thinking*. Princeton, N.J.: D. Van Nostrand Co., Inc., 1957.

AMERICAN DOCUMENTATION INSTITUTE.   *Parameters of Information Science*. Washington, D.C.: Spartan Book Co., 1964.

ANSHEN, RUTH N.   *Language: An Enquiry into Its Meaning and Function*. New York: Harper & Row, 1957.

BAR-HILLEL, Y.   *Language and Information*. Reading, Mass.: Addison-Wesley Publishing Co., Inc., 1964.

BLACKMUR, R. P.   *Language as Gesture*. New York: Harcourt, Brace & Co., 1952.

BORKO, H.   *The Analysis and Design of Information Systems*. Santa Monica, Calif.: System Development Corporation, 1966.

BURLINGAME, J. F.   "Information Technology and Decentralization," *Harvard Business Review*, Vol. 39 (1961), pp. 121–26.

CARROLL, J. B.   *Language and Thought*. Englewood Cliffs, N.J.: Prentice-Hall, Inc., 1964.

Computer Technology—Concepts for Management.   Monograph No. 25. New York: Industrial Relations Counselors, Inc., 1965.

CUADRA, C. A. (ed.).   *Annual Review of Information Science and Technology*. Vol. 1. New York: Interscience, 1966.

DEARDEN, J.   "Can Management Information Be Automated?" *Harvard Business Review*, Vol. 42 (1964), pp. 128–35.

DIEBOLD, J.   *Beyond Automation: Managerial Problems of an Exploding Technology*. New York: McGraw-Hill Book Co., 1964.

FODOR, J. A., and KATZ, J. J.   *The Structure of Language*. Englewood Cliffs, N.J.: Prentice-Hall, Inc., 1964.

FRIES, C. C.   *Linguistics and Reading*. New York: Holt, Rinehart & Winston, 1962.

FURTH, H. G.   *Thinking Without Language*. New York: Free Press, 1966.

GREENBERGER, M.   "The Uses of Computers in Organizations," *Scientific American*, Vol. 215 (1966), 193–96 ff.

HOIJER, H. (ed.).   *Language and Culture*. Chicago: University of Chicago Press, 1954.

HOUKES, JOHN M. (ed.).   *Management Information Systems and the Information Specialist*. Lafayette, Ind.: Krannert Graduate School of Industrial Administration and the University Libraries, Purdue University, 1966.

HOWARD, J. H.   *Electronic Information Displays for Management*. Detroit: American Data Processing, Inc., 1966.

JACOBS, N. J.   *Naming Day in Eden: The Creation and Recreation of Language*. New York: Macmillan Co., 1959.

KRIEBEL, C. H.   *Operations Research in the Design of Management Information Systems*. Management Sciences Research Report No. 73. Pittsburgh: Carnegie Institute of Technology, April, 1966.

LUHN, H. P.   "A Business Intelligence System," *IBM Journal of Research and Development*, Vol. 2 (1958), pp. 314–19.

McLUHAN, M.   *Understanding Media*. New York: McGraw-Hill Book Co., 1965.

MILLER, R. B.   "Psychology for a Man-Machine Problem-Solving System," in L. Thayer (ed.), *Communication: Theory and Research*. Springfield, Ill.: Charles C Thomas, 1967.

NEWMAN, J. R.   *Extension of Human Capability through Information Processing and Display Systems*. Santa Monica, Calif.: System Development Corp., 1966.

Peterson, G. E. "Basic Physical Systems for Communication between Two Individuals," *Journal of Speech and Hearing Disorders*, Vol. 18 (1953), pp. 116–20.

Proceedings of the Western Joint Computer Conference: Extending Man's Intellect. New York: National Joint Computer Committee, 1961.

Read, Herbert. *English Prose Style*. Boston: Beacon Press, 1952.

Richards, I. A. "Communication Between Men: The Meaning of Language," in Heinz Von Foerster (ed.), *Transactions of the Eighth Conference on Cybernetics*, March 15–16, 1951. New York: Josiah Macy, Jr., Foundation, 1952.

Rosenblith, W. A. (ed.). *Sensory Communication*. Cambridge, Mass.: MIT Press, 1961.

Sinaiko, H. W. (ed.). *Human Factors in the Design and Use of Control Systems*. New York: Dover Publications, Inc., 1961.

Smith, F., and Miller, G. A. (eds.). *The Genesis of Language: A Psycholinguistic Approach*. Cambridge, Mass.: MIT Press, 1966.

Solomon, I. I., and Weingart, L. O. *Management Uses of the Computer*. New York: Harper & Row, 1966.

Spiegel, J., and Walker, D. (eds.). *Information System Sciences: Proceedings of the Second Congress*. Washington, D.C.: Spartan Book Co., 1965.

Thompson, H. *Joint Man/Machine Decisions*. Cleveland: Systems & Procedures Association, 1965.

Zipf, G. K. *The Psycho-Biology of Language*. Boston: Houghton Mifflin Co., 1935.

18

On Communication Methods
and Techniques

EXPLICIT OR IMPLICIT in all of the preceding chapters has been the proposition that "successful" (e.g., effective) communication depends first upon one's conceptual abilities, then upon one's attitudes and orientations, and only then upon the kinds of techniques one actually employs—*in that order*. This order of relative importance or impact holds true whether one is the originator or the receiver.

In this chapter, it will be our purpose to consider a useful approach to the wide-ranging body of literature which sets forth methods and techniques of communication, and to consider some useful means for appraising the relevance and applicability of those methods and techniques that are available. We will be concerned not so much with how best to communicate as with how to comprehend and evaluate the potential usefulness of methods and techniques in different kinds of communication situations.

At this stage in our study of communication, we probably have at our disposal many more methods and techniques than we have sound bases for evaluating and using them. Thus the establishment of a framework for ordering and assessing their relevance and applicability will be our primary concern.

A Framework for Organizing Communication Methods and Techniques

We need some way of getting a better "handle" on the great bulk of communication methods and techniques which pour forth in ever-increasing quantities from students, scholars, and practitioners in the field. We need the sort of perspective which would enable us first to define and assess the nature of the communication situations that confront us, and then to take-into-account the applicable methods and/or techniques in a systematic manner.

To establish this much-needed perspective, it will be necessary to review three of the basic concepts from the first part of this book, and to show how their interrelationships provide a convenient framework for ordering the nature of communication situations, and for determining the relevance of specific methods and techniques to those situations.

Basic Processes

From Chapter 3, we need to recall the four basic processes (or subprocesses) of communicating as we commonly understand that term:

1. Generating.
2. Disseminating.
3. Acquiring, and
4. Processing or consuming data (i. e., "information").

So that we do not fail to appreciate the interlocking nature of these processes, it may help to visualize their relationship to each other as in Figure 17. The small vertical rectangles at each end represent the *decoding*

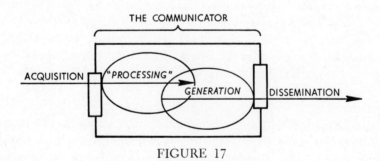

FIGURE 17

that must occur before processing and the *encoding* that must take place before disseminating. What is processed and generated is information to the originator, but what is disseminated and acquired are data for the receiver.

Additionally, it may be helpful to add a simple visualization of how the basic processes relate to each other in *intercommunication* (Figure 18).

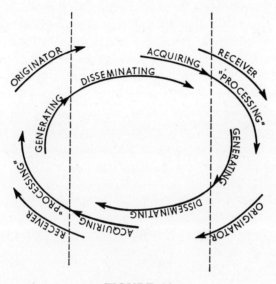

FIGURE 18

Figure 18 is intended to remind us that the message the originator *disseminates* is not the message the receiver *acquires*; that what the receiver *acquires* is a message he can "*process*" (i.e., can comprehend in some way); that the shift from *receiver* to *originator* and back again in intercommunication is not always a clear-cut or discernible one; that the *processing* of acquired data overlaps the *generation* of ideas (new data) in often very complex and intricate ways; that *dissemination* and *acquisition* can and do occur simultaneously in the overall communication process; that what a person *acquires* may have varying degrees of usefulness for his *generating* purposes; and so on.

Also, this visualization may help to remind us that what one acquires may functionally serve either *feedback* or *feedforward* purposes. That is, one may acquire data about the situation, about the receiver, etc., prior to or concurrent with initiating his generating-disseminating sequence (feed-forward); or he may acquire data as a means of determining how effective his last generation-dissemination sequence was (feedback).

LEVELS OF ANALYSIS

Next, we need to recall the crucial significance of the *level of analysis* from which we want to look at the communication process. If, for example, we are concerned only with those factors which are pertinent to a single individual, that level of analysis is what we have referred to as the intrapersonal level. At this level, we are interested in knowing more about how the individual functions in communicating, about related processes (e.g., decisioning and problem-solving, comprehending, etc.), and about the potentials and the limitations which are imposed upon the communication process by the nature of the organism in general, and by the unique characteristics of individual psychological systems.

The next level of analysis is the interpersonal. At this level, we move from our focus upon the functioning of a single individual to the inter-functioning or intercommunication of two or more persons in communication encounters. The next level is the organizational level of analysis. At this level, we concern ourselves with the functioning of larger than face-to-face human organizations, and with the different orders of problems and opportunities which derive from the fact that human organizations are rationally designed, that various task-functions within an organization are interrelated in nonpersonal ways, with the circumstances and conditions of mass communication to vertically and horizontally segmented audiences, and so forth.

The fourth level of analysis considered in Chapter 3 was the techno-logical level. For our immediate purposes, it would be advantageous to limit our consideration of the organizational level to things like employee communication, of functionally "getting the word" around, and the like. Then we can combine certain total organizational communication factors (those which relate to the organization qua total system) with certain technological factors, and establish a convenient hybrid level of analysis we can refer to as the *communication systems* level.

With this slight modification, we could then visualize the relevant levels of analysis for our purposes here as in Figure 19.

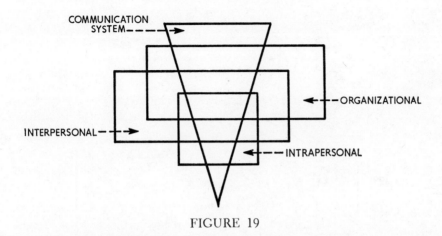

FIGURE 19

COMMUNICATION COMPETENCIES

From Chapter 8, finally, we need to recall the two communication competencies—*strategic* and *tactical*.

Strategic competence in communication refers to an individual's conceptual abilities, to his abilities to assess accurately the state-relationships between himself and others (in the context of his intentions and objectives), to his think-abilities, to his cerebral or intellectual "horsepower," to his abilities to comprehend, to the veridicality of his models and "maps" of his environments, and similar abilities and characteristics of one's central information-processing and information-generating capabilities.

Tactical competencies, by contrast, are the aggregate of an individual's skills, techniques, capacities, etc., (a) for effectively and efficiently converting the information which he generates (and wishes to disseminate) into consumable forms, and (b) for effectively and efficiently converting the data which he acquires and wishes to consume into expediently self-consumable forms. Or, in other words, one's *tactical* competencies are those abilities and capabilities one has at his command to implement his strategic competencies.

TOWARD UNDERSTANDING METHOD AND TECHNIQUE: THE INTERRELATIONSHIPS OF PROCESS, LEVEL OF ANALYSIS, AND COMPETENCE

Given this brief review of the pertinent basic concepts, we can now turn to the description of a useful analytic framework for ordering and assessing the relevance of methods and techniques to varying communication situations. We can begin by visualizing the ways in which the basic processes of communication, the levels of analysis, and the two types of communication competence are interrelated (as in Figure 20).[1]

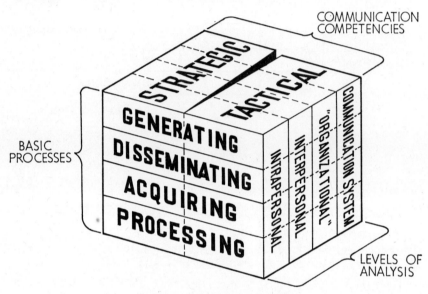

COMMUNICATION COMPETENCIES

BASIC PROCESSES

LEVELS OF ANALYSIS

A Framework for Organizing
Communication Methods and Techniques

FIGURE 20

This simple visualization is intended primarily to illustrate that all communication situations:[2]

1. Occur at one or more of the four levels of analysis we have identified.
2. Involve the competencies of either the receiver or the originator, or both; and
3. Involve one or more of the basic communication processes identified here—i.e., generating, disseminating, acquiring, processing.

Second, it is intended to imply that particular communication methods and techniques are applicable to one or more of the cells of this matrix.

---

[1] A fourth dimension could be added to bring in the variables of synchronic versus diachronic communication. But that would overly complicate the task of visualizing these three central interrelationships.

[2] At least all of those communication situations we are concerned with in this book.

Third, it is intended to suggest that communication methods and techniques do not have a fixed value, but that their usefulness varies according
to the way in which they "interact" with the other elements of any
communication situation.

Perhaps the best way to gain an appreciation of the usefulness of this
analytic tool would be to consider some examples. Suppose we looked at
the three "cells" labelled (1), (2), and (3) in Figure 21. How would we
interpret the significance of these particular cells of the matrix?

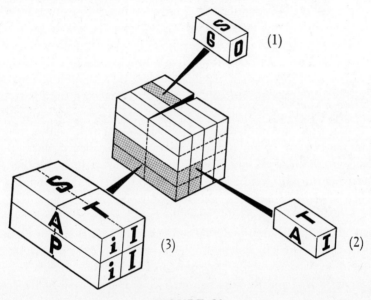

FIGURE 21

Let us look first at "cell" (1)—the "GOS cell." What is implied is that
there are those communication situations at the organizational level to
which methods and techniques for developing or deploying strategic
competencies in generating information would be particularly applicable
and relevant.[3] That is, there are methods and techniques which could
improve the strategic competencies of the originators of messages within
organizations, and the application of those methods would thereby en-

---

[3] The reader may recall that every communication event involves intrapersonal
factors—whether the focus is upon the originator, the receiver(s), or both. For
example, the "AOS cell" identifies those communication situations at the "organizational" level of analysis for which there are methods and techniques peculiarly
applicable and relevant to the development or deployment of the receiver's (or
receivers') strategic competencies for acquiring consumable information.

hance the potential communication effectiveness (and/or efficiency) of those originators.

The "AIT cell"—(2) in Figure 21—is intended to draw our attention to those communication situations on the interpersonal level for which *tactical* methods and techniques for acquiring information would be especially relevant and applicable. For example, there are techniques of listening effectively in face-to-face encounters which would be pertinent.

We might consider one larger unit—(3) in Figure 21—to gain some appreciation of the various multiple interfaces that are possible. What this aggregate of eight cells identifies are those communication situations which involve both intra- and interpersonal factors, and for which some set of methods and techniques for improving both the strategic and tactical competencies of the participants, and for improving both the acquiring and processing of information, would be especially relevant and applicable. For example, some education and training (perhaps even sensitivity training) in the nature and dynamics of interpersonal relations enhance the participants' strategic competencies. Some education and training in listening and in the art of questioning others could enhance their tactical competencies. When we say, "People just don't listen to each other," we are referring to the complicated mix of conditions suggested by this particular block of "cells" in the matrix.

From these few illustrations, it may be apparent that the framework for organizing communication methods and techniques visualized in Figure 20 could be used as well to isolate problems—from the most elementary and unidimensional (one's ability to speak intelligibly, for example) to the most sophisticated and multidimensional (one to which all of the factors represented in the total matrix contribute).

However, this way of organizing our thinking about the relevance and applicability of methods and techniques should also serve as a caution. Simple methods and techniques may be relevant and applicable at the simplest levels of the matrix—i.e., at the level of a single cell of the matrix. But the more cells which are involved, the more complex and multidimensional must be the set of methods and techniques which might be applied, and the longer the time factor involved. For example, if a chief executive wanted to concern himself with all of the communication which goes on in his organization (in order to improve it "across the board"), the training, educational, procedural, organizational, and operational program of methods and techniques that would have to be designed and employed would in some way and at some time involve every member of the organization. And that program would necessarily be extremely long-term in scope. On the other hand, if that same administrator were to determine that one of the weakest spots in his organization's functioning were his own inabilities to write effectively, then the appropriate method would probably be that of developing his writing skills to his satisfaction.

Perhaps this will suffice to establish the usefulness of this way of organizing our thinking about communication methods and techniques. It is a conceptual tool for ordering some very complex aspects of communication situations which might otherwise get confused or glossed over. A method or a technique has no value beyond the appropriateness of its application. This conceptual scheme is intended to help the reader in determining the appropriateness of any methods and techniques he might employ in specific communication situations.

As indicated previously, the potential usefulness of this same tool for isolating the sources of communication *problems* may be obvious. For example, the inadequate functioning of a communication system might be attributable to the way it is designed (a dissemination problem), or it might be attributable to some specific incompetencies of its users to make full and effective use of it (an acquisition and/or a processing problem.) Or it might be attributable to both. Determining the source of the problem before solving it determines whether we will likely be treating symptoms or causes. If methods and techniques are arbitrarily applied, we will in fact more likely be treating symptoms than causes. Thus the approaches implied in Figure 20 may help us to get at causes rather than symptoms.

Communication Skills and Competencies

Traditionally, people have often looked upon communication methods and techniques in terms of communication skills—predominantly those of reading, writing, speaking, and, occasionally, listening. To deal with the total communication process, however, we will need to develop some modifications of these traditional ways of looking at communication skills.

The major difference in point of view can perhaps be pinpointed most directly by considering the competencies any one individual has for generating, disseminating, acquiring, and processing information (all of the front layer of cells in Figure 20).

An individual either has or does not have adequate competencies for generating, disseminating, acquiring, and processing or consuming information—as measured against his goals, task assignments, aspirations, his potentials, his abilities to adapt to a wide range of environmental or problematical conditions, etc. When we train an individual to write according to the forms and conventions of certain media, we do not *thereby* develop his ability to generate intelligent, useful, or valuable ideas (messages). The same holds true for training in the other skills. For example, we may train a person how to read, or even expose him to speed reading. But that skill does not thereby guarantee that what the individual selects (acquires) for his own consumption will be valuable or useful to him in terms of his goals, adaptation problems and opportunities, etc.[4]

Skill training as such is therefore only a part of what is necessary to improve one's communicate-abilities. Because *what* an individual communicates can't be any better than his ideas or his thinking abilities (in spite of his dissemination or transmission skills), his *generating* abilities need also to be developed and trained. Because *what* an individual thinks about, and because *how* he thinks are ultimately both enabled and limited by what he *acquires* (educes from his environment) and how he *processes* what he acquires, it follows that developing his reading and/or listening skills as such is only a part of the training and/or education he needs to improve his communicate-abilities.

There are many other—probably obvious—examples that may come to mind and that could serve to illustrate the disadvantages of thinking only in terms of traditional communication skills. One's skills are indeed necessary or desirable tactical competencies. But as we have seen, tactical competencies advantage him only to the extent that his strategic competencies are adequate to the task at hand. Tactical competencies cannot successfully compensate for strategic *incompetencies*, although superior strategic competencies may sometimes compensate successfully for tactical incompetencies.

A second misassumption that would seem to be fairly prevalent is that high tactical performance in one skill area (e.g., speaking) implies equivalently better perform-abilities in the other skill areas (i.e., reading, writing, listening). One's strategic competencies may generalize somewhat across all of the means employed to disseminate and to acquire informa-

---

[4] Someone has characterized the issues at stake in this particular example quite dramatically (and quite soundly): there are two ways to improve one's reading of a 50,000-word book. One is to learn how to read faster, perhaps up to 2,500 words per minute. The other way may be even better: it is to *learn how to assess the relative value* of the book for oneself, given one's immediate and long-range purposes, etc. Thus one could spend 15 minutes determining that the book is of no particular value to him at this time, and lay it aside in favor of a more useful or valuable one. By doing so, his reading speed would be in excess of 3,000 words per minute!

tion. But tactical competencies are fairly process-specific. An effective reader is not necessarily an effective listener.

There are few communication training programs—if any—designed to develop our individual strategic *and* tactical take-into-account-abilities. Yet this is the basic process in communication. So it is clear that much remains to be done in redefining communication skills and their development in a manner more consistent with the process of communication itself.

Education and Training

One of the basic methods to be employed to achieve certain communicative ends is the education and/or training of the originators and receivers involved. Specially designed courses and educational programs could be looked upon as a prime method for facilitating long-range communication objectives or for solving long-range communication problems when:

1. The objective or the source of a problem is some educable or trainable individual (or set of individuals); or when
2. The weakness or the source of the inefficacy of a communication system can be located in the strategic incompetencies of the individual(s) responsible for designing that system, or who is (are) located within it in a way that makes them crucial to the system's efficacy. For example, if managers do not comprehend the nature and the dynamics of the communication situations they face—and in a way which enhances their strategic competencies—then the appropriate method for achieving the ends sought would *not* be to create a new medium for internal communication. It would be to utilize or create an educational/training program which would in fact develop those managers' strategic competencies to the level desired or required.

Some Neglected Areas

We can then conclude, then, that the methods and techniques we have at our disposal for communicating more effectively

a) do not necessarily relate to the basic communication processes or competencies, and
b) do not cover all of the important areas or dimensions of those processes and competencies.

It would not be possible to review and classify here all of the principles, rules, techniques, etc., that have been set forth over the years for communicating effectively. Further, such a review would not properly emphasize the fact that most of our techniques and principles are not empirically-founded, but are normative in derivation.

So it would be more in keeping with our purposes here to note some major factors that have commonly been overlooked or neglected. The list of sources at the end of this chapter will refer the reader to a wide range of existing documents which outline available methods and techniques for dealing with various communication situations.

PURPOSE AND ADAPTATION

Perhaps the two most basic and general of all the methods and techniques of communication are those (a) of determining in advance a specific purpose for either disseminating or acquiring information, and (b) of adapting all of the elements of the communication situation to each other and to that specific purpose.

It is a strange fact that a great many attempts to communicate-to others fail (or are relatively ineffective or inefficient) simply because the originator did not fix clearly and firmly in his own mind exactly the objective he was seeking. Setting down a specific purpose does not in any way guarantee effective communication. But it does serve to organize the originator's own thinking (generating skills and capabilities) in such a way that the receiver can more readily comprehend and more appropriately react. In addition, a specific purpose is the only target against which an originator can measure his effectiveness. Articulating a specific purpose also forces the originator to plan and to prepare. It is impossible to plan carefully how to achieve an unspecified objective.[5] So defining one's specific purpose, or defining specifically the consequences intended *prior to* any attempt to communicate-to others, is paramount among all communication methods and techniques.

---

[5] Obviously people engaged in face-to-face conversations are not going to plan and prepare for their next statements in the same way that one might plan and prepare a letter, or an address, or a statement of policy. The participants in a face-to-face encounter must have completed all of their planning and preparation before entering into the encounter. Whether or not they are equipped and prepared for the encounter will be evident in their performances. Yet most task-related conversations would be more effective and more efficient if each participant remained silent for the two or three seconds that might be required to formulate a specific purpose or objective for his next statement-in-response to the other.

A considerable degree of ineffectiveness and inefficiency is also incurred by our failure to specify in advance a definite purpose or objective as *acquirers* or *receivers*. For example, few people read or listen in a truly purposive way. Still fewer people set about consciously establishing and creating the input channels of the communication systems within which they are personally in-formed and maintained.

Thus our failure to establish and pursue specific purposes in acquiring and consuming information may have negative consequences of a magnitude equal to our failure to determine in advance a specific purpose for communicating-to others.

Enhancing the effectiveness and/or the efficiency with which one can be communicated-with through more purposive acquisition and consumption is therefore equally important.

ADAPTATION

From our initial analyses, we know that the basic functions of communication are those intended to enable one to adapt to his environment or to adapt some part of one's environment to oneself. But when inter-communication is involved (i.e., two or more people), adapting one's receiver to oneself depends upon how well one has first adapted himself conceptually to his receiver (and conversely). In other words, the success one has in communicating-to another person (or in being communicated-with by another person) depends to a considerable degree upon how well one has adapted himself to all of the elements of that communication encounter.

Specifically, the originator (or receiver) needs to adapt himself, and other aspects of the anticipated communication encounter, to his purpose, to the circumstances, to his subject, and to his receiver (or, if he is the receiver, to the originator).

If one's purpose is to inform another, or to be informed by another, he must adapt his tools and techniques to *that* purpose. His assessment of all of the circumstances which may have some bearing on the outcome (i. e., his strategic competence) will determine the kinds of adaptations he will undertake in order to capitalize on any facilitating conditions and to compensate for any disfacilitating conditions.

It would seem obvious that originator or receiver would have to adapt their tools and techniques to the subject matter to be "communicated" (acquired or disseminated). But people often adapt in the opposite direction. That is, they often adapt their subject matter to their habitual and familiar tools and techniques—rather than the other way around. The tools and techniques we have at our command often determine the kinds of subjects we communicate about. For example, if reading is a particularly difficult and laborious enterprise for a given individual, he will likely favor other media. Or, if one finds writing an onerous task, he may deliver orally many messages he perhaps should have written down. And so on. Communication effectiveness requires adapting one's communication tools, techniques, media, forms, etc., to one's subject and purpose, not conversely.

Similarly, it should probably also be obvious that communication effectiveness depends in part upon the originator's adaptation of his tools, techniques, media, etc., to his receiver(s)—(or upon a receiver's adapting his tools and techniques to the originator). But that doesn't always happen. Often an originator anticipates how *he* would react were he the receiver rather than how *that* receiver is most likely to react. "Empathy" is frequently misunderstood in this way.

It seems that communicative familiarity may breed adaptive indifference. It is commonplace that the longer the period of time over which people intercommunicate, the less concern they give to the need to adapt to each other. A consequence: the same amount of talk but less communication.

The descriptors we use to define those with whom we want to communicate-to also determine the sorts of adaptations we undertake. Those descriptors may be more characteristic of the way *we see him* than they are of the way *he sees himself*. If so, no matter how good our intentions, the resulting adaptation will probably block rather than facilitate communication.

The only stereotype that is useful for purposes of adapting to one's receiver(s) is that one which is valid. One's strategic competencies will thus be the ultimate determinant of his definition of the apparent-state-of-affairs with regard to his receiver(s), and will therefore determine the efficacy of the adaptation he achieves.

What the originator needs to adapt to are *the receiver's* take-into-account-susceptibilities, not his own.[6] It is what *the receiver* can comprehend, and will comprehend, that determines the originator's effectiveness, not what the originator can comprehend. It is what *the receiver* views as valid and relevant that counts, not what the originator considers valid and relevant. It is what has utility for *the receiver* that determines what he will consume, not what has utility for the originator.

---

[6] Or, if one is receiver, what he needs to adapt to are the originator's communicate-abilities and predilections, not his own.

It is therefore *functional* adaptation that makes a difference in communication effectiveness. It is not adapting "correctly" that makes a difference. It is adapting in a way that brings about the consequence intended that makes a difference. For example, it is not the structure or the manner of a letter as such that makes it effective (or not); it is the adequacy and the accuracy with which structure, content, timing, presentation, medium and the other elements of the situation have been adapted to each other and to the purpose and the intended receiver.

INTERACTION OF VARIABLES

The interdependence and interaction of the different elements or variables involved in every communication event have probably also been somewhat neglected in the past.

Our inclination to think of communication in stimulus-response, cause-effect $(A \rightarrow B = X)$ terms has deflected our attention from the *interaction* effects of the variables in every communication encounter. To consider two relatively simple examples: we have a tendency to overlook the fact that ineffective writing could as well be attributed to the receiver's ineffective or inadequate reading abilities. We could as reasonably attempt to adapt the reading abilities of an organization's members to the writing abilities of those who originate messages in that organization as to adapt writing abilities to existing reading abilities in that organization. The two skills are interdependent. They therefore *mutually* determine communication effectiveness.

Or, consider a second and similar example: if a given executive is "overloaded," we would have at least three alternatives for alleviating the problem. First, we could set out to improve his acquisition-consumption skills (tactical competencies). Second, we could attempt to improve his acquisition-consumption strategies and capacities (strategic competencies). Or third, we could alter the input side of his communication system in such a way that he actually receives less volume without any loss of pertinence (e.g., through some specially-developed selective dissemination scheme for this particular receiver).

A communication event or encounter is itself a dynamic system of elements. When two or more people are involved, and mutual adaptation is attempted, those people co-determine each other. Hence the efficacy of any communication technique or method varies with the people involved, the circumstances, the occasion, the methods or techniques employed by the other person(s), and other such key variables.

The point is that these variables do not function independently of each other or upon each other in any fixed way. They are *interdependent*. The *mix* of the variables involved determines the consequences. Methods and techniques cannot therefore be successfully applied in a cause-effect fashion. They are not tools of fixed value; their value or consequence varies from situation to situation. They are interdependent.

TECHNOLOGICAL CHANGE

A fourth area of concern which has perhaps been neglected in the past is the *systemic* effects of the introduction of new technologies into existing communication systems.

Perhaps this would be an illuminating example. The invention of pictographs made it possible for one cave man to tell another about the beasts he had encountered while out hunting. Prior to the introduction of that new technology of communication, he would have had to drag those beasts back to his cave so he could physically show others what he wanted to communicate-to them. Or, imagine what it would have been like to receive your mail only once every two or three months—when that was the only means you had of getting news about your family. Then along came the telegraph—which made it possible to establish contact in a matter of hours or minutes. Whole patterns of intercommunication changed as a result.

These early innovations seem more dramatic than those which have evolved in recent years. But their impact upon the people involved and upon the structure and functioning of their communication systems was no greater than the impacts being made today by the advent of pocket radios, the speed of long distance telephoning, automatic data-processing equipment, and the like.

To point is this: the introduction of new technology into existing communication systems has some impact upon all of the other elements and upon the functioning of that communication system—including changes that occur in the people themselves. Whether it is a new language, new forms or conventions, or new media, any new technology brought into an existing system has its effects throughout that system.

Thus the methods and techniques we use in communication must be reevaluated each time some new technology is added to a communication system—for those methods and techniques have their relevance, and can be assessed, only in the context of that system. Our failure to reassess the applicability of all methods and techniques in use when a communication system is technologically altered in some way often leads to the application of the "right" method or technique in the "wrong" system. That imbalance could lead in turn to certain communication failures and breakdowns, and therefore to some lessening of the efficacy of the communication system itself.

Validity and Generalizability

Whether for practice or theory, the two questions we need to ask of any communication method or technique are: *Is it valid* (i.e., is it based upon something more substantial than anecdote)? and *Is it generalizable* (i.e., could it be reliably employed in other "similar" communication situations)?

Taken together, as previously suggested, there are probably more principles about how to communicate successfully than there are substantial facts or theories upon which to base those principles. In fact, those principles that are most widely exhorted are typically the most normative or consensual in derivation. These would probably have to be classed as part of the folklore of the field rather than as systematically developed, empirically defendable knowledge.

There is actually nothing wrong with that state of affairs. Musical scholars have not yet come up with the formula for composing music-to-make-one-great-by. And the art of communication must in many instances be altogether as difficult and as unpredictable as the public reaction to the composition and performance of a new opus.

Perhaps the difference lies in the fact that everyone "communicates"—and that the field of communication can therefore never take its place as one of the arts, nor can it be taken out of context long enough to gain a place alongside the sciences. Perhaps the difficulty of dealing systematically with communication is that it isn't, and can't be, either one or the other.

This is not the place to try to deal with that question. But awareness of it may serve to remind us that, while the principles and successful practices of communication we read about are perhaps more *valid* than those that occasionally get perpetrated in the arts, they do not have the kind of validity that we have come to expect in the sciences.

How valid are our methods and techniques? Typically, any method or technique offered as an across-the-board principle for successful communication is of questionable validity. As anecdotes, they may be useful. As folklore, they may be better than anything else we could turn to. But unless the "confidence limits" of their validity are offered along with the suggested techniques themselves, no user could reliably assess their validity —except in terms of his own experiences or predilections.

The complementary question is that of the generalizability of our methods and techniques.

As we have seen, all of the elements of a communication encounter are interdependent; they interact with each other, and thereby co-determine each other in often quite complex and as-yet unpredictable ways. In short, every communication situation is unique. It has never occurred before, and will never occur again.

We have *similar* experiences from time to time, of course. But it is in the nature of living things, and of living systems, to pass through an experience but once. We are never the same again.

So it is with communication.

Sometimes a method or technique which seems successful in one situation will be successful in another; sometimes it will not. The general technique of *adaptation*, which we discussed earlier in this chapter, is in fact based upon the expectation that every communication encounter will be different in *some* way and to *some* degree.

But perhaps the point is sufficiently made: adopting a particular principle (or method or technique) for use in a particular communication situation should be done with a substantial awareness of how the present situation *differs* from the one in which that principle (or method or technique) seemed to "work." If those differences seem slight or insignificant, then some comparable success might reasonably be expected (assuming that the technique in question is also *valid*).

All of this is not intended to present a gloomy picture of the state-of-the-art with respect to communication methods and techniques. Quite the contrary. It is only because recent years have seen some serious questioning of the validity and generalizability of our traditional "principles" that we can look forward to significant and highly useful breakthroughs in this area in the years just ahead.

Some of what portends in this respect will emerge in our succeeding examination of some current research and problems in human communication. For some useful inventories of methods and techniques, the list of sources which follows this chapter can be consulted.

SUGGESTIONS FOR FURTHER READING

The large body of literature devoted to communication methods and techniques has not generally grown out of perspectives like those in this book. So it is not always easy to relate a given method or technique to the conceptual framework upon which this book has been based. Nonetheless, students, teachers, and practitioners as well may find the following selected reading lists basically useful in furthering their study of these aspects of communication. For the most part, references which appear elsewhere are not repeated here.

For convenience, this list has been divided into several categories (although some of the entries necessarily overlap):

1. On reading and listening (inputting; acquisition).
2. On speaking and writing (outputting; generation).
3. On human information processing (problem-solving, thinking, decisioning, etc.).
4. On managerial and organizational communication.
5. On communication and information systems and their technology.

On Reading and Listening (Inputting; Acquisition)

Adler, Mortimer J.   *How to Read a Book.* New York: Simon and Schuster, 1940.

Altick, Richard D.   *Preface to Critical Reading.* New York: Henry Holt & Co., 1956.

American Management Association, Inc.   *Are You a Good Listener?* New York, 1955.

Barbara, Dominick A.   *The Art of Listening.* Springfield, Ill.: Charles C Thomas, 1958.

Carter, Homer L., and McGinnis, Dorothy J.   *Effective Reading for College Students.* New York: Henry Holt & Co., 1957.

Chall, Jeanne S.   *Readability: An Appraisal of Research and Application.* Monograph No. 34. Columbus: Bureau of Educational Research, Ohio State University, 1958.

Chase, Stuart.   *How to Read an Annual Report.* New York: Standard Oil Company, 1962.

Cosper, Russell, and Griffin, E. Glenn (eds.).   *Toward Better Reading Skills.* 2nd ed. New York: Appleton-Century-Crofts, 1959.

Huse, H. R.   *The Illiteracy of the Literate: A Guide to the Art of Intelligent Reading.* New York: D. Appleton-Century Co., Inc., 1933.

Johnson, Wendell H.   "Do You Know How to Listen?" *ETC.: A Review of General Semantics,* Vol. 7, No. 1 (Autumn, 1949).

Judson, Horace.   *Techniques of Reading.* New York: Harcourt, Brace & Co., Inc., 1954.

KLARE, GEORGE R., and BUCK, BYRON. *Know Your Reader: The Scientific Approach to Readability*. New York: Hermitage House, 1954.

LANG, CHARLES H. "Practice Perfects the Fine Art of Listening—Try It," *American Business*, March, 1958.

LARKE, ALFRED G. "How to Learn by Listening," *Dun's Review and Modern Industry*, April, 1955.

MCDONALD, ARTHUR G., and ZIMNY, GEORGE H. *The Art of Good Reading*. Indianapolis: Bobbs-Merrill Co., 1963.

MILLER, LYLE L. *Increasing Reading Efficiency*. New York: Henry Holt & Co., 1956

———. *Maintaining Reading Efficiency*. New York: Henry Holt & Co., 1959.

NICHOLS, RALPH G., and STEVENS, LEONARD A. *Are You Listening?* New York: McGraw-Hill Book Co., 1957.

QUILLER-COUCH, SIR ARTHUR. *On the Art of Reading*. Cambridge (England): Cambridge University Press, 1933.

RICHARDS, I. A. *How to Read a Page*. Boston: Beacon Press, 1959.

SHELDON, WILLIAM D., and BRAAM, LEONARD S. *Reading Improvement for Men and Women in Industry*. Syracuse, N.Y.: Syracuse University Press, 1959.

SMITH, NILA BANTON. *Read Faster and Get More from Your Reading*. Englewood Cliffs, N.J.: Prentice-Hall, Inc., 1958.

———, and BERG, PAUL C. *Faster Reading for Business*. New York: Thomas Y. Crowell Co., 1958.

SPACHE, G. D. *Toward Better Reading*. Champaign, Ill.: Garrard, 1963.

STEWART, NATHANIEL. "Listen to the Right People," *Nation's Business*, January, 1963.

STRONG, LYDIA. "Do You Know How to Listen?" *Management Review*, August, 1955.

WIKSTROM, WALTER S. "Lessons in Listening," *The Conference Board Record*, April, 1965.

WITTY, P. A. *How to Become a Better Reader*. Chicago: Science Research Associates, 1953.

ZELKO, HAROLD P. *Are You a Good Listener?* New London, Conn.: National Foremen's Institute, 1955.

ON SPEAKING AND WRITING (OUTPUTTING; GENERATION)

AMERICAN MANAGEMENT ASSOCIATION, INC. *How to Prepare and Publish an Employee Manual*. New York, 1948.

————. *Preparation of Company Annual Reports.* New York, 1946.

APPEL, F. S.   *Write What You Mean.* New York: Henry Holt & Co., 1938.

AYERS, WALDEMAR A.   "Writing Reports That Get Action," *Factory Management,* Vol. 113 (1955), pp. 138–40.

BABCOCK, C. MERTON.   *The Harper Handbook of Communication Skills.* New York: Harper & Bros., 1957.

BARZUN, JACQUES.   "Architects of Babel: Techniques in the Interchange of Ideas," *Saturday Review,* July 1, 1944, pp. 7–9.

BRADEN, WALDO W., and BRANDENBURG, ERNEST.   *Oral Decision Making.* New York: Harper & Bros., 1955.

BRADFORD, CURTIS, and MORITZ, HAZEL.   *The Communication of Ideas.* Boston: D. C. Heath, 1951.

BRITISH ASSOCIATION FOR THE ADVANCEMENT OF SCIENCE.   *The Languages of Science: A Survey of Techniques of Communication.* New York: Basic Books, Inc., 1963.

BROOKS, CLEANTH, and WARREN, ROBERT PENN.   *Fundamentals of Good Writing.* New York: Harcourt, Brace & Co., Inc., 1959.

BURY, CHARLES.   *How to Write Great Letters.* Chicago: National Research Bureau, 1957.

CADY, EDWIN LAIRD.   *Creative Communication.* New York: Reinhold Publishing Corp., 1956.

CARR, JACK.   *How to Become a Letter Writer in One Easy Lifetime.* New York: Graphic Books, 1947.

CASEY, ROBERT S.   *Oral Communication of Technical Information.* New York: Reinhold Publishing Corp., 1958.

CHARNLEY, MITCHELL V.   *Reporting.* New York: Henry Holt & Co., 1959.

COMER, D. B. III, and SPILLMAN, R. R.   *Modern Technical and Industrial Reports.* New York: G. P. Putnam's Sons, 1962.

COOPER, JOSEPH D.   *How to Communicate Policy and Procedure.* New London, Conn.: Bureau of Business Practice, National Foremen's Institute, 1956.

CORT, ROBERT P.   *How to Get an Idea Across.* New York: American Management Association, Inc., 1951.

DAVIS, RICHARD M.   *Effective Technical Communications: Mechanical Description—Experiment II.* AFIT TR65-1. Air Force Institute of Technology, Wright-Patterson AFB, Ohio, 1965.

DEAN, HOWARD H.   *Effective Communication.* Englewood Cliffs, N.J.: Prentice-Hall, Inc., 1953.

DOUBT, JOHN J.   "Let's Take a New Look at Reports," *Advanced Management Journal,* April, 1965.

DOVER, C. J.   *Effective Communication in Company Publications.* Washington, D.C.: Bureau of National Affairs, Inc., 1959.

DRACH, HARVEY E.   *American Business Writing.* New York: American Book Co., 1959.

ELFENBEIN, JULIEN (ed.).   *Business Journalism.* New York: Harper & Bros., 1950.

FEDERAL ELECTRIC CORP.   *How to Write Effective Reports.* Reading, Mass.: Addison-Wesley Publishing Co., Inc., 1965.

FIELDEN, J.   "What Do You Mean I Can't Write?" *Harvard Business Review,* Vol. 24 (1964), pp. 144–56.

FLESCH, RUDOLF.   *How to Make Sense.* New York: Harper & Bros., 1954.
———, and SASS, A. H.   *The Way to Write.* New York: McGraw-Hill Book Co., Inc., 1955.

FROMAN, ROBERT.   "How to Say What You Mean," *Nation's Business,* May 1957.

GLIDDEN, H. K.   *Reports, Technical Writing, and Specifications.* New York: McGraw-Hill Book Co., 1964.

GOWERS, ERNEST.   *Plain Words: Their ABC.* New York: Alfred A. Knopf, Inc., 1954.

GRACE, WILLIAM J., and GRACE, JOAN C.   *The Art of Communicating Ideas.* New York: Devin-Adair Co., 1952.

GRAVES, ROBERT, and HODGE, ALAN.   *The Reader over Your Shoulder.* New York: Macmillan Co., 1944.

A Guide to More Effective Communication.   Engineering Services, General Electric Company, n. d.

GUNNING, ROBERT.   *How to Take the Fog out of Writing.* Chicago: The Dartnell Corporation, 1956.

HACKETT, HERBERT: ANDERSEN, MARTIN; FESSENDEN, SETH; and HAGEN, LESSIE L.   *Understanding and Being Understood.* New York: Longmans, Green & Co., 1957.

HAKE, DAVID L.   "Selective Reporting of Scientific and Technical Information," *Research/Development,* Vol. 17 (1966), pp. 35–36.

HAY, ROBERT D.   *Written Communications for Business Administrators.* New York: Holt, Rinehart & Winston, 1965.

HICKS, TYLER G.   *Successful Technical Writing.* New York: McGraw-Hill Book Co., 1959.

HOLSCHER, H. H.   *How to Organize and Write a Technical Report.* Toledo, Ohio: Administrative Division Research Department, Owens-Illinois, 1958.

KAPP, REGINALD O.   *The Presentation of Technical Information.* New York: Macmillan Co., 1957.

KILDUFF, EDWARD JONES. *Words and Human Nature: How to Choose and Use Effective Words.* New York: Harper & Bros., 1941.

KOCH, FELTON J. "The DIDO Technique for Effective Communication," *Advanced Management,* October, 1956.

LARSEN, SPENCER A. (ed.). *Better Business Communications.* Detroit: School of Business Administration, Wayne University, 1951.

LEE, IRVING J. *How to Talk with People.* New York: Harper & Bros., 1952.

LINTON, CALVIN D. *How to Write Reports.* New York: Harper & Bros., 1954.

MACRORIE, KEN. *The Perceptive Writer, Reader, and Speaker.* New York: Harcourt, Brace & Co., Inc., 1959.

MARTIN, JOHN M. *Business and Professional Speaking.* New York: Harper & Bros., 1956.

MENNING, J. H., and WILKINSON, C. W. *Communicating Through Letters and Reports.* Homewood, Ill.: Richard D. Irwin, Inc., 1967.

MEREDITH, P. *Instruments of Communication: An Essay on Scientific Writing.* London: Pergamon, 1966.

MERRILL, PAUL W. "The Principles of Poor Writing," *Scientific Monthly,* January, 1947.

MILTON, H. H. *Steps to Better Writing.* Washington, D.C.: Spartan Books, Inc., 1959.

NORINS, H. *The Compleat Copywriter.* New York: McGraw-Hill Book Co., 1966.

PAYNE, STANLEY LeBARON. *The Art of Asking Questions.* Princeton, N.J.: Princeton University Press, 1951.

PHILLER, T. A.; HERSCH, R. K.: and CARLSON, H. V. (eds.). *An Annotated Bibliography of Technical Writing, Editing, Graphics and Publishing.* Washington, D.C.: Society of Technical Writers and Publishers, Inc., 1966.

QUILLER COUCH, SIR ARTHUR. *On the Art of Writing.* New York: C. P. Putnam's Sons, 1916.

RALPH, R. G. *Put It Plainly.* New York: Thomas Y. Crowell Co., 1952.

REID, J. M., JR., and WENDLINGER, R. M. *Effective Letters: A Program for Self-Instruction.* New York: McGraw-Hill Book Co., 1964.

SAWYER, THOMAS M. "Organizing Explanatory Speeches," *Michigan Business Review,* Jan., 1961, pp. 9–12.

SCHWARZ, FRED C. "Developing Interview Skills with TV Replay," *Research/ Development,* Oct., 1966, pp. 30–31.

SHIDLE, NORMAN G. *Clear Writing for Easy Reading.* New York: McGraw-Hill Book Co., 1951.

SHURTER, ROBERT L. *Written Communication in Business.* New York: McGraw-Hill Book Co., 1957.

SIMMONS, H.   *How to Talk Your Way to Success.* Englewood Cliffs, N.J.: Prentice-Hall, Inc., 1954.

SONDEL, BESS.   *Speak Up! A New Approach to Communication.* 2d ed. Chicago: University of Chicago Press, 1944.

STRUNK, W. J., and WHITE, E. B.   *The Elements of Style.* New York: Macmillan Co., 1959.

TICHY, H. J.   *Effective Writing.* New York: John Wiley & Sons, Inc., 1967.

TUTTLE, R. E., and BROWN, C. A.   *Writing Useful Reports.* New York: Appleton-Century-Crofts, Inc., 1955.

URIS, AUREN.   "How You Can Improve Your Business Writing," *International Management,* March, 1966.

WEATHERS, W., and WINCHESTER, O.   *The Strategy of Style.* New York: McGraw-Hill Book Co., 1967.

WHITNEY, E. (ed.).   *Symbology: The Use of Symbols in Visual Communication.* New York: Hastings House, 1960.

ZELKO, HAROLD P.   "How to Be a Better Speaker," *Nation's Business,* Vol. 53 (1965), pp. 88–103.

ON HUMAN INFORMATION PROCESSING (PROBLEM-SOLVING, THINKING, DECISIONING, ETC.)

BOIS, J. SAMUEL.   *The Art of Awareness.* Dubuque, Ia.: Wm. C. Brown, 1966.

BROSS, IRWIN.   *Design for Decision.* New York: Macmillan Co., 1953.

CHASE, STUART.   *Guides to Straight Thinking.* New York: Harper & Bros., 1956.

COOPER, J. D.   *The Art of Decision-Making.* Garden City, N.Y.: Doubleday & Co., Inc., 1961.

CRAWFORD, R. P. *Techniques of Creative Thinking.* New York: Hawthorn Books, 1954.

DIMNET, E.   *The Art of Thinking.* New York: Simon and Schuster, 1928.

FEARNSIDE, W. W., and HOLTHER, W. B.   *Fallacy: The Counterfeit of Argument.* Englewood Cliffs, N.J.: Prentice-Hall, Inc., 1959.

HODNETT, EDWARD.   *The Art of Problem Solving.* New York: Harper & Bros., 1955.

HUTCHINSON, E. D.   *How to Think Creatively.* New York: Abingdon-Cokesbury, 1949.

McDONALD, JOHN.   *Strategy in Poker, Business and War.* New York: W. W. Norton & Co., Inc., 1950.

OSBORNE, ALEX F.   *Applied Imagination.* New York: Charles Scribner's Sons, 1953.

PEIRCE, C. S.   "How to Make Our Ideas Clear," *Popular Science Monthly*, Vol. 12 (1878), pp. 286–302.

RUBY, LIONEL.   *The Art of Making Sense: A Guide to Logical Thinking*. Philadelphia: J. B. Lippincott Co., 1954.

SONDEL, BESS.   *Power-Steering With Words*. Chicago: Follett Publishing Co., 1964.

————.   *The Humanity of Words: A Primer of Semantics*. Cleveland: World Press, 1958.

STEBBING, SUSAN.   *Thinking to Some Purpose*. Baltimore: Penguin Books, Inc., 1959.

THOULESS, ROBERT HENRY.   *How to Think Straight*. New York: Simon and Schuster, 1950.

WALLAS, GRAHAM.   *The Art of Thought*. New York: Harcourt, Brace & Co., Inc., 1926.

WERTHEIMER, MAX.   *Productive Thinking*. New York: Harper & Bros., 1945.

ON MANAGERIAL AND ORGANIZATIONAL COMMUNICATION

AMERICAN MANAGEMENT ASSOCIATION, INC.   *Effective Communication on the Job*. Rev. ed. New York, 1963.

————.   *A Guide to Successful Conference Leadership*. New York, 1948.

————.   *Improving Management Communication*. General Management Series, No. 145. New York, 1950.

————.   *Strengthening Management's Channels of Communication*. Personnel Series, No. 116. New York, 1948.

————, Staff of the Executive Communications Course.   "Ten Commandments of Good Communication," *Management Review*, Vol. 44 (1955), pp. 704–5.

ARMSTRONG, T. O.   "Developing Effective Supervisor-Employee Communication," *Personnel*, Vol. 27 (1950), pp. 70–75.

ARNOLD, JOHN D.   "Six Guides to Help You Get Across," *Management Methods*, March, 1961.

BALINSKY, B., and BURGER, RUTH.   "Help Your Message Get Through: Knowing Why Communication Can Fail Is a Big Step Toward Making It Work," *Nation's Business*, March, 1959.

————, and ————.   *The Executive Interview*. New York: Harper & Bros., 1959.

BARNLUND, D. C., and HAIMAN, F. S.   *The Dynamics of Discussion*. Boston: Houghton Mifflin Co., 1960.

BERGHOFF, G. "Measuring the Results of Employee Communication Programs," *Management Review*, Vol. 39 (1950), pp. 457–58.

BINGHAM, WALTER VAN DYKE; MOORE, B. V.; and GUSTAD, J. W. *How to Interview*. 4th ed. New York: Harper & Bros., 1959.

BOYD, WILLIAM P., and LESIKAR, RAYMOND V. *Productive Business Writing*. Englewood Cliffs, N.J.; Prentice-Hall, Inc., 1959.

BUSHNELL, DAVID S., and WOOD, WILLIAM R. "Are You Getting Across to Employees?" *Nation's Business*, July, 1965.

CASSELS, LOUIS. "How to Be Believed," *Nation's Business*, April, 1959.

————, and RANDALL, R. L. "Help Workers' Views Come Through," *Nation's Business*, January, 1960.

Catalogue of Publications on Paperwork Management. Kansas City: General Services Administration, National Archives and Records Service, Records Management Division, 1965.

Communication in Business and Industry. New Brunswick, N.J.: Johnson and Johnson, 1949.

CORTRIGHT, RUPERT, and HINDS, GEORGE. *Creative Discussion*. New York: Macmillan Co., 1959.

CROWNFIELD, A. C., and GRANT, E. S. "Communication Techniques in Labor-Management Relations—Their Development and Application," *Mechanical Engineering*, Vol. 72 (1950), pp. 392–96.

DAVIS, KEITH A. "How Supervisors Can Communicate Better," *Personnel Journal*, Vol. 31 (1943), pp. 417–20.

DE LA OSSA, E. "Informing Employees," *Personnel Journal*, Vol. 26 (1947), pp. 104–8.

DOOHER, M. JOSEPH, and MARQUIS, VIVIENNE (eds.). *Effective Communication on the Job*. New York: American Management Association, Inc., 1956.

DOVER, C. J. "Silence—An Employee Relations Pitfall," *Advanced Management*, September, 1957.

————. "What to Do When Controversy Comes," *Nation's Business*, February, 1960.

DRUCKER, PETER F. "Communications—What Employees Are Really Interested In," *Advanced Management*, Vol. 16 (1941), pp. 7–9.

EMERY, D. "How to Sell Your Employee Communications," *Personnel*, Vol. 32 (1955), pp. 118–22.

Employee Communications for Better Understanding. New York: Industrial Relations Division, National Association of Manufacturers, 1959.

ESCHER, A. J. "Which Communications Methods Are 'Best' for Your Company?" *American Business*, December 1, 1959.

Esso, Inc. *Conference Leadership.* Elizabeth, N.J.: Esso Training Center, 1947.

Exton, William, Jr., "Semantics of Industrial Relations," *Personnel,* Vol. 26 (1950), pp. 418–23.

Fisher, Waldo Halder. *Management Conferences—How to Run Them.* Report No. 10. Philadelphia: Wharton School of Finance, University of Pennsylvania, 1947.

Goetzinger, Charles, and Valentine, Milton. "Improving Executive Communication," *Public Administration News,* Vol. 14 (1964).

Halley, William C. *Employee Publications: Theory and Practice of Communications in the Modern Organization.* Philadelphia: Chilton Books, 1959.

Himler, Leonard E. "Interviewing: Guides from a Psychiatrist," *Management of Personnel Quarterly,* Winter, 1966.

Hodnett, Edward. *The Art of Working with People.* New York: Harper & Bros., 1959.

Ivens, M. H. "A Formula for Good Communication," *Personnel Management,* Vol. 20 (1954), pp. 522–23.

Janis, J. H. *Writing and Communicating in Business.* New York: Macmillan Co., 1964.

King, C. W. *Getting Information to Employees and the Public.* New York: American Management Association, Inc., 1947.

Kolb, H. D. "Creating the Organizational 'Atmosphere' for Improved Communication," *Personnel,* Vol. 30 (1954), pp. 482–87.

Latham, Earl G. "The Technique of Administrative Reporting," *Public Administration Review,* Spring, 1943, p. 3.

Lee, Irving J., and Lee, Laura L. *Handling Barriers in Communication.* New York: Harper & Bros., 1956.

Lindgren, Henry Clay. *The Art of Human Relations.* New York: Hermitage House, 1953.

Lindh, A. E. "Plain Talk About Communicating in Business," *Business Management,* April, 1964, 91–95.

Loney, Glenn M. *Briefing and Conference Techniques.* New York: McGraw-Hill Book Co., Inc., 1959.

McGuire, Delbert. *Technical and Industrial Journalism.* Harrisburg, Pa.: Stackpole Books, Co., 1956.

McKersie, R. B., and Shropeshire, W. W., Jr. "Avoiding Written Grievances: A Successful Program," *The Journal of Business,* Vol. 35 (1952), pp. 135–52.

McLaughlin, T. J.; Blum, L. P.; and Robinson, D. M. *Communication.* Columbus, Ohio: C. E. Merrill, 1965.

MacRury, K. "How to Communicate with Employees," *Personnel Journal*, Vol. 25 (1946), pp. 186–202.

Magee, Richard H. "The Employment Interview—Techniques of Questioning," *Personnel Journal*, May, 1962.

Mahoney, T. A. "How Management Communicates with Employees," *Personnel*, Vol. 31 (1954), pp. 109–14.

Maier, N. R. F. *Problem-Solving Discussions and Conferences: Leadership Methods and Skills.* New York: McGraw-Hill Book Co., 1963.

————. *The Appraisal Interview: Objectives, Methods, and Skills.* New York: John Wiley & Sons, Inc., 1958.

Maloney, Martin. "Semantics: The Foundation of All Business Communication," *Advanced Management*, July, 1954.

Marting, E., et al. (eds.). *Effective Communication on the Job.* Rev. ed. New York: American Management Association, Inc., 1963.

Menninger, William C., and Levinson, Harry. *Human Understanding in Industry: A Guide for Supervisors.* Chicago: Science Research Associates, 1956.

Merrihue, W. V. *Managing By Communication.* New York: McGraw-Hill Book Co., 1960.

Myers, C. A. "Communication in Industry—How to Make It Effective," *Industrial Relations* (Calcutta), Vol. 7 (1955), pp. 43–49.

National Industrial Conference Board, Inc. *Communicating with Employees.* Studies in Personnel Policy, No. 129. New York, 1952.

————. *Communication Within the Management Group.* Studies in Personnel Policy, No. 80. New York, 1947.

Newcomb, R., and Sammons, Marg. *Employee Communications in Action.* New York: Harper & Row, 1961.

————, and ————. *Speak Up, Management!* New York: Funk & Wagnalls, 1951.

Nilson, Thomas R. "Twenty-Four Ways to Better Communication," *Personnel Journal*, Vol. 34 (1955), pp. 171–72.

Patton, J. A. "Management's Channels of Communications with Employees," *Modern Management*, Vol. 7 (1947), pp. 20–22.

Phillips, David C. *Oral Communication in Business.* New York: McGraw-Hill Book Co., Inc., 1955.

Pigors, Paul. *Effective Communication in Industry.* New York: National Association of Manufacturers, 1949.

Sexton, R., and Staudt, Virginia. "The Clinic Approach to Business Communication," *Journal of Psychology*, Vol. 44 (1957), pp. 109–10.

SHUTTE, W. M., and STEINBERG, E. R. *Communication in Business and Industry.* New York: Holt, Rinehart & Winston, 1959.

SINGER, T. E. R. *Information and Communication Practice in Industry.* New York: Reinhold Publishing Corp., 1958.

STRONG, LYDIA. "Meetings and the Manager," *Management Review,* July, 1956.

TOSKETT, JOHN D. "Do You Get Maximum Benefit from Your Executive Meetings?" *International Management,* January, 1966.

TRULL, SAMUEL G. "Strategies of Effective Interviewing," *Harvard Business Review,* Vol. 42 (1964), pp. 89–94.

URIS, AUREN. *Mastery of People.* Englewood Cliffs, N.J.: Prentice-Hall, Inc., 1964.

WEAVER, ROBERT G., and ZELKO, HAROLD P. "Talking Things Over on the Job," *Supervision Magazine,* May–July, 1958.

WEISMAN, H. (ed.). *Proceedings of the 1964 [et seqq.] Institute in Technical and Industrial Communications.* Ft. Collins: Colorado State University, 1965.

ZELKO, H. P. "Downward Communications: A Survey of Company Practices," *Management Review,* Vol. 45 (1956), pp. 344–45.

———. "Make Your Meetings More Worth While," *Nation's Business,* September, 1964.

———. *Successful Conference and Discussion Techniques.* New York: McGraw-Hill Book Co., 1958.

———, and O'BRIEN, H. J. *Management-Employee Communication in Action.* Cleveland: Howard Allen, 1957.

———, and WEAVER, R. G. *Communicating with Your Employees.* Personnel Leaflet No. 6, Society for Personnel Administration, October, 1961.

ZETLER, R. L., and CROUCH, W. G. *Successful Communication in Science and Industry: Writing, Reading, and Speaking.* New York: McGraw-Hill Book Co., 1961.

ON COMMUNICATION AND INFORMATION SYSTEMS AND THEIR TECHNOLOGY

BELLO, FRANCIS. "How to Cope with Information," *Fortune,* Vol. 62 (1960), pp. 162–90.

DEARDEN, JOHN. "How to Organize Information Systems," *Harvard Business Review,* Vol. 43 (1965), pp. 65–73.

EVANS, MARSHALL K., and HAGUE, LOU R. "Master Plan for Information Systems," *Harvard Business Review,* Vol. 40 (1962), pp. 92–103.

FIELD, JOHN W.   "Management Information Systems: A Report on Techniques," *Advances in Management Information System Techniques.* New York: American Management Association, Management Bulletin No. 16, 1962.

KRIEBEL, C. H.   "Operations Research in the Design of Management Information Systems," Management Sciences Research Report No. 73. Pittsburgh: Carnegie Institute of Technology, 1966.

MORAVEC, ADOLPH F.   "Using Simulation to Design a Management Information System," *Management Services,* Vol. 3 (1966), pp. 50–58.

SOLOMON, I. I., and WEINGART, L. O.   *Management Uses of the Computer.* New York: Harper & Row, 1966.

SPENCER, S. A.   "The Dark at the Top of the Stairs: What Higher Management Needs from Information Systems," *Management Review,* Vol. 51 (1962), pp. 4–11.

STAHL, N.   "Information Networking," *Mechanical Engineering,* Vol. 86 (1964), pp. 34–37.

SWANSON, ROWENA W.   *Information System Networks—Let's Profit from What We Know.* Arlington, Va.: Office of Aerospace Research, United States Air Force, June, 1966.

Appendix A: How to Write

This is not a "how-to" book. No one can learn to write by reading any or even all of the how-to-do-it books available on the subject. Writing well enough to be readily understood is something anyone *could* do. The reason that not many *do* write well consistently is that most would-be writers are looking for the "secret" or the "inspiration." About the first, they are misinformed; about the second, they are simply attempting to rationalize away laziness. There are no secrets. No one is *inherently* more talented than any other person to write in such a way as to be readily understood. Writing is like golfing or tennis or chess: You might have "beginner's luck," but consistently good performance requires study and practice. Doing anything well requires effort. So it is with writing well. No one who is not willing to put out the necessary effort to practice and to learn will ever write well consistently, no matter how many books or courses he subjects himself to.

But here are some thoughts which may nonetheless be useful to the reader in *thinking* about writing and writing "problems."

THE FIRST essential prerequisite to the ability to write adequately I take to be the ability to think adequately and clearly. All talk of techniques is futile if the would-be writer has not learned to think straight. Those who have difficulty putting their thoughts down on paper have this difficulty because:

1. They do not have a clear thought to put down on paper;
2. They fear exposing their poor thinking even to themselves, and this fear provides an emotional block that keeps them from trying.

And if they will not face up to these basic difficulties, no other training or teaching will be effective.

To write effectively, then, one must be able to think effectively.

The second essential prerequisite to the ability to write adequately I believe to be that of simply having something to say. We talk about communication as if it were something to be done well or poorly without regard to the value of its sources or referents. Those who concern themselves most with their "communication problems" may have nothing to say. No one can write well about that which is of no consequence to him or his audience. Anyone can write well about that which is of some consequence to him or his audience.

Third, one cannot write well unless he has a *specific purpose* for doing so. Not even the best techniques will compensate for the absence of a specific purpose. That purpose must be stated in terms of the receiver's response, not in terms of the qualities or form the message may have. If one sets out "to write a letter," or "to write clearly," the results can never be measured in any functional way. To write well, one must write to achieve a specific response or reaction by the receiver.

Fourth, the effective writer relies upon a thorough knowledge of his subject. Imperfect knowledge or inadequate information can lead to no better than imperfect or inadequate communication. He also relies upon an awareness of the communication process, which in turn rests upon an adequate knowledge of the qualities, functions, tools, and techniques of communication.

These are the things one must *know*. To write well, one must also *have* the kinds of attitudes toward himself, his subject, and his receiver which will facilitate the receiver's understanding and acceptance of the message. In short, these attitudes are all those feelings the originator has which incite in the receiver mutual feelings of confidence and trust. One's attitudes toward his subject or his receiver can never be completely hidden, and rarely successfully feigned. The receiver seeks cues to the originator's attitudes because a knowledge of them is necessary to his complete understanding of the message and its intent. Fifth, then, is the necessity of having appropriate attitudes toward the task.

Sixth, the writer needs now but adapt, organize, and present his material in such a way as to cause the receiver to react, respond, or comprehend precisely as desired. How can this be done? Only, I believe, by projecting oneself into the receiver's position as receiver, assuming *his* knowledges, attitudes, and perceptions of the situation. If there is a particular talent connected with the ability to write well, it is this simple ability to understand the receiver's frame of reference and project oneself into it before, during, and after writing.

Last, but frequently neglected, is the superior of all techniques: proofreading. Presumably, anything worth writing is worth reading—first by the writer. It gives him the opportunity to edit his message and to eliminate errors, inconsistencies, and ambiguities. But more than that, it offers him a perfect opportunity to sit back and play the role of the receiver—reading the message as if he had just received it. In this way, the writer *pretests* the message for its qualities and the probabilities of its success in achieving the specific purpose for which it was conceived and designed.

These I take to be the essentials of writing adequately. From the functional point of view, one writes to achieve a specific purpose. If he achieves his purposes rather consistently, he is successful. If he does not, he is not successful. The ultimate criterion exists not in the writing itself, but in the receiver's reaction to it. The ultimate measure of success is the degree to which the originator achieves his purpose for writing.

Appendix B: Managerial Reporting

CONSISTENT WITH the concept of communication developed in this book, managerial reporting refers to all reporting originated by any member of the organization and called for or utilized by the managers or leaders of that organization. An administrative report is thus any report originated or received by authority of a manager in his management of an organization.

An administrative report may be visual or oral. It may occur in any form—conversation, letter, conference, memo, picture, graph, and so on. The formal typed or printed report about which so much has been written is actually a less frequently used form than some others (oral reporting, for example).

The important thing about a report is not its style or form, as one might be led to believe, but its *utility*.

By postulate, if not by practice, the value or worth of a report is measured only by its ultimate usefulness to the manager in his planning, decision making, and control. (Naturally a report must be effective if it is ever to be useful.)

Good managerial reports, then, represent the primary inputs to a manager in the performance of his job. Good managerial reports also represent the most effective secondary or collateral outputs to owners and directors, employees, customers and suppliers, and the public at large.

While upward-directed reports are usually those that are emphasized—sometimes to the exclusion of any other direction of reporting—it is my view that good reporting *across, down,* and *out* is equally important to the organization's integrity and ultimate success.

Reports *to* managers are generally believed to serve these purposes:

1. To inform the manager about the status of all plans, projects, and operations.
2. To provide the manager with all the information he needs from all sources for adequate decision making.
3. To report potential problems or problem areas.

The parallels in the other directions of reporting may suggest the perspective desired. The purposes of reporting *downward* to employees (including subordinate managers) might be:

1. To keep them informed as to the long-range and short-range plans of the company, and of any changes required in their implementation.
2. To inform employees of the status of current plans and operations—and problems.
3. To provide employees with all the *current* information they may need to perform adequately their own jobs.

The purposes of reporting *across* (horizontally), and to customers and suppliers, are these:

1. To inform equal-level managers, or customers or suppliers, of the status of all major company plans and projects which do or might affect them directly or indirectly.[1]

---

[1] Traditional concepts of organizations would call for such reports to move up in the organization to the top of each functional division, then across, then back down in some modified or edited form. Sometimes, this roundabout way of keeping people informed may be necessary because of the nature of the organization or the personalities of the people involved. But if this indirect way is not necessary, or directed, then there are conspicuous advantages in reporting across in the manner described.

2. To identify those current problems which may be common to all or several functional divisions.
3. To provide other managers with information about department plans, policies, or operations which may be useful to them.

Reporting *out* to owners and directors would serve these purposes:

1. To inform them of the status of their investment.
2. To inform them of current and future operations and plans.
3. To refer to them organizational and managerial problems beyond the scope of the company's management (e.g., the implications of new government regulations, changing general economic conditions, etc.).

Outward reporting to the public would be useful for these purposes:

1. Informing the public of the company's social, philanthropic, personnel, and economic activities.
2. Reporting the social and civic activities of employees.
3. Reporting the company's particular successes, with a view toward showing how these relate to the community's and the general economy's well-being.

These are not, of course, the only purposes of reporting in all directions. But these examples may indicate the possibilities for viewing managerial reporting from this point of view. Other functions and types are suggested in Chapter 11, "Administrative Reporting," of Charles E. Redfield's *Communication in Management;*[2] and in Robert D. Gray's article, "What Your Boss Wants to Know."[3]

The Organization of Reports

What has been said in this book about the nature and functions of communication is altogether applicable to the preparation and presentation of reports. No separate description is desired or required.

Frequently, however, essays or books devoted to report writing tell the report writer *how* to organize the report. In my view, reports should be planned and organized no differently from other forms of communication. Tradition and custom may be important only because the receiver has developed certain expectations. The customary or traditional way of organizing reports, however, may be both inefficient and ineffective.

Even policy or regulation to the contrary, the most effective organiza-

---

[2] Rev. ed.; Chicago: University of Chicago Press, 1958.

[3] In M. Joseph Dooher and Vivienne Marquis (eds.), *Effective Communication on the Job.* New York: American Management Association, Inc., 1956.

tion of reports is that which is suggested by the subject, the circumstances, and the receiver. The best report organization is that organization which best serves the originator's purpose.

The Coordination of Upward-Directed Reports

Since the manager depends greatly upon the information provided him through reports, he needs to learn as much as he can from them. Yet, as the organization grows larger and specialization of functions increases, he likely receives more reports than he can possibly read and study. He must have the information he *needs* to make adequate decisions; but he must be spared all the information which he *does not need* to make adequate decisions.

The problem: how to reduce the quantity of the reports routed to him without missing any of the pertinent information which may be scattered through them.

Three conditions must obtain before this problem can be solved:

1. Those who provide the manager with reports must have a better idea of the plans, problems, and decisions for which the information is being provided. Subordinates are not mind readers. If they are not thoroughly aware of the manager's needs (in the way of information), they can hardly be expected to provide data at the right time in the right amount.
2. Those who originate reports must become better communicators. They must learn how better to analyze the situation in order to infer reporting needs.
3. The managers themselves must become better communicators. Research shows that, while they are superior communicators, they still listen and read at less than 50 percent efficiency.

In addition, coordination may sometimes be achieved through some physical means, such as integrating related reports, or adding a special staff to coordinate and brief all incoming reports. These are frequently no more than crutches, however, and serve to cover up the real source of the problem —poor communicators at all levels.

The need for considerable research in managerial reporting is clearly indicated by the nature and magnitude of typical problems in the handling of information for managerial decision making.

PART V

Theory and Research: Problems and Issues

19

Communication Theory and Research: Tributaries and Trends

THERE HAS NEVER BEEN a time in history when communication has not been of *some* concern or interest. We tend to think of our popular or scientific interest in communication as a phenomenon of the 20th century. But this is clearly not the case.

Because communication is basic to all of man's transactions, and crucial to his transactions with his fellows, the process of communication has fascinated or frustrated thoughtful men of all walks of life throughout history. Confucius, for example, was perhaps the first to write about "communication problems" in human organizations—and that was nearly 2500 years ago.

Concern with human communication problems was evident in the Bible:

> But let your communications be, Yea, yea; Nay, nay: for whatsoever is more than these cometh of evil.
>
> *St. Matthew, 5, 37*

About 1500, the great scholar da Vinci wrote in his *Notebook*:

> Man has a great power of speech, but the greater part thereof is empty and deceitful. The animals have little, but that little is useful and true; and better is a small and certain thing than a great falsehood.

Late in the 17th century, the characters of Wycherly's comedy, *The Country Wife*, found themselves embroiled in complex interpersonal

305

misunderstandings. The suggestion made by one of the characters to all of the others for getting things straightened out and back to normal? "Communicate, man, communicate!"

Shakespeare was apparently very much aware of the difference between the mere use of words and fruitful intercommunication:

"What do you read, my lord?" Polonius asked.

"Words, words, words," answered Hamlet.

Toward the end of the last century, Henry James noted that "all life therefore comes back to the question of speech, the medium through which we communicate with each other. . . ." In England, the poet Swinburne wrote:[1]

> Who hath given man speech? Or who hath set therein
> A thorn for peril and a snare for sin?
> *Atalanta in Calydon, 1865*

The emergence of "bureaucratese" and "gobbledygook" has often been attributed to the growth of huge organizations in our own century. But we might have good cause to wonder just how much progress we've made over the years in discovering, defining, and coping with our "communication problems" when we consider this quotation from Oscar Wilde's *Lady Windermere's Fan* (first presented in 1892):

THE DUCHESS: "Do, as a concession to my poor wits, Lord Darlington, just explain to me what you really mean."

LORD DARLINGTON: "I think I had better not. Nowadays to be intelligible is to be found out."

What this terse scanning of some reflections on communication from 2500 years of history is intended to point up is simply this: that we are probably fascinated or frustrated by the very same *communication* problems today as our predecessors were 10 or 50 or 200 or 2000 years ago.

Communication problems are nothing new. Hence our interest in the process of communication is nothing new.

What can we deduce of value from the perspectives on our subject afforded by these facts? Perhaps there are two useful conclusions which can be drawn.

First, there is the obvious conclusion that he who doesn't know his

---

[1] For interesting and cogent analyses of some concerns with communication in contemporary literature, see W. Weathers, "Communications and Tragedy in Eugene O'Neill, "*ETC*, 19 (No. 2), 148–160; and "An Exemplary Theory of Communication in Modern Literature," in L. Thayer (ed.), *Communication: Theory and Research* (Springfield, Ill.: Charles C Thomas, 1967).

history is destined to repeat it. The record of our progress in communication thought (until very recently) has been one of recurrently rediscovering the same problems and just as recurrently reinventing the same "principles" for the solution of those problems. To use an analogy, the record of our understanding of the processes of communication has been one of constantly reinventing the wheel; for example, now and then someone comes along and rediscovers that the receiver is an active and not just a passive element in the communication process. If we assume that the fascinations or the frustrations communication holds for us are unique to us or to our organizations, then we are probably destined to perceive them and deal with them in ways which likely have already been tried and found wanting— in the last century or the first century of man's existence.

Second, one might usefully conclude that the lack of substantial progress in the accumulation of substantive knowledge about communication could be attributed to the absence or the inadequacy of any theoretical foundations on which to build. If so, he would be right.

There has not been, and still is not, a single comprehensive theory of human communication on which those involved or concerned with communication could reliably base their perceptions of and solutions to communication problems.

There are a great many reasons—and perhaps good reasons—why this is so.

One of those reasons is that what we want to talk about—human communication in all of its forms—is exceedingly complex. The process of communication is comprised of a wide array of distinguishable components; and we don't have substantial knowledges even of those components. For example, we don't know *how* sensory data get translated into meaningful forms; nor do we yet have sufficient knowledge of how the brain and/or the nervous system process data in such common human functions as learning, remembering, forgetting, etc. Without substantial and reliable knowledge of these crucial aspects of communication, there is no sound way to develop valid and reliable criteria for communication system efficacy, or for a multitude of everyday applications of communication. So the sheer complexity of the process has been a significant impediment to the development of a comprehensive theory.

Another reason, of course, is simply that there has been no clearly defined field of communication—as such. Thus there has not been the systematic effort to develop theory and applications that, for example, physicists have profited from for the past one or two hundred years. Scholars and practitioners in a wide and increasing range of disciplines and fields of interest have pursued their own separate interests in the communication process in a piecemeal way. The freshman composition teacher is not likely to be aware of what psychologists are studying that might have some bearing on the development of his student's thinking or writing skills. Those psychologists may not be aware of the current research in cybernetics or mass communication that must inevitably relate in some way to their own research. And it's quite possible that neither the psychologist nor the writing instructor are aware of what is going on in the study of reading or listening—which, again, must ultimately relate to their own interest in some way. Or, perhaps if they were aware of these other pieces of the puzzle which is the total process of communication, they might not see any relevance in it. Each more or less necessarily goes his own way, developing theories and models of that part of the process which interests him, unconstrained by the necessity of fitting all of those pieces of knowledge together in such a way that a single, comprehensive theory might evolve.

Kenneth Boulding once said that we ought to stop looking at the world as if it were organized in the way our curriculums are. That *caveat* could hardly be more pertinent than it is to the way in which the process of communication—which underlies all specifically human functioning—has been chopped up into little pieces to be scrutinized by people whose fields of interest are often so alien that they couldn't fully comprehend each other even if they wanted to.

So it is that the absence of a single, integrated field or discipline of communication has stultified the growth and development of truly substantive and scientific knowledge of the process.

It may be useful to consider a further reason for the lack of a comprehensive theory of communication.[2] Communication is too common; too ubiquitous. Everyone "does it." And what is common to everyone is difficult—if not impossible—to approach scientifically. Why? Because if people are already "doing it," they feel no need to understand it in any *different* way, and usually feel resentful if someone else does under-

---

[2] I have elsewhere detailed a number of other possible reasons why we do not as yet have a single, unitary theory (or even a common conceptual scaffolding for that theory), and would refer the interested reader to them: L. Thayer, "On Theory-Building in Communication: I. Some Conceptual Problems," *Journal of Communication*, 1963, 13 (No. 4), 217–235; and "On Theory-Building in Communication: II. Some Persistent Obstacles," based on an address at the Annenberg School of Communications, Colloquium Series, University of Pennsylvania, November, 1965 (in press).

take to study it. So it is with love and seeing, walking and communica-tion.[3]

Thus, not only is the process more complex than perhaps any process known to man; and not only has the lack of a single discipline precluded the systematic accumulation of scientific knowledge; but the comfortable familiarity that all of us have with the process has stood in the way of our developing a substantial knowledge of it. These are all very good reasons for the state-of-the-art with respect to our fractionated knowledges of some parts of the process of communication, and to the lack of a single comprehensive perspective from which to understand and more artfully apply our understanding of that process.

Those reasons are equally good reasons for doing what we are going to do in this chapter. We could not trace the history of *the* theory of communica-tion. Nor could we trace the significant breakthroughs that have been made in communication research. Anyone who would concern or interest himself with the process of communication *as such* today must necessarily be cognizant of the fact that the field of study exists *only* in terms of its major tributaries and current trends. There is no single body of knowledge to which he can turn. Even if his interest is in one applied area of study— say "organizational communication"—he must necessarily recognize that the pertinent knowledge he seeks is available *only* in that array of tributary knowledges which bear in some partial way upon the phenomena he wants to comprehend.

So the purpose of this chapter will be to provide a very selective cross-section of the sources of substantive knowledge and research on part-aspects of the communication process, and thereby to suggest what the major tributaries are. When that is done, a look at some current trends may throw some additional light upon the nature and the magnitude of the task facing the communication theorist/researcher, and upon some implications therein for the practitioner.

Tributaries

As emphasized above, the sources of substantive knowledge about the various part-aspects of the communication process are many and varied. There are, as well, those studies which are best identified simply as "communication studies"—and which are carried out from the perspective

---

[3] A. N. Whitehead once observed that "It requires a very unusual mind to undertake the analysis of the obvious." Cf. A. Maslow, *The Psychology of Science.* New York: Harper & Row, 1966.

of the interface(s) of two or more of the traditional disciplines. We will look first at some representative studies from tributary fields, and then at some recent research and attempts at integration in the field of communication studies itself.[4]

REVIEWS AND COMPILATIONS

There are some recent reviews and compilations which should serve to suggest the range and the scope of the domains and tributaries to which one might turn in his study of the total process of communication. While none of these is intended to be exhaustive, they nevertheless do reflect the kinds of biases that exist in the way the study of communication is to be boundaried. They may also serve to emphasize the many hundreds of individual phenomena that will probably have to be taken into account by any ultimate theory of communication.

Cherry, C., *On Human Communication*. 2d ed. Cambridge, Mass.: MIT Press, 1966.

Dance, F. E. X. (ed.), *Human Communication Theory: Original Essays*. New York: Holt, Rinehart & Winston, 1967.

Handy, R., and P. Kurz, "A Current Appraisal of the Behavioral Sciences. Communication: Information Theory, Cybernetics, Linguistics, Sign Behavior." *American Behavioral Scientist*, 1964, 7 (No. 6), Supplement.

Johnson, F. C., and C. R. Klare, "General Models of Communication Research: A Survey of the Developments of a Decade." *Journal of Communication*, 1961, 11 (No. 1), 13–26 ff.

Rioch, D. Mck., and E. A. Weinstein (eds.), *Disorders of Communication*. Baltimore: Williams & Wilkins, 1964.

Schramm, W. (ed.), *The Science of Human Communication*. New York: Basic Books, 1963.

Smith, R. L., "General Models of Communication" (dittoed). Lafayette, Ind.: Communication Research Center, Purdue University, 1962.

---

[4] To provide the most meaningful cross-section of both direct and indirect study and research in communication, the representative documents selected (with few exceptions) have all been published since 1960. This necessarily meant the omission of a few earlier studies which have had considerable impact—e.g., J. Ruesch, "Synopsis of the Theory of Human Communication," *Psychiatry*, 1953, 16, 215–43; and B. H. Westley & M. S. MacLean, Jr., "A Conceptual Model for Communication Research," *Audio-Visual Communication Review*, 1955, 3, 3–12. But it is not the history of the development of our thinking about communication that is of importance here. What I would like to get across is a *feeling* for the scope and the range of the tributaries to which one would *currently* have to turn if he were interested in the process of communication as *such* (i.e., not the process as viewed from the partial point of view of neurophysiology, or information systems, or linguistics, etc.).

Thayer, L. (ed.), *Communication: Theory and Research*. Proceedings of the First International Svmposium on Communication Theory and Research. Springfield, Ill.: Charles C Thomas, 1967.

Thayer, L. (ed.), *Communication: Concepts and Perspectives*. Proceedings of the Second International Symposium on Communication Theory and Research. Washington, D.C.: Spartan Books, Inc., 1967.

NEUROLOGICAL AND BRAIN RESEARCH

Beyond such reviews of the "field," there are a number of specialized areas in which concepts are being developed or research conducted which have some relevance to any comprehensive understanding of the communication process.[5] It might be useful to revert to the framework provided by our earlier consideration of the *levels of analysis* from which to approach communication phenomena. Although not all of the tributaries we will want to consider are so named as to fit nicely into the scheme of levels we have used throughout this book, it will nonetheless provide a basic frame of reference.

Thus, our first perspective will be upon those tributaries which might be useful resources in the study of the *intrapersonal* aspects of the communication process. Most obvious here would be the relevant work being done in neurological and brain research—for it is difficult to imagine how one could be communicated-with outside the functioning of these internal systems. Perhaps representative of the scope and the magnitude of recent work in these areas are the following:

Broadbent, D. E., "Information Processing in the Nervous System." *Science*, (Oct.) 1965, 150, 457–62.

Chase, R. A., "Sensory Feedback Mechanisms and Speech." Bethesda, Md.: Neurocommunications Unit, National Institute of Mental Health, 1963.

Fields, W. S., and W. Abbott (eds.), *Information Storage and Neural Control*. Springfield, Ill.: Charles C Thomas, 1963.

George, F. H., *The Brain as a Computer*. London: Pergamon, 1962.

---

[5] It will probably be apparent that the categories employed are not by any means mutually exclusive. They overlap and interpenetrate each other in many dimensions. Too, there are those tributaries which are basic enough to overrun several of the categories described here—e.g., cybernetics, systems and general systems theory, information theory, and so on. Hence they are not singled out for separate attention. However, the interested reader may find useful vantage points on cybernetics in M. E. Maron, *Cybernetics* (Santa Monica, Calif.: The RAND Corp., 1965), and C. R. Dechert, "The Development of Cybernetics," *The American Behavioral Scientist*, 1965, 8 (No. 10), 15–20; and on systems and general system theory in the yearbook, *General Systems*, published annually by the Society for General Systems Research since 1956.

Gibson, J. J., *The Senses Considered as Perceptual Systems*. Boston: Houghton Mifflin Co., 1966.

Gregory, R. L., *Eye and Brain: The Psychology of Seeing*. New York: McGraw-Hill Book Co., 1966.

Pribram, K. H., "How the Brain Controls Its Input." In L. Thayer (ed.), *Communication: Theory and Research*. Springfield, Ill.: Charles C Thomas, 1967.

Rosenblith, W. A. (ed.), *Sensory Communication*. Cambridge, Mass.: MIT Press, 1961.

Schmitt, F. O., and T. Melnechuk (eds.), *Neurosciences Research Symposium Summaries*. Cambridge, Mass.: MIT Press, 1966.

Wooldridge, D. E., *The Machinery of the Brain*. New York: McGraw-Hill Book Co., 1963.

Bionics, Communication Pathologies, Human Factors

Closely related in many respects is the study and research being done in the new hybrid field of *bionics*, the "*communication sciences*" (primarily through the study of the pathologies of speech, hearing, writing and reading), and the hybrid field of *human factors*. From attempts to model the structures and functions of living systems in transactions with their environments, from a better understanding of organically based inabilities to communicate effectively, and from a continuous analysis of man-machine relationships—have come some further insights into the process of human communication. As is the case with most of the tributaries cited in this chapter, each is a field in itself, and therefore defies full coverage here. But these representative studies will perhaps be indicative of the resources to be tapped under this heading:

Bennett, E., et al. (eds.), *Human Factors in Technology*. New York: McGraw-Hill Book Co., 1963.

Bionics Symposium. Research and Technology Div., A.F. Systems Command, U.S. Air Force, Wright-Patterson Air Force Base, Ohio, 1966.

Chapanis, A. *Man-Machine Engineering*. Belmont, Calif.: Wadsworth Publishing Co., Inc., 1965.

Gaaze-Rapoport, M. G., et al. (eds.), *Bionics*. Moscow: Nauka Publishing House, 1965.

Gagné, R. M., *Psychological Principles in System Development*. New York: Holt, Rinehart & Winston, 1962.

Luria, A. R., *The Role of Speech in the Regulation of Normal and Abnormal Behavior*. TT 66 60821. Washington, D.C.: U.S. Department of Commerce, Institute for Applied Technology, 1966.

Mason, Stella E. (ed.), *Signs, Signals, and Symbols.* Springfield, Ill.: Charles C Thomas, 1963.

McCormick, E. J., *Human Factors Engineering.* 2d ed. New York: McGraw-Hill Book Co., 1964.

Miller, R. B., "Psychology for a Man-Machine Problem-Solving System." In L. Thayer (ed.), *Communication: Theory and Research.* Springfield, Ill.: Charles C Thomas, 1967.

Sinaiko, H. W. (ed.), *Human Factors in the Design and Use of Control Systems.* New York: Dover Publications, Inc., 1961.

Media Technology

Also closely related are those studies which attempt to measure man-medium (and form and convention) relationships. Again, to be comprehensive enough to cover all of the media and message forms would take us afield from our present purpose of presenting exemplars from the various tributaries. So the list must necessarily be extremely limited. The first two studies cited are studies of report-form/reader interactions, while the third is exemplary of those studies, now beginning to appear, which address themselves to what we have earlier referred to as human take-into-account-abilities.

Davis, R. M., *Effective Technical Communications Mechanical Description—Experiment II.* AFIT TR 65–1. Wright-Patterson AFB, Ohio: Air Force Institute of Technology, 1965.

Ronco, P. G. et al., *Characteristics of Technical Reports that Affect Reader Behavior: A Review of the Literature.* Medford, Mass.: Institute for Psychological Research, Tufts University, 1966.

Zipf, P., "More on Understanding Understanding Utterances." Paper SP–2504. Santa Monica, Calif.: System Development Corp., 1966.

Verbal Learning and Verbal Conditioning

It is but a short step from such studies as those just cited to the domain of verbal learning and verbal conditioning, and to the analysis of "meaning." The following are no more than suggestive:

Ausubel, D. P., *The Psychology of Meaningful Verbal Learning.* New York: Grune & Stratton, 1963.

Cofer, C. N., and Barbara S. Musgrave (eds.), *Verbal Behavior and Learning.* New York: McGraw-Hill Book Co., 1963.

Creelman, Marjorie B., *The Experimental Investigation of Meaning: A Review of the Literature.* New York: Springer Publishing Co., Inc., 1966.

Krasner, L., "Verbal Conditioning and Psychotherapy." In L. Krasner & L. P. Ullmann (eds.), *Research in Behavior Modification*. New York: Holt, Rinehart & Winston, 1965.

Werner, H., and B. Kaplan, *Symbol Formation*. New York: John Wiley & Sons, Inc., 1963.

LANGUAGE, LINGUISTICS, AND SEMANTICS

There is an obvious overlap between the study of verbal conditioning and the study of language—linguistically, psycholinguistically, and semantically. Yet each tributary brings a somewhat different perspective to bear on the communication process. Thus they are separately identified here. The study of language is perhaps the oldest, and therefore the largest, of all the tributaries we are concerning ourselves with in this chapter. So some violence to its significance will necessarily be done (a) by virtue of not indicating established subgroupings, and (b) by virtue of lumping together what specialists in the various subdisciplines within language and linguistics might insist are entirely different fields. Nonetheless, our purpose here is not to do justice to the structure of each of the tributaries to be considered, but to cite some exemplars of the current scope of work in each tributary—so as to establish a *feeling* for the manner in which the phenomenon of communication stretches across most of our traditional disciplines in the life, social, and behavioral sciences. The few studies cited here were therefore selected only on the basis of their potential contribution to that objective.

Austin, J. L., *How to Do Things with Words*. Cambridge, Mass.: Harvard University Press, 1962.

Carroll, J. B., *Language and Thought*. Englewood Cliffs, N.J.: Prentice-Hall, Inc., 1964.

Fodor, J. A., and J. J. Katz, *The Structure of Language*. Englewood Cliffs, N.J.: Prentice-Hall, Inc., 1964.

Glasersfeld, E. V., *An Approach to the Semantics of Propositions*. ILRS–T–12, 651115. Milan (Italy): Istituto di Documentazione dell'Associazione Meccanica Italiana, 1965.

Haney, W. V., *Communication and Organizational Behavior*. Homewood, Ill.: Richard D. Irwin, Inc., 1967.

Herdan, G., *The Advanced Theory of Language as Choice and Chance*. Berlin: Springer-Verlag, 1966.

Lenneberg, E. H. (ed.) *New Directions in the Study of Language*. Cambridge, Mass.: MIT Press, 1966.

Lyons, J., and R. J. Wales (eds.), *Psycholinguistics Papers: Proceedings of the 1966 Edinburgh Conference*. Edinburgh University Press, 1966.

Osgood, C. E., "On Understanding and Creating Sentences." *American Psychologist*, 1963, 18, 735–51.

Osgood, C. E., and T. A. Sebeok (eds.), *Psycholinguistics: A Survey of Theory and Research Problems*. Bloomington, Ind.: Indiana University Press, 1965.

Rosenberg, S. (ed.), *Directions in Psycholinguistics*. New York: Macmillan Co., 1965.

Salomon, L. B., *Semantics and Common Sense*. New York: Holt, Rinehart & Winston, 1966.

Sebeok, T. A., "The Informational Model of Language: Analog and Digital Coding in Animal and Human Communication." In P. L. Garvin (ed.), *Natural Language and the Computer*. New York: McGraw-Hill Book Co., 1963.

Sebeok, T. A., et al., *Approaches to Semiotics*. The Hague: Mouton, 1964.

Smith, F., and G. A. Miller (eds.), *The Genesis of Language: A Psycholinguistic Approach*. Cambridge, Mass.: MIT Press, 1966.

COGNITION, THINKING, PROBLEM-SOLVING

Whatever the particular point of view we might take in looking at language, we would undoubtedly agree that the acquisition and use of language is to some end. The terms we have used in this book are "processing" and "consuming." But the central information-processing that we engage in has been named in several different ways over the years—usually in terms of its consequence or purpose (e.g., in the service of solving a problem). So the tributary is a broad and variegated one, and the terms greatly proliferated. But the general function we are concerned with is the central information-processing which occurs in the service of the organism's adaptive needs and goals. Some studies that may help to illustrate the current flavor of the directions being taken in this tributary are these:

Berlyne, D. E., *Structure and Direction in Thinking*. New York: John Wiley & Sons, Inc., 1965.

Bruner, J. S., et al., *Studies in Cognitive Growth*. New York: John Wiley & Sons, Inc., 1966.

Furth, H. G., *Thinking Without Language*. New York: Free Press, 1966.

Hunt, E. B., *Concept Learning*. New York: John Wiley & Sons, Inc., 1962.

Klausmeier, H. J., et al., *Concept Learning and Problem Solving: A Bibliography, 1950–1964*. Technical Report No. 1. Madison: Research and Development Center for Learning and Re-Education, University of Wisconsin, 1965.

Maron, M. E., "On Cybernetics, Information Processing, and Thinking." P–2879. Santa Monica, Calif.: The RAND Corp., 1964.

Mowrer, O. Hobart, *Learning Theory and the Symbolic Processes.* New York: John Wiley & Sons, Inc., 1960.

Reitman, W. R., *Cognition and Thought.* New York: John Wiley & Sons, Inc., 1965.

Schon, D. A., *Displacement of Concepts.* London: Tavistock, 1963.

Personality, Psychological, and Psychiatric Studies

There are areas of concern to personality theorists, psychologists, and psychiatrists that have little relevance for the communication scholar or practitioner. Yet there are other areas of their interests which bear directly upon communication and intercommunication phenomena—e.g., attitude formation and change, psychological structure, nonverbal influence, etc. Representative of some current work in these areas of relevance are:

Beier, E. G., *The Silent Language of Psychotherapy.* Chicago: Aldine Publishing Co., 1966.

Cohen, A. R., *Attitude Change and Social Influence.* New York: Basic Books, Inc., 1964.

Garner, W. R., *Uncertainty and Structure as Psychological Concepts.* New York: John Wiley & Sons, Inc., 1962.

Harvey, O. J., D. E. Hunt, and H. M. Schroder, *Conceptual Systems and Personality Organization.* New York: John Wiley & Sons, Inc., 1961.

Powers, W. T. et al., "A General Feedback Theory of Human Behavior." *General Systems Yearbook,* 1960, 5, 63–73, 75–83.

Sherif, C. W., M. Sherif, and R. E. Nebergall, *Attitude and Attitude Change.* Philadelphia: W. B. Saunders Co., 1965.

Taylor, D. W., "Toward an Information-Processing Theory of Motivation." In M. R. Jones (ed.), *Nebraska Symposium on Motivation.* Lincoln: University of Nebraska Press, 1960.

Tomkins, S. S., and C. E. Izard (eds.), *Affect, Cognition, and Personality.* New York: Springer Publishing Co., Inc., 1965.

Interpersonal Behavior

From those tributaries of thought and research which are focused primarily upon *intrapersonal* factors, we will shift our attention now to those studies which focus upon *interpersonal* factors. The line dividing the two levels is rarely clear-cut. And certainly interpersonal encounters involve participants at the intrapersonal as well as the interpersonal level. But when the focus is upon the interpersonal transaction *as such*, new and useful insights and constructs derive from this additional tributary into that delta of confluence with which we are concerned—communication theory and research. Suggested here for illustrative purposes are but a few examples of this very rich field of study. Three of these (marked with *) are themselves reviews of the field, however, and would therefore "map" this field in a way we needn't duplicate here.

*Bennis, W. G. et al. (eds.), *Interpersonal Dynamics: Essays and Readings on Human Interaction*. Homewood, Ill.: Dorsey Press, 1964.

Foa, U. G., "Differentiation in Cross-Cultural Communication." In L. Thayer (ed.), *Communication: Concepts and Perspectives*. Washington D.C.: Spartan Books, Inc., 1967.

*Harvey, O. J. (ed.), *Motivation and Social Interaction*. New York: Ronald Press Co., 1963.

Kanfer, F. H., "Structure of Psychotherapy: Role Playing as a Variable in Dyadic Communication." *Journal of Consulting Psychology*, 1965, 29 (No. 4), 325–32.

Laing, R. D. et al., *Interpersonal Perception: A Theory and a Method of Research*. London: Tavistock, 1966.

Lipham, J. M., and D. C. Francke, "Non-Verbal Behavior of Administrators." *Educational Administration Quarterly*, 1966, 2, 101–9.

McCall, G. J., and J. L. Simmons, *Identities and Interactions*. New York: Free Press, 1966.

*Zaleznik, A., and D. Moment, *The Dynamics of Interpersonal Behavior*. New York: John Wiley & Sons, Inc., 1964.

SMALL GROUP STUDIES AND COMMUNICATION "NETS"

It is in some respects a minor shift of focus that would turn our attention from interpersonal factors to the concerns of those whose interests are in the study of small groups and/or communication "nets." Not all communication networks are face-to-face, however, and this variation does indeed introduce some new variables.

Again, the literature emanating from these fields is vast. But since four of those selected as representative of current perspectives in these fields (marked with *) are reviews, the interested reader could expediently use them as springboards for deeper inquiry.

*Cohen, A. M., "A Model of Group Adaptation to Organizational Change in Communication Networks." In L. Thayer (ed.), *Communication: Theory and Research*. Springfield, Ill.: Charles C Thomas.

Collins, B. E., and H. Guetzkow, "Communication and Interaction" in *A Social Psychology of Group Processes for Decision Making,* Ch. 6. New York: John Wiley & Sons, Inc., 1964.

*Glanzer, M., and R. Glaser, "Techniques for the Study of Group Structure and Behavior: II. Empirical Studies of the Effects of Structure in Small Groups." *Psychological Bulletin,* 1961, 58, 1–27.

*Hare, A. P., *Handbook of Small Group Research.* New York: Free Press, 1962.

Lyle, J., "Communication, Group Atmosphere, Productivity, and Morale in Small Task Groups." *Human Relations,* 1961, 14 (No. 4), 369–79.

*Raven, B. H., *A Bibliography of Publications Relating to the Small Group.* Los Angeles: Department of Psychology, University of California, 1965.

ORGANIZATIONS, ORGANIZATION THEORY, ORGANIZATIONAL BEHAVIOR, MANAGEMENT THEORY

There are those who believe that small group and communication net studies can be directly generalized to the study of larger organizations. There are others who would argue to the contrary.[6] Whichever point of view one might prefer, it would seem indisputable that there are factors to be considered at the *level of organization* which do not obtain at the interpersonal or intrapersonal levels of analysis. As one might expect, these several fields of interest, which seem to have a common domain of study but somewhat different perspectives on that domain, comprise a very heterogeneous body of literature. That heterogeneity is perhaps reflected in these few exemplars:

Chapline, J. D. (ed.), *The Manager's Role in Organizational Communications.* Proceedings of the 1963 IEEE/MSU Colloquium. New York: Institute of Electrical and Electronics Engineers, 1964.

Cooper, W. W. et al. (eds.), *New Perspectives in Organization Research.* New York: John Wiley & Sons, Inc., 1964.

Jones, W. M., *On Decision Making in Large Organizations.* Memorandum RM–3968–PR. Santa Monica, Calif.: The RAND Corp., 1964.

Katz, D., and R. L. Kahn, *The Social Psychology of Organizations.* New York: John Wiley & Sons, Inc., 1966.

---

[6] For a short discussion of this issue, see L. Thayer, "Communication and Organization," in F. E. X. Dance (ed.), *Human Communication Theory: Original Essays* (New York: Holt, Rinehart & Winston, 1967). Cf. J. A. Seiler, "Toward a Theory of Organization Congruent with Primary Group Concepts," *Behavioral Science,* 1963, 8 (No. 3), 190–98; and R. T. Golembiewski, *Behavior and Organization: O & M and the Small Group* (Chicago: Rand McNally, 1962).

Likert, R., *New Patterns of Management.* New York: McGraw-Hill Book Co., 1961.

Litterer, J. A., *The Analysis of Organizations.* New York: John Wiley & Sons, Inc., 1965.

McGuire, J. W., *Theories of Business Behavior.* Englewood Cliffs, N.J.: Prentice-Hall, Inc., 1964.

McLaughlin, C. P. *et al., Technology Transfer and the Flow of Technical Information in a Large Industrial Corporation.* Committee on Space, American Academy of Arts and Sciences. 1965.

March, J. G. (ed.), *Handbook of Organizations.* Chicago: Rand McNally, 1965.

Marting, E. *et al.* (eds.), *Effective Communication on the Job.* Rev. ed. New York: American Management Association, 1963.

Newcomb, R., and Marg Sammons, *Employee Communications in Action.* New York: Harper & Row, 1961.

Read, W. H., "Communication in Organizations: Some Problems and Misconceptions." *Personnel Administration,* (Mar.–Apr.) 1963, 26, 4–10.

Redding, W. C., and G. A. Sanborn (eds.), *Business and Industrial Communication: A Source Book.* New York: Harper & Row, 1964.

Rome, S., and B. Rome, *Communication and Large Organizations.* SP–1690. Santa Monica, Calif.: System Development Corp., 1964.

Scott, W. G., *Organization Theory: A Behavioral Analysis for Management.* Homewood, Ill.: Richard D. Irwin, Inc., 1967.

Thayer, L., "Communication and Organization." In F. E. X. Dance (ed.), *Human Communication Theory: Original Essays.* New York: Holt, Rinehart & Winston, 1967.

Tompkins, P. K., "Communication in Business and Industry—A Summary of Research Findings" (mimeoed preprint). Industrial Communication Research Council. Lafayette, Ind.: Purdue University, 1963.

Walter, B., *Bureaucratic Communications: A Statistical Analysis of Influence.* Chapel Hill: Institute for Research in Social Science, University of North Carolina, 1963.

Walton, E., *A Magnetic Theory of Organizational Communication.* China Lake, Calif.: U. S. Naval Ordnance Test Station, 1962.

Zajonc, R. B., and D. M. Wolfe, "Cognitive Consequences of a Person's Position in a Formal Organization." Tech. Report No. 24. Ann Arbor, Mich.: Institute for Social Research, 1963.

COMMUNICATION AND INFORMATION SYSTEMS, INFORMATION SCIENCES AND TECHNOLOGY

At the organizational level of analysis, we would be remiss if we did not take adequate account of the surfeit of study and research now emerging from the broad areas of information systems and information sciences. For convenience, we can include under this heading some representative examples of current treatments of the hardware aspects of information technology—as those media and devices bear upon our main concern with human communication.

American Documentation Institute, *Parameters of Information Science.* Washington, D.C.: Spartan Books, Inc., 1964.

Bello, F., "How to Cope with Information." *Fortune,* (Sept.) 1960, 62, 162 ff.

Bennett, E. et al. (eds.), *Military Information Systems.* New York: Frederick A. Praeger, Inc., 1964.

Bonini, C. P. et al. (eds.), *Management Controls: New Directions in Basic Research.* New York: McGraw-Hill Book Co., 1964.

Carey, J. W., "Communication Systems and Social Systems: Two Economic Postulates Applied to a Theory of Communication Systems." Unpublished doctoral dissertation, University of Illinois, 1963.

Dearden, J., and F. W. McFarlan, *Management Information Systems.* Homewood, Ill.: Richard D. Irwin, Inc., 1966.

Diebold, J., *Beyond Automation: Managerial Problems of an Exploding Technology.* New York: McGraw-Hill Book Co., 1964.

Diebold, J., "What's Ahead in Information Technology." *Harvard Business Review,* (Sept.–Oct.) 1965, 43, 76–82.

Greenberger, M., *Computers and the World of the Future.* Cambridge, Mass.: MIT Press, 1962.

"Information Systems Summaries." ONR Report ACR–113. Washington, D.C.: Office of Naval Research, 1965.

Johnson, R. A. et al., *The Theory and Management of Systems.* New York: McGraw-Hill Book Co., 1963.

Kriebel, C. H., "Operations Research in the Design of Management Information Systems." Management Sciences Research Rep. No. 73, Carnegie Institute of Technology, 1966.

McDonough, A. M., *Information Economics and Management Systems.* New York: McGraw-Hill Book Co., 1963.

Mesarovic, M. D. (ed.), *Views on General Systems Theory.* New York: John Wiley & Sons, Inc., 1964.

Neeland, Frances, *A Bibliography on Information Science and Technology for 1966–Part I.* Report TM–3008/001/00. Santa Monica, Calif.: System Development Corp., 1966.

Proceedings of the Western Joint Computer Conference: Extending Man's Intellect. New York: National Joint Computer Committee, 1961.

Rothstein, J., "Entropy Concepts for Complex Systems." Boston: Laboratory for Electronics, 1966.

Ruesch, J., "Technology and Social Communication." In L. Thayer (ed.), *Communication: Theory and Research.* Springfield, Ill.: Charles C. Thomas, 1967.

Spiegel, J., and D. Walker (eds.), *Information System Sciences.* Washington, D.C.: Spartan Books, Inc., 1965.

Stahl, N., "Information Networking." *Mechanical Engineering,* 1964, 86, 34–37.

Toda, M., and E. H. Shuford, Jr., "Logic of Systems: Introduction to the Formal Theory of Structure." Tech. Doc. Rep. No. ESD–TDR–64–193. Bedford, Mass.: Decision Sciences Lab., A.F. Systems Command, L. G. Hanscom Field, U.S.A.F., 1964.

Walker, C. C., *A Study of a Family of Complex Systems: An Approach to the Investigation of Organisms' Behavior.* Tech. Rep. No. 5. Electrical Engineering Research Laboratory, University of Illinois, 1965.

Wilson, I. G., and M. E. Wilson, *Information, Computers, and System Design.* New York: John Wiley & Sons, Inc., 1965.

Yovits, M. C. et al., (eds.), *Self-Organizing Systems, 1962.* Washington, D.C.: Spartan Books, Inc., 1962.

Mass Communication, Sociocultural, and Sociopolitical Studies

Still at the organizational level of analysis, but having some relevance for the understanding of communication at all levels, are those studies which derive from those scholars and researchers whose interests are in mass communication,[7] and the sociocultural and sociopolitical aspects of communication. A few of these studies are cited here to suggest something of the usefulness of these tributaries to the study of communication qua communication.

Crane, E., *Marketing Communications.* New York: John Wiley & Sons, Inc., 1965.

Danielson, W. A. (ed.), *Paul J. Deutschmann Memorial Papers in Mass Communications Research.* Cincinnati: Scripps-Howard Research, 1963.

Davison, W. P., *International Political Communication.* New York: Frederick A. Praeger, Inc., 1965.

---

[7] As previously suggested, what differentiates "mass" communication is not necessarily the size of the audience or the medium employed, but (a) the nonface-to-face or nondirect nature of the encounter (which would imply a relatively nondiachronic mode, and relatively nondynamic "movement"), and (b) the condition that the receiver(s) has (have) no established interpersonal relationship with the originator. Thus my telephone conversation with a friend is not mass communication, whereas a letter I might write to someone I do not know personally is necessarily one kind of mass communication.

DeFleur, M. L., "Mass Communication and Social Change." Social Forces, 1966, 44 (No. 3), 314–26.

Dexter, L. A., and D. M. White (eds.), People, Society, and Mass Communications. New York: Free Press, 1964.

Duncan, H. D., Communication and Social Order. New York: Bedminster Press, Inc., 1962.

Easton, D., A Systems Analysis of Political Life. New York: John Wiley & Sons, Inc., 1965.

Eisenstadt, S. N., "Communication and Transformation of Symbolic Systems —Some Problems of Communication in Developing Societies." In L. Thayer (ed.), Communication: Theory and Research. Springfield, Ill.: Charles C. Thomas, 1967.

Gerbner, G., Mass Communications and Popular Conceptions of Education: A Cross-Cultural Study. Institute of Communications Research, University of Illinois, 1964.

Hall, E. T., The Hidden Dimension. Garden City, N.Y.: Doubleday & Co., Inc., 1966.

Hertzler, J. O., A Sociology of Language. New York: Random House, 1965.

Hymes, D., Language in Culture and Society: A Reader in Linguistics and Anthropology. New York: Harper & Row, 1964.

Jansen, B. D., "A System for Content Analysis by Computer of International Communications for Selected Categories of Action." American Behavioral Scientist, 1966, 9 (No. 7), 28–32.

Klapper, J. T., The Effects of Mass Communication. New York: Free Press, 1960.

Lerbinger, O., and A. J. Sullivan (eds.), Information, Influence, and Communication. New York: Basic Books, Inc., 1965.

Milbrath, L. W., "Lobbying as a Communication Process." Public Opinion Quarterly, 1960, 24, 32–53.

Pye, L. (ed.), Communications and Political Development. Princeton, N.J.: Princeton University Press, 1963.

Robinson, E. J., Communication and Public Relations. Columbus, Ohio: Charles E. Merrill Books, Inc., 1966.

Robinson, J. A., Congress and Foreign Policy-Making. Homewood, Ill.: Dorsey Press, 1962.

Schramm, W., Mass Media and National Development. Stanford, Calif.: Stanford University Press; 1964.

Windlesham, Lord, Communication and Political Power. London: Jonathan Cape, 1966.

OTHER RESOURCE AREAS

There are other areas of study which the student of communication may find useful to draw upon from time to time. Because they are not readily subsumable under any of the other headings, they can be dealt with here. But this separate treatment should not be taken as any evidence of exceptional relevance. Each tributary has its unique usefulness to the study of communication, a usefulness which may be circumstantially neither more nor less than any of the other resource tributaries.

Animal Communication. Studies of animal communication can provoke a wide range of different insights into the communication process. Three recent publications are:

Altmann, S. A. (ed.), *Social Communication Among Primates.* Chicago: University of Chicago Press, 1967.

Frings, H., "Animal Communication." In L. Thayer (ed.), *Communication: Concepts and Perspectives.* Washington D.C.: Spartan Books, Inc., 1967.

Frings, H., and M. Frings, *Animal Communication.* New York: Blaisdell Publishing Co., 1964.

Simulation. Another area of activity which will increase in usefulness to the student of communication in the years just ahead is that of *simulation.* Intrapersonal processes, interpersonal processes, group and organizational processes, complex system processes—all are being simulated now with greater and greater degrees of sophistication. Some examples of the fruits of these inquiries are:

Bonini, C. P., *Simulation of Information and Decision Systems in the Firm.* Englewood Cliffs, N.J.: Prentice-Hall, Inc., 1963.

Feigenbaum, E. A., and J. Feldman (eds.), *Computers and Thought.* New York: McGraw-Hill Book Co., 1963.

Garvin, P. L. (ed.), *Natural Language and the Computer.* New York: McGraw-Hill Book Co., 1963.

Guetzkow, H. (ed.), *Simulation in Social Science: Readings.* Englewood Cliffs, N.J.: Prentice-Hall, Inc., 1962.

Hoggatt, A. C., and F. E. Balderston (eds.), *Symposium on Simulation Models.* Cincinnati: South-Western Publishing Co., 1963.

Hunt, E. B. et al., *Experiments in Induction.* New York: Academic Press, 1966.

Tomkins, S. S., and S. Messick (eds.), *Computer Simulation of Personality.* New York: John Wiley & Sons, Inc., 1963.

Quantitative Analysis and Methodology. Another resource area pertinent to the interests and concerns of the student of communication is that of methodology and quantitative analysis. Because quantitative analysis requires the learning of a language (a different order of technological tool), we could not presume to characterize here any more than the sorts of documents that are presently available—and which themselves review the relevant methodologies—e.g.,

Binder, A., and B. Wolin, "Informational Models and Their Uses." *Psychometrika*, 1964, 29 (No. 1), 29–54.

Chapple, E. D., "Quantitative Analysis of Complex Organizational Systems." *Human Organization*, 1962, 21 (No. 2), 67–80.

Miller, G. A., and N. Chomsky, "Finitary Models of Language Users." In R. D. Luce *et al.* (eds.), *Handbook of Mathematical Psychology*. Vol. II. New York: John Wiley & Sons, Inc., 1963.

Rapoport, A., "Mathematical Models of Social Interaction." In R. D. Luce, *et al.* (eds.), *Handbook of Mathematical Psychology*. Vol. II. New York: John Wiley & Sons, Inc., 1963.

Webb, E. J. *et al.*, *Unobtrusive Measures: Nonreactive Research in the Social Sciences*. Chicago: Rand McNally, 1966.

COMMUNICATION STUDIES

In addition to the several tributaries suggested to this point, there is one further area that should be given especial consideration here. This is the area of "communication studies," so called because they derive not from any one of the traditional fields of study as such, but from various hybrid combinations of disciplines which aggregatively are often referred to as "communication." There is a burgeoning flow of papers, studies, and research from a wide range of such interdisciplinary hybrids. The short list cited here does not in any way reflect the magnitude (or the importance) of this tributary. But it may serve to suggest the kinds of cross-disciplinary thinking which give rise to this group of studies, and to suggest something of the broad range of documentary sources in which these studies might appear.

Barnlund, D. C., and C. Harland, "Propinquity and Prestige as Determinants of Communication Networks." *Sociometry*, 1963, 26 (No. 4), 467–79.

Carter, R. F., "Communication and Affective Relations." *Journalism Quarterly*, 1965, 42 (No. 2), 203–12.

Haney, W. V., "A Comparative Study of Unilateral and Bilateral Communication." *Academy of Management Journal*, 1964, 7 (No. 2), 128–36.

McMurry, R. N., "Clear Communications for Chief Executives." *Harvard Business Review*, (April) 1965, 131–47.

Mulder, M., "The Power Variable in Communication Experiments." *Human Relations*, 1960, 13, 241–57.

Smith, A. G., *Communication and Status: The Dynamics of a Research*

Center. Eugene: Center for the Advanced Study of Educational Administration, University of Oregon, 1966.

Zajonc, R. B., "The Process of Cognitive Tuning in Communication." *Journal of Abnormal & Social Psychology*, 1960, 61 (No. 2), 159–67.

Attempts at Integration

There have been, over the years, several attempts at integrating the relevant knowledge of all of the pertinent tributaries in such a way as to formulate a single, unitary conceptual/theoretical statement. Perhaps in some way representative only of those which have appeared since 1960 are these:

Bemis, J. L., and G. M. Phillips, "A Phenomenological Approach to Communication Theory." *Speech Teacher*, 1964, 13, 262–69.

Gerbner, G., "A Theory of Communication. . . ," in *The Nature of Teaching, A Symposium*. Milwaukee: University of Wisconsin, School of Education, 1963.

MacKay, D. M., "The Science of Communication—A Bridge between Disciplines," Inaugural Lecture, University of North Staffordshire, Keele, England, February, 1961.

Miller, J. G., "Living Systems: Basic Concepts; Structure and Process; Cross-Level Hypotheses," *Behavioral Science*, 1965, 10, 193–237; 337–79; 380–411.

Ruesch, J., "Principles of Human Communication," in *Therapeutic Communication*. New York: W. W. Norton & Co., Inc., 1961.

Shands, H. C., "Outline of a General Theory of Human Communication. . . ," in L. Thayer (ed.), *Communication: Concepts and Perspectives*. Washington D.C.: Spartan Books, Inc., 1967.

A Recapitulation

Certainly this list of exemplary studies from the various tributaries that will ultimately have to converge in any comprehensive theory of communication in no way reflects the scope or the magnitude of all that is available —and indispensable—to the student of communication. But, for all of its limitations, and its likely errors of omission as well as commission, it may serve its primary purpose: that of leaving the reader with a feeling of the great range and diversity of tributaries which he must have some cognizance of if his own comprehension and understandings of the communication process are not to be unnecessarily inadequate to the nature of the task which every student of communication faces.

The task is a formidable one.

It is not the task of being an "expert" in all of the resource fields or tributaries identified in the previous pages. It is more the task of (a) making better determinations of what needs to be known, and (b) knowing where to look for and how to assess the validity and usefulness of what is found there. And, if we take the tip from Whitehead, it is not so much the superiority of the mind making the inquiry that counts—as it is the unusualness of that mind which puts itself to the task of exploring what is familiar and commonplace to all of us . . . communication.

What is one to gain from coldly apprehending the major resources for that task, as we have done in this chapter? Certainly not much new knowledge of the relevant or useful ideas and concepts available through those tributaries. Perhaps no more than a vague *feeling* for the fragmented structure or form of the field as it exists today. If so, that is the gain.

For, as we will examine in more detail in Chapter 20, what the serious student or practitioner needs today are not better ways of solving communication problems, but better ways of perceiving them, better ways of structuring his apprehension and comprehension of them. "Solving" problems is easy. It is understanding them that is difficult.

And the point of all that has preceded in this chapter is this: that one's understanding of the processes and problems of communication depends upon how the knowledge from all of these tributaries fits together at the point of their confluence for him—i.e., in the way he comprehends their relationships and their relevance for his task. What is needed is a perspective which encompasses all of the intellectual domains throughout which the process of communication extends. What was intended in the preceding was gaining some appreciation for the scope of that needed perspective.

Some Trends

It is to one's advantage to be aware of a number of trends in communication theory and research developed during recent years. Different authors might concern themselves with somewhat different trends. Here we will simply want to identify four trends which seem most relevant to the consequences and implications of the conceptual framework developed in this book, and which are evidenced in the preceding description of the tributaries. They are:

1. The continuing influence of information theory, cybernetics and general systems theory, and the evolving tradition of communication "net" studies.

2. The impact of the technological hardware and software of information systems and information sciences.
3. The continued proliferation of hybrid fields of interest—arising primarily out of the need to solve new problems in applied fields (e.g., bionics).
4. Emergent and perhaps accelerating attempts at broader and broader integration of the field.

A few explanatory remarks about each of these trends will serve our purposes here.

From 1948 to about 1951, four of the most important tributaries emerged and were given impetus: Information Theory,[8] cybernetics,[9] general systems theory,[10] and the tradition of communication "nets" studies.[11]

These new fields of interest have had an immediate and continuing influence on communication thought. This trend will likely continue. But the question of the exact nature and extent of their relevance to *human* communication and to communication in human organizations is yet to be settled. The temptation to reach into the physical sciences for theoretical and/or conceptual panaceas for something as complex and as difficult to systematize as human communication is an understandable one—and perpetuates a long tradition in the life and behavior sciences. But "uncertainty reduction" and "feedback," while useful as *concepts*, do not alone explain the process of human communication. Nonetheless, the trend has been a fuitful one for other reasons, and will likely persist.

Another continuing trend will be the impact of the technological hardware and software of the "information sciences" on thinking about human communication. There is no question of the appropriateness or the legitimacy of studying human communication in the technological contexts in which that communication is going to occur—i.e., in the context of the technological hardware and software in which it occurs. But there has been, and probably will continue to be, a disproportionate interest in the hardware and procedural aspects to the possible detriment of our interest in the human aspects of communication. It is much easier to design an

---

[8] C. E. Shannon and W. Weaver, *The Mathematical Theory of Communication* (Urbana, Ill.: University of Illinois Press, 1949).

[9] N. Wiener, *Cybernetics* (New York: John Wiley & Sons, Inc., 1948).

[10] Bertalanffy, L. von, "The Theory of Open Systems in Physics and Biology." *Science*, (Jan. 13) 1950, 111, 23ff.

[11] A. Bavelas, "A Mathematical Model for Group Structures." *Applied Anthropology*, 1948, 7, 16–30.

organizational data system than it is to design an efficacious communication system. And our proclivity toward easy solutions would predict to the continuing impact of these concerns upon our thinking. Thinking of communication and communication problems in terms of applied technology will likely be a continuing trend.

Hybrid fields of interest, arising primarily out of the need to deal with the problems of new human endeavors (such as space and ocean exploration), will undoubtedly continue to proliferate. The problems that must be solved to enable new human endeavors typically cut across disciplinary boundaries—for example, biochemistry, human engineering, etc. Hybrid problem areas already exist in the "field" of communication, of course (such as advertising and interpersonal selling and "information transfer"), but they typically do not have the aura of legitimacy that would attract many leading scholars and researchers. But there may be hybrids or amalgams such as *intrapersonal communication* evolving in the years ahead, forcing the issue of theoretical integration across the relevant disciplinary boundaries.

Finally, for the reasons just suggested, there will likely be more attempts to integrate broader and broader theoretical and research domains. This trend will not inhibit the concurrent fractionization of the field into smaller domains of interest, however. Both trends will likely continue on into the future, and movement will be in both directions simultaneously. Just as there will be a need to comprehend smaller and smaller units of the overall process, there will be an increasing need to deal with practical problems at more and more comprehensive levels of understanding.

Given the kinds of perspectives on communication theory and research offered in this chapter, it would seem a logical next step to turn our attention to the major problems and issues in communication in the next, and last, chapter of this book.

SUGGESTIONS FOR FURTHER READING

References to theory and research in human communication are to be found in the reading lists which follow every chapter. And a cross-section of current thought from the perspectives of different levels of analysis has been presented in this chapter. Yet there are additional documents which for one reason or another have some special pertinence as supplementary readings for this chapter and those are suggested here.

ACKOFF, R. L.   "Towards a Behavioral Theory of Communication," *Management Science*, Vol. 4 (1958), pp. 218–34.

ANGRIST, A. W. "A Study of the Communication of Executives in Business and Industry," *Speech Monographs*, Vol. 20 (1953), pp. 277–85.

BAKER, HELEN. *Company-Wide Understanding of Industrial Relations Policies: A Study in Communications*. Princeton, N.J.: Industrial Relations Section, Princeton University, 1948.

———; BALLANTINE, J. W.; and TRUE, J. M. *Transmitting Information through Management and Union Channels*. Princeton, N.J.: Industrial Relations Section, Princeton University, 1949.

BAVELAS, ALEX, and BARRETT, DERMOT. "An Experimental Approach to Organizational Communication," *Personnel*, Vol. 27 (1945), pp. 366–71.

BEER, S. *Decision and Control*. New York: John Wiley & Sons, Inc., 1966.

BERELSON, BERNARD. *Content Analysis in Communication Research*. New York: Free Press, 1952.

BIRDWHISTELL, RAY L. *Introduction to Kinesics: An Annotation System for Analysis of Body Motion and Gesture*. Washington, D.C.: Foreign Service Institute, Department of State, 1952.

BONINI, C. P.; JAEDICKE, R. K.; and WAGNER, H. M. (eds.) *Management Controls: New Directions in Basic Research*. New York: McGraw-Hill Book Co., 1964.

BUCKLEY, W. F. *Modern Systems Research for the Behavioral Scientist*. Chicago: Aldine Publishing Co., 1967.

BURNS, TOM. "The Directions of Activity and Communication in a Departmental Executive Group: A Quantitative Study in a British Engineering Factory with a Self-Recording Activity," *Human Relations*, Vol. 7 (1954), pp. 73–97.

CARTWRIGHT, D., and ZANDER, A. (eds.) *Group Dynamics: Research and Theory*. 2nd ed. Evanston, Ill.: Row, Peterson & Co., 1960.

DAVIS, KEITH A. "A Method of Studying Communication Patterns in Organizations," *Personnel Psychology*, Vol. 6 (1953), pp. 301–12.

DORSEY, JOHN T., JR. "A Communication Model for Administration," *Administrative Science Quarterly*, Vol. 2 (1957), pp. 307–10.

FEARING, FRANKLIN. "Toward a Psychological Theory of Human Communication," *Journal of Personality*, Vol. 22 (1953), pp. 71–88.

FESTINGER, L.; BACK, K.; SCHACHTER, S.; KELLEY, H. H.; and THIBAUT, J. *Theory and Experiment in Social Communication*. Ann Arbor: Research Center for Group Dynamics, University of Michigan, 1950.

FRESHLEY, D. L. *A Study of the Attitudes of Industrial Management Personnel toward Communication*. Unpublished doctoral dissertation, Ohio State University, 1956.

HARRAH, D.   *Communication: A Logical Model*. Cambridge, Mass.: MIT Press, 1963.

JACOBSON, E., and SEASHORE, S.   Communication Practices in Complex Organizations," *Journal of Social Issues*, Vol. 7 (1951), pp. 28–40.

JAFFE, J.   "Language of the Dyad: A Method of Interaction Analysis in Psychiatric Interviews," *Psychiatry*, Vol. 21 (1958), pp. 249–58.

KATZ, ELIHU.   "The Two-Step Flow of Communication: An Up-to-Date Report on an Hypothesis," *Public Opinion Quarterly*, Vol. 21 (1957), pp. 61–78.

KEOWN, W. H.   *Some Dimensions of Company-Union Downward Communication*. Madison: University of Wisconsin Press, 1955.

LAFFAL, J.   *Pathological and Normal Language*. New York: Atherton Press, 1965.

LASSWELL, H. D.; LERNER, D.; and DE SOLA POOL, I.   *The Comparative Study of Symbols*. Stanford, Calif.: Stanford University Press, 1952.

McCULLOCH, W. S.   *Embodiments of Mind*. Cambridge, Mass.: MIT Press, 1965.

MacKAY, D. M.   "Linguistic and Non-Linguistic 'Understanding' of Linguistic Tokens," Memorandum RM–3892–PR. Santa Monica, Calif.: The RAND Corp., 1964.

MELCHER, A. J., and BELLER, R.   "Toward a Theory of Organizational Communication," *Academy of Management Journal*, Vol. 10 (1967), pp. 39–51.

MEREDITH, P.   *Instruments of Communication*. London: Pergamon, 1966.

NEWCOMB, T. M.   "An Approach to the Study of Communicative Acts," *Psychological Review*, Vol. 60 (1953), pp. 393–404.

————.   *The Acquaintance Process*. New York: Holt, Rinehart & Winston, 1961.

NEWELL, A., and SIMON, H. A.   "Simulation of Human Processing of Information," *American Mathematical Monthly*, Vol. 72 (1965), pp. 111–18.

NILSEN, THOMAS R.   "Research Problems in Communication in Industry," *Journal of Communication*, Vol. 4 (1954).

ODIORNE, G. S.   "An Application of the Communications Audit," *Personnel Psychology*, Vol. 7 (1954), pp. 235–43.

OSGOOD, CHARLES E. (ed.)   *Psycholinguistics: A Survey of Theory and Research Problems*. Report of the 1953 Summer Seminar sponsored by the Committee on Linguistics and Psychology of the Social Science Research Council. Baltimore: Waverly Press, 1954.

OSGOOD, CHARLES E.; SUCI, G. J.; and TANNENBAUM, P. H.   *The Measurement of Meaning*. Urbana: University of Illinois Press, 1957.

PEABODY, R. L.   *Organizational Authority: Superior-Subordinate Relationships in Three Public Service Organizations*. New York: Atherton Press, 1964.

PRONKO, N. H. "Language and Psycholinguistics," *Psychological Bulletin,* Vol. 43 (1946).

QUASTLER, H. (ed.). *Information Theory in Psychology.* New York: Free Press 1956.

RAMSÖY, O. *Social Groups as System and Subsystem.* New York: Free Press, 1963.

RAPOPORT, A.; WEAVER, W.; GERARE, R. W.; SAMSON, E. W.; and KIRK, J. R. "Information Theory," *ETC.: A Review of General Semantics,* Vol. 10 (1953), pp. 241–320.

ROSS, RAYMOND S. "Using Communications Research in Industry," *Personnel,* Vol. 33 (1957), pp. 514–20.

ROTHSTEIN, JEROME. "Discussion: Information and Organization as the Language of the Operational Viewpoint," *Philosophy of Science,* Vol. 29 (1962), pp. 406–11.

RUBENSTEIN, A. H. "Problems in the Measurement of Interpersonal Communication in an Ongoing Situation," *Sociometry,* Vol. 16 (1953), pp. 78–100.

SCHRAMM, WILBUR (ed.). *Communication in Modern Society.* Urbana: University of Illinois Press, 1948.

SEXTON, RICHARD, and STAUDT, V. "Business Communication: A Survey of the Literature," *Journal of Social Psychology,* Vol. 50 (1959), pp. 101–18.

USHENKO, A. P. *The Field Theory of Meaning.* Ann Arbor: University of Michigan Press, 1958.

VON NEUMANN, J., and MORGENSTERN, O. *Theory of Games and Economic Behavior.* Princeton, N.J.: Princeton University Press, 1947.

WALTON, E. "A Study of Organizational Communication Systems," *Personnel Administration,* Vol. 26 (1963), pp. 46–49.

WEAVER, C. H. "The Quantification of the Frame of Reference in Labor-Management Communication," *Journal of Applied Psychology,* Vol. 42, (1958) pp. 1–9.

WESTLEY, BRUCE H., and MacLEAN, M. S., JR. "A Conceptual Model for Communications Research," *Journalism Quarterly,* Vol. 34 (1957), pp. 31–38.

20

Problems and Issues

Not all problems that are labelled "communication problems" are com-
munication problems. Conversely, there are many communication problems that get labelled by other names, and still others that don't get
identified at all. So it is that many situations we concern ourselves with as
communication problems should probably be approached as problems of
another kind. At the same time, our failure to concern ourselves with
certain basic ramifications of communication and communication systems
gives rise to other kinds of problems which we *must* deal with.

As a very important conclusion to all that has gone before, therefore, it
will be our purpose in this chapter to piece together some further insights
into what constitutes a communication problem, to gain some additional
perspectives from which to better analyze communication problems, and
finally to characterize some current and pressing issues in the study of
communication.

Some Preliminary Reconsiderations

It is possible—and likely—that the factor which has contributed most
to our present confusion regarding the nature of communication problems
has been *faulty or inadequate conceptions of the process itself.* A look at
the most common and universal models of the process[1] upon which our
perspectives have been based will undoubtedly be convincing of one thing:

---

[1] E.g., R. L. Smith, "General Models of Communication." Mimeoed. Lafayette,
Ind.: Communication Research Center, Purdue University, 1962.

few if any of those models or theories adequately take into account the subtle ways in which the *receiver and the message* (and, of course, the originator and the message) *co-determine each other communicatively.* With inadequate conceptions of the process itself, we could hardly hope to be able to identify and deal effectively with communication problems.

Second, the history of the field has been dominated by the *apparent need to deal with communication as a problematical rather than as a natural phenomenon.* For example, much of the impetus for our concern with communication problems has come from the need to deal with problems of immediate concern in formal organizations—i.e., business and industry, government, the military, etc. Thus it is that our understandings of and our approaches to the processes of communication have generally derived from the need to solve specific problems rather than from the study of the basic phenomena as natural events.

To solve a particular communication problem is not necessarily to understand the underlying process in any basic or general way. So our problematic approach has undoubtedly also contributed to the present unsystematized state of the field of study.

Third, *communication has typically been treated as if it were a unidimensional rather than a multidimensional phenomenon.* The significance of *level of analysis* has frequently been ignored. Similarly, the different functions which communication subserves at those different levels have typically also been neglected both in study and in application. For example, what goes on *intrapersonally* is an inevitable aspect of every communication event. We might choose to disregard those intrapersonal factors when concerned with mass communication; but if we do so, it should be clear *what* we are disregarding, and what kinds of differences that choice would make in any analysis. The phenomena we might focus upon at the mass communication level could be quite different from those we might focus upon at the intrapersonal level. Therefore, the theory or model we have of the communication process should either accommodate *both* levels of phenomena in some reliable way, or—if not—we should be prepared to discover (sooner or later) that the two are different orders of phenomena, only one of which should therefore properly be referred to as communication.

In a like manner, we have neglected the multiple functions of communication. Writers have variously characterized communication as having *only* informative or *only* persuasive functions. Yet, as we have seen, the command and integrative functions of communication in organizations are as important as the informative and persuasive functions. Indeed, as we have also seen, most of our attempts to communicate-to or to be communicated-with may simultaneously serve all four of these functions. How we might go about *informing* someone could be quite different from the manner in which we would engage him in some verbal fencing. The fact that our conceptions of the communication process have not adequately accommodated the several functions of communication has also contributed to our present limited ability to specify the *nature* of communication problems as such, our present limited ability systematically to distinguish certain communication problems from other sorts of problems, and our present limited ability to deal with complex as well as simple communication problems in a consistently effective manner.

Fourth, as proposed in the preceding chapter, the field has long been plagued by some considerable *ambiguity about its raison d'etre:* Is the phenomenon to be studied purely an art, and hence not amenable to "scientific" approaches? Is the field purely an applied one, in which the criterion is performance and not understanding? These are not incidental questions. They are basic. How they are answered determines how "communication problems" will be identified and dealt with. Normative and anecdotal orientations to problems and their solution are situationally adequate if *applied* communication is the only end sought. But something theoretically more substantial and viable is necessary if the end sought is a thorough and reliable understanding of the *process*—whatever its application may be. Such indefiniteness about the purposes of the field of communication as a field of study have, then, further contributed to the difficulties we experience in identifying and dealing effectively with communication problems.

Similarly, a fifth point that should be raised here for reconsideration is a *general tendency to think and act on symptoms rather than sources of communication problems.* For example, there has been concern with the isolation of top executives and administrators. The rationale goes something like this: the higher in the organization a manager rises, the further removed he is from the action, from "the facts" of any situation—and, at the same time, the more reason his subordinates will have to screen from him those data which reflect negatively on their own performances, or his performance as a manager. That such conditions do exist in large organizations (and in small ones as well) is indisputable. But those conditions are *symptoms;* their *sources* lie elsewhere—in this case in the faulty design of the communication system serving those executives. That is, such problems could be anticipated and therefore compensated for in the design of executive communication systems. The treatment of symptoms may be quite as necessary in formal organizations as coping with the sources of communication problems. But failure to clearly distinguish the one from the other has probably impeded our understanding of communication phenomena, and our attempts to develop more useful concepts and theories.

A Priori Misassumptions

In addition to the preliminary reconsiderations briefly raised above, there are at least three a priori misassumptions which may be clouding our perceptions of, and our typical approaches to, communication problems.

We seem to suffer a broad range of consequences which stem from a misassumption made long ago that *people invariably want to understand and be understood.*[2] This assumption is not a tenable one. People do in fact engage in intercommunication for all sorts of reasons besides wanting to understand or be understood. In formal organizations, simply generating and transmitting data in the required form is often considered the sole criterion for "communicating." Understanding or being understood is not the major criterion. Husbands and wives don't always want to understand each other, and it happens that many such relationships would be jeopardized if somehow each person really succeeded in understanding the other. The error is in assuming that there is something intrinsic to the process which provides clear evidence for this primary criterion of understanding and being understood. This is not so. The process itself is without values or goals of its own. As a process, it can be brought into the service of whatever ends people may have in mind vis-à-vis themselves and each other. And these ends are not always understanding or being understood.

A second possible misassumption that often seems to be harbored in the way we look at communication problems is that *communication problems have their origin in present or prior communication* encounters. Again, this is a very questionable assumption. It often happens that we are tempted to look for the origin of certain communication problems in prior encounters between the persons or groups involved, when in fact their origin may be in the intersection or juxtaposition of conditions which are not only beyond the control of those involved, but may even be imperceptible to them. For example, intergroup communication problems may not have

---

² See, e.g., J. Church, "Cognitive Differences as Impediments to Communication, with Some Uneasy Hindthoughts on the Questions What? and Whether?" in L. Thayer (ed.), *Communication: Theory and Research* (Springfield, Ill.: Charles C Thomas, 1967).

their origin in the *individuals* involved, but in the unavoidable machinations of group identification and integration.[3] The "communication problems" that often obtain between management and labor negotiators are a function not so much of the specific individuals involved, but a function of the cultural and group boundaries that have been drawn. The problem is sourced in the necessity each has (in order to maintain his own identity and group membership) to speak from orientations and interests that sometimes conflict because of the way each group has come to characterize its basic values and interests. Such conflicts of interest and intention as these sometimes make intercommunication difficult or inefficient—and sometimes impossible.

Such an impasse should bring us face to face with another misassumption: that the *source of communication problems is in the present or the past.* Many communication problems have their origin in the expectations that one or all participants have about the possible *consequences* of the way they interpret and respond to one another. Thus the origin of a communication problem may be some *future* condition considered inimical to his own interests by one or another of the participants.

Two further misassumptions that should perhaps be noted before moving on to a consideration of some specific problems are these:

1. That there are techniques or methods which will bring about one's communicative intentions more or less immediately, if he only knew what they were; and
2. That techniques can be substituted for strategic competencies in communication.

To the first assumption: the timetable by which one might attempt to achieve certain communicative intentions vis-à-vis another has to reflect the nature of those intentions in the context of the consequences for the receiver—as *he* sees them. Persuading others to change their basic attitudes or orientations or identity anchorages would require as much time and effort as persuading them to change their I.Q.'s. Time is always a variable which must realistically be reckoned with.

Then to the second assumption: accurately assessing the *nature* of the communicative task (in terms of its probable and possible outcome) is a key factor in communication. For example, failure to identify a particular situation as *impossible* can lead to attempts which end in frustration. Similarly, too much time and too much effort can be spent in achieving

---

[3] See M. Sherif *et al., Intergroup Conflict and Cooperation.* (Norman, Okla.: Institute of Group Relations, University of Oklahoma, 1961).

results which were *inevitable* at the outset. If one's communicative intentions are *possible*, then the tactical competencies he can bring to bear will make a difference in the relative effectiveness and efficiency of his attempt. But no set of tactical methods or techniques, no matter how sophisticated, can compensate very far for the lack of such strategic competencies in communication as assessing the specific nature of the task facing the originator. It is ultimately disadvantageous to believe that tactical skills or techniques can offset a lack of strategic competencies.

On the Nature of Communication Problems

Being able to distinguish communication problems from other kinds of problems is of considerable advantage to those who have set themselves to the task of managing themselves and/or larger organizations to some desirable end. To get a good grasp of what is involved, we will need to call upon some basic concepts from earlier chapters.

Particularly, we will want to recall the relationships among communication competencies, basic communication processes, and levels of analysis as described by Figure 20; the four categories of consequence (given the initial mutuality of participants' goals) presented in Figure 11; and the scheme for plotting relative "pay-offs" for the participants illustrated in Figure 13.

Consider the four categories of consequence: the inevitable, the serendipitous, the possible, the impossible. Those situations which are clearly either serendipitous or inevitable cannot logically lead to communication problems. Those situations that are strategically *impossible* should not be considered problematic, for what is truly impossible can not be problematic. So we are rightfully left to focus upon those communication situations which are *possible*—but which are more, or less, difficult.

In those situations in which it is *possible* for one to achieve his objectives or intentions, his *strategic* communication competencies would be called into play, first to determine the state-relationships that obtain and hence the nature of the communicative task confronting him, and, second, to create or establish state-relationships which would enable him to achieve his objectives or intentions *given the limits of his own tactical competencies*. Because *communicative facilitation* is beyond the control of originator or receiver in intercommunication, the application of strategic competencies at this level is essentially to the end of enhancing or increasing *metacommunicative facilitation*. At the intrapersonal level, strategic competencies determine one's communicate-abilities and adaptabilities. At the level of organization and communication systems, strategic competencies determine the efficacy designed into the communication systems serving the users of those systems.

With the help of these perspectives and those developed throughout this book, we can now make explicit what has been implicit in much of the previous discussion. We can usefully characterize six different types of basic communication problems, their ultimate source(s), and corrective measures for their solution (Figure 22).

To further enhance understanding of this scheme for comprehending the nature of the several basic communication problems, a brief description of each may be useful.

1. The problems that any individual has in fulfilling his own goals and/or adaptive needs—logically have their origin in the adequacy and the appropriateness of his own strategic and/or tactical communication competencies. For example, a manager's lack of strategic competencies for acquiring and processing statistical data may be the source of certain faulty adaptations he might make to the conditions of his enterprise or its environment. Or, one's poor diction may be the source of certain failures to achieve one's goals vis-à-vis others.

2. At the interpersonal level,[4] communication problems may be sourced in the relative inadequacy or inappropriateness of the communication competencies of *any* or *all* of the participants. That is, any given problem may be attributable to one or the other, or to *both* persons engaged in a two-person communication encounter. For example, the difficulty that a manager may have in communicating to a particular subordinate may be attributable to his own incompetencies as a communicator; it may be attributable to some defect or inadequacy in the subordinate's strategic or tactical acquisition and/or processing competencies; or it may be attributable to the relative *mix* of their particular competencies and/or incompetencies in that relationship. It is important to appreciate fully the subtle ways in which mutual skills and comprehend-abilities (or inadequacies therein) give rise to communication problems sourced in *both* originator and receiver.

3. An originator or a receiver may fail to achieve his communicative goals or intentions for reasons other than the skills and/or comprehend-abilities involved. There are those situations in which intercommunication

---

[4] The reader should recall that all higher order levels incorporate lower level phenomena, and that any higher order problem may thus have one or more lower level problems as components.

FIGURE 22
Basic Communication Problems

Level of Analysis		Problem	Source(s)	Corrective Measures
	Intrapersonal	1. An individual is not adequately fulfilling his own communicative goals and/or adaptive needs.	His own strategic and/or tactical *incompetencies* for generating, disseminating, acquiring, and/or "processing" information.	Improvement and/or modification of faulty or inadequate competencies.
	Interpersonal	2. Same.	One's own relative *incompetencies*, the other's (others') relative *incompetencies*, or some combination of both.	Development of strategic and/or tactical communication competencies that would adequately *compensate* for the other's incompetencies; where possible, development of the other's communication competencies as required; or both.
	Intrapersonal or Interpersonal	3. Same.	Any condition or set of conditions *other* than originator's and/or receiver's communication competencies (e.g., negative "pay-off" for receiver, prospects of loss of identity anchorages, organization "ethic," etc.).	Development of communication competencies of all participants as in 1 and 2 above; *then* alteration or modification of source conditions as necessary and as possible.
	Interpersonal or Organizational	4. Communication system inefficacy (or economy, or both).	a) Inappropriate criterion. b) Faulty design. c) Inadequate or improper use.	a) Establish appropriate criteria of efficacy. b) Proper design through enhanced strategic competencies of designer(s). c) Analysis and corrective measures as in 1, 2, and 3.
	Organizational	5. Incompatibility of communication systems at their interfaces.	Inherent adaptational and/or goal-seeking incompatabilities (a) between any intra- and interpersonal communication systems; (b) between any interpersonal and formal organizational communication systems; and/or (c) both.	
	Composite	6. Those problems which involve two or more of these basic problems in any combination.	Component problems separately sourced.	Component problems separately treated as suggested above.

is satisfactorily achieved, but the consequences anticipated by the receiver for doing or thinking or feeling as intended by the originator are so negative as to preclude the fulfillment of the originator's intentions. In such cases, the source of the problem is located in conditions other than the participants' communication competencies as such. That is, if doing or thinking or feeling as intended by the originator would lead to possible loss of identity anchorages by the receiver (as anticipated by him), to some "loss of face" (as anticipated by the receiver), to some uncharacteristic effort on his part, etc., then the originator's intentions vis-à-vis that receiver are not likely to be fulfilled. For example, a manager may *disunderstand* what a subordinate is saying because the appearance of understanding would be detrimental to the manager's prestige in some way (as anticipated by him—consciously or nonconsciously). Or, a subordinate may fully understand what his boss said, but still fail to do what the boss intended—for the reason that doing so would have required a degree of effort he (the subordinate) wasn't prepared or inclined to put forth. And so on; the list of such examples would be endless.

4. The communication systems which link two or more people together communicatively may be more (or less) efficacious, more (or less) economical, or both. Often the source of this order of communication problems is in the inappropriate designation of criteria by which the system's performance is to be assessed. For example, if two people create a communication channel (and hence a communication system linking them communicatively), but each establishes as the sole criterion of the system's efficacy its usefulness to him individually, then that system is likely to be inefficacious, uneconomical, or both. The efficacy of a communication system has to be determined at the level of the system, not at the level of any one individual user of that system.

Second, the system may be improperly or faultily designed. For example, the informal communication system that is created when a group of managers get together for a meeting may simply be poorly suited to the purposes of that meeting in some way. Or, a formal organization's communication systems may be inadequate or inappropriate for the goal-seeking and adaptive needs of that organization vis-à-vis its environment.

A third possible source of communication problems at the level of system efficacy is that of inadequate or improper use of the system by its users. For example, if a manager fails to acquire and consume information available to him in the system—information which is pertinent to his deliberations—then there is at least some loss of economy in the system, if not some lessening of that system's efficacy. Or, if one member of a system continuously places extraordinary stresses and demands upon it, that system may suffer in both efficacy and economy of functioning.

5. A still higher order of communication problem complexity is the organizational level of analysis. It is at this level of analysis that we would contemplate problems which are sourced in the relative incompatibility of communication systems at their interfaces. Those incompatibilities may emerge at the interface of different levels of systems. For example, the problem may be that an interpersonal communication system is incompatible with a formal organizational system, or that one's personal communication system is incompatible with certain interpersonal or organizational communication systems within which he may be called upon to communicate on-behalf-of . . . his role or position.

Or, two or more interpersonal or organizational communication systems may be incompatible at their interfaces. For example, the operational communication system serving one organization may be incompatible with its counterpart in another organization, thereby giving rise to communication problems when an attempt is made to link the two systems together in some way.

6. Finally, there is that highest order of complexity—those communication problems which are composites of a number of lower order problems. Our present inability to deal with such complex problems conceptually would seem to necessitate dealing with them at the level of their component basic problems.

With this scheme for identifying and dealing with the basic communication problems as a backdrop, we can profitably conclude this chapter with a consideration of some current problems and issues in communication at the various levels of analysis.

Some Current Issues and Problems

Perhaps a good way of proceeding with this highly selective inventory of current issues and problems in communication would be to broadly categorize those few to be discussed here as either *intrapersonal, interpersonal, organizational,* and *systemic* and/or *technological*—with the full understanding that these levels overlap and interact in various subtle and intricate ways. However, for our purposes here, while such categorization may do some violence to the manner in which some of the problems and issues to be discussed do overlap each other, its usefulness will probably offset that potential disadvantage.

A great many communication problems and issues of current interest have previously been identified and discussed. For the most part, those will not be repeated here—except as their overriding importance may warrant such repetition.

INTRAPERSONAL ISSUES AND PROBLEMS[5]

Because our concern in this book has been primarily with communication in organization, management, and interpersonal relations, the kinds of issues to be raised under the heading of "intrapersonal" are those which are likely to give rise to symptoms at higher-order levels of analysis—either as a matter of inevitability or as a result of our failure to understand them.

1. The implications of "Ashby's theorem"—that an individual must have at least the same *requisite variety* of take-into-account abilities as those communicative situations which he would (or has to) encounter— are basic to many emergent communication problems. On the one hand, we are limited to what we can take into account by our comprehend-*abilities*, and on the other we are constrained by what we *must* take into account by our take-into-account-*susceptibilities*. The ramifications of this basis circumstance for every individual's (and certainly every manager's) communication behavior, and for the design of communication systems, are manifold. For example, the fact that receiver and message co-determine each other is a matter for considerable theoretic and practical concern.

2. A second factor has also been touched upon previously. It is that an individual *will* comprehend that which he would or should comprehend— and will freely make inferences and extrapolate in order to create a consumable *gestalt*—a message which is adequately meaningful *to him*. The more ambiguity he has to cope with, the more freedom he has to create the message he "gets." Yet overly constraining his freedom to create the message he gets will lead to increased dependence upon literal interpretations—a condition which can be just as disadvantageous. Here is indeed one of the dilemmas of human communication.

3. A third factor is also one which is being reemphasized here. People do engage in what might be called *retroactive reconceptualization*—an elaborate name for something we all do very commonly. On the basis of something A says or does today, B reconsiders his model or image of A, and reconstrues his whole opinion of A in (typically) a much more negative

---

[5] There is no significance to the order in which these problems and issues are presented. There is no way of ranking them, for they are general problems which might concern any of us at one time or another.

direction. This is a communication analog of the "sour grapes" (and its opposite) phenomenon.

4. Many problems arise because we all too frequently overlook the fact that our own and others' communication behavior is essentially *autómatos* —nonconscious, automatistic, a matter of habit or preprogramming. The communicate-abilities each of us has are as basic and as resistant to change as are our basic attitudes, our personality styles, our intelligences, our postures, and our countenances. At any given moment in time, they are given. Thus we are forced to cope with these more or less fixed aspects of our communicative behavior by compensating for them in some way, or by systematically altering them over time.

5. It would seem that *information* is looked upon as intellectual or cerebral, and that one's feelings and emotions sometimes "get in the way of" successfully "communicating." A number of problematic consequences befall us because we do not fully realize that communicative inputs are all of the same sort—sensory data—and that there is nothing sacrosanct about pure information which would preclude its being reacted to in highly emotional ways by particular receivers in particular situations. The fallacy is to assume that "factual" information does not pass through exactly the same functional pathways *within* every receiver as does every other sort of communicative input.

6. Typically, communication training focuses upon generating and disseminating, to the relative neglect of the other two processes: acquiring and consuming or processing. Courses and programs devoted to producing data for others' consumption, and skill training in disseminating those data (e.g., through letter-writing or speech-making), are considerably more common than courses and programs intended to improve individual strategic and tactical competencies in acquiring (and educing) and critically determining the utility of potentially consumable information. As one consequence, we characteristically listen and read with less effectiveness than we talk or write (or perhaps just with greater ease).

7. There is, of course, the *necessity* by which we are all constrained to see and deal with the world communi-centrically (i.e., in a communicatively egocentric fashion). When we disseminate a message, we commonly fail to adapt in advance to the *contrary* messages which the receiver may have been subjected to. Each of us is the center of his own communicative universe, and we often fail to appreciate that every other person is equally and just as necessarily the center of *his* communicative universe. To an originator, a receiver may be but one of hundreds of elements in his communicative universe. But to the receiver, the *originator*

will be but one of hundreds of elements in *his* communicative universe. Small wonder we sometimes subject ourselves to communication problems stemming from the exigencies of our own intrapersonal characteristics!

8. Closely related is this condition of our own functioning: people *will* comprehend that which they want to deal with in some way. In other words, if you want to "consume" what has been written here, you *will* do so in some way, whether that way approximates what was intended or not. We typically create scopic and complex concepts of other people and events of the world on what is often the flimsiest evidence. We often piece together a few clues as to what something is really like, or as to what the speaker really said—and handily extrapolate from those few clues to a whole universe of private comprehensions of those people or their utterances.

So we are frequently faced with communication problems that stem directly, and perhaps inevitably, from the conditions by which our comprehending systems *must* function. As a direct consequence of the structure and/or the functioning of our comprehending systems, we are all of us inveterate jumpers-to-comprehensions. In our necessary obliviousness to that data which might alter our comprehensions of things, we inherit a wide range of consequent communication problems.

INTERPERSONAL ISSUES AND PROBLEMS[6]

Interpersonal issues in communication may have their roots in the conditions of *intrapersonal* functioning, and their consequences in organizational or communication systems problems. But it is nonetheless helpful to focus upon some factors unique to this level of analysis.

1. Perhaps the most significant issue at stake in our understanding of interpersonal communication and its attendant problems is that of escaping from the bonds of stimulus→response, cause→effect thinking long enough to realize the *interdependence*←→of the participants, and thus the many subtle and intricate ways in which they separately but aggregatively contribute to their own communication problems. One or the other person

---

[6] Certain commonly recognized problems of interpersonal communication in management and organization have been dealt with by a number of other writers. Those problems probably need not be repeated here. See, e. g., C. Argyris, "Interpersonal Barriers to Decision Making," *Harvard Business Review*, 1966, 44 (No. 2), 84–97; C. Goetzinger and M. Valentine, "Problems in Executive Interpersonal Communication," *Personnel Administration*, 1964, 27 (No. 2), 24–29; and L. Sayles, "On-the-Job Communication: Why Isn't It Easier?" *Supervisory Management*, (July) 1962, 6, 2–15. Other useful references are listed at the end of this chapter.

may indeed be the *primary* cause of a problem between them. But inter-communication requires at least two—whether for success or failure.

2. Closely related is the fallacy of "the proper meaning." Our communi-centricities would lead us to believe that our own understanding of what was said—whether we were originator or receiver—is the proper interpre-tation of that message. Problems stem from the difficulty of realizing that in every encounter there are at least three messages—what the originator thought he said, what the receiver thought the originator said, and what was said (which, of course, is subject to as many interpretations as there are receivers or interpreters).

3. Similarly, many interpersonal communication problems arise from discrepancies between what an individual says and what he does. When-ever the receiver is faced with such dissonance, he must choose; unless he has major psychological problems of his own, he will weight what the originator does over and above what the originator says. There are thus two problems: (a) to the extent we cannot or do not make our words consis-tent with our actions—or our actions consistent with our words—we open up a whole range of potential communication problems; but (b) on the other hand, to the extent that a receiver holds an originator to the receiver's interpretations of his actions, the originator is thereby greatly limited in what he *can* communicate-to the receiver—even if to the receiver's own personal advantage.

4. Other interpersonal communication problems stem from the assumption we often make that all communication is intended to "com-municate." This is not so. People often say what is currently "sayable" and topical, for doing so serves integrative functions for them. As suggested in the chapter on integrative functions, we err (i.e., create communication problems) if we listen to people engaged in this sort of behavior as if they intended to communicate something related to the "content" of their utterances.

5. Still other interpersonal communication problems derive from our abilities to initiate encounters easily, but our relative inabilities to termi-nate them when they become dysfunctional. Oliver Wendell Holmes has well characterized the essence of this problem:

Talking is like playing on the harp; there is as much in laying the hands on the strings to stop their vibrations as in twanging them to bring out their music.[7]

---

[7] *The Autocrat of the Breakfast Table*, 1, 1858.

6. Interpersonal relationships are created and maintained by the communication system which links the participants communicatively. As such, interpersonal relationships are subject to a peculiar communication problem. While the participants may have some difficulty from time to time in communicating-to one another and being communicated-with by the other, the opposite condition of too-easy intercommunication has perhaps equally deleterious consequences. That is, if the participants have no difficulty at all communicating-to and -with each other, it is probably because they are so well "synchronized" with each other in terms of their take-into-account-abilities and -susceptibilities that a certain level of effective communication (as such) is *inevitable*. But such circumstances are inimical to the growth and viability of each of the participants and to the relationship as well. It is a form of successive communicative inbreeding—with all of the negative consequences that analogy may conjure up.

Thus too-efficient and/or too-effective communication in interpersonal relationships has problem-inciting consequences that are not often or widely understood.

7. Interpersonally, the participants in any communication encounter will likely concern themselves with the other's intentions.[8] Each will, as well, likely concern himself with what he believes to be the other's concern with his intentions, and so on. Strategies of intention and counter-intention can be played at many levels of depth, just as they are in poker. The problem: to the extent such strategies "work," they place constraints upon the strategies to be employed by each at the next encounter, and so on in a continuously restricting (or, occasionally, enlarging) spiral. For example, if a supervisor believes that a subordinate intends to misinform him, and such a possibility turns out to be "true" (as perceived by the superior) the supervisor is likely to assess that subordinate's statements as less valid on the next occasion. The subordinate, accurately perceiving this communicative bias, then builds into his messages a counter-bias, and so on and on. At a certain point—as many labor negotiators know—it becomes impossible to be believed even if one wants to reveal his full and honest intentions. Interpersonal relationships are evolutionary, and thus are irreversible. This basic fact has a wide range of implications for interpersonal communication problems.

8. In the same way, the climate of the relationship will have consider-

---

[8] ". . . the problems of communication are not, in the main, linguistic problems. It is our intentions in the use of language, not the language itself, which hinder or facilitate communication" (P. Meredith, *Instruments of Communication* [London: Pergamon, 1965], p. 36).

able bearing upon what can and cannot be "communicated," what will and will not be "communicated." This factor is crucial when the relationship is a vertical or hierarchical one. One's authority to command another brings with it as many potential disadvantages as advantages. There is nothing in the nature of authority itself which would guarantee its proper use either for the good of the people involved or of the organization they may both be serving. In the same way that parents may especially enable or disable their children by the manner in which they exercise their authority, organizational superiors may contribute especial abilities or disabilities to the larger organization by the manner in which they exercise their authority in their vertical relationships with subordinates.

9. People vary greatly in their abilities and inclinations to educe and usefully consume "feedback" about their impact upon others. Most of us would be very surprised to learn how we impact other people communicatively—and particularly nonverbally, which is at least as important interpersonally as are verbal interactions.[9] Thus many intercommunication problems undoubtedly emerge from these sorts of inabilities or disinclinations.

10. Perhaps an equally large number of interpersonal communication problems could be traced to the assumption participants typically make that communication is something one *does to* people. To the extent that the parties to any interpersonal relationship do not comprehend the process of communication as a process which joins them together in a mutual enterprise of some designable sort, there will inevitably be problems to cope with.

ORGANIZATION AND COMMUNICATION SYSTEMS PROBLEMS AND ISSUES[10]

Before we delve too deeply into the communication problems of organizations and the problems of communication systems, we should take

---

[9] For one revealing case, see A. J. Marrow, *Behind the Executive Mask* (New York: American Management Association, Inc., 1964).

[10] Again, some of the more universally recognized problems and issues in managerial-organizational communication have been dealt with by a number of other writers, so it should not be necessary to repeat those here. Cf., e.g., J. D. Chapline, "Problems in Management Communications," in *The Manager's Role in Organizational Communications* (New York: Institute of Electrical and Electronics Engineers, 1964); E. Planty and W. Machaver, "Why Doesn't Somebody Tell Me These Things?" *Supervisory Management*, 1958, 3, 2–9; B. B. Boyd, "An Analysis of Communication between Departments—Roadblock and By-Passes:," *Personnel Administration*, December, 1965; A. E. Lindh, "Plain Talk about Communicating in Business," Special Report No. 6,

careful cognizance of this point: *that so-called communication "problems"
are not necessarily dysfunctional to the organization within which they
occur.* The reason is simple enough. As suggested by Figure 21, communication ineffectiveness at the intra- or interpersonal levels may or may not
affect the larger system (the organization) in any detrimental way—since
what occurs or does not occur at one level does not necessarily predict to
like consequences at contiguous levels of analysis. In fact, communication
problems and difficulties within organizations do on occasion contribute
positive long-run advantages. To consider a mundane example: if a subordinate fails to understand a superior's order and therefore does not carry
it out; and if in fact carrying out that order as intended by the superior
would have been ultimately disadvantageous to the organization (which
does happen); then that "communication breakdown" has advantaged the
organization. When concerned with effectiveness and efficacy, levels
should be clearly distinguished. For what is effective or efficacious at one
level may be disadvantageous or inefficacious at the next lower or next
higher level of analysis.

2. One of the major issues in organizational communication is this one:
how far to rationalize the systems of communication which subserve that
organization in its tasks and goal-seeking, and its adaptational needs and
hazards. There are problems in each direction. If under-rationalized,
people improvise communication systems and communication encounters.
If over-rationalized, people are constrained from that very improvisation
that might be necessary to the organization's efficacy and viability vis-à-vis
its environment.

For example, members of organizations often turn to fortuitious ex-
pediencies for getting or giving task-related information when task channels and their use are not rationally and fully specified. One person
happens to see another in the hall and says, "Oh, yes, I've been meaning to
talk to you about. . . ." Neither is fully prepared for the encounter; and
perhaps neither is the appropriate person in the organization to be giving
or receiving that particular information.

We probably err on the side of under-rationalizing communication
systems. Few organizations have deliberately-designed operational, regulatory, and maintenance communication systems. The consequent loss of

Business Management Council, 1965; G. A. Sanborn, "Communication in Business: An
Overview," and W. Charles Redding, "The Organizational Communicator," in *Business and Industrial Communication: A Source Book* (New York: Harper & Row,
1964); J. G. March and H. A. Simon, *Organizations* (New York: John Wiley & Sons,
Inc., 1958); and L. Thayer, "Communication and Organization," in F. E. X. Dance
(ed.), *Human Communication Theory* (New York: Holt, Rinehart & Winston, 1967).

economy is great, and the loss of efficacy, while not so easily determined, is probably equally great.

3. Another condition which is perhaps the source of a considerable number of communication problems in organizations is the necessity of communicating on-behalf-of . . . the position one holds in an organization. Whether role or formalized task, communicating on-behalf-of . . ." other than oneself has its inevitable consequences in the communication problems that arise in organizations. Whether one's organizational assignment is information- or product-processing, the exigencies of organizational life place upper and lower limits on the what, the when, and the where of one's performance—and thus upon the valence of one's involvement. At white-collar levels, as we have seen, these constraints have far-reaching consequences for the investment one makes in his communicative encounters. However it is to be described, the necessity of communicating on-behalf-of . . ." the organization is (a) either adequately compensated for in the design of organizational communication systems, or, if not, (b) the problems which consequent must be dealt with in some other fashion.

4. How managers and/or administrators of formal organizations conceive of their communicative functions in those organizations is a determinant of the kinds of problems that will likely arise.[11] For example, if the managers of a particular organization conceive of their function as that of policing the performances of all of those subordinate to them, various problems of a communicative "misdemeanor" sort are likely to arise. If, on the other hand, they conceive of their communicative role as one of catalyzing ideas, then a different order of communicational opportunities and problems will emerge.

Those managers who cannot conceive of the various functions of communication being subserved in certain communication encounters will unwittingly contribute to communication problems that must sooner or later be dealt with by themselves or by other managers in that organization.

5. In recent years the notion of full and "open" communication has gained some momentum. There are faulty assumptions behind such a notion.

For one, as was previously suggested in this chapter, it is just as important to have the strategic competence to stay or impede message generation and dissemination as it is to facilitate acquisition and consumption. "Full and complete communication" is no panacea. Not only are there data

---

[11] Cf. G. L. Hinds, "The Communicative Behavior of the Executive," *The Journal of Communication*, 1957, 8, 29–34.

which those at superior or subordinate levels in the organization should *not* have, there are those data which they *cannot* have simply because they are not known to those persons who are supposed to reveal them (or are temporarily not revealable by them for good reasons). For example, a superior does not always know just why a certain decision (even his own) has been made, so he could not reveal the reasons for that particular decision simply because he doesn't know what they are. Similarly, it is possible that complete revelation would be detrimental to one's relationship with others, to the organization which both serve, or both. The assumption that free and open communication will preclude communication problems in organizations would likely give rise to at least as many communication problems as it precludes.

6. A part of the same family of assumptions is the assumption that eliminating organizational barriers will eliminate organizational communication problems. This could hardly be true. Eliminating organizational barriers would be tantamount to eliminating the organization itself. Certain lateral task-specialization and certain vertical points of authority consolidation are an inevitable aspect of organizing human enterprises. To look upon what is necessary to organization-ness as problematic could hardly lead to diminishing communication problems. As Simon has aptly pointed out,[12] organization is innately hierarchical in structure; to the extent one looks upon certain communicative consequences of that structuring as "problematical," he is destined to deal with symptoms rather than causes.

7. Created and designed typically in the tradition of accountancy, some contemporary enterprises suffer the consequent problems of trading short-term fluidity for long-range viability. As suggested in Chapter 10, the efficacy or viability of an organization (qua organization) may or may not be congruent with measures of its fiscal histories, as portrayed by its financial statements. The point is this: that the short-term criteria by which enterprise performance is determined financially are not the same criteria by which organizational efficacy and viability must be determined. The profitability of an enterprise is a function of some unspecifiable interaction between that enterprise and its environment. Its efficacy (and/or its viability) is a function of many conditions other than its short-term profitability. Thus certain other kinds of communication problems may arise—those which have their origin in the conflict between fiscal and long-range-viability orientations.

---

[12] H. A. Simon, *The New Science of Management Decision* (New York: Harper & Row, 1960).

8. Every organization has its "ethic"—an unwritten, practice-derived code, to which its members can turn to determine what pays-off for whom, under what circumstances, etc. Formally stated policies and philosophies may provide guidelines for goal-orientations and daily operations. But people are equally concerned with such questions as "How do people *actually* get promoted in this organization?" "What's the best way to stay out of trouble?" "Who really has the power around here?" "What rules and regulations and procedures do 'they' actually enforce?" "What are some of the unwritten policies that guide the thinking and behavior of the people in this organization?" "How is one *supposed* to behave at this management level?" And so on. These are quite natural questions one might expect of a person who must adapt himself to his organizational environment, and to the social realities he must internalize if he is to get along.

If another term is preferred, these are, of course, the *norms* of the organization—the unwritten thought, attitude, and behavior specifications which emerge from the actual practices of the organization's members over time. The issue: to the extent that these norms are not properly internalized by the organization's members, and/or to the extent that this unwritten code conflicts with or contradicts formal policies and specifications, various communication problems inevitably arise.

9. In an earlier chapter, the concept of proprietary information or "information ownership" was discussed. The issue is clear enough. Since certain kinds of information withheld from those who need or want it endow its "owners" with power,[13] the phenomenon of information ownership as a source of communication problems in organizations could easily be anticipated.

The machinations by which such communication problems are sourced are given in the nature of people and the nature of organizational life. One could hardly do away with the needs and appetites people may have for security and power over others. And the organizational ethic may indeed sanction information ownership. So the corrective measure for this as for so many similar-sourced communication problems in organizations is one of *compensatory design* of the communication systems serving the organization. That is, one could design into the organization's communication

---

[13] Cf. J. W. Forrester, "A New Corporate Design," *Industrial Management Review*, 1965, 7 (No. 1), p. 11: "To possess information is to possess power. A monopoly of information can give a form of security. There are, in all organizations at all levels, a selective withholding and extending of information . . ."; and W. H. Read, "Upward Communication in Industrial Hierarchies," *Human Relations*, 1962, 15 (No. 1), 3–15.

systems certain compensatory mechanisms to offset the deleterious effects of information ownership.

10. A whole host of communication problems undoubtedly arises from the fact that organizational communication systems (and all supporting subsystems) are not purposefully and intentionally designed for the uses to which they will be put. For example, the absence of an overall design, which would serve the organization, *qua* living system, in the information acquisition, consumption (or processing), generation, and dissemination processes necessary or desirable to its adaptive and/or goal-seeking needs in its complex environment, invariably gives rise to communication problems of all sorts and at all levels in the organization. If none of an individual manager's superiors knows exactly how his particular communication-decision functions fit into the overall communication-decision functions of the organization, it is not surprising that he doesn't perform his communication-decision functions properly.

11. Some misassumptions about perfect communication and/or perfectly reliable human communication may themselves serve as sources of communication problems in organizations. When an industrial manager buys a machine to do work in an organization, he buys that machine which comes closest to having the characteristics required for the work to be done, and he accepts the fact that the machine is not going to do its work perfectly—that some *tolerances* simply have to be accepted. Yet we have not commonly selected and placed people in organizations with a similar order of acceptable communicational tolerances in mind. If a part can be machined to within only $\pm.003''$, then perhaps communication can be carried out to within only 60 percent effectiveness (perhaps $\pm$ 20 percent). Whatever these tolerances *should* be, communication problems do occasionally arise from misassumptions about just how effective synchronous communication *could* be.

12. The *efficacy* of organizational communication systems is often sacrificed unwittingly for the effectiveness of individual encounters by organization members. In contemplating "organizational communication" problems, managers often mistake intercommunication effectiveness for system efficacy, thereby creating the conditions for the evolution of other kinds of communication problems. People do suffer "psychological" problems in the context of organizational life. But solving those problems without regard for the potential consequences therein for the communication systems involved is simply to trade one set of problems for another (and perhaps organizationally more detrimental) set of problems.

13. Clearly, the crux of the matter—at least as far as the *operational*

communication system of organizations is concerned—is one of getting the right information to those who need it, when they need it, in the consumable form in which they need it, in the quantity and of the quality needed, and so on. What complicates this otherwise simple paradigm, however, is the fact that most of an organization's members cannot specify in advance what information they are going to need. Nor do they have clear-cut rationales for determining the other criteria for their own task-related information acquisition and consumption. Add to this the fact that there is usually some ambiguity about goals and individual task-functions. Looked at from this perspective, it would seem that organizational communication problems are simply of the magnitude one might expect as a consequence of "muddling through."

The dilemma is, of course, that there is no simple, rational alternative. Adaptiveness, from the intrapersonal through the organizational level, requires a relatively high degree of flexibility. And flexibility is possible only where constraints are not perfect. Thus "muddling through" is not only a necessary but a desirable condition within organizations. For the needed flexibility, every organization must pay the price of some degree of ineffective and inefficient communication. The alternative would be a rigidity which could severely lessen the organization's adaptability and goal-seeking capabilities.[14]

14. There is probably a misplaced faith in the magic of communication amongst those who design and manage organization.[15] The best-constructed communiqué will not offset poor planning or the negative consequences of an inefficacious relationship between a boss and his subordinate. Communication can be no better than the channels through which people intercommunicate, no better than the total context in which that communication occurs. There is no magic in communication which does not exist *in* the people who are involved. To assume that "good" communication can compensate for poor management paradoxically creates more real communication problems than it solves.

---

14 Cf. various related papers in O. J. Harvey (ed.), *Experience, Structure, and Adaptability* (New York: Springer Publishing Co., Inc., 1966); and, for one specific study, L. T. Alexander and A. S. Cooperband, "The Effect of Rule Flexibility on System Adaptation," *Human Factors*, 1964, 6 (No. 2), 209–20.

15 Suggests J. Harold Janis: "Businessmen tend to put too much faith in the power of the written word. Often they write as if the very act of writing will cure what is wrong policy, an overcomplex procedure, or a bad decision" ("Writing Skills Cut Management Waste," *Nation's Business*, April, 1958). Cf. E. C. Bursk (ed.), *The Management Team* (Cambridge, Mass.: Harvard University Press, 1955), who warns of the need to take the mystery out of communication.

15. Some believe that the increasing size of organizations is in itself a problem. I don't agree. Our failure to cope adequately with the consequences of the increased size and complexity of organizations may be the source of certain problems, but size alone cannot be problematical.[16] To the extent that managers and communication system designers can think at the level of the mass as well as at the level of individuals and aggregates of individuals, size alone will not present problems which cannot be compensated for in the design or operation of the communication systems serving that organization.

SOME TECHNOLOGICAL ISSUES

Even though we should be reluctant to attribute problems to communication technology as such, there are perhaps five issues which can usefully be considered here.

1. In the same way that organization size cannot in and of itself be a problem, the increasing magnitude of information generation and dissemination cannot in and of itself be a problem. The often-referred-to "information explosion" has without question altered the conditions of human and organizational life. But it is not the sheer magnitude of data which gives rise to communication problems; it is our relative inability to cope with and to compensate for the kinds of changes these magnitudes have brought about. For example, the fact that there are approximately 1 million pages of new documents being produced every minute of every day, or that our paperwork is inceasing at the rate of 62 million new file-drawers filled per year[17]—these facts and hundreds of others that characterize the information explosion are not themselves a problem. The problem is sourced in our inabilities to redesign the man-information interface satisfactorily. To the extent we do not learn how to cope with or compensate for our increasing information-producing capacities, we will suffer the problems that consequent from them.

2. By contrast, a great many organizations are operating today under the

---

[16] Cf. W. G. Scott, "Organization Size: Some Theoretical Issues," *Management International*, 1961, 5, 41–51.

[17] See E. J. Leahy & C. A. Cameron, "Paperwork Explosion: Can We Control it?" *Nation's Business*, 1965, 53 (No. 9), 103 ff.; R. A. Shiff, "Presidents and Paperwork," *Dun's Review and Modern Industry*, April, 1959; J. G. Miller, "Coping with Administrators' Information Overload," Mental Health Research Institute, University of Michigan, 1963; D. R. Daniel, "Management Information Crisis," *Harvard Business Review*, 1961 (Sept.–Oct.), 39, 111–21; and "The Information Revolution," *Dun's Review and Modern Industry*, Sept., 1966, 130 ff.

severe disadvantages of obsolete or dysfunctional equipment for disseminating information and technologically linking members together. There are those missile-age enterprises trying to keep up the pace with horse-and-buggy-days equipment. To fail to acquire and utilize the best of the recent technological advances in devices and equipment is to create what are really unnecessary communication problems in organizations.

3. An immediate corollary, however, is the necessity for reorganizing and redesigning relationships and communication systems before or concurrent with the introduction of new technology into the organization, an issue discussed in the chapter on communication technology.[18] The speed and the coverage of data dissemination technologies, particularly, are critical factors. Linking everyone to a common medium does in fact change people and their relationships. Putting "real-time" data[19] into a manager's hands does in fact require modification of many of our cherished concepts about managing, about organizational structures, and so on. These are the problems that must be dealt with if completely new generations of human communication problems are not to arise.

4. The languages we use as tools of intercommunication are a part of our communication technology software. There are two aspects of language qua technology which pervade our communicative behavior that have their origin in language.

The first of these is simply that the words we use as "instruments" of intercommunication do not refer to things or events; they refer to *categories* of things and events. Every word is therefore a stereotype, and conversely. Our failure to remain cognizant of this simple fact undoubtedly makes for a wide range of communication problems intrapersonally, interpersonally, and organizationally.

5. As someone once said: "The trouble with 'is,' is *is!*" He was right about one thing: the word "is"—is probably the most dangerous and slippery of all of the thinking and intercommunication tools we have available. *Is* always implies far more in the way of "objective" fact than any human or group of humans is capable of. It is an illusion-provoking word, a deluding word. With it we perpetrate all sorts of ills upon ourselves, and all sorts of problems upon our relationships with others and upon the

---

18 Cf. F. J. Jasinski, "Adapting Organization to New Technology," *Harvard Business Review*, 1959 (Jan–Feb.), 37, 79–86; J. F. Burlingame, "Information Technology and Decentralization," *Harvard Business Review*, 1961 (Nov.–Dec.), 39, 121–26.

19 See J. Dearden, "Myth of Real-Time Management Information," *Harvard Business Review*, 1966 (May–June), 44, 123–32.

organizations to which we belong. *Is*—is a source of communication problems *par excellence*.

Perhaps this is an especially useful note on which to conclude this inquiry into the nature of communication in organization, management, and interpersonal relations.

What *is* communication?

What *is* there about it which leaves us oblivious to its functions except when we are frustrated or fascinated by it?

Why *is* that, indeed?

SUGGESTIONS FOR FURTHER READING

The problems and issues in communication theory and communication research have been dealt with at various points throughout the book. So the purpose of this list of suggested additional readings is only to supplement this particular chapter. Most of the other reading lists contain several references which address themselves to the problems and issues of the field, and they should also be consulted.

BRIDGMAN, P. W.   *The Way Things Are.* Cambridge, Mass.: Harvard University Press, 1959.

CHASE, STUART.   "Executive Communications: Breaking the Semantic Barrier," *Management Review*, Vol. 46 (1957), pp. 58–66.

DEXTER, L. A., and WHITE, D. M. (eds.).   *People, Society, and Mass Communications.* New York: Free Press, 1964.

GREENBERGER, M.   *Computers and the World of the Future.* Cambridge, Mass.: MIT Press, 1962.

HENLE, M., and HUBBELL, R.   "Egocentricity in Adult Conversation," *Journal of Social Psychology*, Vol. 9 (1938), pp. 227–34.

HIGHAM, T. M.   "Is 'Communications' a Sacred Cow?" *Personnel Management*, Vol. 35 (1953), pp. 219–24.

HOSLETT, S. D.   "Barriers to Communication," *Personnel*, Vol. 28 (1951), pp. 108–14.

JACKSON, JAY M.   "The Organization and Its Communications Problems," *Advanced Management*, February, 1959.

KATZ, DANIEL.   "Psychological Barriers to Communication," *Annals of the American Academy of Political and Social Science*, Vol. 250 (March, 1947).

LIPPITT, R. "Administrator Perception and Administrative Approval: A Communication Problem," *Sociatry*, Vol. 1 (1947), pp. 209–19.

MAIER, N. R. F.; HOFFMAN, L. RICHARD; and READ, W. H. "Superior-Subordinate Communication," *Personnel Psychology*, Vol. 16 (1963), pp. 1–11.

MICHAEL, D. N. "Some Long-Range Implications of Computer Technology for Human Behavior in Organizations," *American Behavioral Scientist*, Vol. 9 (1966), pp. 29–35.

MINTEER, CATHERINE. *Words and What They Do to You*. Evanston, Ill.: Row, Peterson & Co., 1953.

MYERS, C. A. (ed.). *The Impact of Computers on Management*. Cambridge, Mass.: MIT Press, 1967.

NILSEN, THOMAS R. "Some Assumptions that Impede Communication," *General Semantics Bulletin*, Nos. 14 and 15, Winter–Spring, 1954.

PYE, L. (ed.). *Communications and Political Development*. Princeton, N.J.: Princeton University Press, 1963.

READ, W. H. "Communication in Organizations: Some Problems and Misconceptions," *Personnel Administration*, Vol. 26 (Mar.–Apr., 1963), pp. 4–10.

ROETHLISBERGER, F. J. "Barriers to Communication between Men," in S. I. HAYAKAWA (ed.), *Language, Meaning, and Maturity*. New York: Harper & Bros., 1954.

————. "Human Relations in Industry: A Problem of Communication," *General Semantics Bulletin*, Nos. 14 and 15, Winter–Spring, 1954.

ROGERS, C. R. "Communication: Its Blocking and Its Facilitation," in S. I. HAYAKAWA (ed.), *Language, Meaning, and Maturity*. New York: Harper & Bros., 1954.

————, and ROETHLISBERGER, F. J. "Barriers and Gateways to Communication," *Harvard Business Review*, July–August, 1952.

SCHRAMM, W. *Mass Media and National Development*. Stanford, Calif.: Stanford University Press, 1964.

SCOTT, W. G. "Communication and Centralization of Organization," a paper presented before the Summer Conference of the National Society for the Study of Communication, 1962.

SEILER, J. A. "Toward a Theory of Organization Congruent with Primary Group Concepts," *Behavioral Science*, Vol. 8 (1963), 190–98.

SEXTON, RICHARD, and STAUDT, VIRGINIA. "The Communication Clinic: A Proposed Solution to the Business Communication Problem," *Journal of General Psychology*, Vol. 60 (1959), pp. 57–62.

SIMON, H. A. *The Shape of Automation for Men and Management*. New York: Harper & Row, 1965.

STIEGLITZ, H. "Barriers to Communication," *Management Record*, Vol. 20 (1958), pp. 2–5.

STRYKER, PERRIN. "A Slight Case of Overcommunication," *Fortune*, March, 1954.

THAYER, L. "On Theory-Building in Communication: I. Some Conceptual Problems," *Journal of Communication*, December, 1963.

INDEXES

Author Index

Subject Index

A

Adaptation, 55, 255, 278 ff.
Ambiguity, 342
  of consequence, 167
  of intention, 166
  of meaning, 166
Anchorages, 227
Animal communication, 323
Attention, 51 ff.
Authority, 85

B

Barriers
  channel and media, 201
  economic, 201
  geographic, 201
  individual, 199
  interpersonal, 197 ff.
  organizational, 195
  technological, 202
  temporal, 201
Basic functions, 33 ff.
Basic phenomenon, 26 ff.
Basic processes, 268
Behavior control, model of, 60 ff.
Behavior regulation, 95
Bionics, 312
"Brain-washing," 83 n.

C

Ceremony and ritual, 245
Change, least rate of, 56
Channel efficiency, 159
Channel and media barriers, 201
Channels vs. media, 131, 260
Climate, 198
Cognition, 315
Cognitive dissonance, 63 n.
Command and control systems, 205 n.
Command and instruction functions, 205 ff.
Communication
  adaptation, 55

Communication—*Cont.*
  appetite, 78, 84
  barriers, 195 ff.
  basic functions, 33 ff.
  basic phenomenon, 26 ff.
  basic problems, 339
  channels vs. media, 131
  vs. communicating, 39
  competence, 5 ff., 131–33
  competence and control, 131–33
  competencies, 271, 275
  consequences of, 121
  consummatory vs. instrumental, 34
  control, 85 ff., 132
  vs. data and information, 28 ff.
  defined, 17, 26
  diachronic, 129
  diachronic vs. synchronic, 129, 141
  dynamics, 3 ff., 81 ff.
  effectiveness, 7 ff., 137 ff., 348
  efficiency, 158
  facilitators and barriers, 128 ff.
  forms and conventions, 261
  functions of, 187 ff.
  instrumental vs. consummatory, 34
  interdepartment, 115
  interorganizational, 115
  interpersonal, 26 ff., 113
  intrapersonal, 111 ff.
  and management, 19 ff., 94 ff.
  managerial, 103
  mass, 115
  media vs. channels, 131
  metabolism, 32, 82
  methods and techniques, 267 ff.
  nature of, 3 ff., 23 ff., 111 ff.
  occasions of, 119 ff.
  "on-behalf-of . . . ," 105, 349
  organizational, 18, 103, 114, 142
  "packaging," 262
  phatic, 241 n.
  problems and issues, 332 ff.
  "recipes" for, 166 n.

371

Roles, 79 ff., 231
Rules, 79 ff., 95 ff.

S

Self-organization, 55
Semantic universals, 255 n.
Semantics, 314
Silence, 125
Simulation, 323
Skills, 275
Small group studies, 104 n., 317
Social evolution, 257
Social structure, 244
Sociocultural studies, 321
Sociopolitical studies, 321
Speaking and writing, 286
Strategic competence, 131
Stress-resolution, 68 ff.
Study of communication, basic premises, 3 ff.
Subjectivity vs. objectivity, 45 n.
"Subliminal communication," 230 n.
Symbiosis, 82, 175
Synchronic communication, 129
Synchronic vs. diachronic communication, 129, 141, 272 n.
Synergy, 82, 178
System
  adaptability, 179
  adequacy, 178
  compatibility, 181
  efficiency, 160
  organization as, 101 ff.
  reliability, 180
Systems
  communication, 173 ff.
  communication and control, 116–17
  theory, 61 ff., 62 n., 311, 327

T

Tactical competence, 131
Take-into-account-abilities, 50, 83, 111–12, 120
Task functions, 96
Technique, validity and generalizability, 283
Techniques and technology, 253
Technological
  change, 282
  issues, 354 ff.
Technology and techniques, 253 ff.
"Theory" vs. "practice," 6 ff.
Thinking, 247, 255, 315
"Thought control," 83 n.
Timeliness vs. speed, 179 n.
Timing, 126, 234
"TOTE" unit, 63 n.
Training and education, 217, 277

U

Uncertainty, 168 n., 327
Unintentional information, 194
Utility, 170 ff.

V

Validity, 168 ff.
Verbal fencing, 246
Verbal learning and conditioning, 313
Viability, 182

W

Who's Afraid of Virginia Woolf?, 90
Writing, 296 ff.
Writing and speaking, 286

This book has been set in 10 and 9 point Electra, leaded 3 points. Part numbers and titles are 24 point Bernhard Modern Bold; chapter numbers are 36 point Bernard Modern Bold and chapter titles are 18 point Bernard Modern Bold. The size of the type page is 27 by 45 picas.